The House of Lords in the
Parliaments of
Edward VI and Mary I

The House of Lords in the Parliaments of Edward VI and Mary I

An institutional study

MICHAEL A. R. GRAVES
Senior Lecturer in History, University of Auckland

CAMBRIDGE UNIVERSITY PRESS

Cambridge

London   New York   New Rochelle
Melbourne   Sydney

Published by the Press Syndicate of the University of Cambridge
The Pitt Building, Trumpington Street, Cambridge CB2 1RP
32 East 57th Street, New York, NY 10022, USA
296 Beaconsfield Parade, Middle Park, Melbourne 3206, Australia

First published 1981

Printed in Great Britain by
Western Printing Services Ltd, Bristol

British Library Cataloguing in Publication Data

Graves, Michael A. R.
The House of Lords in the Parliaments of
Edward VI and Mary I
1. Great Britain – Parliament – House of Lords – History
I. Title
328.41′07′109   JN621   80–42225
ISBN 0 521 23678 9

CONTENTS

TO MY MOTHER

PREFACE

This book is the belated end-product of Professor S. T. Bindoff's suggestion in 1964, when he directed me towards the mid-Tudor House of Lords. As I had been educated in the parliamentary tradition of A. F. Pollard and J. E. Neale, I made parliamentary politics my first priority. Also I initially accepted the thesis that the Commons advanced its authority, whilst the Upper House took a back seat. Consequently I approached the subject with little enthusiasm, not relishing the prospect of sifting through the sources on a parliamentary backwater. Sixteen years have changed all that. Hence the two salient characteristics of this study: that it is essentially an institutional and not a political study; and that it restores the Lords to its rightful place in the parliamentary trinity. Although this reformation of attitudes and the shift in priorities were effected in physical isolation, twelve thousand miles from the sources, that isolation was more apparent than real. For this I am deeply indebted to Professor G. R. Elton. Not only has he lent me advice and encouragement over the years but in the process both he and his wife, Sheila, have become valued friends – never more so than during my sabbatical year in Cambridge in 1979–80 when I completed this volume. Their warm hospitality will be one of my most cherished memories.

The other debts incurred in the preparation of this book are inevitably too numerous to itemise. However it would be churlish not to proffer a special vote of thanks to M. F. Bond and his colleagues at the House of Lords Record Office. In its deceptively relaxed atmosphere they have always been attentive, efficient and helpful. I am also grateful to the members of the History of Parliament Trust and the generous manner in which they made available to me the accumulated results of many years of research.

It was through the Trust that I met Norah Fuidge in 1966. Since then I have frequently called upon her help, both as a friend and as an historian with an unrivalled knowledge of members of the Tudor House of Commons – and she has always turned up trumps.

Working on my own in New Zealand, I have come to depend on my postgraduate students for criticism and simply the opportunity to talk Tudor 'shop': especially Terry Bates, David Dean, Kadia Horgan, Judith Mason and Claudia Wysocki. Together they jumped on any signs of pomposity or pretentiousness and prevented me from losing sight of comparative standards. Above all I must mention two academic lawyers, Anne and Dick Webb of Auckland University. Without their support in the few 'ups' and many 'downs' of the last few years, this book would never have come to fruition.

Its weaknesses and limitations are of course my responsibility. I am fully conscious that one limitation may incur criticism: the omission of a detailed study of convocation. The decision to exclude it was taken for two reasons: partly because there was not enough surviving material but also – more importantly – because of the existing state of ignorance about the Lords. The first priority was to rehabilitate the Upper House as a parliamentary institution – as one of the three essential parties to the legislative process. There existed no systematic research or published study about its composition, quality, procedure or legislative activity. These are the priorities of this book which is, after all, only the initial step in the restoration of the Lords to its rightful place in the Tudor parliamentary trinity. The relationship between convocation and parliament has its place in the parliamentary politics of the sixteenth century but it deserves, indeed demands, a separate study.

M. A. R. Graves
Cambridge
January 1980

PARLIAMENTARY SESSIONS, 1547-58

	Calendar dates	Regnal year
Edward VI		
1st parliament	4 November – 24 December 1547	1 Edward VI
	24 November 1548 – 14 March 1549	2/3 Edward VI
	4 November 1549 – 1 February 1550	3/4 Edward VI
	23 January – 15 April 1552	5/6 Edward VI
2nd parliament	1 March – 31 March 1553	7 Edward VI
Mary		
1st parliament	5 October – 6 December 1553*	1 Mary
2nd parliament	2 April – 5 May 1554	1 Mary
3rd parliament	12 November 1554 –	
	16 January 1555	1 & 2 Ph. & Mary
4th parliament	21 October – 9 December 1555	2 & 3 Ph. & Mary
5th parliament	20 January – 7 March 1558	4 & 5 Ph. & Mary
	5 November –	
	17 November 1558	5 & 6 Ph. & Mary

* Mary's first parliament was briefly prorogued on 21 October 1553, after the queen had given her assent to three bills (which are described as H.L.R.O., Orig.Act, 1 Mary, st. 1 in the Original Acts). The acts passed in the remainder of this parliament are designated *ibid.*, 1 Mary, st. 2. The enactments of the following parliament are simply labelled H.L.R.O., Orig.Act, 1 Mary.

I

INTRODUCTION

It should be stressed at the outset that this is an institutional rather than a political study. Its particular institutional emphasis is the consequence chiefly of past neglect by historians who have persistently ignored the fact that parliament was a trinity. At best the House of Lords has been treated as a kind of constitutional longstop or a compliant managerial tool wielded by the Crown; at worst it has received a cursory nod of recognition before being consigned to oblivion. However, the comfortable assumption that it could be thus dismissed derived from ignorance, and not from a considered judgement arrived at by a systematic study of its parliamentary performance. More reprehensible, though doubtless a natural consequence of this assumption, is the fact that no attempt has yet been made to answer questions which are of elementary yet fundamental importance: *how* it carried out its functions, *why* legal assistants were summoned to the Lords, and *what* contribution they made to its business. It is surprising that, as the role assigned to it was a subordinate and managerial one, no detailed study was made even of the way in which it performed *this* supposed service to the Crown. The first responsibility of any pioneering study of the House of Lords is therefore to compensate for this past neglect. Information must be collected, collated and systematically presented about such obvious institutional characteristics as its composition and the rights of membership, the officers of the House, the legal assistants, its procedures and their continuing refinement.

However, an institutional study cannot rest there. The Lords must be invested with the realities of people and political activity. Any assembly, no matter what its institutional assets are, is only as lively and efficient as its membership. So a good deal of space has been devoted to the quality of that membership, its record of attendance (which is, after all, the prerequisite of parliamentary activity), and the enmities and rivalries, loyalties and alliances, which affected the Lords' performance by both their divisive and their cohesive impact. Secondly, the Lords ought not to be studied in a vacuum. To do so would be to commit all over again the consistent error of previous Commons-orientated historians. Therefore bicameral comparisons figure frequently, especially on such matters as quality, attendance and procedure – above all in the examination of the Lords' legislative role. It is a sobering, even depressing, reflection that it was only in 1970 that a major Tudor parliamentary study was conceived in bicameral terms.[1] Nor was S. E. Lehmberg a pioneer in this respect alone. He rightly recognised that the concurrent meetings of the Canterbury convocation were an integral part of the parliamentary process and, so far as the sources permitted, he gave due attention to their composition and deliberations.[2] The lean scraps of information about the Edwardian and Marian convocations render pointless any attempt at a systematic and detailed study. The only solution – admittedly an unsatisfactory one – represents a practical compromise: to examine them at appropriate points in the text when both relevance and evidence make it a worthwhile exercise. Thus it is possible and pertinent to treat of the calls which convocation and the Upper House made on the bishops' time, and bills inspired by convocation proceedings. In contrast the public religious disputations held there – as in October–December 1553 – were official propaganda exercises and belong to a political rather than an institutional history.

On the other hand, politics cannot be excluded from a study of the House of Lords. To pursue the marital metaphor so pleasing to Sir John Neale,[3] we must wed together the institution and its politics. Politicking was, and always has been, a natural ingredient in the law-making process. This is equally true both of matters of great moment and of the private, personal and local bills which threatened to inundate parliament in the second half of the sixteenth century. However, it should not be conceived of in the antithetic structure of modern two-party politics. Politicking is no more than the art of making an institution work to one's own advantage. When, as in the sixteenth century, there was a broad area of agreement and essential unity of purpose between the Crown and the governing class, the politics of conflict and opposition were, more often than not, absent. This did not mean a decline into a state of political passivity, but rather a direction of such energies towards positive and constructive ends.

Politicking also meant parliamentary management, not designed to head off or stifle opposition but usually to ensure efficient productive parliaments in which the speedy transaction of official business was a first priority. In order to fulfil that objective, the privy council had to cope successfully with competing priorities. Members of the governing class had projects of their own to promote. Some of them were of a general nature, designed to benefit the commonweal, but usually they were intended to advance the interests of their proposers or, in the case of the House of Commons, of the cities, boroughs and counties which they represented. However, bills beneficial to individuals, sectional interests and communities might, in the process, adversely affect others. So politicking often meant the tactical manoeuvring, mustering of support, and even confrontation between rival interests. It all consumed precious time and could jeopardise the official ideal of productive sessions.

Nor should it be thought that the House of Lords was largely excluded from this process. Peers and bishops had their own bills to promote. Tactically conscious boroughs and economic lobbies sometimes deemed it politic to submit their bills to the Upper House first. In any case bills which successfully negotiated the Commons eventually came under its scrutiny too. The Lords was fully involved in both the legislative process and the political activity which accompanied it. This was particularly true of Edward VI's and Mary's reigns. Furthermore, although competing priorities rather than conflict and opposition were the prevailing characteristics of Tudor parliaments, negative, obstructive and destructive political activity ran at a higher level during the weak regimes and disturbed political environment of the mid-sixteenth century. The resistance to official objectives (and even, on one occasion, the sabotage of royal measures) centred on the Lords rather than on the Commons.

A corpus of facts about the mid-Tudor House is already part of the commonstock of our knowledge of Tudor parliaments, and only needs brief repetition here. It was the heir of the earlier king-in-council-in-parliament, and the occupant of its parliament chamber. It was also the beneficiary of the services which the

early parliaments had received from the king's permanent
council and the clerical organisation of chancery clerks. In 1547
the Lords was composed solely of bishops and peers (though not
all of them), and it constituted one of the three partners in the
enactment of legislation.[4] The presence in parliament of the
Crown, the elites of Church and State, and the elected representatives of local communities accorded well with the contemporary political theory of mixed government: 'a combination,
blending and balancing of the three main types of government
. . . derived from Aristotle – monarchy, aristocracy, and
democracy'.[5] In theory and in law the House of Lords was equal
with the Commons.

Beyond this we have to proceed with caution in a twilight
world of ignorance only occasionally illumined by shafts of light.
It was not until 1894 that L. O. Pike published what is still
virtually the only general history of the Lords, and certainly the
earliest work of any relevance to the mid-Tudor House.[6] However,
it is primarily concerned with the tenurial origins and evolution
of rights of membership, rather than with the institution *per se*,
and its main emphasis is pre-Tudor. Likewise the chief thrust of
J. H. Round's interest was peerage law and genealogy, not the
peerage in parliament.[7] Apart from one monograph on writs of
assistance and others by A. F. Pollard, no significant contribution to our knowledge of the mid-Tudor Lords appeared until
the 1950s.[8] To do him justice, Pollard did verse himself in the
institution of parliament, as well as its politics, and he acquired
considerable technical expertise in the way in which both Houses
conducted their affairs.[9] Yet he remained orientated towards the
Commons. He was convinced, not only that the sixteenth century
saw the growth of parliament's importance, but also that there
occurred, within it, a shift in authority from the Upper to the
Lower House.[10]

Pollard was one of the most prominent historians – and
certainly the earliest – to postulate a thesis which became, and
until very recently remained, the orthodox explanation of Tudor
parliamentary developments. It was political in emphasis,
focussed on the Commons, and concerned with opposition and
conflict. Tudor parliamentary history became retrospective
history, as historians searched for the origins of Stuart conflict
and found them in the sixteenth century. Pollard and his suc-

cessors,[11] tarred with a whiggish brush, were prompted to detect the rise of parliament and within it the Commons – the commencement of that lengthy process which eventually neutralised the monarch, subordinated the Lords, and culminated in the unchallenged supremacy of the Lower House. Most influential of the 'orthodox' practitioners was J. E. Neale, whose declared purpose was 'to banish the old illusion that early-Stuart Parliaments had few roots in the sixteenth century', and whose most notable discovery was the phenomenal growth in the Commons', authority.[12] In contrast, the Lords slithered from its former superiority into a long decline. Parity in the mid-Tudor period gave way to Elizabethan inferiority, when the House played 'second fiddle' to the Commons, complied obsequiously with the monarch's wishes, and assisted it in controlling the other House. Indeed it was a mark of its lack of importance that very little can be learned about its procedures.[13] The classic contrast is that between an amenable Marian and Elizabethan Upper House and an independent-tempered, even truculent Commons, where organised opposition manifested itself as early as 1555, and became regular and persistently troublesome in the next reign.[14]

This version of sixteenth-century developments went unchallenged until the mid-sixties, when a tentative revision got under way. In order to be effective it needed to rid itself of the constraints and distortion imposed by the knowledge of future Stuart conflict, to open its eyes to the existence and possible significance of the House of Lords, and to rearrange its priorities – in particular to recognise that a knowledge of the institution is a prerequisite to an understanding of its politics. However, the early revisionists fired wide or short of the mark. J. S. Roskell rightly criticised the fashionable assumptions about the rise of parliament, the upward political progress of the Commons, the Lords' decline, and the growth of conflict and opposition.[15] Yet he too adopted a political not institutional framework of reference for his attack, concentrating on politics not business. In the process he became a prisoner of the very tradition which he was attempting to overthrow. Four years later the historical world was treated to the startling novelty of a book by J. Enoch Powell and Keith Wallis, entirely devoted to the House of Lords. Regrettably, however, it had little to do with the conduct of its members, with its legislative procedures or with its parliamentary role. Instead the chief thrust of its interest lay in earlier theories of membership qualification and the incidence of creations, in rank, precedence and ceremonial, genealogy and heraldry.[16] During the later sixties Vernon F. Snow contributed to the stirring interest in the Lords with a series of articles on absenteeism, proctorial representation, and conciliar management.[17] Unlike Powell and Wallis, whose study terminated in 1540, he extended his examination to the end of Edward VI's reign. He was, in sentiment at least, a revisionist, simply because he recognised that the Lords was important enough to warrant detailed treatment. Yet when he argued that, between 1510 and 1553, the crown-in-council exploited licensed absenteeism and proctorial representation in order to secure effective and un-challenged control of the Upper House, his conclusion was in harmony with the older, orthodox interpretation: that the House of Lords was effectively muzzled.[18] However, an undue reliance upon dubious sources weakened his argument, his methodology has been questioned, and his conclusions have been seriously challenged.[19]

Revision is still in its infancy, but the most important obstacle to a more sensible, balanced, and realistic assessment of Tudor parliaments has already been removed. The overriding and wrong-headed concern with the politics of parliament, especially that search for the seeds of Stuart conflict, is being displaced in favour of an institutional emphasis: in particular how parliament transacted its business, and what kinds of business it handled. There is already emerging a new image of parliament, charac-terised by general harmony, co-operation, the onerous and detailed business of legislation, and often its grinding tedium and ennui. As the equal partner in the making of statute, the Lords is naturally emerging from the shadows and receiving its just recognition. S. E. Lehmberg pointed the way by giving the Upper House an equal place in his study of the Reformation Parliament.[20] A body of specialist and critical literature remains a thing of the future; but, chiefly as a consequence of G. R. Elton's work in the seventies, the fundamental rethinking about the functions and business of parliament, and the role of the Lords therein, is already well advanced.[21]

The new concentration on parliament as an institution – its business, procedures and records – has rendered innocuous, even irrelevant, the assumption that it was not worth studying the Lords because there were no sources on which to base such a study – a register of its insignificance.[22] Of course it lacks the diaries and personal journals which add so much flesh to the political bones of the Elizabethan Commons, and it must be admitted that it would be difficult, even impossible, to write an illuminating political history of it. However, the journals of the two Houses, the original acts, and parliament pawns,[23] do provide adequate materials for an institutional study. There are lacunae.[24] There are, inevitably, clerical errors, inconsistencies and omissions.[25] Furthermore it should not be forgotten that the journals of the two Houses were intended to satisfy the clerks' requirements and not those of historians.[26] Nevertheless, these sources constitute, together, a vital record of legislative activity, which is, after all, what parliament was all about. The parliament pawns served as a master list in chancery for the drawing and despatch of writs to eligible bishops and peers, to the assistants, and to the sheriffs for the holding of elections; the journals were a record of bill proceedings and proxies; and the original acts were successful bills, engrossed on parchment after the second reading and committee stage (if any) in the House of origin. These must always constitute the chief and vital working aids for any institutional study. Proceedings can then be fleshed out with the assistance of State papers (both domestic and foreign), and other government records, miscellaneous manuscript collections (both public and private), parliamentary treatises, and chronicles. In addition we are blessed with the rare and inestimable advantage of a journal which includes a daily attendance register. Despite its shortcomings,[27] and an occasional disaster,[28] the attendance record is a reliable one. Where it has been possible to check its accuracy, from other sources relating to the whereabouts of bishops and peers at time of parliament, its reliability is almost always confirmed. As we shall see, the attendance register tells us a good deal about the workings of the Upper House.[29] It simply will not do to use, as an excuse for neglect, the argument that nothing of value can be gleaned from existing sources.

At the end, after many more years of revisionist writing and research, we may come to the reluctant conclusion that the practitioners of the 'orthodox' interpretation were right after all: that the Lords' parliamentary role seriously declined in the

sixteenth century. Yet this can only be measured by its legislative
performance, not, as in the past, by its political activity. To
argue that, in the Upper House, 'a government bill which was
known to have the backing of the Sovereign was tantamount to a
royal command', may be to confuse abject compliance with
political responsibility.[30] The only legitimate yardstick of the
Lords' importance and success is its effectiveness as a legislator:
how efficient and productive it was in the handling of bills
before it, and what integrity, responsibility and reasonableness
it displayed in its relations with Crown and Commons, its
partners in the legislative process. Even then Sir John Neale may
have been right. In 1588, for example, Sir Christopher Hatton
wrote that 'the use of the higher House is not to meddle with any
bill until there be some presented from the Commons'.[31] And in
1610 the earl of Salisbury, addressing the Commons' committees
during a joint-conference, told them that 'the number of judges
you are more, besides you have more lawyers than we, and for
eloquence you are too hard for us, and for our places the greatness
of us makes not the argument the stronger'.[32] A lord keeper
acknowledging the Lords' impotence as an initiating chamber and
a lord treasurer avowing the Commons' superiority in the appropriate parliamentary skills: it all makes one wonder. However,
our contemporary awareness of the straitened integrity of
politicians makes for a healthy scepticism. Thus, if Hatton was
speaking the truth, he was describing a very novel state of affairs.
The Lords' originating role had certainly declined since the
early Marian parliaments. Yet in 1563 it had initiated one-third
of all bills and 63% of all acts;[33] and in the three-session parliament of 1572–81 its record read thus: 22% and 40%.[34] If the
figures point to a continued decline, it remains improbable that,
only seven years and two sessions later, Hatton was right when he
said, in effect, that it was *customary* for the Upper House not to
initiate bills. One can only ponder on his motives. Likewise with
Salisbury who, in 1610, was probably only playing the parliamentary game and flattering the Lower House to his own advantage. Whether or not they accurately reflect the diminishing
role of the House of Lords[35] is, perhaps, beside the point, for there
can be no doubts about its prominence in the mid-Tudor parliaments. And that is the particular concern of this exercise.

THE COMPOSITION OF THE HOUSE

Membership of the mid-Tudor Upper House was confined to those who were lords of parliament, either spiritual (the bishops[1] and, until 1540, a number of abbots and priors[2]) or temporal (the peers). They did not, however, constitute two separate orders or estates each of which was required to assent to matters placed before the House. Prelates, regulars and peers were all members of one House of parliament in which the assent of a majority of those present was sufficient. In 1516 this received weighty confirmation when the judges declared that a parliament could be held without the lords spiritual. Their judgement was historically sound. After all, the lords of parliament, spiritual as well as temporal, were in origin no more than *barones* holding lay baronies in chief of the Crown, and there was a direct association between baronial tenure and summons to parliament

However, even as the judges reached their verdict – and certainly by the middle of the sixteenth century – the association of territorial possession and membership of the Lords was being discarded. During the fifteenth century it had become the practice to summon a noble family regularly or not at all, and the distinguishing mark of the Tudor peerage became a personal one: the right of individual summons to the Lords, not a territorial one, the possession of baronial tenure.[3] Contemporary legal opinion also clung to the traditional doctrine when, in 1516, the judges declared that 'the Spiritual Lords have a place in the Parliament House not in virtue of any spiritual office, but solely in virtue of their temporal possessions'.[4] Even in Elizabeth's reign William Lambarde could still echo them when he wrote that the bishops sat in the Lords 'in respect of their Baronies, and not of their Churches'.[5] Despite the weight of learned opinion, however, mid-Tudor bishops were summoned as *sapientes*, by virtue of their ecclesiastical offices, and not as landholders *per baroniam*. When Henry VIII created six new bishoprics by letters patent in 1540–2, the new prelates were summoned to parliament as occupants of their respective sees.[6] The increasing recognition of Tudor parliaments as 'a representative institution whose decisions bound everyone because everyone was present in it either in person or by proxy' also affected the bishops' position. When, in 1565, Sir Thomas Smith wrote that 'the bishoppes for the clergie bee present' he was expressing what may have been a common opinion, that they were there specifically as representatives of the clergy.[7] The original basis and nature of Upper House membership were undergoing significant change in the sixteenth century and that change had already gone far by 1547.

The Tudor peerage comprised a small social elite which, after an initial increase, remained stable in numbers throughout the sixteenth century: 43 in 1509, 54 in 1529, and 55 in 1603. Between the first parliamentary session of Edward VI's reign and the last of Mary's it was no less constant: 54 in 1547, rising to 58 in 1554/5, and standing at 57 in November 1558.[8] Such changes as occurred in the size and especially in the composition of the mid-Tudor peerage were dependent on the relationship between the two processes of attrition and recruitment. Attrition was sometimes the simple consequence of natural causes, in particular the lack of male heirs whereby a title became extinct (if the rule of descent was to heirs male) or fell into abeyance (where the descent was to heirs general). Altogether seven titles were extinguished or became abeyant when holders died without male heirs: Lord Parr of Horton (1547), the earl of Bridgewater (1548), Lord Grey of Powis (1551), the earl of Devon (1556) and Lords Bray and Conyers in 1557; in 1551 the Brandon line also came to an end when Henry, the second duke of Suffolk, and his brother Charles, both unmarried, died of the sweating-sickness on the same day.[9]

State action also took its toll, usually through the process of attainder for treason whereby a dignity became forfeit. Two of the victims – the third duke of Norfolk and the marquess of Northampton – were unusually fortunate in that they escaped death and were eventually restored to peerage rank. Only Norfolk, however, was restored to his dignity before the death of Queen Mary.[10] In contrast, three peers suffered the full penalties for treason. Lord Seymour of Sudeley was executed in 1549 for 'High Treason, great falsehodes, and marvelous heynous misdemeanours against the Kinges Majestes person and his Royall Crowne'. The duke of Northumberland died for his attempt to alter the succession in 1553. And another duke, Suffolk, suffered less than a year later for his pathetic and abortive attempt to raise the Midlands against Mary and her proposed Spanish marriage. In December 1551 a third duke, Somerset, successfully defended himself against a charge of treason but was condemned and executed for felony. He was posthumously attainted by statute, whereby all honours were forfeit.

One other line was corrupted in blood for a felony committed, the Wests, Lords De la Warr. The villain of the piece was William West, the nephew and heir-designate to the childless Thomas ninth Lord De la Warr. His uncle accused him of endeavouring to hurry his inheritance along by the application of poison, and he secured a private act which disabled William from all honours.[11] William challenged its validity. When he was implicated in the Dudley conspiracy in 1556, two years after his uncle's death, he would not answer to his name of William West esquire, but only as Lord De la Warr. Moreover, he demanded to be tried by the peers. But 'the judges there with the heraldes proved he was no lorde, because he was never created nor made a lorde by anye writt to the Parlement, nor had anye patent to shewe for his creation'.[12] It was not until Elizabeth's reign that he was restored in blood and created Baron De la Warr.[13]

This steady wastage in the peerage, which removed fourteen lines between 1547 and 1558, was more than offset by new creations and restorations. In February 1547 four barons were created. This action might be regarded as a postcript to Henry VIII's reign, because they were ennobled on Sir William Paget's testimony as to the late king's unfulfilled intentions. Paget recollected that Henry had determined upon 'thadvauncement of divers to higher places of honour' because 'the nobilitie of this realme was greately decayed, somme by atteyndours, somme by their own misgovernaunce and riotous wasteng, and somme by sickenes and sondrie other meanes'.[14] He then recapitulated 'a booke of such as [the king] did chose to advaunce': six promotions and the creation of ten barons. But, again according to Paget's testimony, when the king later finalised the arrangements for the augmentation of the nobility the list of intended barons was whittled down to six. Even this reduced list did not remain intact, for the executors of Henry's will approved the ennoblement of only Thomas Seymour, Richard Rich, William Willoughby and Edmund Sheffield.[15] Thus was Henry's original intention to enlarge the peerage by about one-fifth reduced to the modest addition of four junior peers. And the rest of Edward's reign saw only three more elevations to peerage dignity: Paget himself in 1549, and Sir Thomas Darcy and Sir William Herbert, both in 1551.

The pattern of creations in Mary's reign was, coincidentally, similar: a batch of new barons in March and April 1554 – the new lord admiral Lord William Howard, Sir John Bridges, Sir Edward North and Sir John Williams – but only two other ennoblements during the reign: Sir Anthony Browne (who became Viscount Montagu) and Sir Edward Hastings (who was advanced to a barony).

The restorations to titles raise certain problems, if only because there were varying forms and procedures of restitution. The Crown could pardon an attainted offender (if he was still alive); it could also return to him or to his heirs such property as had been confiscated by virtue of the attainder and which remained in the Crown's possession. It could not, however, terminate the corruption of blood, nor could it restore the original peerage dignity to the offender or his heirs until the corruption had been removed – in other words it could not reverse the attainder nor cancel some of its most serious impediments. This could only be accomplished by a reversal of the original judgement in the law-courts or by parliamentary enactment, that is by an act of restitution. Moreover there were two degrees of restitution, which Sir Edward Coke termed *secundem quid*, or partial, and *restitutio in integrum*, or complete. The former restored in blood the heir(s) of an attainted person. The latter extended the restitution to dignities and honours as well, though not necessarily to the property forfeited as a consequence of the attainder.[16]

Altogether six titles were restored during the reigns of Edward VI and Mary, two by letters patent and four by act of parliament. Edward Courtenay was the son of Henry marquess of Exeter, who had been executed for treason in 1538. Edward passed the next fifteen years in the Tower but was then released by Mary, who, in September 1553, raised him to the earldom of Devon. It was a strangely premature action because his corruption in blood was not reversed until parliament met a month later, but it was doubtless in anticipation of this formality that Mary ennobled him. Although the earldom had been one of his father's dignities, the terms of the letters patent designated this a creation not a restoration. He was, however, also granted a warrant of precedence permitting him and his heirs 'to enjoy in Parl[iament], as well as in all other places whatsoever, such place and precedence as any of the ancestors of the said Earl, heretofore Earls of Devon, had ever had or enjoyed';[17] the creation was thus transformed into a restoration. Thomas Percy's restitution followed similar lines and differed only in its procedural sequence. He was first restored in blood by act of parliament in 1549, and then in 1557 he was created earl of Northumberland by letters patent. It was, however, a creation with a clause of precedence and he took his seat in the Lords as second in precedence amongst the earls. In effect it was a restoration too. Despite the unusual procedural sequence adopted for Courtenay, the Crown enjoyed no independent power of restoration; the validity of its letters patent ultimately depended on the statutory reversal of the corruption in blood. Therefore it was more convenient to secure an act of restitution which restored blood and honours at the same time.

Between 1547 and 1558 there were 32 such acts, 16 of which concerned attainted peers, their heirs or other relatives.[18] With very few exceptions each act had the same form and scope. It acknowledged the validity of the original attainder but released the heir from some of its penalties, by restoring him in blood and enabling him to acquire and possess property and protect it in the law-courts. Whilst the act was the *sine qua non* for the restoration of honours, in most cases it did not actually restore them. The restitutions for John Lumley, Henry Stafford and George Darcy, however, were exceptions,[19] for they restored them in honours as well as in blood. In each case it was enacted that they should 'have and enjoye in and att all parlyaments, and other places the rowme, name, place and voyce of a baron'.[20]

There remained some uncertainty whether this part of the enactment constituted a restoration or a creation. Lumley was admitted to the Lords in such place as if he was heir to the previous and fourth baron, whereas Henry Stafford in 1548 and George Darcy in 1549 were placed last among the barons as befitted new creations.[21] The inconsistencies were not immediately ironed out. On 12 February 1558, however, the Lords resolved that Stafford's rightful place was 'next unto, and under, the Barons Talbot', and thereupon raised him from thirtieth to tenth baron in the order of parliamentary precedence.[22] And in the following year George Lord Darcy's successor was eventually admitted 'to the ancient seat and rank formerly enjoyed by his attainted ancestor'.[23] The House had clearly decided that the regrant of a title to the male heir, who would have succeeded to it but for its forfeiture by attainder, was a restoration not a new creation.

Although these acts were exceptional, they were at least free from the complexities associated with the rehabilitation of Thomas Howard, third duke of Norfolk. In January 1547 Norfolk's son and heir, Henry earl of Surrey, had been brought to trial, convicted, and executed for treason. The duke himself, charged with the same offence, had been condemned by an act of parliament which also confirmed Surrey's attainder.[24] Norfolk's life, however, was spared by the death of Henry VIII and he survived, a prisoner in the Tower, until Queen Mary released and pardoned him in 1553. He now sought rehabilitation for himself, the attainted person, as well as for his heirs – in itself an unusual circumstance. Moreover he appealed, not for his restoration as an act of royal grace, but for a declaration that his attainder was null and void on the grounds that it was both unjust and technically invalid. It was this which endowed his restitution with such an unusual character. Normally a restitution act did not deny the justice of the original attainder, but simply released the heirs of the offender from some of the consequences of his treason or felony. But Norfolk's bill argued the injustice of the charges against him. And it sought to invalidate the attainder for technical reasons too. The royal assent had been given by four commissioners appointed by the absent king, whereas 'the Lawe of this Realme is and allwayes hath been that the royall assent . . . to any Acte of parlament ought to be geven in hys owne Royall presence being personallie present in the higher howse of the parlament'. Furthermore the warrant appointing the commissioners 'was not Signed with his Highnes' hand but with his stampe putt thereto in the nether parte of the said Commission and not in the upper parte of the saide commission as his Highnes was accustomed to doe'.[25]

Norfolk's bill passed: the 'pretended' act of attainder was accordingly declared void and 'no acte of parlament'; Thomas Howard was recognised as rightful duke of Norfolk and the statutory confirmation of his son's attainder was reversed. But Surrey's actual attainder, his condemnation at law, was not reversed. It meant that the earl's children – Norfolk's grand-children and heirs – were still subject to the penal consequences of his attainder. This problem was resolved in the same parliament by the usual form of restitution act which, whilst acknowledging Surrey's treason, restored his son Thomas and his heirs in blood.[26]

The reversal of Norfolk's attainder, together with the res-torations and new creations, more than offset the losses incurred by State action and natural causes. This is reflected in the slight increase in the size of the peerage from 54 in November 1547 to 57 eleven years later. Recruitment and attrition also affected the composition of the peerage, as old lines were extinguished and new peers were created, whilst promotions altered its structure: when four nobles were elevated in 1547[27] and six more in 1550/1.[28] The structural impact of these elevations, however, was limited and temporary because, within three years, four of them were executed or deprived.[29] As promotion was the reward for success, so attainder and forfeiture of honours were frequently the penalties for failure.

Whereas the number of peers was limited only by royal policy or inclination, the size of the episcopate was determined by the number of existing dioceses. In normal circumstances the creation of new sees would have depended on an awareness of the ad-ministrative needs of the Church. In the mid-sixteenth century, however, the exigencies and opportunities of Reformation politics influenced, even dictated, the size of the episcopate. The duke of Northumberland whittled down the number of bishops, ostensibly in the cause of reform but really for the sake of profit and power. Westminster was absorbed into London in 1550 and two years later Worcester and Gloucester were amal-gamated under John Hooper.[30] Durham was suppressed by statute in March 1553.[31] Fortunately for the best interests of the Church, Northumberland's rule was shortlived. Although Mary did not revive Westminster, Durham was restored,[32] and the amalgamation of Worcester and Gloucester was terminated when Nicholas Heath was restored to Worcester in August 1553 and James Brooke was consecrated bishop of Gloucester after John Hooper's deprivation in March 1554.[33] This raised the number of bishoprics to 26, a total which remained unaltered for the rest of Mary's reign.[34]

Within the limit imposed by the number of existing sees, the size of the episcopate at time of parliament depended on the Crown's rapidity in filling vacancies. In the flanking reigns of Henry VIII and Elizabeth most vacancies were caused by the death or translation of incumbents, all part of the normal process of change on the episcopal bench. Not so, however, between 1547 and 1558 when religious conflict and change produced a spate of deprivations, a more rapid turnover of bishops, and a consequent increase in the number of vacancies. The Edwardian and Marian episcopate experienced nearly 50 changes. Eighteen deaths and nine promotions were the simple consequences of the inexorable march of time. But the remainder, 17 deprivations and three resignations, were the products of successive changes in religion. With two exceptions[35] they occurred when first Northumberland and then Mary attempted to bring the episcopal bench into line with the prevailing religious complexion of the government. Thus, between 1550 and 1552, Northumberland's regime deprived four conservative bishops,[36] compelled John Veysey to surrender Exeter, and forced William Repps to resign Norwich.[37] In 1553/4 positions were reversed when the Marian government carried out a purge of Protestants. Eleven bishops were deprived, four for clerical marriage and the rest because the Crown maintained that they had no right to episcopal office.[38] A twelfth, William Barlow of Bath and Wells, forestalled deprivation by resignation, perhaps in the hope that this would expiate his sins and appease his Catholic queen.[39]

As the religious pendulum moved back and forth, the successive crops of victims accelerated the rate of change. The Henrician bishops' average tenure of office had been almost eleven years; the Edwardian and Marian prelates, however, managed only five years and seven months, just over half. Thus there was a sharp increase in the incidence of vacancies. On the other hand the exigencies of Reformation politics required that the vacancies be filled as rapidly as possible. Consequently the duration of each vacancy averaged no more than seven or eight months and the episcopal bench was seldom seriously undermanned for long. The Marian purge serves to illustrate the point. A spate of deprivations in mid-March 1554 left seven sees without bishops, yet within a month five of these vacancies were filled.[40] Only in the latter half of 1558 did numbers seriously decline: from 23 in January to 21 in November and 17 by the end of the year.

Therefore, despite the frequency of changes and vacancies, there were relatively few empty bishoprics when parliamentary sessions began. In the Edwardian sessions, for example, there was only one vacancy in 1547 and 1549/50, and none in 1548/9, though the total rose to three in 1552 and 1553. It is true that the Marian incidence of vacancies was higher. Although, when her first parliament assembled in the autumn of 1553, only two sees required to be filled, Mary's systematic removal of reformers temporarily depleted the episcopal bench during the following year. Strenuous efforts were made to replenish their numbers: six new bishops were consecrated on 1 April 1554, on the very eve of parliament,[41] whilst Robert Warton was translated from St Asaph to Hereford (left vacant by John Harley's deprivation in March). Yet there were still four vacant sees when her second parliament opened on 2 April 1554 and as many as six[42] when the third one began in November. By the time parliament reassembled in 1555, the purge was almost complete and the bench had been replenished with reliable conservatives.[43] During the two sessions of 1558, however, vacancies were again on the increase. This development probably reflected a combination of circumstances, particularly the government's absorption in war against France, the estranged relations with the pope (who granted the bulls of consecration), and the physical decline and mortal illness of both Queen Mary and Cardinal Pole.

The dissolution of the monasteries removed the parliamentary abbots and priors from the House of Lords in 1540. Thereafter, but for a brief interlude in 1558/9,[44] the membership consisted exclusively of a majority of peers and a minority of bishops. However, it never corresponded exactly with the size of the peerage and episcopate. In order to determine the effective membership of the Lords it is essential to discover the difference between, on the one hand, the number of peers and bishops (who constituted what may be termed the *nominal membership* of the House), and, on the other, the lords temporal and spiritual, those peers and prelates who were deemed eligible to attend and therefore received a summons to parliament (the *actual membership*). The disparity was the simple consequence of certain conditions disabling a 'nominal' member from receipt of a writ of summons to which, in normal circumstances, he was entitled.

The commonest reason for the temporary disqualification of a peer was possession of title during minority. It was not until 22 May 1685 that the Lords formally resolved 'that no Lord under the Age of One and Twenty Years shall be permitted to sit in the House'.[45] A scrutiny of minorities in the mid-sixteenth century, however, reveals that, long before that resolution, the Crown was already observing the twenty-first birthday or thereabouts as the terminal date of a minority.[46] Fifteen mid-Tudor peers were ineligible for at least one session because they were under age. One of them, the second duke of Suffolk, died of the sweating-sickness at Cambridge when he was only 15.[47] Most of the others were duly called to the Upper House for the first session following the attainment of their majority, though precise information is lacking about the birthdates of four of them. There were, however, two exceptions. The earl of Southampton did not come of age until five months before the parliamentary session of 1566 and therefore his case really lies outside the chronological limits of this study. Nevertheless it is worth observing that, in 1566, he was a royal ward[48] and that his Roman Catholic sympathies and connections may explain why his first summons to the Lords was not issued until the next parliament in 1571. It suggests that the Crown still exercised a certain discretionary power. The same may be true of Robert sixth Lord Ogle. Although his twenty-first birthday fell on 30 May 1550[49] he was not summoned to the last two sessions of Edward's reign. Perhaps he was unsympathetic to Northumberland's regime. Or his services as deputy warden might have been required in the middle march,[50] though this explanation is improbable because the Crown normally issued writs to the marcher wardens before instructing them to stay at their posts if the situation warranted it. Political exclusion is a more plausible explanation. At the age of 24 Ogle's name was omitted from the list of those to be summoned to the abortive Edwardian assembly of September 1553. The list was dated 19 June, only eight weeks before a writ went out to him for Mary's first parliament.[51] Ogle's case confirms that the Crown enjoyed a discretionary authority in the issue or deferment of first writs to peers who had just attained their majority.

Poverty was another, though less frequent, disability.[52] Henry Grey, who succeeded his brother as fourth earl of Kent in 1523, surrendered the earldom 'by reason of his slender estate'. Thereafter he styled himself Sir Henry Grey.[53] When his grandson Reginald succeeded him in 1562, the relinquishment of the title continued to be recognised and effective in law. Reginald was not summoned to the Lords but sat instead in the Commons, as M.P. for Weymouth, in 1563–7.[54] There is some uncertainty, however, about the second case, that of John Sutton, third Lord Dudley. He was heavily indebted on his own account and encumbered with his father's debts as well, when he succeeded to the barony in 1532. Matters went from bad to worse. He mortgaged the family estates and finally parted with them altogether – and it is this, we might assume, which explains why he was never summoned to parliament. Yet he was also reputed to be mentally unstable, even 'half-witted'[55] and it was not unknown for the Crown to disqualify a peer from membership of the Lords on those grounds too.[56] This might serve to explain why his father Edward had been summoned to the Upper House as recently as 1529. It seems improbable that the family fortunes had declined so rapidly that only three years later, when John succeeded to the title, he could have been disqualified for poverty alone. But mental incapacity remains an unsatisfactory explanation. There are no contemporary descriptions of John's mental state and the story of his incapacity derives solely from Dugdale,[57] a fact which does not inspire special confidence.[58] Unfortunately the story has been accepted and repeated, even as recently as 1970.[59] Poverty would seem to be the only plausible explanation. In any case if he was 'a weak man of understanding'[60] this would simply account for the intemperate way in which he rapidly alienated his patrimony. The slide to financial ruin was certainly spectacular: heavily indebted to Sir John Dudley in 1532, attempting to raise money on his wife's

jointure in 1533, and finally alienating Dudley Castle in 1537. A
year later his wife was lamenting that 'by the meanes of my
lorde my husbond I and all myne ar utterly undone'. By then she
was dependent on the charity of the prioress of Nuneaton. He
too subsisted on the charity of friends, thereby earning the
nickname of *Lord Quondam*. The final proof that poverty was the
reason for his disqualification is to be found in Mary's reign.
John's son, Edward, who succeeded him in September 1553, was
not summoned to the first two Marian parliaments. It was not
until Mary had restored to him much of the Sutton patrimony,
including the ancestral seat of Dudley Castle, on 4 November
1554, that she issued his first writ of summons.[61]

It is clear, from the Crown's treatment of the Suttons, father
and son, that it retained some discretionary power in such cases
and that it decided each one on its particular merits. The Greys
and the third Lord Dudley were excluded. But John eighth
Lord Audley and Thomas eighth Lord De la Warr were regularly
summoned despite their pressing and persistent financial embarrassment. Far from displaying any fears that poverty might
disqualify them from lordship of parliament, they paraded their
financial hardship in support of requests for licences of absence.
Thus, in December 1531, Audley sought permission to stay
away because he lacked the money 'to maintain his status
among his peers'. Forty years later William third earl of Worcester
was described by Reginald Grey's mother-in-law as one of those
'noblemyne off long countenuens and ansent honor [w]hos landes
be so dekayd as beseydes ther offesses and fyes have not muche
gretter lyvinges then me sonys'. Yet he had been regularly
summoned to parliament since his succession to the title in
1549.[62] Whatever reasons swayed the Crown to summon one
peer or exclude another, there was no question that it alone had
the right to make the decision, though, as a general rule, the
Tudors would have concurred with the duchess of Suffolk's
opinion: 'Yet God forbeyde, wylste the[y] deserve it not, that
they shold lysse ther honors for ther small lyvinges.'[63]

Minority, poverty and lunacy do not exhaust the catalogue of
conditions over which the monarch exercised a discretionary
power. If, for example, a nobleman was out of the kingdom when
the writs went out, what was the Crown's response? In April 1554
the earl of Bedford and the heir of the earl of Sussex, Lord

FitzWalter, were despatched to Spain to ratify the marriage treaty with Philip of Spain. With them went the earl of Worcester, in an unofficial capacity though with the queen's approval. All three of them received writs. By 1558 FitzWalter (now third earl of Sussex) was chief governor of Ireland. Not only did he receive a summons but he actually returned to England to attend the Lords, only returning to Ireland after parliament had been prorogued. Mary's military commanders at Guisnes, Calais and Hammes[64] were accorded similar treatment. Although they were on duty in the French marches for much of Mary's reign (and in Grey's case for the second Edwardian parliament too), the government could not be accused of dereliction of duty, for, like Sussex, they continued to receive their writs even though the increasingly urgent priorities of defence usually prevented them from returning to take their seats.[65]

Worcester apart, however, they were all engaged in the queen's business, and it would have been churlish for Mary to have denied them writs, simply because their duties took them to foreign parts. On the other hand it would be naive to expect the government to extend its generosity to peers in self-imposed or enforced exile. Edward earl of Devon paid for his complicity in Wyatt's rebellion with a year's imprisonment followed by a spell of involuntary exile in Italy. When he sought permission to return, in order to see the queen and his mother, it was refused. And although his name was included in the list of those to be called to the parliament of 1555, the queen's learned counsel were consulted touching the despatch of his writ, and it was finally decided to refuse him permission to return. Doubtless some members of the council preferred to keep him at arm's length, as his presence in parliament might have rallied once again the forces hostile to Mary's Spanish husband.[66]

Devon was not the only aristocratic exile of the reign. Francis second earl of Bedford was a staunch adherent of reformed doctrines. He suffered a short spell in prison in 1553 for his part in the duke of Northumberland's July treason, and his summons to the Edwardian Lords as his father's heir was not renewed by Mary.[67] Thus relations between Francis and the government were already devoid of affection and trust when, in 1555, he was suspected of complicity in a plot involving the earl of Devon. It was this particular circumstance which encouraged him to contemplate and undertake a spell of travel abroad.[68] In April 1555 the government, no doubt pleased to be rid of him, equipped him with an official passport, and he toured the Continent for the next two years. During that time Mary's fourth parliament met. Bedford's name was listed amongst the intended recipients of writs[69] but whether one was actually sent to him is another matter. Certainly he did not return to take his seat in the 1555 parliament. It is difficult to imagine the government exerting itself to seek out exiles such as Bedford and furnish them with summonses to the Lords. Absentee peers were enrolled on the parliament pawn as a kind of registration or confirmation of that most important criterion of peerage, the right to receive an official summons; beyond this, however, the decision whether or not to send out writs in questionable cases was a matter for the Crown's discretion.

That discretionary power in the issue of writs was at its greatest with peers who had been placed under restraint – and it mattered little what form the restraint took, whether it was close imprisonment, house arrest or just enforced exile in the country. Each case was decided on its merits. When the pawn for Mary's first parliament was drawn up in August 1553 the leaders of the abortive July coup, the duke of Northumberland and the marquess of Northampton, were left off – it was pointless to summon them on the eve of their attainder although neither of them had actually been convicted when the writs were issued on 14 August. Their confederate, the duke of Suffolk, was likewise omitted from the pawn. But otherwise he got off lightly: three days in the Tower followed by a heavy composition and a spell of enforced retirement at his home in East Sheen. In mid-November the imperial ambassador, Simon Renard, was able to report to Charles V that Suffolk 'has made his confession as to religion, and the Queen has therefore remitted his composition . . . and reinstated him by means of a general pardon'. His name was duly inserted in the left-hand margin of the pawn, presumably as a record of the belated issue of a writ to him.[70]

The queen displayed remarkable clemency towards Suffolk, but he had learned no lessons. On 17 February he was attainted for attempting to cause a stir in Leicestershire against her intention to marry Philip of Spain. When the writs for Mary's second parliament went out on the same day he was not summoned.[71] At the same time George ninth Lord Cobham was in the Tower, waiting to learn whether he too would be punished for his ambiguous conduct during Wyatt's rebellion. It must have been an ill omen when he received no call to the Upper House. When the queen ordered his release on 24 March, however, he was then summoned, and indeed he attended all but three of the sittings.[72]

The exclusion of Suffolk and Cobham from the Lords was no more than an incidental consequence of their imprisonment. In contrast, however, the earl of Devon's detention served the specific purpose of keeping him away from parliament. Although his involvement in the anti-Spanish conspiracy provided the public justification for his imprisonment, the government displayed more concern for what he represented than for what he had done. He was regarded by many as a more suitable consort than Philip. He had become the focal point of religious and xenophobic fears and resentments about the Spanish marriage.[73] Therefore he posed a serious threat to the queen, not by virtue of his political talents, which were meagre, but because he was the figurehead of opposition to her policies. In these circumstances she might have been expected to proceed harshly against him, and she was not lacking advisers who favoured his execution.[74] Devon owed his life and the leniency with which was treated to powerful defenders at Court, in particular his mother, a confidante of the queen, and Bishop Gardiner, the lord chancellor.[75] Perhaps too the queen's own moderation benefited him. His treatment represents a compromise between the political necessity of removing him from the political scene during the fulfilment of Mary's policies and her personal reluctance to administer condign punishment. Thus he stayed in the Tower until May 1554 when he was transferred to Fotheringhay for a year. And he received no writs to the two parliaments held during that time.[76] When he was eventually released the queen still dared not risk his appearance in future parliaments nor even his continued presence in England where he might continue to be the rallying point of anti-Spanish sentiment – hence his enforced exile.

It was nonetheless rare for the mid-Tudor regimes to resort to imprisonment as a justification for the denial of writs. During the turbulent days before and after Edward VI's death a large body of peers was implicated in one way or another in Northumberland's treason. In most cases their treasonable activity extended no further than confirming the letters patent limiting the succession or signing the engagement to maintain the amended succession.[77] Furthermore the privy councillors' action in proclaiming Mary queen on 19 July helped to make amends,[78] and many others hurried to her to beg their pardons. Mary displayed considerable political common sense when she overlooked their indiscretions. It would have been impolitic in any case to commence her reign conducting a pogrom against her nobility. She needed support for her new regime and even felt obliged to appoint some of the most prominent Edwardians to her council.

Her clemency did not stop there, however, but was even extended to most of those who had been more deeply involved in the July treason. Suffolk, the earl of Huntingdon, and Viscount Hereford were sent to the Tower and the earl of Rutland went to the Fleet Prison, whilst the marquess of Winchester and Lords Bray and Darcy of Chiche suffered the gentler and more comfortable constraints of house arrest. Lord Clinton too was arrested and may have suffered a short spell of imprisonment.[79] But the pains and penalties inflicted upon them were brief in duration and of the mildest kind. We have already witnessed the clemency extended to Suffolk. In August Winchester was not only freed but reinstated in all his offices, including the lord treasurership and a place on the council. Clinton lost his office of lord high admiral and was fined £6,000 but he was rapidly restored to favour and his son was knighted at Mary's coronation. After six weeks Rutland was released from the Fleet and, although he was confined to his town house at 'Hallywell', he was pardoned a month later. Huntingdon served a longer spell of imprisonment after which the privy council, on 12 October, ordered him to confine himself to his home at the queen's pleasure. But by mid-November he too had been pardoned. Bray's fate followed the familiar pattern: arrest, followed by a council order to return to his house 'and there to remayne and not to passe from thens untyll [he knows] further . . . the Queen's Highnes' pleasure'. In Bray's case, however, the duration of his house arrest is not known. Hereford, like Clinton, suffered in his pocket, but when, on 6 September, he was 'delevered and dyscharged of the Towre with a grett fyne' he had been there for only a month.[80]

Thomas Lord Darcy of Chiche, however, did not make his peace with the queen as easily as most of the other delinquents had done. It is hardly surprising. He had stood high in Northumberland's regime, serving as lord chamberlain of Edward VI's household. After the duke's fall he adopted an obdurate and provocative manner towards the new government. On 30 July the privy council felt compelled to order him 'to dysperse the numbre of reteynors which [it] is informede he haith nowe in forcyble maner assemblede'. Yet in early September he was still accumulating arquebuses and other weapons in his house. Mary even suspected him of fomenting 'rebellious intrigues'. Despite such foolish provocation, however, he did not suffer the rigours of the Tower or the Fleet and on 1 November he was actually pardoned.[81] If the queen's gentle treatment of Darcy seems remarkable, it might be recalled that even Suffolk, a central figure in the attempt to rob Mary of the crown, received a pardon in the same month

Most of the delinquent peers were in detention when the writs for Mary's first parliament were issued on 14 August but, with the exception of Northumberland (marked down for execution), Northampton (who was degraded) and Suffolk (who received a belated summons at a later date), all of them were then called to the Upper House.[82] And (with the possible exception of Bray) all of them were released and pardoned in time to attend at least part of the session. Mary may have been guided less by scruples about the right of peers to be summoned than by the political necessities of the moment. When she pardoned some peers and remitted the compositions of others[83] it was probably all of a piece with her policy of securing aristocratic support for the Spanish match. It seems to have paid dividends. In November 1553 the imperial ambassador noted that her policy had already secured promises of loyalty and support for her marriage from Suffolk, Huntingdon and other peers.[84] Insincere their protestations may have been, but presumably few would risk offending the queen again so soon after their recent experiences and her clemency. Whatever her motives, and despite the Crown's considerable discretionary power in the issue of writs to peers who were accused or suspected of treason or sedition, Mary wielded that power with remarkable moderation during the critical weeks of July–August 1553 and January–February 1554.

The parliamentary disability of imprisonment was not always the consequence of political offences such as treason and sedition. Because personal monarchy was the contemporary form of English government, the line between political offences against the State and actions personally offensive to the ruler was not always a distinct one. Marriages contracted without the monarch's approval might offend royal prejudices – witness Elizabeth's treatment of Bishop Fletcher and Sir Walter Ralegh. Or they might be regarded as politically dangerous – the view which Elizabeth took of the earl of Hertford's marriage to Katherine Grey and which resulted in his imprisonment and exclusion from the Upper House in the 1560s. Felony too could disable a peer, though it might also bring him to his death: the third Lord Dacre of the South was executed in 1541 for killing a gamewarden during the exhilarating, youthful and aristocratic pastime of poaching royal game; the duke of Somerset was acquitted of treason but beheaded in 1552 for felony (albeit in this case his punishment for felony was in reality the penalty for a political offence); and Charles eighth Lord Stourton was hanged in 1557 for the brutal murder of his neighbours, the Hartgills.[85]

No Edwardian or Marian peer was penalised for personal offences against the monarch, whilst the two peers convicted for felony – Somerset and Stourton – were imprisoned, convicted, and executed between parliamentary sessions. Consequently neither of these causes of disability had any practical effect upon the membership of the Edwardian and Marian Lords. Nevertheless they remain significant as limitations upon the privileges of peers and on their rights of membership of the Upper House.

There was a closer correlation between the numbers of lords spiritual and bishops than between lords temporal and peers. This was because the commoner disabilities of the peers were not applicable to the episcopal office. No Edwardian or Marian bishopric was occupied by a lunatic or a minor. And though many of the sees were progressively impoverished by the policies and appetites of Reformation governments, poverty did not release a bishop from the performance of his parliamentary duties. The occupants of the poorest Welsh sees were summoned no less regularly than those from the wealthier dioceses of Winchester, Durham, Salisbury and London. In this respect the official attitude to them was quite different from that adopted towards the peers, whose possession of adequate estates was considered necessary for the maintenance of their status and dignity, in parliament as elsewhere.

Furthermore, whilst the dangers attendant upon the episcopal office were considerable in the forties and fifties, when a bishop became a victim of the shifting fortunes of Reformation politics he was usually penalised not merely by imprisonment but by deprivation. In other words he did not become a disqualified prelate but ceased to be one altogether; whereupon the Edwardian and Marian governments usually attempted to fill the vacancy as quickly as possible. These conditions produced a higher rate of change and yet a lower incidence of disability amongst the bishops.

The cavalier manner in which successive mid-Tudor governments coerced and deprived bishops contrasts with their general respect for the parliamentary rights of peers. To some extent this difference may be accounted for by the prelates' decline in prestige and status under Royal Supremacy and by their reduction to the position of civil servants in the State's employ.[86] But necessity too played a part. Their key role in the furtherance of both Edwardian reformation and Marian reaction obliged the government of the day to remove opponents and appoint supporters as rapidly as possible. The exception was the protectorate government. It imprisoned Stephen Gardiner of Winchester during the sessions of 1547 and 1548/9 so that he could not head a parliamentary opposition against religious reformation. But it did not deprive him. Both Northumberland and Queen Mary displayed a greater willingness to purge the episcopate, but sometimes even they did not have the time to deprive and replace a disabled bishop before parliament met. During the parliamentary session of 1549/50 Gardiner remained in the Tower whilst Warwick (Northumberland) consolidated his power after the recent overthrow of the protectorate. By the time Edward VI's first parliament met in 1552 for the fourth and last time, however, Gardiner had been deprived[87] and Tunstall was in the Tower, charged with misprision and awaiting proceedings for deprivation.[88]

Mary's accession was the signal for a thoroughgoing purge of the episcopate. When her first parliament met on 5 October, less than three months later, the process was only half complete. The two archbishops (Thomas Cranmer and Robert Holgate), Ferrar of St David's and John Hooper of Gloucester were all in custody.[89] John Taylor of Lincoln actually attended the service which preceded the formal opening of parliament on 5 October but when he withdrew at the celebration of mass, 'not abiding the sight thereof', he was examined and commanded to attend. Later, when they were in the parliament house, 'hys parlament robe was tane from hym and he was commy[tted] to the tower'.[90] John Harley of Hereford, who joined Taylor in his protest, escaped imprisonment but was likewise excluded from parliament.[91] Two other reforming bishops, John Bird of Chester and Thomas Goodrich of Ely, may also have been 'discharged from parliament' despite their possession of writs, although the evidence for Goodrich's enforced absence is slender and suspect.[92] He was not deprived, being summoned to Mary's next parliament. By then the purge was almost complete. Only Cranmer remained in prison. When he was finally deprived, Mary's third and fourth parliaments had also run their course, and he had been denied writs to all of them.[93]

The Crown's treatment of delinquent bishops therefore assumed two forms: some were denied writs; others were summoned and then disabled, usually – though as we have seen by no means always – at some time between the issue of writs and the assembling of parliament. The same variations occurred in the case of reliable prelates who had been despatched overseas on royal business. Thomas Goldwell, the Marian bishop of St Asaph, received his writ to the 1555 parliament although he was unable to attend, having been sent by Cardinal Pole to report to Pope Paul IV on the state of England after the reunion.[94] In contrast Thomas Thirlby was regarded as ineligible because, when the writs went out for the second Marian parliament, he was serving the queen as ambassador to the imperial Habsburg Court. His writ was sent instead to his custodian of spiritualities.[95] However, even when these loyal Marians are added to the delinquents the incidence of ineligibility remains low. Apart from Mary's first parliament, when six bishops were excluded from parliament for their religious opinions or the offence of clerical marriage, the difference between the nominal and actual membership was very modest, no more than one or two in each session.[96]

In very obvious ways the Crown could alter the size and composition of the Upper House: positively, by the creation of new peers and new dioceses, or negatively, by attainder and the amalgamation or suppression of sees. Yet there is no evidence that the mid-Tudor regimes, politically shaky though they were, commonly resorted to such crude managerial devices in order to procure a tractable Upper House. To tamper with the size of the political elite or to alter the number of dioceses merely in the interests of parliamentary expediency would have offended all the canons of common sense and good governance. On the other hand the Crown did dispose of one weapon which might be employed to strengthen its support in the Lords: it could summon the heir apparent of a senior peer, *vita patris*, in his father's junior dignity, whereby he became a lord of parliament. It was a practice of recent origin, probably stretching back no further than Edward IV's reign.[97] And in this the Crown retained complete and untrammelled freedom of action. It should come as no surprise that, whereas Somerset did not exercise this undoubted royal right, Northumberland did. Nevertheless even he felt the need to justify his action. He dealt with the matter at length in a letter to William Cecil on 19 January 1553, in which he stressed that it could only be done 'with the Kinges ma[tes] plesser'; or again 'howe often yt shall plese his highnes to call [them]'; and yet once more 'yf it shall please his highnes to call any . . . of his ma[tes] grace'. And he justified their summons because they would 'be the better able to occupye the places [of their] parentes'.[98] Five days before he had used a similar theme when corresponding with the lord chamberlain, Thomas Lord Darcy; he argued that by 'the bringinge in by writ some heyres apparent into the parliment hows', they would 'the better be able to serve his ma[te] and the realme hereafter'.[99] These letters constituted an apologia, which is hardly surprising because heirs were being summoned for the first time in Edward's reign, and one of them was Northumberland's own son.

It remained, however, an irregular practice. The eldest sons of Bedford and Shrewsbury were called to Edward's second parliament in the paternal baronies of Russell and Talbot, along with

Northumberland's heir, who was summoned in his father's earldom of Warwick. Mary continued the practice, calling the earl of Sussex's heir in October 1553 and the marquess of Winchester's son in November 1554. Yet no son of Pembroke was called as Lord Herbert or of Westmorland as Lord Neville. Successive heirs were not necessarily summoned. Although Henry Radcliffe, heir to the first earl of Sussex, was styled Lord FitzWalter from 1529 to 1542, he was never in receipt of a writ, whereas his son was. Nor was the Crown under any obligation to summon an heir to successive parliaments. Warwick and Russell were dropped by Mary who summoned Lord FitzWalter instead.[100] The issue of a summons to the heir of a peer was entirely and without question a matter of royal grace. As such it could be utilised selectively to bring reliable men into the Upper House – though it should be added that it was always used sparingly.[101]

Manipulation of the Lords' membership by creations, attainders and deprivations offered no watertight solution to the unstable and divided mid-Tudor regimes, uncertain as they were of the loyalty of the House and fearful for the fate of cherished legislative measures. Not that they sought to pack the House or systematically purge it of critics and opponents. Head-counting, division lists and the totting up of majorities belonged to a future age of emergent parliamentary government and a new breed of parliamentary managers such as Danby, Walpole and Newcastle. Quality was the concern of Tudor managerial politicians: the creation of an effective leadership and, if necessary, the silencing of prominent critics around whom an opposition might crystallise. A more effective and less provocative means of achieving the latter than resort to the extreme course of attainder or deprivation was the manipulation of writs. Unfortunately for the jittery regimes of the late forties and fifties, the Crown no longer possessed the freedom to summon and exclude peers at will which it had once enjoyed. Not that it had been divested of all discretionary power in the issue of writs, for it was not until Charles I's reign that the Lords would presume to inform the king that writs should be withheld only from those members of the House who were made incapable to sit 'by Judgement of Parliament or any other legal Judgement'.[102] Nevertheless its discretion was, in practice, strictly circumscribed and confined to such disabilities as minority, poverty, lunacy, absence abroad or imprisonment at the king's pleasure. Undoubtedly it enjoyed a certain licence to discriminate between individuals. And although the Crown denied writs only to opponents of royal policies when they had incurred one of the customary disabilities, this could amount to the same thing; it simply had to find a suitable pretext for incarcerating an offending member or despatching him into exile or service abroad. Nevertheless it did so only occasionally, and even then very selectively.

The Crown was particularly careful to avoid deliberate and systematic tampering with the composition of the lay element in the Upper House by the denial of writs. In the sixteenth century the process was completed whereby nobility became identified with peerage and peerage with lordship of parliament. The right of summons became the distinguishing mark of a peer. It could not have been recognised and expressed more clearly than in a letter of Lord Chancellor Audley in 1536. He instructed Arthur Viscount Lisle, who was Henry VIII's deputy of Calais, that he must remain at his post during the coming parliament; 'but', he added, 'I send you the wrytt, bycause it ys the order that every nobilleman should have his wrytt of somonz of a parlament'.[103] It would have been impolitic for the Crown to have ignored this. And although it allowed itself greater licence in its treatment of the lords spiritual, it usually withheld a writ only when a deprivation was impending. When the government overstepped the mark it was liable to receive a sharp reminder that it had done so. Bishop Goldwell of St Asaph querulously defended his right to a writ when he wrote to Sir William Cecil in December 1558. He sought a licence to absent himself. Nevertheless he thought it strange that he had not received a summons to the coming parliament, as he considered himself still bishop of St Asaph.[104]

Another and more discreet way of removing undesirables from the parliamentary scene was to issue writs, thereby observing the right of members to be summoned, and then to incapacitate them by imprisonment or exile. This too, however, was becoming less and less acceptable to members of the Lords, spiritual no less than temporal. Stephen Gardiner, bishop of Winchester, was summoned to Edward VI's first parliament on 2 August 1547, but before it met he had been imprisoned in the Fleet. From prison he protested 'that nowe the Parliamente is begonne wherof I am a member . . . and wherunto I was called by wrytte, which I received before my comming hether'. During the third session of this parliament he complained again, this time from the Tower. 'And being now the time of Parliament, wherof I am a member in my degree, called unto it by writ, and not cut from it by any fault, but only by power kept heere, it is a double calamitie to be detained in prison by so intolerable wrong, and excluded from this assembly so much against right.'[105] Gardiner's protest is symptomatic of the growing awareness and insistence of members of the Lords on their rights of membership so long as they enjoyed peerage status or episcopal office. And it must have compelled the mid-Tudor regimes to exercise the royal discretionary power with increasing caution, both in the discriminatory issue of writs and the suspension of those rights once the writs had been issued.

The Edwardian and Marian Upper House therefore was a small working assembly whose composition was subject only to selective and, for the most part, unexceptionable control by the Crown. Its nominal membership ranged between 77 and 84 whilst its actual membership fluctuated between 65 and 79. There were no dramatic sessional fluctuations which might point to unusual manipulative activity by the Crown. The dramatic changes had already occurred in Henry VIII's reign, when the dissolution of the monasteries had removed the regulars and decisively confirmed a lay predominance in the House. In its initial size in 1547 and its barely perceptible rate of growth thereafter, the mid-Tudor Lords contrasts vividly with the Commons which expanded from 343 to 400 members in the same period.[106] Altogether no more than 145 adult males were actual members of the mid-Tudor Lords, men who were in receipt of writs and not disabled at time of parliament: 52 bishops, one abbot and a lay prior, 88 peers sitting in their own right, and three heirs summoned *vita patris* in junior paternal dignities.[107] Of course they were not all eligible for every one of the five Edwardian and six Marian sessions. But together they constituted the membership of the Upper, more honourable, prestigious, and ancient House of parliament during those reigns.

3

THE QUALITY OF THE HOUSE

A substantial majority of the mid-Tudor House of Lords consisted of a social elite of hereditary peers. It is an obvious truth that an hereditary elite is unlikely to possess exceptional qualities unless there exists the means to recruit new members, thereby maintaining vitality by the infusion of fresh blood, and ensuring adaptability to changing political and social conditions. In practice the Upper House was not afflicted with the deadening political consequences of a closed, self-perpetuating, noble caste. Peers constituted a majority, but they did not enjoy a monopoly of membership. The bishops sat there, not by virtue of high birth, ennoblement or heredity, but by possession of office. Doubtless a bishopric was sometimes the reward for political compliance (as was the case with the appointment of several ex-regulars to Henry VIII's new sees in 1540–2). It was, on some occasions, no more than one of the benefits of Court connections. For others, however, it was a recognition of talent or a reward for services in diplomacy and administration. In any case the peerage itself was not an exclusive, closed order, conscious and sensitive though peers were about status and rank, precedence and lineage. Dreams of an aristocratic caste were not unknown in the sixteenth century,[1] but they were unrealistic and unlikely ever to be realised. The Upper House was never in danger of transmutation into the stronghold of an exclusive noble oligarchy.

In Reformation England, moreover, political necessity and common sense precluded any such possibility. Although both the Edwardian and the Marian governments purged the episcopal bench of opponents, the result was not a decline in the quality of the lords spiritual. When Bonner, Gardiner, Heath, Tunstall and the other prominent Henrician diplomats and lawyers were

deprived, the Upper House received replacements, such as
Coverdale, Hooper and Ridley, who were poles apart from their
predecessors in religious position and tradition but were no less
impressive in their intellectual calibre and parliamentary activity.
Their services were lost to the Marian Upper House, but the
deprived Henricians returned, whilst the gradual extinction of
those amenable ex-regulars (whose parliamentary record was
singularly unimpressive) was accompanied by the emergence of
a new conservative type. Baynes, Brooks, Goldwell, Holyman,
Hopton and the other new Marians were intellectually more
impressive than the conformers and theologically better equipped
than the Henricians. The non-hereditary nature of the episcopal
office, coupled with the vicissitudes of Reformation politics,
ensured a regular recruitment of new and often energetic bishops
to the House.

The mid-Tudor nobility was no more impervious to change,
because it proved to be politic for the Crown to reward servants
and supporters with peerages. Henry VIII's creation of a batch
of peers in 1529 was the opening act of a major infusion of new
blood during the next 30 years. One of them, the Tailboys
barony, did not survive even until Edward VI's reign, and five
other creations between 1529 and 1558 had disappeared before
Elizabeth's accession.[2] Nevertheless 32 of the 88 peers who were
'actual' members of the mid-Tudor Lords were ennobled in or
after 1529 – and all but eight of them were of the first generation.[3]
The majority of them – 18 – did not rise above baronial rank,
but one became a viscount, three acquired earldoms and two
marquessates, whilst two achieved ducal status.[4] Henrician
creations made up half the total of new peers, beginning with
Bray, Wentworth and Windsor in 1529, Mordaunt in 1532, and
Viscount Beauchamp four years later. Three new barons – Parr,
St John, and Russell – were made on the same day, 9 March
1539; and on 18 December 1540 Gregory Cromwell was created
baron by patent, less than five months after his father's execution.[5] Viscount Lisle (1542) and Lords Eure, Wharton and
Wriothesley (1544) were the last additions of the reign although,
if we are to believe Paget's testimony shortly after Henry's
death, the late king had determined upon further creations.[6]
Henry's original intention to create ten barons was later reduced
first by him and then by the Edwardian privy council, to only

four. Three more peerages were added during the reign, whilst
Mary added four barons and one viscount, Montagu, in 1554,
and another baron, Hastings of Loughborough, during the last
year of her life.[7]

As a result of this steady recruitment about one-third of the
Edwardian and Marian lords temporal consisted of new peers.
More important than the volume of recruitment, however, was
its quality. With certain exceptions the new members brought
with them to the Lords the mixture of special skills, general
competence and experience necessary for the effective fulfilment
of its parliamentary functions. The motives for many of these
creations were, admittedly, not very encouraging. The advancement of Edward Seymour and William Parr was assisted, if not
actually caused, by their kinship with Henry's queens, whilst
Thomas Seymour rose with his brother at the beginning of
Edward VI's reign. William Willoughby was raised by Henry
VIII's posthumous favour, and not by virtue of long and dedicated service as a bureaucrat, diplomat or general.[8] As for the
conferment of a barony on Gregory Cromwell, whose mediocrity
must have been a constant embarrassment to his father,[9] it may
have been an exercise of royal conscience after Thomas's execution.

The decision to ennoble was sometimes influenced or deter-
mined by political expediency. Thomas Wharton and William
Eure were instruments of policy, promoted by Henry VIII to
counter-balance and diminish the power of the old quasi-feudal
dynasties of Percy, Clifford and Dacre.[10] The advancement of
Paget and Herbert to peerages and Russell's promotion to
Bedford were in the nature of political rewards for deserting
Somerset or adhering loyally to Northumberland (Warwick).
Paget was summoned to the Lords on 3 December 1549, two
months after his acquiescence in the fall of his former political
boss; Russell became an earl after the overthrow of the protectorate; and Herbert's blood-money, the earldom of Pembroke,
was granted on 11 October 1551, the eve of Somerset's final
downfall.[11] Concurrently with Paget's ennoblement, Sir Thomas
Darcy, who was a Dudley supporter, was appointed vice chamberlain of the household; in January 1550 this was followed by
admission to the privy council and in April 1551 by a barony.[12]

Mary's reign too had its politically inspired honours list. Sir

John Bridges and Sir John Williams received due reward for
their prompt adhesion to her in July 1553 and for their loyalty
in the critical February days of Wyatt's rebellion.[13] Though
Sir Anthony Browne (Viscount Montagu) and Sir Edward
Hastings could not be credited with such dramatic demonstrations
of loyalty,[14] they were nonetheless trusted Marians and devout
Catholics. Montagu was Mary's emissary to the pope in 1555
and the only peer who consistently opposed the parliamentary
passage of the Elizabethan Settlement in 1559.[15] If Hastings's
ardent Catholicism was a subject for mirth in Edward Underhill's
autobiography,[16] it was nonetheless genuine. Therefore it was an
understandable and politic action for the queen to elevate such
convinced co-religionists and unswerving loyalists who were also
among the more prominent gentry in their respective counties.

Sometimes Mary was moved to act by other considerations.
Noble title equipped Sir John Williams with the status and
dignity which he required for his new office of chamberlain to
her husband. It also served as compensation for his loss of the
treasurership of the court of augmentations. Likewise, Sir Anthony
Browne's appointment as master of the horse to Philip became
superfluous when the prince arrived with a household staffed
by Spaniards – and Mary was doubtless aware that any grief
which he experienced would be quickly stifled with a peerage
and a pension.

It is clear that the decisions governing additions to the political
elite (and therefore recruitment to the Lords) were frequently
short term and expedient. Yet this does an injustice to Henry
VIII and Mary, and even to the regents who governed for
Edward VI. These were experienced men with lengthy careers
in royal service which averaged more than two decades and
ranged from Russell's 40 years to Parr's seven. Edward Seymour,
John Dudley, William Herbert and Thomas Wriothesley had all
entered government service during the 1520s. Sir John Bridges
may have been rewarded as a direct consequence of his loyalty in
1553/4, but he had first fought for Henry VIII at the battle of
the spurs in 1513, and in the intervening forty years he had
served three Tudors as a royal attendant, military administrator
and local official.[17] Wharton and Eure may have been instruments of policy; they were nevertheless sensible choices, schooled
in the harsh realities of marcher warfare, politics and admini-

stration. Both held marcher wardenships and sat at the board of
the council in the north, Eure for nearly 23 years.[18] Eure had
served as marshal of the rearward army against Scotland in
1523, and Wharton had commanded the force which routed the
Scots at Solway Moss in 1542.[19] Even by the time of his elevation,
and more so by the end of Mary's reign, Wharton possessed an
unequalled experience and knowledge of marcher conditions:
a veteran campaigner, and a hard-bitten negotiator treating with
Scottish commissioners over the division of the 'Debateable
Land'.[20]

Paget is the prime example of the peer whose title was a
political reward, but who, more than most, deserved it for his
sheer professionalism. By 1547 he was a diplomat, a civil servant,
and a councillor with twenty years of service already behind
him.[21] In the last years of his life, Henry VIII so valued Paget
that 'as it is well knowen he used to open his plesour to me
alone in many thinges'.[22] Henry's confidence was well founded.
When Paget gave testimony to the Edwardian privy council
of the late king's intentions, he fabricated no peerage for himself.
He attempted to serve Somerset faithfully, with sound advice[23]
which was persistently ignored. Even then he did not join the
wolf-pack and turn on the protector during the October crisis of
1549; he simply stood aside and accepted the inevitable. For that
he received his peerage. Nevertheless it was a mark of his ability
and prominence in government that such a reward was considered
to be desirable.

John Williams's administrative record is hardly less impressive.
Despite his armed demonstration on Mary's behalf in July 1553,
his record is that of the professional civil servant rather than of
the politician or the general. He retained a key post in the
financial administration, as treasurer of the court of augmentations, during the shuffling for power in Henry VIII's closing
years, the Protestant Reformation and faction fights of Edward's
reign, and the Marian reaction. Characteristically, his tenure of
office was terminated only by administrative reorganisation,
when the court of augmentations was dissolved and its responsibilities were transferred to the exchequer. When he took his
seat in the Lords for the first time in 1554, he had served the
Tudor dynasty continuously for over a quarter of a century
and he brought to the Upper House considerable experience

(albeit a questionable competence and integrity) in matters financial.[24]

Amongst the new peers there were those who, like Williams and Paget, were tried and trusted professionals in the royal administration, but who, unlike them, did not receive their titles out of expediency or for specific and isolated political services. Peerage dignity and a seat in the Upper House represented the pinnacle of a long upward toil through the bureaucratic hierarchy. William Paulet, marquess of Winchester, was *par exellence* the professional civil servant whose career dwarfed even that of Paget and Williams. It spanned 60 years from 1511, when he was pricked sheriff, to 1572 when, hoary, deaf, and in his late eighties,[25] he died after 22 years as lord treasurer.[26] From 1526 he occupied a succession of offices, major and minor, in the financial administration, royal household and local government; he served as a privy councillor for 30 years,[27] and inevitably he became entangled in the multifarious activities and responsibilities which were stacked upon the backs of Tudor royal servants.[28] Paulet's greatest achievement was to absorb some of the Cromwellian courts into the exchequer, thereby re-establishing exchequer supremacy whilst, at the same time, incorporating some of the Cromwellian reforms. By the later 1550s he must have donned the mantle of father of the House.

Yet he was not a lone figure in the Lords. He was joined there by fellow professionals for whom the charter of creation or writ of summons was the culmination of a civil servant's career. Richard Rich followed him in 1547[29] and Edward North in 1554.[30] In a lower key was William Lord Howard of Effingham, though he too had a varied record as diplomat, soldier, military administrator and councillor behind him.[31] At a more modest level the continued loyal service of prominent local gentry was recognised by the occasional elevation of one of their number. Characteristic of this group was John Lord Mordaunt. He was created a baron in 1532, in the middle of a career spanning a half a century (1513–62) as a trusted local official of the Crown. During that time he served as surveyor of woods in Crown lands, and he was employed on numerous commissions of the peace and of oyer and terminer. The government could confidently impose on his kind an almost infinite number and variety of duties: in the late twenties he was organising the provision of timber for the fortification of Calais; in the last year of Henry VIII's reign he was assessing contributions in Bedfordshire for defence against a possible French invasion, and in 1551 he was investigating the high prices of foodstuffs.[32] A peer who retained the mentality of a local gentleman, Mordaunt's horizon was the county and his interests did not extend to national politics. He seems to have acquiesced in each turn of the Reformation wheel, and he was decidedly uninterested in parliamentary matters: the clerk of the parliaments records him as present in the House on only one day during all the Edwardian and Marian parliaments.[33] Nevertheless the 'Mordaunt type' was essential for the maintenance of effective royal authority in the counties. There was still a place for the local peer and in this role he seems to have acquitted himself admirably.

It would be misleading, however, to represent the influx of new members as a picture of unrelieved talent and industry. William Parr was little more than a competent mediocrity who profited from his sister's marriage to the king[34] – the weather-beaten courtier rather than the seasoned professional civil servant. Thomas Seymour was another beneficiary of a royal marriage, useful enough in diplomatic service for Henry VIII.[35] However, he was emotionally unstable – a peer whose jealousy of his brother led him to neglect and then to abuse his office of lord admiral for his own political ends.[36] These were small fry,[37] yet doubts must also be cast on the ability of such a prominent royal servant as Sir Thomas Wriothesley, created baron in 1544, appointed lord chancellor in May of the same year, and elevated to the earldom of Southampton on 11 February 1547.[38]

The sorry tale of incompetence and negligence does not end there. John Lord Russell may have been a reliable viceroy in the west, but his repeated and extravagant demands for more and yet more assistance against the west-country rebels in 1549 pose questions about his military capacity.[39] William Herbert, first earl of Pembroke, enjoyed a martial reputation and a creditable military record. Perhaps this is why the Crown groomed him as a provincial viceroy, its representative in Wales and the marches. He received extensive western and marcher properties, stewardships and the custody of royal castles, the attorney-generalship of Glamorgan and, most important, the presidency of the council in the Welsh marches.[40] Yet in 1558 Mary had cause to complain to Pembroke 'that the Marches of Wales are in disorder for want of a President residing there'[41] – a reprimand which raises doubts about his personal attention to business.

It would be unjust, however, to demand that Tudor servants should have displayed an equal competence and energy in all of the tasks heaped upon them by the Crown. In any case there was undoubtedly sufficient talent and political acumen amongst the new recruits to revitalise the house and mould its attitudes in pace with the changes going on around it. After all they included Winchester, Eure, North, Paget, Rich, Wharton and Williams. In addition there were those whose future rather than past record of service justified their promotion to the peerage. So Edward Seymour and John Dudley[42] became the most successful military commanders of the forties,[43] whilst Willoughby served as deputy of Calais (1550–2), chief steward of the duchy of Lancaster in the north (1553–70), and a lord-lieutenant under both Edward VI and Mary.[44] Finally it should be remembered that those whose performance was below par in one office usually more than compensated by outstanding or enduring service in others: Pembroke's neglect of his duties in the Welsh marches must be set against his long military record both before and after his ennoblement.[45] Russell's demands for overwhelming superiority before moving against the Prayer Book rebels in 1549 are counterbalanced by his long record of diplomatic service; and Wriothesley's suspect record as lord chancellor must be weighed against his previous service as clerk to the coffer, joint-clerk of the signet, a privy councillor from 1540 and secretary of State from 1540 to 1544.[46] Obvious mediocrities and incompetents were few.[47]

It should not be assumed that these new recruits provided a necessary injection of energy and talent into a House of Lords suffering from a conspicuous dearth of such qualities amongst the old nobility. There was, however, a vital and obvious distinction between a newly created peer and one who inherited his title. The act of ennoblement was a product of the royal will, a result of the monarch's decision to reward. Whilst the motives were many and varied, the great majority of new dignities in this period were conferred on royal servants of experience, loyalty and at least a modicum of ability. Moreover they were usually conferred not for isolated and dramatic services – a victory in battle, or the suppression of a rebellion – but for long, hard, grinding labour in the departments of State, diplomatic and military service, provincial and local government, council and parliament. In contrast later generations did not sit in the Lords by virtue of such qualities, but simply in the right of the peerages which they inherited. Succeeding generations might well have exhibited a lack of precisely those qualities which justified the ennoblement of the original grantee – it was a matter of mere chance. For this reason alone the augmentation of the lords temporal with experienced civil servants, politicians and military experts, together with the rapid changes in the membership of the lords spiritual, was important for the continued vitality of the Upper House. It ensured that the assembly would not be afflicted with the somnolence and mental fossilisation which might otherwise have resulted from undisturbed life-occupancy of episcopal office, or from the statistical probability that, in an hereditary peerage, a considerable number would be mediocrities, wastrels and incompetents. Certainly the Lords was not without its share of the aged and infirm (Salcot and Veysey), incapacitated (the third Lord Dudley) and afflicted (De la Warr). Nevertheless the quality of an assembly which received a steady flow of vigorous and often talented recruits, both spiritual and temporal, could hardly be stigmatised as apathetic, slavishly obedient to the royal will, divorced from political realities, mediocre, or incapable of fulfilling its parliamentary responsibilities with efficiency, independence and despatch.

Natural ability alone would not have sufficed to make the Lords an efficient House. Sir John Neale, writing of the Elizabethan Commons, was justified in asserting that 'While native talent will display itself whatever a man's education and stupidity be tempered but unchanged after even the best training, it still remains true that the effectiveness of an assembly is inevitably and profoundly affected by the quality of education its members have received.'[48] He then proceeded to chart a dramatic increase in the number of Commons' members possessed of a higher education. In this he was in harmony with those, such as J. H. Hexter, Lawrence Stone and M. H. Curtis,[49] who identified a dramatic expansion of education amongst the peerage and gentry in the middle and later years of the sixteenth century –

even though they differ on questions of chronology and timing, when the dramatic expansion occurred and how long it continued. Whether or not this phenomenon warrants the description of an 'educational revolution' is of no consequence here, but the phenomenon itself seems beyond question: that during the sixteenth century an increasing number of the governing class availed themselves of the existing educational opportunities.

The 'explosion of higher education' charted by Stone[50] was essentially the response of that class to changed circumstances. Its members were simultaneously bombarded with humanist propaganda and faced with the practical necessity of equipping themselves educationally if they hoped to secure preferment and advancement in the service of the State. Criticism of an unlettered nobility was common to Erasmus and Vives, Edmund Dudley and Sir Thomas More, Sir Thomas Elyot, Thomas Starkey and Roger Ascham. Education was necessary for the attainment of the good life, and the fulfilment of their duty to serve the prince and the commonwealth. Ancient lineage, gentility and chivalric accomplishments would no longer suffice as prerequisites for employment by the State. Nobility and gentry who failed to educate themselves to the end of royal service would find themselves displaced from office, power and the counsels of the Prince in favour of men of meaner origins.

Humanist propaganda might have been ineffective but for the fact that it coincided with (or reflected and was provoked by) this very process. Edmund Dudley had early sounded a warning note when he wrote that, because the nobles were ignorant and unlettered 'the children of poor men and mean folk are promoted to the promotion and authority that the children of noble blood should have if they were meet therefore'.[51] Thomas Cromwell, William Paget, Richard Rich, Edward North and Thomas Wriothesley are only the more dramatic examples of the triumph of education and training over the noblemen of great substance and little learning. A peer like Edward first Lord Monteagle, for whom the 'camp was his school' and whose 'learning was a pike and sword' could not hope to compete with them for high office.[52]

The response to this situation was a mixed one. It aroused a conservative response of bitterness and resentment,[53] and it produced the more significant and constructive response of education for royal service. So from the 1540s on, peers, gentry, and their heirs entered universities and inns of court in increasing numbers. Their motives were probably much more complex and divers than the simple object of preparation for royal office: perhaps to acquire 'social cachet',[54] or to establish useful connections with other members of the governing class. Whatever their motives were, the important practical consequence of the twin pressures – humanist propaganda and the increasing demand for an educated administrative elite – was that many nobles and gentlemen at least went through the motions of a classical humanist education, either by private tuition or in public institutions of learning. The connection between this process and the educational quality of parliament is necessary to an understanding of the political and legislative capabilities of its membership: the value of a trained mind and a knowledge of the common law in the enactment of statute; and a skill in rhetoric which might produce a higher standard of parliamentary debate. It is probable that both Lords and Commons became more competent in direct proportion to the improvement in their educational standards.

When Sir John Neale argued that the educational quality of the Elizabethan House of Commons rose dramatically, he based it on a numerical assessment of the members who had been admitted to Cambridge or Oxford or one of the inns of court. Between 1563 and 1593 the proportion of knights and burgesses who had tasted the fruits of higher education rose from 33% to just over 54%. 'Little wonder', he concluded, 'that the House of Commons showed initiative and ability.'[55] If the nature of his evidence admits of this conclusion about the Commons, then the same argument can be applied to the Upper House. As early as the first session of Edward VI's first parliament in 1547, 17% of the peers and 96% of the bishops (or 44% of the House) had attended institutions of higher learning. Eleven years later, the second session of Mary's last parliament assembled: by then 29% of the lords temporal and all of the lords spiritual (or 50% of the House) had been enrolled either at a university or an inn of court or both[56] – a record which was proportionally superior even to the House of Commons in 1584.

The educational 'backbone' of the Upper House was provided by the bishops. Even so there was a quantitative upward trend amongst the peers: from 17% to 29% in eleven years. Although no systematic study of the Elizabethan Upper House has yet been made, all the evidence suggests that this trend continued. The first earl of Bedford, the second earls of Bath, Cumberland and Huntingdon, and the sixteenth earl of Oxford did not attend university, but their heirs and successors did.[57] The heir of the merely literate first earl of Pembroke was schooled at Peterhouse under Whitgift and became a noted patron of Elizabethan antiquaries.[58] Unlike their immediate predecessors, the sixth earl of Westmorland was admitted to the Inner Temple, the second Lords Wentworth and Willoughby and the third Lord Monteagle matriculated from St John's College, Cambridge, the second and third Lords Sheffield went to university and the eleventh Lord Zouche attended Cambridge and Gray's Inn.[59] The list could be extended to include the heirs of the first Viscount Hereford, the eighth Lord Scrope and the first Lord Darcy of Chiche, all of whom attended the inns of court, and of course Lord Burghley (Cambridge and Gray's Inn) whom Lawrence Stone describes as 'the key figure in the transformation of the education of the aristocracy'.[60] A systematic and comprehensive examination would doubtless unearth other examples: those cited simply suggest that the Elizabethan increase was a continuation of a process which was pre-Elizabethan in its origins.

If the assessment of educational quality rests on no more than the arithmetical technique employed by Sir John Neale, it is evident that the mid-Tudor House of Lords was enjoying the benefits of the novel addiction to learning and letters, and that it certainly matched (and was probably superior to) the Lower House. Yet a qualitative assessment cannot be satisfactorily achieved by the mere counting of heads. The totals of those enrolled or admitted to public institutions of higher learning must be related to the purpose and effectiveness of the formal educational process, its relevance to the needs of bishops and aristocratic governors, the degree to which universities had adopted classical humanist canons, and the alternative forms of education – especially private tuition in the great noble households – adopted by those who eschewed public education.[61] In any case lurking in the wings is the villain of the piece, human nature, which can upset a quantitative analysis and make nonsense of the psephological technique. Enrolment, even attendance, is not evidence of education.[62] If they enrolled did they attend? If they attended did they work or play?

The only solution is to submit the results of the crude arithmetical technique to a number of qualitative tests: for example, who graduated? Of the 52 bishops, one abbot, one prior and 91 peers who sat in the mid-Tudor lords, 58 received degrees. All but six of these were lords spiritual, most of whom advanced beyond a first degree. In contrast only one of the peers earned his degree and did not receive it as a mere honour. The exception was Henry tenth Lord Morley whose baccalaureate of music at Oxford could hardly be regarded as an appropriate preparation for a career in the service of the Prince.[63]

On the other hand it is probable that some of the 15 peers who had enrolled at a university – for example the sons of Thomas Cromwell and John Russell[64] – had been sent in order to equip themselves for public service and so were not entirely idle when in residence, whilst the ambitious careerists of modest origins, such as North, Paget and Rich, must have viewed higher education as the ladder to a profitable career in law or government. In contrast the scions of well-established families often fell into that category of students described by a seventeenth-century Cambridge tutor, Richard Holdsworth, as men who had 'come to the university not with the intention to make scholarship their profession, but only to get such learning as may serve for delight and ornament and such as the want whereof would speak a defect in breeding rather than scholarship'.[65] Indeed the three peers of ancient lineage who had attended Oxford or Cambridge – John Lumley, Henry Parker (tenth Lord Morley) and Henry Stafford – were numbered amongst the most cultivated of the mid-Tudor peers.[66]

Therefore it is probable that the ambitions of new men with their way to make, and the disinterested dilettantism of antique peers, caused most of them to approach higher education with a serious sense of purpose and a genuine interest. Nevertheless it it questionable whether the contemporary university adequately equipped either group to serve a State which now placed a premium on administrative skill, knowledge of the law and diplomacy, rather than skill in the martial arts. Most of the peers who sat in the Edwardian and Marian parliaments were educated before the full and prolonged impact of the humanist

campaign was felt.[67] Elyot's *The Governour* was only published in
1531. The regius professorships in divinity, Greek, Hebrew,
civil law and physic were not established until 1540. Starkey,
Moryson, Cheke and Ascham and the university reforms of
1549–53 all lay in the future. So did the supplementary and
extra-statutory university courses of study which did not make
their first appearance until Elizabeth's reign. On the other hand
we must not underestimate the impact of classical humanism on
the lords temporal. Thus the fluency of William Paget and Henry
Stafford in Latin, the second earl of Bedford's skill in languages,
North's poem (written in the style of Lydgate and treating of
the moral decay of the realm), Thomas Wriothesley's highly
commended performances in the comedies of Plautus and
Lumley's translation of Erasmus's *Institution of a Christian Prince or
Ruler*, may be accounted amongst the fruits of their university
education.[68]

The contribution of the inns of court to the educational
calibre of members of the Lords (and no less of the Commons) is
more problematical. Only 14 peers[69] were admitted, one less
than the number enrolled at a university. Moreover the admission of this small band did not necessarily imply attendance
and serious study any more than it did at Cambridge and Oxford.
Motives were mixed and diverse, serious and frivolous, academic
and social. The studies of even dedicated students of the law were
hampered by the progressive neglect of the moots and readings,
the benchers' failure to fulfil their duties and, equally, the failure
of the inns to exercise an adequate academic and moral supervision.[70] As if in compensation for these deficiencies, however, the
inns encouraged an increasing range of extra-curricular activities,
which included geography, history, mathematics, languages and
other subjects of obvious utility to future governors.[71]

Of course the nature of the benefit which individuals derived
from the inns ultimately depended on whether they were serious
or 'social' students. In fact they were a mixed bag. The six
commoners, some from families of very modest status, later
acquired a variety of central and local offices – the end-product
of a vocational approach to their education.[72] Although the
Windsor brothers, William and Edward, later succeeded to the
family barony by virtue of the accidents of death, neither was
heir to a title or estate at the time of his admission to an inn:

they were faced with the challenge of carving out careers.[73] Edward Dudley was burdened with poverty as a consequence of the disastrous financial mismanagement of his father, John third Lord Dudley. Circumstantial evidence suggests a pressing need to profit from their studies.

There is, however, another side to the coin: the abrupt termin- ation of Thomas Wentworth's studies after only one year, when he succeeded to his father's barony in 1551;[74] and the serious speech impediment of Thomas ninth Baron De la Warr which must have been a severe hindrance in the system of oral exercises on which legal education was based.[75] Doubt may even be cast upon the dedication of one of the 'careerists'. Sir Thomas More's scathing description of Rich as a student at the Middle Temple cannot be dismissed lightly: 'We long dwelled both in one parish together when . . . you were esteemed very light of your tongue, a great dicer and of no commendable fame. And so in your house at the Temple, where hath been your chief bringing-up were you likewise accompted.'[76] However, later criticisms of Thomas Wriothesley should be treated with caution,[77] even though they lend apparent support to the contemporary case for his dismissal from the office of lord chancellor in March 1547. In fact he was guiltless of the charges of misconduct formulated against him: that he had issued a commission (contrary to common law) authorising 'certaine persones, the more parte whereof be Civilians . . . autorising them to heere and determyne all matters and cawses exhibited into the saide Court of Chauncery', thereby enlarging its jurisdiction and harming the common law. The real motive for his removal was his resistance to Somerset's assumption of the office and dignity of lord protector, in violation of Henry VIII's will. Moreover recent research has defended his performance in chancery.[78]

The most that can be said with confidence, therefore, is that a formal and public education beyond the grammar-school level was experienced by 23, just over one quarter of the 91 Edwardian and Marian lords temporal[79] – a total which includes the oc- casional student at a foreign university.[80] Yet this is obviously not the whole story, because some of the most cultivated, curious and academically accomplished peers had acquired their skill in Greek and Latin, modern languages and rhetoric from private tutors. The fact that many noble families opted for a private education is not surprising. It was no more than the continuation of a late-medieval tradition which was being reinforced rather than weakened by the influence of the early-Tudor educational reformers. There was a sharp division of opinion amongst them. Thomas Starkey, writing between 1533 and 1536, recommended 'the bringing up of youth in common discipline and public exercise'. He eschewed the practice whereby 'every man privately in his own house hath his master to instruct his childer in letters', a sentiment echoed by Richard Mulcaster in Elizabeth's reign.[81] Starkey went further when he advocated special schools for the nobility.[82] Nor was he alone. There followed a succession of schemes for the creation of aristocratic academies: by Nicholas Bacon at Henry VIII's direction, by Hugh Latimer during Edward VI's reign, and by Sir Humphrey Gilbert and Bacon (again) under Elizabeth.[83]

Nothing came of these conservative, hierarchically conscious proposals for aristocratic schools[84] and the great weight of humanist opinion displayed a marked preference for private tuition. Erasmus argued that even advanced education should take place in a small school or the home; Thomas Lupset envisaged an education which excluded both grammar school and university; and Sir Thomas Elyot charted a programme of private education from the child of seven to the adult of twenty-one. Elyot set great store by the study of rhetoric. 'The utility that a nobleman shall have by reading these orators is that when he shall hap to reason in counsel, or shall speak in a great audience . . . he shall not be constrained to speak words sudden and disordered, but shall bestow them aptly and in their places.' Private tuition would train the young noble to be an effective debater in the Upper House, unlike 'famous schools and universities which be so much given to the study of tongues only, that when they write epistles, they seem to the reader that, like to a trumpet, they make a sound without any purpose'.[85]

Despite the invasion of the grammar schools by the gentry, lawyers and merchants, and although a growing number of peers' sons went up to university in Elizabeth's reign, the educational record of the Edwardian and Marian peerage demonstrates that the tradition of private tuition proved to be hardy and resistant to change. Thomas third earl of Sussex, John Dudley (the duke of Northumberland's heir), Henry marquess of Dorset, Edmund Sheffield, the sixteenth earl of Oxford, the tenth Lord Cobham and Gregory Lord Cromwell had all been placed in the care of tutors.[86] At least three men undertook the instruction of Thomas Howard, the future fourth duke of Norfolk: Hadrianus Junius, a scholar of European reputation, John Foxe, and finally John White, later bishop of Lincoln.[87] Provision was even made for the education of Edward Courtenay, the son of the attainted marquess of Exeter, during his long imprisonment in the Tower.[88]

Others were placed in private schools within aristocratic households. If Sir William Cecil's was the exemplary Elizabethan model, then it found its earlier counterparts in the establishments of Sir Thomas More and Edward earl of Derby. During the 1540s sons of noblemen were being tutored in the households of Thomas earl of Southampton, William Lord St John at Basing, and Henry Stafford at Stafford Castle.[89] The most prestigious of these private 'academies' was of course at Henry VIII's Court, where Lords Lumley and Mountjoy shared with Prince Edward the attentions of Roger Ascham, Sir John Cheke, Sir Anthony Cooke and Richard Cox.[90] These examples constitute no more than the tip of the iceberg. Beyond them it is not possible to give specific examples or precise numbers. It becomes apparent, however, that the private educational process was still preferred by many noble families especially those of more 'respectable' lineage.

Moreover tutorial instruction could be as rigorous and effective as the public and formal alternative. It was broadly based, combining a classical humanist content with religious instruction and a utilitarian training in those skills appropriate to a future governing class.[91] Accomplished nobles, ranging from Edmund first Lord Sheffield ('a great Musitian' who 'wrote a Book of Sonnets according to the Italian fashion') to Henry second earl of Cumberland, a man of scientific bent but 'very studious in all manner of learning', may have contributed little to the arts of government and the transaction of parliamentary business.[92] Against them, however, must be set the more practical value of the first earl of Bedford's 'remarkable gift of tongues' and Thomas Seymour's diplomatic despatches (in both Latin and English) to Henry VIII.[93] Such examples can be repeated many times over and and attest to the importance of both private and public education in equipping a sizeable proportion of the lords temporal with the kind of training demanded by the humanist propagandists.

There is, perhaps, a darker side to the picture, especially in the north and the marches. It would be wrong to conclude a general condition of ignorance and illiteracy *a silentio*. On the other hand there is no evidence that any, other than Cumberland and Lumley, enjoyed an advanced education. The more typical northern magnates were Conyers, Dacre of the North, the first and second Lords Eure, and Barons Ogle, Scrope and Wharton.[94] They were innately conservative men, a body of near-professional soldiers none of whom, apart from Dacre, was possessed of more than modest wealth. Their correspondence with the privy council, especially on marcher matters, bears witness to their literacy, though in November 1551 the privy council complained that certain articles received from Robert sixth Lord Ogle were 'so evell writton that they could not be understanded'.[95]

More serious perhaps were the educational deficiencies of peers who rose to high places and great authority in government, or who served the Crown abroad: the third duke of Norfolk had but a meagre formal schooling; the duke of Northumberland, who had not proceeded beyond grammar school, confessed his incompetence in Latin, whilst the first earl of Pembroke's ignorance of any classical or modern language must have severely restricted the range of his usefulness to the government.[96] Despite a succession of tutors and a spell at Cambridge, the fourth duke of Norfolk remained so 'ashamed of my unskilfulness' in Latin that on one occasion early in Elizabeth's reign he had to ask a fellow councillor to negotiate with the Spanish ambassador 'because his own Latin tongue was not ready'. In 1553 no less a man than the cultivated earl of Arundel admitted that 'he understood Latin better than he spoke it'.[97]

So the educational quality of the mid-Tudor lords was patchy and variable. They ranged across the spectrum, from the unlettered nobility scorned by the humanists to the exemplars of classical humanism. In between were those for whom their families had provided the opportunities but who had not seized them. In any case even a rigorous educational programme could not act the alchemist and transmute lead into gold. Despite the care which Thomas Cromwell lavished on his son, Gregory, his

Cambridge tutor John Chekyng could only describe him in 1528 as 'rather slow but diligent'. Six years later Chekyng's successor, Henry Dowes, lamented 'forcause summer was spent in the service of the wild gods'. In 1541, his formal education completed, Gregory was described by a contemporary as 'almost a fool'.[98] The best that can be said of this ill-assorted mixture is that at least there is no evidence of illiteracy amongst the lords temporal, and although their educational record fell short of the ideal of the humanist propagandists, the mid-Tudor House was nonetheless graced with the presence of dilettante peers[99] and served by a small pool of active men of business.[100] The latter included skilled linguists, common lawyers, peers conversant with the law, versed in the art of rhetoric and acquainted with the oral exercises of the inns. Fortunately, perhaps naturally, they were amongst the most active of the lords temporal.

Any educational shortcomings in the peerage were in any case compensated in large measure by two other groups in the House: the legal assistants[101] who equipped the Lords with a panel of technical advisers at the pinnacle of the legal profession; and the lords spiritual. Episcopal status and the role of bishops in secular government declined during the Reformation. So did the number of lords spiritual in the House of Lords. Apart from the brief reappearance of a solitary abbot and the lay prior of the order of St John of Jerusalem in Mary's reign, the regular clergy disappeared after 1539. The lords spiritual were reduced to a permanent minority, comprising no more than about one-third of the House under Edward VI and Mary.[102] These circumstances, however, should not lead us to assume their parliamentary impotence or insignificance. Indeed quite the reverse: the bishops' educational 'quality' was not matched by the lawyers or country gentry in the Commons, the peers, or any other group within parliament.

Most of the lords spiritual had had a public and formal school education, over twenty of them as novitiates in monastic houses, the rest at free grammar schools. Thus Thomas Cranmer's father 'did sett hym to scole with a mervelous severe and cruell scolemaster [and] after this his bringing upp at gramer-scole he was sent to the universitie of Cambridge'.[103] With only two exceptions,[104] every one of the lords spiritual attended university[105] and, unlike the peers, they all completed their statutory

courses of study and graduated. Of course it cannot be assumed
that university courses were any more relevant to the needs of
bishops than peers. Cranmer at Cambridge, for example, 'was
nosseled in the grossest kynd of sophistry, logike, philosophy
morall and naturall, (not in the text of the old philosophers, but
chefely in the darke ridels, and quidities of Duns and other
subtile questionestes)'.[106] Criticisms of this kind, no matter how
justified they were, could not detract from the performance of
the lords spiritual, most of whom had proceeded to higher degrees
and 37 of whom had been awarded doctorates in divinity or canon
and civil law.[107] The study of divinity by 40 future bishops could
hardly have been irrelevant to their professional needs, whilst
their legal studies opened the door to diplomatic careers for
Bonner, Gardiner, Sampson and Thirlby.

The mid-Tudor bishops had an impressive record, not only as
scholars but also as teachers and administrators: 17 were masters
of colleges or occupied other collegiate offices, eleven held
university posts, two were professors,[108] and two more future
bishops – John White[109] and John Harley[110] – held other responsible teaching positions. Moreover their experience of the
world was not, in all cases, confined to ivory-tower scholarship
and the petty politics of an introverted Oxbridge society. Nine of
them had studied abroad,[111] and six had endured lengthy
periods in exile – Reginald Pole for more than twenty years.[112]
Their greatest collective parliamentary asset, however, was their
long academic training. It equipped a number of them with the
knowledge and some of the special skills which the Tudor State
now required in its officers – in particular their theological
expertise which was at a premium during the Reformation.
That expertise made the rest of parliament – Crown and Commons as well as peers – dependent on them at each religious
change, especially when that change had to be incorporated in
statute. For evidence of this we need to look no further than the
Prayer Book debate of December 1548,[113] the public disputations
in October 1553 and March–April 1559,[114] Mary's concern to
remodel the episcopal bench in 1553–4, and the recall of Thirlby
from the imperial court in order to sit in the Lords.[115]

It also fell to the bishops of the opposing faith to lead the rearguard actions against officially sponsored religious change. During
Edward VI's reign it was the conservatives Aldrich, Bonner,

Day, Heath, Repps, Skip, Tunstall and even the circumspect Thirlby, who performed this task.[116] In 1559 Heath combined with two Marians, Cuthbert Scott and Abbot Feckenham, to mount a cogently argued resistance to the Elizabethan Settlement.[117] John Jewell lamented that they and their episcopal supporters 'are a great hindrance to us, for being, as you know, among the nobility and leading men in the upper house, and having none there on our side to expose their artifices and confute their falsehoods, they reign as sole monarchs in the midst of ignorant and weak men, and easily overreach our little party, either by their numbers, or their reputation for learning'.[118] His letter was an exasperated commentary on the theological and intellectual superiority of the lords spiritual in the Upper House. It serves also as a reminder of their ability to deliver both set orations and extempore speeches – perhaps a legacy of their training in rhetoric and their experience as preachers.

Ten of the mid-Tudor bishops were trained in canon and civil law rather than in theology. The importance of this group was considerable, because it included those formidable Henricians Bonner, Gardiner, Sampson, Thirlby, Tunstall and the underrated Veysey. Their prestige derived partly from their reputation for classical learning: Erasmus was an admirer and intimate friend of Sampson; Sir Thomas More extolled the learning of Tunstall and Veysey; and John Leland sang Gardiner's praises.[119] However, this does not explain either their value to the State or the contribution which they could make to the House of Lords. It was their training in law which drew them into royal service. Canon law was one prerequisite for promotion in the Church. Civil law was the basis of international diplomacy. As canonists, civilians and Latinists they were regularly employed on diplomatic missions and in administration and the judiciary. Bonner, Gardiner, Sampson, Thirlby and Tunstall were amongst the more experienced diplomats in the Upper House.[120] At home, the service of Veysey and Sampson as presidents of the council in the Welsh marches and Tunstall's succession of offices suggest the utilitarian value of their legal education.[121]

The lords spiritual were educated men not merely in the narrow technical sense of an expertise in divinity or law. They were 'rounded' men with a diversity of interests which extended to the standard humanistic studies of Latin, Greek and Hebrew, and beyond. Bush was architect and chemist, botanist and poet. Ponet and Goldwell applied themselves to mathematics, and Tunstall's new arithmetic was prescribed as a text for the arts course, during the Cambridge visitation of 1549.[122] Naturally there is no way of determining whether this diversity did constitute a political or parliamentary asset. Nor is it possible to measure the practical value of their qualifications and specialised skills in the House of Lords. It is however, clear that collectively they were the educational and intellectual superiors of the peers. Furthermore their formal education was not merely esoteric but also practical and of wider application. They brought to the House a broad-ranging experience in matters administrative, judicial and diplomatic.

One other distinguishing characteristic of the lords spiritual was significant: that there was a 'generation gap' between peers and prelates. In January 1558 the average age differential narrowed to 11 years and 5 months, but in all other sessions the gap fluctuated between 13 and 20 years. Occasionally old grey hairs resulted in the parliamentary inactivity of individuals such as Robert King (Oxford) or John Veysey (Exeter). This was more than counterbalanced by the fact that the bishops had a maturity in years and experience which the peers only enjoyed in much smaller measure.

Nonetheless it would be misleading to convey the impression that, so far as the arts of secular government were concerned, the lords spiritual enjoyed some kind of monopoly or even primacy in the Upper House. The bishops had a positive and important contribution to make to the legislative process: in drafting, debate and revision (and sometimes in a negative and obstructive way too, as an opposition). However, apart from those canonists and civilians who were long-time royal servants, the bishops' influence seems to have been largely confined to measures concerning the Church, religion, or local matters which fell within the geographical confines of their dioceses. When the clerk of the parliaments read out the text of a bill dealing with administration, national security, common-law reform or the army, then the lords temporal naturally came into their own. The continuing laicization of government was progressively diminishing the bishops' role and experience in the council and departments of State and confining them more and more to certain specialised activities, such as diocesan and regional administration, diplomacy and equitable jurisdiction. Yet this development was, to some extent, masked during the mid-Tudor reigns. So long as the Henrician canonists and civilians survived, the bishops were a potent force in the enactment of all kinds of legislation. This was reinforced by the parliamentary enthusiasm of some of those bishops schooled in divinity not law and, as we shall see later, by the short-lived Marian episcopal 'revival'. Clearly the secularising process should not be exaggerated when six of the mid-Tudor bishops were privy councillors[123] and three held the office of lord chancellor.[124]

Yet most of the Edwardian and Marian privy councillors, officers of State, bureaucrats and Court officials were laymen, and many of the more prestigious or important offices were noble preserves: the lord great chamberlain, lord admiral, lord treasurer, steward of the royal household, earl marshal and lord president of the council. Others were often in their hands: the lord chancellor, keeper of the privy seal, lord chamberlain of the household, and master of the court of wards and liveries. Furthermore 30 peers sat at the council board for varying periods between 1547 and 1558. Inevitably they carried with them into the Upper House a much greater and more diverse knowledge and experience of both matters of State and the bureaucratic process than the bishops could hope to muster.

This immediately brings us into confrontation with the double standard so commonly applied in Tudor parliamentary studies. It is frequently assumed that an assembly of bishops – State servants of a king who was also supreme head – and peers who were intimately involved in national government and closely connected with the Court, naturally constituted an obedient, even subservient house. Although this assumption may satisfy those historians who read Tudor parliaments in terms of the rise of the Commons, of the decline of the Lords, and of opposition and conflict,[125] it has never been adequately tested. It ignores the independent temper of many members of a powerful social elite. It forgets the bishops' stiffening of faith in the face of unwelcome religious changes. It neglects to observe that many of the most vigorous figures who sat in the supposedly independent-tempered Commons were elevated to the Upper House. John Dudley, William Paulet, John and Francis Russell, William

Herbert, Thomas Wriothesley, Anthony Browne, John Bridges, Thomas Darcy, Edward Hastings, Edward North, William Paget, Richard Rich, Thomas Wentworth, Thomas Wharton and John Williams were only the most prominent members of a steady flow of recruits. Are we to assume that, once they had taken their seats, they too were suddenly cowed and complaisant like the rest of the House? It is an unlikely proposition and, as we shall see, an unacceptable one. It should be added that the intimate association of bishops and peers with the State was an asset to the House rather than a liability or constraint. It provided members with a detailed knowledge of the workings of government which was of practical value when dealing with many of the bills before them.

Two other characteristics of the Lords' membership deserve mention. The House consisted of men with a relative permanence of tenure: bishops (once appointed) and peers (once created or having succeeded) could look forward to life tenure, unless they fell victims to Reformation politics or royal disfavour. Sir John Neale drew attention to the emergence of the long-serving 'parliament men' in the Elizabethan Commons:[126] for example 54% of the knights and burgesses who sat in the 1584 parliament served in three or more sessions;[127] yet in the mid-Tudor Upper House the total was 81%, 22 being eligible for 20 sessions or more.[128] Because of the very nature of its membership, the Lords' fund of parliamentary experience far outweighed that of the Lower House.

Nor was the experience of the lords temporal confined to their own house. Twenty-six peers[129] (nearly 29%) had been elected to the Commons at some time in the past. Inevitably their experience varied considerably. Thomas Wentworth represented Suffolk in the parliament which met on 3 November 1529, but within a month he was summoned to the Lords as a baron.[130] In contrast to this fleeting appearance in the Commons, seven other future peers were eligible for eight sessions,[131] three more for nine,[132] Edward Hastings for eleven and Richard Rich for 13. These men brought to the Lords a knowledge of Commons' procedures, and they may have played a part in a process of procedural cross-fertilisation whereby the Commons followed the established practices of the older House, which in turn adopted refinements developed in the lower chamber.[133]

A small group of bishops and peers also served in the parliamentary bureaucracy. Their names are familiar. North was clerk of the parliaments from 1531 to 1540.[134] In July 1541 the office was granted to William Paget who held it until 1543 when it was regranted in survivorship with Thomas Knight. In December 1549 Paget was summoned to the Lords, and in the following year he relinquished the office.[135] Wriothesley, Rich[136] and three bishops[137] served as lord chancellor (who was the presiding officer in the Upper House). That indefatigable trimmer Rich actually enjoyed the distinction of presiding over both Houses, having been elected speaker of the Commons in the parliament of 1536. As might be expected, his tenure of the office was distinguished by the fulsome flattery of his addresses to the king.[138]

The same names appear repeatedly in any qualitative study of the Lords' membership. Nevertheless the assets of the House, as represented in the training and experience of bishops and peers, encompassed a large proportion of the members. Although any attempt to make a precise comparison with the Commons would be futile, it would be foolish to underrate the quality of the Upper House or to write it off as compliant or ineffectual. On the contrary there is every indication that it was well equipped to perform its parliamentary functions in an efficient and responsible manner – and probably more so than the Commons.

4

ATTENDANCE AND ACTIVITY, ABSENTEEISM AND MANAGEMENT

An examination of the quality of a parliamentary assembly acquires substance and meaning only when it is related to actual performance. The fact that the Lords was blessed with a wide spectrum of talents, abundant experience and the appropriate legislative skills, becomes irrelevant if the members endowed with these particular qualities did not attend regularly and shoulder the main burden of business. Even if they did, a second question interposes itself: did they enjoy freedom of action or did they simply bow to royal directives? The conundrum can be expressed in institutional terms: was the Upper House efficient in practice, and was it something more than a rubber stamp to royal policies and a constitutional support to the Crown's authority?

The Lords' attendance record provides a precise record of who turned up and who stayed away. More problematical is the motivation: whether their presence or absence was determined by the political interests of the Crown. Vernon Snow and Helen Miller disagreed about the pre-Edwardian situation,[1] the former arguing that the privy council perfected its managerial techniques in the early forties by manipulating attendance, and the latter denying that, by then, there existed serious managerial problems.[2] Whatever the answer, it sheds no light on the problem whether the Upper House was effectively controlled in the two succeeding reigns. There are other subsidiary and related considerations too: whether the active membership was recruited mainly from the lords spiritual or temporal, from old or new peers, and from the abler and more experienced members; whether, too, the legislative burden was spread broadly or was concentrated in the hands of a dedicated minority of active 'parliament-men', in particular the privy councillors. The answers to such questions will provide at least a pointer to the mid-Tudor Lords' business efficiency, and the extent to which it enjoyed a freedom of initiative, action, and decision.

As soon as comparative and qualitative assessments are applied to a quantitative analysis of attendance, arbitrary decisions have to be made, in particular, where to position the boundaries between those who attended occasionally, infrequently and regularly. Helen Miller isolated two groups in her study of Henrician attendance: those who appeared at some time during the session, and those who attended regularly. Her line of de-marcation was 75%[3] of business sessions in which attendance is recorded in the Lords' Journal.[4] Whilst her choice has been adopted here to facilitate comparison, it would be no less realistic to adopt 80%, 70% or 66% as a lower limit for the regulars.

The application of what we might call the 'Miller index' to the attendance register of the mid-Tudor Lords' Journals reveals that a high proportion of the House (77%)[5] put in an appearance in each session. In contrast, and as might be expected, the regulars constituted a smaller group of just over 42%. Of course there are sessional variations: the proportion who turned up at some time during a session fluctuated between 89% in the second protectorate assembly of 1548/9 and 54% in November 1558.[6] The relatively low figure for the last Marian session probably reflects the loosening discipline, administrative relaxation, and anxiety about the political future as the queen approached death and the reign drew to a close. This session apart, the great majority of eligible members did participate in each of the mid-Tudor parliaments. The proportion of 'regulars' inevitably fluctuated too. Apart from the session of 1548/9 and the parlia-ment of March 1553 it was always a minority. On the other hand, only twice did it fall below a third: in January 1558 – partly because of the military demands on the peerage – and in November of the same year.[7]

The fact that many bishops and peers made only infrequent or occasional appearances meant that the daily attendance was small and invariably lower than the general attendance figures: for example 82% of eligible members turned up for at least part of the 1547 session, but the daily attendance ran at only 57%[8] or an average of 15 bishops and 26 peers each day. The most striking impression is that of a small and intimate body, more akin in size to a committee and in stark contrast to the House of

Commons. In May 1979 the new Conservative prime minister appointed a cabinet of 22 members; the daily attendance of the Lords in November 1558 averaged only four more than this, and in all but two of the mid-Tudor sessions was less than double that number. This doubtless explains why many of the Lords' procedures were characterised by an apparent flexibility which was possible, permissible and even desirable in such a small gathering.[9]

On the other hand there were normally sufficient members present to carry on the business of the House, averaging between 35 and 48, again with the exception of the last Marian session.[10] Admittedly, sessional averages do conceal the fact that on particular days the attendance could fall dangerously low: 14 on 24 November, and eight on 21 December 1548, whilst the clerk recorded only 17 on 18 February 1558.[11] However, the presence rarely fell below 20, and only in the session cut short by Mary's death did it frequently fail to reach 30. Strangely enough crucial debates and votes did not result in an unusually crowded chamber. When, for example, the bill for confirmation of the first Edwardian Prayer Book was read, on 7, 10 and 15 January 1549, the turnout of about 49 was almost identical with the daily average for the entire session.[12] Daily attendance seldom exceeded two-thirds of the eligible membership, even when important or contentious measures were before the House, and parliamentary business was normally transacted by an active minority, afforced by a number of 'irregulars'. Despite this, daily absenteeism did not become so serious that, in the absence of an official quorum, a sitting had to be abandoned simply for lack of members.

The attendance registers also record a significant regnal contrast. The proportion attending the Edwardian sessions was 82%, a figure which dropped to 72% in the following reign. The regulars' attendance record under Edward VI ranged between 66% and 39%, with a regnal average of 51%, whereas no Marian session rose above 44% and the average was only 34% for the reign. The constantly inferior Marian record may be politically significant and it is certainly characteristic of a parliamentary decline, manifested in a number of ways.[13] Particularly serious was the decline in regular attenders, the group on which the legislative effectiveness of the House really depended. In November 1554, for example, 80% made at least one appearance, perhaps to signify publicly their conformity and loyalty during the parliament which reunited England with Rome. Thereafter, a steady procession of withdrawals, expressive of dissatisfaction with royal policies, lowered the proportion of regulars to only 34%. Nor was the erratic and inferior Marian performance restricted to this one parliament.[14]

There are two possible explanations for the regnal contrast.[15] Successive Edwardian governments *may* have exercised a more effective supervision over parliamentary attendance. There is no significant difference between the protectorate sessions[16] and those held during Northumberland's supremacy, the fall in the general attendance level in March 1553 being compensated by the increased proportion of regulars. Both the Edwardian and Marian regimes were characterised by bitter political in-fighting. Yet, despite its particular ferocity under Edward VI, it probably had a less deleterious effect on parliament. Each of Northumberland's coups, which toppled the protector in 1549 and sent him to his death in 1552, was carried through before parliament assembled. By the time it met, in November 1549 and January 1552, the victor and his allies were in command and the government was able to project the image of unity and a common purpose. The power-struggle between Bishop Gardiner and Lord Paget in 1553–4, however, split the Marian privy council and disrupted parliament, which was treated to the public spectacle of rival conciliar factions promoting their own designs and even sacrificing the queen's interests to their mutual enmities.[17]

The response of the governing class to royal policies was also of some account. Although the Edwardian religious measures of 1549 and 1552 were guaranteed to offend conservative prelates and peers, none were as contentious, or productive of such widespread hostility, resentment and fear, as either the Spanish match and its consequences or the economic and financial implications of the reunion with Rome.[18] The disunity within Mary's government mirrored the concern of the governing class. Together with the unpopularity of her policies, it inhibited effective parliamentary management, and provoked the varying responses of conflict, resistance, and the absenteeism of those who opted for discretion instead of confrontation.[19]

Two characteristics of attendance have so far emerged: some

participation by a large majority of eligible members, whilst a minority were the dedicated hewers of wood and drawers of water. These latter were the active parliament-men, amongst whom the lords spiritual loomed large: 53% of the mid-Tudor bishops and only 38% of the peers can be accounted so. Again there was a regnal decline (down from 59% to 47% of the lords spiritual and from 47% to 22% of their lay colleagues) but it cannot mask the fact that the bishops' record was consistently more respectable. This was not a new phenomenon – a similar state of affairs had prevailed in medieval parliaments,[20] and in the Henrician sessions of the early forties[21] – nor was it a surprising one. Their presence, as royal servants[22] and theological experts, was demanded in the successive swings of the Reformation pendulum. Consequently a sizeable group figured amongst the most active members of the House – not only Edwardian reformers, such as Cranmer, Ferrar, Goodrich, Holbeach, Hooper and Ridley, but also conservative Henricians and Marians (in particular Bonner, Bourne, Day, Gardiner, Heath, Thirlby, Tunstall and White). Much of the business of the Upper House devolved upon a group of prelates who polarised into two opposing ideological camps but who spent much of their time collaborating in the enactment of bills. They also shared the common characteristic of parliamentary 'busy-ness', despite the concurrent demands of convocation.[23]

The lords spiritual and temporal both included in their ranks a number of privy councillors. Their individual records of conciliar service naturally varied considerably.[24] Some served in only one reign, whereas Winchester (Paulet), Rich and others had a more or less continuous record of service. Some were already experienced councillors in 1547;[25] others no longer sat at the council board but still sat in the Upper House.[26] The mid-Tudor council was large and unwieldly, in sharp contrast to the Henrician and Elizabethan bodies. As it grew, so did the recruitment of bishops and peers to its membership. Collectively the councillors, present and past, embodied the greatest fund of practical experience of public affairs, an asset of obvious importance in an assembly of legislators. The wealth of such experience available is indicated by the figures: that 30[27] peers and seven[28] bishops (over a quarter of the entire actual membership) had been, were, or became councillors between 1547 and 1558. Furthermore the conciliar element in the House steadily grew during Edward VI's reign – from ten (14% of the actual membership) in 1547 to 18 (27%) in March 1553 – and only a modest decline occurred under Mary (15 to 17 or 23% per session).[29]

Most of the councillors possessed a specialised skill and accumulated experience in a particular aspect of government. Southampton, Paget and Rich had been trained in Cromwell's bureaucracy.[30] Others were soldiers,[31] courtiers,[32] experts in diplomacy,[33] finance,[34] law[35] and theology, or were men with a working experience in regional and local administration.[36] However, they were more than mere specialists. By the very nature of the privy council, with its all-embracing interest, activity, and oversight, its members were confronted with an infinite range of problems, and multifarious tasks were heaped upon them. Consequently their administrative experience extended far beyond the duties of any one particular department of State. Moreover, practical knowledge of the working of government was not confined to councillors. A considerable number of other peers and bishops had a record of past or present service on the regional councils,[37] in the French[38] and Scottish[39] marches, and in Ireland.[40] It is unnecessary to labour the point that, in its deliberations, the Lords could call upon a wealth of practical experience of government.[41] This was an undeniable asset. However, the intimate involvement of its membership in the structure and activities of the State could have robbed it of the capacity to adopt an independent stand on matters before it, especially those concerning the Crown. Whilst its efficiency doubtless benefited from the presence of numerous councillors and bureaucrats, these men were royal servants with an obligation to protect and pursue royal interests. This was especially true of privy councillors, whose responsibilities included the successful transaction of the monarch's parliamentary business. They devised the schedules of proposed bills, instructed those learned in the law to draft the appropriate measures, and guided them through *both* houses.[42]

On paper, the very size and composition of the mid-Tudor privy council and bureaucracy should have resolved this managerial challenge, at least so far as the Upper House was concerned. It was an assembly top-heavy with royal servants and led by a sizeable body of councillors. In these circumstances it is not surprising that parliamentary historians have assumed it to be compliant and subservient, with its independence stifled and the occasional rebel easily browbeaten.[43] However, the prerequisite either of a systematic and disciplined control or even just of a general guidance and leadership was regular attendance by councillors. In the absence of attendance figures for the House of Commons, it has been supposed that the majority dutifully fulfilled their obligations of attendance and management there. Naturally that assumption has been extended to the Lords,[44] where the general obligation of members to attend (saving a special exemption from the Crown) reinforced the particular duty of councillors to look to the king's business. Despite this, the council's performance sometimes fell noticeably short of the ideal. Admittedly, and to their credit, the episcopal councillors of Edward VI – Cranmer, Goodrich and Tunstall – had a parliamentary record which was almost impeccable and certainly peerless.[45] Even the noble councillors were rarely absent for an entire Edwardian session: only Warwick in 1547, and Huntingdon and Rich in 1552.[46] Nevertheless the performance of the lay element was variable and, at times, unimpressive. The proportion of days on which they attended Edwardian sessions ranged between 83% (1548/9) and 59% (1549/50). Only once did their Marian average rise above three-quarters of the daily sittings (76% in 1555), whilst twice they dropped below 60% (in 1554/5 and November 1558).

This patchy performance was the consequence of the kaleidoscopic politics of the two reigns. When the first two Edwardian sessions were held, the protector's supremacy was not yet being openly challenged, except by his madcap brother. The relative stability of the regime was reflected in the council's superior attendance record (86% and 81% compared with 71% and 75% by the whole House). Thereafter its chequered performance reflected the aristocratic power-struggle. When parliament reassembled for its third session, on 4 November 1549, the protectorate had collapsed, Somerset and his supporters were in prison, and Warwick's faction had moved into the seats of power. Warwick himself, absorbed in the consolidation of his authority, left parliamentary management to others and attended only nine of the 66 business sittings. Shrewsbury replaced Archbishop Holgate, Somerset's adherent, as president of the council of the north – hence his absence from the Lords from 11 December onwards.[47] The disillusioned conservatives, Arundel and Southampton, who had lent themselves to Warwick's coup in the vain hope of a Catholic 'restoration', and then had failed in their bid to carry through a counter-coup, rarely appeared.[48] The cumulative parliamentary effect was a falling away in the council's attendance record.

The next session also met in the shadow of a political upheaval, engineered by Warwick (now Northumberland) who was intent upon the final destruction of the Somerset interest. The ex-protector was executed on the day before parliament met; Arundel, Paget and Tunstall were in prison; and Rich was conveniently (though genuinely) sick. With the exception of Cobham, Northumberland's noble recruits to the council did not attend regularly.[49] The frequency with which councillors attended (69% of the sittings) was now marginally lower than the average of the whole House.[50] Their improved performance in Edward's second parliament occurred when Northumberland was in undisputed control of government and making strenuous efforts to secure a tractable assembly.[51] Even so their performance was once again slightly inferior to that of the whole House.[52] In practice, however, the variable record of individual councillors was more than offset by the steady increase in the size of the conciliar element in the Lords.[53] The average daily presence of councillors rose from eight to ten in the protectorate sessions, remained constant at that level in the politically disturbed years of 1549–52, and then increased again to 13 in March 1553. In a small House Somerset, and after him Northumberland, was served by a group of councillors large enough to provide a continuous and effective leadership.[54] Furthermore, conciliar divisions were rarely given a public airing in the Lords because, on each occasion, opponents of the ascendant faction were in prison or opted to stay away. The council usually sustained a facade of unity in parliament.[55]

Once again Mary's reign contrasted unfavourably with its predecessor. The proportion of days attended by councillors dropped.[56] The daily presence fell to ten in 1554–5 and continued to decline thereafter.[57] The number of sessional absentees increased – admittedly six (and possibly seven) of these stayed away from that brief addled session abruptly terminated by the queen's death, but ten councillors also stayed away for an entire session between 1554 and 1558.[58] To some extent this reflected the diminishing presence in the Marian Upper House.[59] And there is a simple and innocuous explanation of a number of absences: Wentworth on duty as deputy of Calais in 1554–8,[60] Bedford heading an embassy to Spain in April 1554,[61] and Shrewsbury sick in the following year.[62] Nevertheless decline was a Marian characteristic which continued, albeit erratically, throughout the reign.

More serious than decline was disunity, both in the House at large and amongst the councillors.[63] Concerted and vigorous parliamentary opposition to official policies in Edward VI's reign was restricted to conservative bishops afforced by a handful of peers of like persuasion. They had the courage and conviction (or effrontery and foolish impetuosity) to turn up regularly and offer resistance. But they always constituted a minority, official bills were never at risk, and there was no public split in the council. In contrast, Mary swiftly purged the episcopal bench and transformed it into a loyal, if not tame, body. Opposition to the often divergent policies of the queen and Gardiner was therefore centred on the lords temporal, amongst whom the response was threefold. Some coalesced into a pressure group.[64] Others went further and organised successful resistance to measures desired by Gardiner and Mary.[65] The remainder preferred to dissociate themselves from unpopular policies, whilst avoiding direct confrontation with the Crown. Resorting to a compromise which threaded its way uneasily between conviction and circumspection, they absented themselves as a silent gesture of protest.[66] More sinister was the fact that the most prominent critics and opponents of the queen and her lord chancellor were councillors. The transfer of faction disputes from the council board to the House of Lords[67] during the period of Gardiner's chancellorship (1553–5) destroyed any prospect of effective management, promoted disunity, demoralised the Lords and contributed to absenteeism.

When parliament reassembled in 1555, however, circumstances had changed. Mary's dynastic and religious policies had been largely sanctioned by statute. Gardiner, one of the faction leaders, was dying, his rival Paget and many other peers were tied to the Spanish connection by pensions and military appointments, and

the old faction issues were irrelevant or dormant.[68] The focus of
discontent switched instead to the Commons.[69] The relative
tranquillity of the Upper House may of course be a consequence rather of a lack of evidence than of opposition. However
about one thing we can be certain: that in this parliament the
decline in attendance was arrested.[70] Although, in January 1558,
military exigencies demanded the absence of a number of peers,
the previous attendance levels were maintained.[71] Only in the
peculiar circumstances of that short-lived session later in the
same year did the numbers noticeably drop again.[72] What
comes through quite clearly is that, even at the end, the councillors
constituted a significantly large proportion of the members
present.[73] Even in the unusually disordered conditions of the
years 1547–58, the surrogate kings of Edward VI's reign and
Queen Mary were always served by the regular presence of a
sizeable group of councillors – the prerequisite for an effective
leadership, guidance and even control of the Lords. Nevertheless
this is a reflection of the size and aristocratic complexion of the
mid-Tudor councils, not of the regularity with which all noble
and episcopal councillors attended. Indeed the variable and even
indifferent record of many of them suggests that the Crown may
not have been concerned to compel a larger presence and more
regular attendance – a commentary on either its political inepti-
tude or its awareness that there were always enough councillors
on hand to protect its intersts. Alternatively it may have been
incapable of disciplining councillors to treat their parliamentary
obligations more seriously, a comment on its weakness. In any
case, as other calls of service sometimes took precedence over
parliamentary business, it was impossible to secure the presence
of the full complement of councillors. Even regular attendance
brought few benefits without co-operation and unity, which
were so dramatically lacking in the early Marian parliaments.

It remains then to be considered who constituted the active
membership of the House, how qualified they were to carry the
burden of business, and how prominent the councillors were in
this group. Identification of the active membership is largely
dependent on the tests of attendance, the record of committee
membership, and the occasional evidence of speeches culled
from extra-parliamentary sources. Frequently it is more realistic
to evaluate activity in relative terms – that a peer or bishop was

more (or less) active than others – rather than in the absolute criteria of *active* and *inactive*. On the other hand, it is easy enough to slot men like Nicholas Heath and John Lord Mordaunt into quite different categories. Heath (with an attendance record of 81% and a membership of 14 committees in eight sessions) contrasts with Mordaunt who did not bother to appear and naturally sat on no committees. Mordaunt must be counted amongst the 22[74] parliamentary backwoodsmen of the mid-Tudor Lords. They were conspicuous only by their regular absence, frequently away for entire sessions and perfunctory when they did turn up. They can have contributed little to the business of the House.[75]

The remaining 121 'actual' members of the mid-Tudor Lords fall into two groups: the work-horses, without whom the Lords could not have functioned effectively, and those members who played a less important yet still useful and supporting role.[76] The allocation of members to one or other of these groups sometimes smacks of the arbitrary, but usually their placing is automatically determined by their performance. They ranged from regular attenders with committee experience to those with a lower attendance record yet still frequent nomination to committees. Nevertheless a clearly identifiable active membership emerges, consisting of 22 bishops[77] and 36 peers[78] – over one-third (41%) but still a minority of the House bore the burden of parliamentary business. In that group the bishops stood out by virtue of their superior attendance and committee records. Amongst the lords temporal the new nobles scored over the old families.[79] Although the new, intermediate and old peers constituted groups of similar size in the actual membership (37%, 31% and 32% respectively), nobles of recent creation totalled 21 (or 58%) of the active lords temporal, and in every way their record was superior.[80] There is no question but that the business of the House was borne chiefly on the backs of the bishops and the newly risen, politically conscious members of urban middle-class and gentry families.[81] They attended more assiduously;[82] their names figured more frequently on committee lists;[83] and in every session they comprised well over half of the active membership.[84]

Inevitably a broad analysis of this kind ignores variations in the duration of individual performance: that Holbeach and

Skip died in Edward VI's reign, whilst six 'intruding' Edwardian bishops were deprived by Mary without an opportunity to sit in one of her parliaments;[85] that the mid-Tudor experience of Bishop Gardiner and seven other prelates was confined to Mary's reign,[86] eight peers appeared only in Edwardian sessions,[87] and eight more were created or restored, or succeeded to titles under Mary.[88] No more than five bishops and 20 peers garnered their parliamentary experience in both reigns. Such variations, however, cannot disguise the superior collective performance of the new nobility and, above all, of the bishops. Moreover it was a group rich in qualifications, ability and experience. Every bishop had at least one degree. Six peers had enrolled at a university or inn of court and another five had sampled both, whilst there is evidence of the private education, cultural and intellectual achievements of at least nine others.[89] As might be expected the group included a large number of peers (17)[90] who had served in the Commons at sometime prior to their elevation. There was after all a natural correlation between parliamentary activity and an interest in parliamentary affairs. The quality of the active membership, however, is best demonstrated not by collective virtues but by individual performances. They dominated the politics and government of their day: Bonner, Day, Gardiner, Heath and Tunstall fighting an Edwardian rearguard action in and out of the Lords, before coming into their own under Mary; the Reformation vanguard of Coverdale, Cranmer, Hooper, Ponet and Ridley; prominent politicians such as Somerset, Gardiner and Paget; and the Crown's most experienced diplomats, bureaucrats and household officials.[91] As if this was not enough, the active membership included many with present or previous experience of the privy council, a high proportion of the Crown's military and naval experts,[92] its great regional viceroys,[93] and those ornaments of learning, Arundel, Lumley, (tenth) Morley and Stafford.

It would be misleading to imply that every man of talent, power, reputation or experience was active. The duke of Northumberland, for example, may have detested the parliamentary grind as much as he loathed the monotony of council business.[94] However, such men amounted to no more than a handful. Experience, authority and the requisite skills were concentrated in the active membership. So too were the privy councillors who comprised 19 (or 45%) of active Edwardian members and 15 – just over one-third – in Mary's reign. Such a numerous and prestigious group, bolstered by the Crown's authority, could have managed and manipulated the Lords if it had so desired. It also had to fulfil certain conditions. Councillors could only translate their numerical potential into actual parliamentary muscle if they were organised, united, and agreed on their ultimate managerial objective. Was their prime concern to head off or suppress opposition, or simply to improve efficiency? To invert the question, was the Lords a compliant assembly, immersing itself in the technicalities of legislation and happy to accept the dominance and direction of the council, or was it capable of taking up a neutral, independent, critical, hostile or even oppositionist stand towards official policies and bills?

The answer lies partly in the complementary phenomena of attendance and absenteeism. As we have seen, the Crown's power to deny writs was by now strictly circumscribed. However, the managerial possibilities of attendance-manipulation were much greater because, once the Crown had issued writs of summons, which in normal circumstances it was required to do, it exercised a broad-ranging discretionary power over attendance.[95] It could also pressurise absentees to name reliable men as proctors who would exercise their 'voice' in the House. Yet to assume that the Crown did this, or even contemplated it, is to accept a largely untested hypothesis: that it always feared parliamentary opposition and organised itself to prevent or overcome it.

Past experience, however, indicates that this was not the chief purpose of management. A. F. Pollard[96] and, more systematically, J. S. Roskell[97] demonstrated the alarming absenteeism of the medieval House of Lords. Roskell lamented that fourteenth-century attendance was 'frequently spasmodic, and at times so embarrassingly scanty as to have a very deleterious effect on parliament's capacity to proceed with its business: in fact, now and then, parliament had to be abandoned altogether on this account'.[98] Nor did the fifteenth century witness an improvement and the old deficiencies continued into the reign of Henry VIII: irregularity of attendance, the delayed arrival of many members, a fluctuating but often high incidence of sessional absenteeism. Although there was a marked improvement under Thomas

Cromwell, there occurred, after his fall, a partial reversion to the medieval situation. The common willingness to evade parliamentary responsibilities compelled the government to direct its energies towards the ensurance of a sufficient presence.[99] Whilst it cannot be denied that private instructions and pardons from attendance occasionally excluded political opponents,[100] their use for political reasons was exceptional. To the end of Henry VIII's reign endemic absenteeism remained the continuing concern of the Crown, and the conduct of Edwardian and Marian governments must be considered in the context of this past experience.

There was nothing sinister in absenteeism. Personal reasons such as old age, infirmity, the priority given to royal service elsewhere, distance, poverty, simple lack of interest – these explain most absences before 1547.[101] Nevertheless, absenteeism – and especially sessional absences – could have serious implications. Every peer and bishop had the right as well as the duty to attend, but the Crown held the whip-hand. It could demand attendance,[102] instruct royal servants to stay at their posts;[103] or, as an act of grace, pardon the poverty-stricken, the aged and the sick from attendance. As Henry VIII had demonstrated, it could also exclude opponents under any of these pretexts, or by the simple device of a private letter instructing a member to absent himself.[104] Its ability to regulate attendance remained extensive, and one weapon in its armoury had important managerial potential: that in practice it exercised a power of veto (or direction) over the absentee's choice of a proctor to represent him in the House.[105] The years 1547–58 were a time of crisis akin to the 1530s. Indeed government was faced with even more sustained and widespread opposition than Henry VIII had had to overcome. In those circumstances it is conceivable that the privy council was tempted to go further than Henry's occasional exclusion of opponents and systematically exploit the system of licensed absenteeism and proctorial representation in order to control the Upper House.

Proctorial representation was the procedural consequence of the Crown's power to grant exemptions from attendance to members of the Lords.[106] By 1547 the procedural sequence had been standardised: a written or verbal application to the king, lord chancellor or favoured minister (such as Thomas Cromwell) for leave of absence, stating the reason for the request; and a royal licence or letter of approval which exempted the supplicant from attendance for part or all of a session, a parliament or for life.[107] The licence also instructed the absentee to nominate a proctor (or proctors) invariably appointed from the ranks of the lords spiritual or temporal.[108] The proctor was empowered to execute a general power of attorney, including the right to exercise the absentee's voice and his vote, as well as his own. His authority to act rested on the letter of procuration or proxy sent up by the absentee and delivered to the clerk of the parliaments or his deputy.[109] Upon receipt of the proxy the clerk registered it in his journal.[110] Sometimes he entered it as part of the record for the day on which it was handed to him;[111] but in other sessions the proxies were collated in a composite list, which was later bound in at the beginning of the journal.[112] No matter which technique was adopted, the purpose was the same: it enabled the clerk to obtain the fees due to him for registration of the proxies.[113]

The managerial possibilities inherent in the proxy system are obvious. The Crown could have secured the absence of critics and opponents and ensured that they nominated proctors favourable to its policies. Thus, by a process of political accountancy, it could transfer votes from the debit to the credit column. If this was the case contemporary political commentators and members of the House missed the point. According to Henry earl of Essex in 1529, 'it is accustomed that our voyces shall remayne in the hous for the avancement and furtherance off justice'.[114] Henry Elsynge, writing in the next century, was equally oblivious to its potential as a manipulative instrument: 'Those Lords that could not appear according to their summons, made their Proxies, and even this shews their Right to be summoned, else what needed their Proxies.'[115] In their view a proxy was the confirmation of the right of a bishop or peer to attend, and a formal acknowledgement of his duty to do so. The procedure enabled him to absent himself, whilst ensuring his representation and committing him to decisions taken in his absence.[116]

Inevitably that procedure had its fair share of variations and irregularities: that 45 of the 168[117] licensed absentees under Edward and Mary secured licences for only part of a session; that a member seeking absence for only part of a session (whether for personal reasons or because of the exigencies of royal service elsewhere) might sue out a licence at the requisite moment during a parliament and not before it met;[118] and that the validity of a licence (and therefore of a proctor's authority) might extend to more than one session.[119] Nor, to further complicate matters, did every licensee absent himself immediately after the registration of his proxy, or for all of the remaining business days.[120] It would even be rash to assume that the proctors attended regularly.[121] Their frequently perfunctory attendance was the product of many things, amongst them illness, more pressing business and simple lack of interest. It was a risk which the absentee had to take. However, if the Crown had been concerned to secure a reliable bloc of proxy votes, then presumably it would have concerned itself to ensure the proctors' presence. Yet even councillors such as Arundel with six proxies in the parliament of 1554–5, Pembroke with three in 1555, and Paget and Pembroke with three between them in January 1558, turned up for less than half the morning sittings. The Crown made no move to replace proctors who died or were themselves absent.[122] Successive mid-Tudor regimes displayed a consistently casual attitude to the whole question.[123]

The explanation of this apparently happy-go-lucky attitude is not difficult to find. The proctor exercised the absentee's 'voice', which could be expressed in two ways: by airing his views and (theoretically) by casting his vote.[124] If proxy votes were used in the mid-Tudor Lords, they could have acquired political significance only when cast against an endangered official bill. Dissenting votes, however, were the exception, for bills usually passed with the assent of the whole House. The earliest recorded examples of dissent were in the Henrician sessions of 1542–5.[125] The incidence rose sharply in the two following reigns, but still remained infrequent.[126] Seldom did the number of 'not contents' imperil the passage of a government bill. Nevertheless, supposing that proxy votes were exercised on such occasions, could the dissenters have mustered a sufficient number of them to secure the defeat of an objectionable measure? The question cannot be answered without posing another: *how* were they exercised? The procedure was complicated by the fact that absentees frequently nominated multiple proctors to act *conjunctim et divisim*.[127] This direction to joint proctors, to exercise their votes jointly and severally, might be regarded as a power of attorney entitling them to cast their proctorial votes individually,[128] and even differently if they disagreed. Common sense and the evidence both discourage such a conclusion. If each joint proctor had exercised a separate vote, then the more proctors who were named by each absentee, the more votes would have been created.[129] The result would have been to transform into reality any parliamentary manager's dream and to convert the House of Lords into a royal pocket borough. In fact the earliest recorded account of proxy voting discounts the possibility that joint proctors could cast their votes on opposing sides. Sir Edward Coke described a vote in the Lords in 1559 when one 'gave consent to a Bill, and the two others said, not content'. When the advice of the legal assistants was sought, they resolved that 'this was no voice'.[130] The fractionalisation of votes among joint proctors is equally improbable, and D'Ewes's later description must be accepted as the only practicable procedure: 'if there be two or three Proxies constituted by one absent Lord, as is frequent, then always the first named in the same is to give the Voice if he be present, and if absent then the second, *et sic de reliquis*'.[131]

Whether the addition of proxies to the votes of dissenters ever imperilled a bill before the mid-Tudor House must remain an academic question. The recorded use of proxy votes in the sixteenth century occurs only twice: in Sir Edward Coke's description of events in 1559, which is unsupported by the journal, and on 1 March 1581, when 'the nombers of the contents on the one syde and the nombers of the not contents on the other syde [were] founde to be equall and alyke with their proxyes'.[132] Although the evidence is fragmentary, and is barely reinforced by Sir Thomas Smith's idealised description of Lords' procedure,[133] it is enough to establish that proxy voting was not unknown to the Elizabethans. On the other hand there is no indication that it was practised before then. The Edwardian and Marian journals are silent on the point (as indeed the Elizabethan clerk's record is until 1581), and when the clerk recorded dissenting votes he did not include their proxies. If the deficient record conceals the truth and they were exercised, then the government was curiously lax when it failed to ensure the regular attendance of proctors. If they were not used, however, then the only important function of proctorial representation was not a managerial one. It was no more than a confirmation of the right and duty of lords of parliament to attend.

The Crown's apparent lack of concern to maintain a tight control over absenteeism – and in particular to extract proxies from all who stayed away – is confirmed by the phenomenon of the unlicensed absentee. No parliament was without its quota, perhaps as many as 70 in the two reigns.[134] In fact sessional absenteeism, licensed or otherwise, still ran at a high level in the mid-Tudor Lords, even though its attendance record remained superior to that of its medieval and immediate predecessors. On no occasion did it fall below 10% of the actual membership of the House, fluctuating between 14% in 1548/9 and 49% in November 1558.[135] The benches of the lords spiritual and temporal in the parliament house were appreciably thinned, sometimes by as much as one-fifth or more, by sessional absenteeism. Fortunately few of the ablest, most influential and experienced members stayed away for long periods and such absences affected the quantity rather than the quality of the House.

If, however, sessional absenteeism was politically inspired, it may have left the Lords' quality intact whilst diminishing or suppressing its freedom of action. The phenomenon can be read in two ways. Like the government's casual attitude towards proctors and unlicensed members, the incidence of sessional absenteeism may reflect simply an official lack of concern to manage the House by the manipulation of attendance: in other words that the Crown was confident enough of guiding its measures through the Lords without having recourse to either a general exclusion of critics or the marshalling of proxy votes in order to give it an assured and unassailable majority.[136] This argument has much to commend it, partly because proxy voting remains 'not proven', but especially because 'counting heads' was alien to the sixteenth-century managerial mentality.

The alternative is more sinister. The shaky mid-Tudor regimes, aiming to push through contentious and often unpopular programmes, may have employed more systematically any managerial means to hand, including the exploitation of the licensing procedure, in order to remove unwanted critics. Whatever Northumberland's motive for calling parliament in 1553,[137] for example, the bustle of preparation is unmistakable: his own son and the heirs of two loyal peers were summoned to the Lords;[138] arrangements were in hand for the choice of the Commons' speaker;[139] the sheriffs were circularised in order to secure a general return of official candidates;[140] government intervention was practised in an unusually large number of constituencies: and Northumberland gave advice on how to handle the Lower House when the subsidy was requested.[141] The only possible focal point of serious opposition – Bishops Day, Gardiner, Heath and Tunstall – had already been neutralised. It would afford no surprise to discover that, with a tractable parliament in view, he had extended his managerial activities in order to exclude other undesirables.

Mary's government laboured to achieve the same result in her first three parliaments. The prize – statutory enactment of her religious policies and confirmation of the Spanish marriage treaty – was pursued with an arsenal of weapons: the rapid remodelling of the episcopal bench, which guaranteed a conservative bloc in the Lords;[142] the circular letters to sheriffs and others (before the elections to the parliament of 1554/5) instructing them to secure the return of 'the wise, grave, and Catholic sort',[143] the creation of new peers,[144] deprivation of reforming bishops[145] and consecration of Catholic prelates.[146] Mary's managerial resources were supplemented by the calculated generosity of the Habsburgs, in a manner and degree which were unique in the sixteenth century. The imperial ambassador, Simon Renard, distributed largesse 'in order favourably to dispose the principal members of Parliament'.[147] By April 1554 fifteen members, almost one-third of the Lords, were in receipt or expectation of Habsburg patronage, in the form of gifts, pensions, chains, or offices in Philip's household.[148] By November the number had grown.[149]

There was, then, a concern on the part of the government to manage both Houses. The conduct of Mary's first lord chancellor, Bishop Gardiner, typifies this bicameral approach. Barely two months after his release from the Tower in August 1553, the Commons in Mary's first parliament included a dozen[150] or more[151] diocesan servants, clients and members of his household.[152] However, he did not neglect the Lords where he also mustered considerable support.[153] In the critical years of the mid-sixteenth century the monarch, or those who governed in his name, and others who, like Gardiner, attempted the difficult feat of pursuing both royal and personal interest, were obliged to give detailed attention to the management of parliament. They did so without the retrospective wisdom of twentieth-century historiography. They clung instead to the unfashionable conviction that *both* Houses had to be supervised. In these circumstances, it is conceivable that the Crown might have resorted to a legitimate managerial instrument such as the licensing procedure in the Upper House. After all there were precedents enough in Henry VIII's reign when the Crown had regularly instructed royal servants to remain at their posts and on several occasions even excluded members for their political sympathies.[154]

A dramatic increase in licensed absenteeism between 1547 and 1558 also has to be accounted for, from 7 to 8 licences per session in 1540–7 to an average of 15 in the Edwardian and 18 in the Marian sessions:[155] altogether 168 licensees, of whom 123 were absent from entire sessions.[156] In addition there were the 70 sessional absentees who were either unlicensed or, at least, whose licences and proxies have not survived.[157] Doubtless some of these simply stayed at home without royal authorisation, especially the 27 who absented themselves in the closing days of Mary's reign. The question remains: did the Crown extend this practice to exclude political opponents, just as Henry VIII had done with Tunstall?[158]

Fortunately a high proportion of the 193 sessional absences (licensed and unauthorised) can be explained.[159] In only 33 cases[160] can no motive be advanced with any confidence. However, the fact that many of these occurred in November 1558, and nine of them were unlicensed, suggests a widespread evasion of parliamentary duties when the government was embroiled in other and more pressing matters.[161] By far the largest group of absences are attributable to advanced age, its concomitant infirmities, and the discouragement of hazardous conditions of travel along atrocious roads and over long distances, in the inhospitable months in which parliament usually met. It should come as no surprise, therefore, either that some members were repeatedly absent or that the bishops (whose average age was always ten years more than that of the peers) figure more prominently in this group.[162] A member's absence, of course, cannot always be explained in the uncomplicated terms of a single motive.

Poverty and a speech impediment may have influenced Lord De la Warr.[163] Tunstall's absence in November 1558 may have been caused by his age or service on the Scottish borders – or an amalgam of the two.[164] Bishops Bulkeley and Warton, and Lord Mordaunt, were probably motivated by a simple lack of interest in parliament and a preference for the comforts of an episcopal palace or country house, demonstrating their loyalty by industrious activity in diocesan or county administration.[165] This multiple explanation can be extended to other bishops too, such as Chambers, King, Kitchin, Veysey and Wakeman, whose deplorable mid-Tudor record ought to be viewed in the longer perspective of their entire parliamentary career.[166] Their regular absenteeism cannot be explained just by age or hostility to religious change in the forties and fifties. Even in their younger days, before the Edwardian reformation, they simply did not relish toiling to London with the dismal prospect of parliamentary chores at their journey's end.

Some of the aged were also ailing in the parliament time, although not all of the halt and the lame were old. Warwick was ill (and may have had a heart attack) in 1547, and both Shrewsbury (in 1555) and Ogle (in November 1558) were licensed on the grounds of sickness. At the time the two earls were in their forties and Ogle not yet thirty.[167] Inevitably sickness and death took their heaviest toll amongst the aged, and the terminal illnesses of seven of them (six bishops and a peer) were a sufficient reason for their absence from entire sessions.[168] Even Bishop Goodrich, lord chancellor under Northumberland and an Edwardian reformer, was not instructed by Mary's government to sue out a licence and stay away from her second parliament. He was in his sixties, and incapacitated, dying only five days after its dissolution.[169]

An undistinguished band of nobles also languished in parliamentary obscurity. Characteristic of them was the earl of Cumberland, whose prestigious marriage to Lady Eleanor Brandon, youngest daughter of the duke of Suffolk and Mary Tudor, had plunged him into debt. When she died he withdrew to his northern estates, a move prompted perhaps by his grief and certainly by the need for economic retrenchment.[170] He was present at only one Edwardian session[171] and one (possibly two) of the Marian parliaments.[172] There can be little doubt too that he found literary and scientific pursuits more congenial, and economic management more important, than the politics of Court and parliament. Others, such as the penurious (eighth) Audley[173] and the frivolous Berkeley[174] were equally uninterested.

Whatever the particular cause in each case – age, sickness, poverty, or just any excuse to avoid the tedium of parliament – all of these men stayed away for personal, not political, reasons, and the initiative to do so must have come from them. The Crown's role was simply to decide whether or not to grant licences to those who sought them – some did not even bother to do so. In contrast, the government alone determined whether royal servants should act upon their writs of summons or remain at their posts. Obviously this applied to those on military or diplomatic service, especially in distant regions or abroad, rather than to officials on hand in Westminster. Nevertheless a number of peers and (fewer) bishops were always in remote parts at parliament time. In this matter Tudor practice was, as usual, variable. On about half the known occasions (21) the council took the initiative, the licence–proxy procedure was by-passed; servants were instructed to waive their parliamentary rights and continue at their posts. Bishop Thirlby and the earl of Arundel, for example, were at the abbey of Cercamp, arranging peace preliminaries between England and France, when parliament sat in November 1558. The privy council gave them an implicit pardon from attendance because it thought that they should remain 'as long as there is any hope of agreement or until the communication shall be utterly ended'.[175] However, a similar number (22)[176] did receive licences, though it should be pointed out that the procedural distinction between the two groups is often a subtle and even hazy one. Thomas Lord Wharton is a good case in point. He was warden of the west marches when he received his writ to Edward VI's first parliament in 1547. On 5 October he sought instructions whether to leave his 'weightie Charge', repeating his request a week later. Finally and belatedly, on 20 October, the lord protector advised him that 'we have . . . resolved for you to remayne uppon your charge this tyme of the parlyament'.[177] The initiative had come from Wharton, even if it was not a specific request for a licence. Nevertheless it matters little whether Wharton and the rest received formal licences or

just commands to remain on duty. The pertinent point is that
they were not the victims of sinister political manipulation by
the Crown, but dutiful servants receiving directions in accordance
with the priorities of good government.[178]

There still remains a residue of absentees who stayed away at a
time when they were opponents, critics, or at least unsympathetic
towards the policies and religious position of the government.
They did not constitute a large group. Nor were they all sessional
absentees. A number secured licences and departed during a
session, and some of them even reappeared before it ended.[179] If,
however, mid-Tudor government is to be charged with heavy-
handed management of the Lords by the forcible exclusion of
those ill disposed towards it, the evidence for conviction must be
sought in its treatment of this group. At this point it is necessary
to differentiate between the complexion, the objectives, and the
conduct of the protectorate, Northumberland's regime, and the
Marian government. Yet, whilst it would be wrong to assume a
behaviour common to all three in this matter, there was, in
practice, little variation in Edward VI's reign. The 'political'
absentees were not prominent politicians, nor were they natural
political leaders. Thus the conservative bishops who stayed away
were men who preferred to take the line of least resistance.
Warton (St Asaph) avoided the debate on the sacrament in
December 1548 and then secured a licence, which enabled him to
depart before the first bill of uniformity entered the Lords.[180]
Sampson (Coventry and Lichfield) at least nailed his conservative colours to the mast in the same debate, but thereafter
he did not take up the obdurate position of Gardiner, Bonner and
Heath. He did not regularly vote against Reformation measures
in 1547–50, and finally he took refuge in licensed absenteeism
in 1552 and March 1553.[181] Sampson was not the stuff of which
martyrs are forged, and it would have been strange for the
government to penalise him whilst allowing stout-hearted conservatives to turn up and oppose official religious bills with
regularity.[182] Bishop Repps, it is true, fell a victim to Northumberland, when he was forced to resign. The ostensible reason
was the spoliation of his see, but his conservative stand during
the protectorate probably encouraged the new regime to act.
His unlicensed absence in 1549–50 was the natural consequence
of his resignation, which was probably pending when parliament

met and which certainly took place during the session.[183] However, it remains a mystery why Repps was singled out in preference to, say, Aldrich or Thirlby.

Apart from Richard Rich, the lay absentees were all barons of little political distinction, without a single great regional peer to grace their ranks. They included men like Thomas second Lord Monteagle, head of a cadet branch of the house of Stanley; and the second Lord Vaux who withdrew from public affairs when Henry VIII broke with Rome and absented himself from parliament for 20 years.[184] De la Warr at least looks a likelier object of government attention: his staunchly conservative, even papalist, position had led to a round of interrogations and a spell in the Tower in 1539;[185] his attendance record was excellent in 1540–3, the years of conservative reaction; thereafter he reverted to his endemic absenteeism of the 1530s.[186] He had all the hallmarks of an opponent of the Edwardian Reformation. Yet if he was, he expressed it only in a passive way, by the silent protest of absence.[187] In any case, his record must be seen in the context of his entire parliamentary career and in such personal handicaps as his poverty, his congenital speech defect and his advancing years.[188] Although he was early in the field on Mary's behalf in July 1553, for which he earned a seat at the council board, he rarely attended its meetings. He was also a licensed absentee from the Lords in April 1554.[189] His conservative record notwithstanding, his absence was probably personally, not politically, prompted; and his frequent nomination of religious critics and political opponents of the Edwardian regimes as his proctors does not suggest that he was acting under official instructions.[190]

There is little to be said about the rest. The tenth Lord Morley[191] and Stafford were undoubtedly conservatives, who could not tolerate the second Prayer Book of 1552. However, they would not meet the government head-on. The day after the bill authorising the new book received its first reading in the Lords, Morley's proxy was registered and he stayed away for the rest of the session.[192] Stafford tried a different tack, turning up after the bill had passed the House.[193] Rich, also a licensed absentee from this session, had sympathised with Somerset at the hour of his fall, and his loss of the great seal may have been the price which he had to pay for backing the wrong horse. He had suffered a prolonged and genuine illness in 1550-1, from which recovery was slow. However, it would not have been out of character for him to capitalise on it, in order to keep out of trouble.[194] Rich apart, these men were of little consequence and unlikely to have been the victims of official coercion. Indeed the circumstantial evidence suggests the contrary.

Mary's reign stands in stark contrast. The 'political' absentees were all peers,[195] eight of whom held senior titles, whilst Lord Talbot was Shrewsbury's heir. The Bedfords in the west, Huntingdon in the midlands, Sussex in East Anglia, and Westmorland in the north were all powerful regional magnates. Bath and Sussex were privy councillors at the time of their absences; so was Bedford, who was also keeper of the privy seal. These were not nobles to be toyed with, and, as the cause of their absenteeism, voluntary or enforced, was political discontent, it must have given the government serious concern.

Westmorland typifies the position and conduct of the alienated peers, most of whom stayed away in 1554-5, when Marian policies were being enacted and discontent was running high. They did not speak in unison but spanned the whole gamut of aristocratic fears, in particular the threats to the reformed faith and secularised property, the spectre of absorption into the Habsburg power-complex, the prospect of war with France and the political eclipse of the native nobility. However, an abiding loyalty to the Crown, and an innate social responsibility, cemented together with a calculated self-interest, imposed strict limits on the extent of their opposition. Most of them, on most occasions, preferred the silent protest of withdrawal or a discreet absence rather than a public and parliamentary confrontation with the government. So it was with Henry fifth earl of Westmorland. Renard thought him unsound in religion. So did Mary who reprimanded him for it.[196] In 1556 he was even suspected of being privy to the Dudley conspiracy to rob the exchequer.[197] Nor were such doubts entirely unjust, because his attitude to the Spanish marriage[198] and the papal restoration were equivocal to say the least. Yet it was he who scotched the amateurish descent on Yorkshire by the anti-Spanish rebel, Sir Thomas Stafford, in April 1557.[199] The ambiguity of his conduct was more apparent than real. He confined his disapproval of royal policies to sessional absences in April 1554 and 1555, and an early licensed departure

from her third parliament.[200] Beyond that he would not go, nor
would he condone treason in others.

Other discontented peers behaved in the same way: the earl of
Bath (in April 1554), John eighth Lord Audley, who fled abroad
after an unlicensed absence in 1555,[201] George tenth Lord
Zouche (in November 1558), and even that prominent Edwardian, Viscount Hereford (absent in April 1554 and departing early
in the following parliament).[202] Francis second earl of Bedford
was in a more delicate, even dangerous and exposed position
than the rest. He was a powerful regional peer, suspected of
complicity in Wyatt's rebellion in 1554 and a plot centred on
Courtenay in the following year. He deemed it politic to travel
for his health, and he did so with royal approval. When the
1555 parliament met, he was still abroad.[203] Not surprisingly
there is no record of either licence or proxy – it was enough that
a powerful critic was out of harm's way, without sending messen-
gers scouring Europe merely to grant him an exemption from
parliament.

The most frequent parliamentary defaulter was Henry Lord
Bergavenny who, even more than Westmorland, represented in
his person the inner contradictions of aristocratic attitudes and
actions. He had been closely identified with the Edwardian
regimes. In the cause of legitimacy, however, he supported
Mary in July 1553, denounced 'the lady Jane, a queen of a new
and pretty invention',[204] and later led the loyalist gentry of
Kent against Wyatt's rebels.[205] Yet he was rapidly and utterly
alienated by Mary's government and all that it strove to achieve.
Like Westmorland, he expressed his disenchantment not by
parliamentary opposition but by absenteeism: only two recorded
appearances during the reign and licences for every session
between April 1554 and January 1558.[206] The imperial ambassador, writing in 1554, described him as an enemy of Spain
and a possible heretic who 'excused [his] absence from Parliament on the ground of ill-health'.[207] As with Bergavenny, so
with the rest: their empty places on the peers' benches were not
the consequence of royal commands but of individual decisions.

The most dramatic example of the personal exercise of the
'politics of discretion' occurred in Mary's third parliament.
Through it she sought the paper fulfilment of a programme
guaranteed to offend and frighten reformers, xenophobic

Englishmen who feared Spain, and owners of secularised Church lands, regardless of their religious persuasion. Events in that parliament also antagonised a peerage which was jealous of its right to participate in any succession settlement and arrangements for a regency government.[208] Nevertheless the lords temporal were in a dilemma. There were only two options open to them: to resist the queen publicly, or to stay away. Absenteeism had its obvious attractions: it would avoid an embarrassing, even dangerous, confrontation, but at the same time it would register a gesture of disapproval. At first glance there is nothing exceptional about this parliament. After all, the nine peers who obtained licences and did not put in a single appearance represent the normal mixed bag: several whose motives cannot be divined, that inveterate backwoodsman Mordaunt, the aged Morley, and four others of Protestant persuasion or anti-Spanish sentiment.[209] The absence of a handful of religious and political dissenters was nothing new. The novelty of this parliament lay in the steady exodus during the session. Seven peers secured the queen's permission to depart,[210] but nine others silently withdrew without authorisation.[211] What is significant about their action is that they did not represent one point of view. Hereford, Bray, the ninth Lord Cobham and Zouche were members of the reforming camp, but Arundel and Vaux were Catholics. Rich moved with the prevailing wind, and Sussex was a loyal Marian conservative who, as lord-lieutenant in Norfolk, endeavoured to drive Protestants back to the Mass. Whereas the loyalty of Westmorland, Bergavenny and Bray was in doubt, Arundel, Pembroke, the first earl of Bedford, the second earl of Sussex and Rich were privy councillors. Bedford, as keeper of the privy seal, and Arundel, who presided over the queen's household and the council, were also prominent officeholders. Moreover some of them – Arundel, Bedford, Pembroke, Sussex, FitzWalter and Grey de Wilton – had recently become Habsburg clients.

The aristocratic 'seceders' clearly lacked a common focal point of political loyalty, religious affiliation, material interest, or priorities. Nor, apart from the admittedly significant exceptions of Bedford and Pembroke, was there any sign of planned and concerted action. For most there was just a painful dilemma, often involving a clash of responsibility and conscience, duty and self-interest. Sussex, the loyal Marian, was no lover of the Spanish marriage.[212] Grey de Wilton, the queen's governor of Guisnes 'tyll by the eares hee was pulled owte of the same' in 1558, had marched against her during Northumberland's attempted coup.[213] Pembroke too had a chequered past, with a record of Protestant sympathies, prominence in Edwardian government, and support for Courtenay in 1553. His desertion to Mary in convenient season and his part in the defeat of Wyatt could not entirely expunge memories of such erratic behaviour.[214] Even that supple, ingratiating but useful politician, Lord Rich, who had survived all the political vicissitudes since 1540 and still remained on the council, had been moved to public protest in the previous parliament.

However, it was Bedford who found himself in the most ambiguous position. His past record, his possession of extensive secularised estates and his sympathy with the reformed religion conflicted with his loyalty to the Crown and his duty as a prominent royal servant. He had opposed Wyatt's rebels, ratified the Spanish match as the chief representative of his royal mistress, welcomed Philip on his arrival in July 1554, and accepted a Habsburg pension. But he remained stiff in his opinion that no monastic lands should be restored.[215] The way in which Bedford resolved this conflict of priorities is central to the following story.

The saga of Mary's third parliament can only be understood by a backward glance at the previous assembly, which had met in the spring of the same year. It had been a turbulent session in which the Lords had given vent to its fears for the fate of secularised property, momentarily panicked, and, in the process, had frustrated both queen and lord chancellor.[216] Since then Philip had arrived, the marriage had been solemnised, and the stage set for the final act in the fulfilment of the Marian programme. In these circumstances one might have expected a dispirited and compliant Upper House when it met in November. However, fears about property, foreign control and religion had not been allayed. Throughout November and early December, as obnoxious bills for the pope's restoration and the persecution of heretics came before the Lords, a trickle of peers posted home. In the light of their past record and present opinions, this is no matter for surprise. Zouche and Bergavenny, Rich, Cobham,[217] Hereford and Bray[218] were, with one exception,[219] Edwardian in their political and religious sympathies.

After Christmas, however, the exodus accelerated. Furthermore it now consisted largely of powerful senior peers and their heirs, a large proportion of whom were members of the official element in the House. The catalyst of change was the regency bill, now under consideration by the Commons.[220] It was certainly not the bill for reunion with Rome which Pembroke and Sussex saw through its concluding stages on 26 December before departing. They were followed in steady succession by Westmorland, Grey de Wilton, Cumberland, FitzWalter, St John and, on 10 January Arundel.[221]

The lords temporal had already expressed their dissatisfaction to the imperial ambassador in no uncertain terms. Renard specifically mentioned Arundel, Pembroke, Westmorland and Cumberland who 'stayed away in order not to give their consent to a measure infringing upon the right hitherto exercised by the nobility to appoint a protector when need has arisen'.[222] The object of their hostility was the aforementioned regency bill which would make Philip protector in the event of Mary predeceasing him when their child was still a minor. Moreover, the initiative to act came from them, not the Crown. Renard, it is true, was an eternal pessimist, moving in a fog of rumour, doubt and suspicion, forever a prey to fears of intrigue, conspiracy and rebellion. On the other hand, he was unusually well placed and well informed as a foreign ambassador. He had Mary's confidence and he was frequently consulted by councillors, officials and peers. There is no reason to doubt his word that the parliamentary exodus resulted from a decision made by the peers themselves. Indeed he was quite firm on this point. He even gives us a glimpse of the discreet manner in which the malcontents withdrew: Arundel, Pembroke and the rest had obtained leave of absence 'some on account of illness, others of private business'.[223] So the real issue was tactfully avoided and therefore a confrontation was prevented.

The activities of one prominent peer escaped Renard's attention. Bedford, too, disapproved of the regency bill, but as keeper of the privy seal he was a prominent royal servant and had to act with particular prudence. As early as mid-December, when the regency bill was before the Commons, he had obtained a licence of absence and registered his proxies.[224] Perhaps it was just an insurance policy, because he continued to attend the Lords frequently until 12 January. Then he absented himself on three successive days when the regency bill was before the House. It concluded its passage through the Lords on the morning of 16 January, whereupon Bedford returned for the closing ceremony of parliament in the afternoon. It was a consummate exercise in the politics of discretion.[225]

The conduct of discontented peers on this occasion was not unique. Arundel, Westmorland, and Bergavenny avoided overt resistance to official policies in other Marian parliaments and obtained licences 'on the ground of ill health';[226] and the practice was not unknown in Edward VI's reign. In every case the decision to withdraw during a session, or not to turn up at all, was taken by individual peers, and there is no evidence that any of the mid-Tudor regimes directed their opponents to absent themselves. The one possible exception to this general pattern was the bizarre case of John fourth Baron Latimer, who did not attend either of the sessions of 1558. However, his absence was not occasioned by his political dissent but by urgent sexual impulses coupled with a sad lack of calculation. In 1557 he was arrested for the attempted rape of his landlady. He compounded the felony when he 'strake the goodman ther. There was such an oute cry . . . that the constables and strete rose and sette hym oute of hys house, and browght hym thorowe Chepsyde to the Maere's and xl boyes at hys heles wonderyng on him.'[227] He was bound over to appear daily before the privy council and duly did so on most days between late August and early November 1557. By then events had taken a more serious turn. The privy council decided that he 'shulde be called into the Starre Chambre towching the deathe of the woman, and his case there to be harde and ordered accordingly'.[228] Official disapproval of his behaviour was probably influenced by his past record: in 1553 he had been imprisoned in the Fleet for his 'misdemeanour' towards Dorothy Wiseman, his servant.[229] The Marian council certainly did not exclude Latimer in the cause of tractable parliaments. It sought only to punish his sexual aberrations[230] which were 'to grete a vellany for a noble man, my thought'.[231]

Throughout the two mid-Tudor reigns, the Crown seemed unconcerned or unable to exercise a detailed and effective control over attendance. This manifested itself in various ways: in unauthorised absenteeism, in the re-appearance of licensed members before a session had expired, and in its casual attitude to proctorial representation. Prominent critics and opponents of the government attended the House freely without let or hindrance.[232] Even Thomas Lord Seymour of Sudeley was free to come and go as he pleased until he was finally arrested for treason, midway through the session of 1548/9. Yet he represented a constant threat to parliamentary and public order. He was consumed with jealousy when his brother was elevated to the office of protector; he 'mislyked that he was not placed in the Parliament House, as woon of the King his Unkills'; and his resentment was intensified by squabbles with Somerset over his wife's precedence and jewellery.[233] Seymour turned to parliament to remedy his grievances and challenge his brother's authority. In 1547 he attempted to persuade Edward VI to subscribe to a letter of his, requesting Lords and Commons to be 'good' to him 'in such suites and matters as he should open and declare unto them'. He was later charged with 'having in both the same howses laboured, stired, and moved a nombre of persons to take part and joyne with him in such things as he wolde sett fourthe and enterpryse, whereby he thought to brede suche a tumulte, uprore and sedycion as well in the saide courte as in the hole realme'.[234] He and his ally, the marquess of Dorset, voted against the ratification of the protector's letters patent which confirmed his plenary authority.[235] However, Seymour was not content to confine himself to mere gestures of dissent. The council accused him of intending to appear in the House of Commons with his 'fautours and adherentes before prepared' and there to cause a tumult.[236] Nor did he neglect the House of Lords, where he intended to make suit to be appointed governor of the young king: 'and he had the names of all the Lordes, and totted them whome he thought he might have to his purpose to labour them'.[237] Seymour himself admitted the accuracy of the council's charge that he sought to make parliament serve his vaulting ambition. He had even threatened that, if his designs were thwarted, 'I wol make the blakest Parlament that ever was in Ingland.'[238]

Seymour's failure cannot alter the fact of his intention to disrupt parliament. Much of his scheming was little more than hot air, exemplified by his boast that he would never agree to a proposed parliamentary tax on sheep.[239] However, he did go so far as to seek Southampton's support and to canvass for the voices of Dorset, Northampton and Rutland in the Lords.[240] In spite of his constant and clumsy intrigues, which must have been widely known, he was allowed to attend the Upper House frequently in 1547 and during the first eight weeks of the following session. Moreover, Dorset and the other peers who had dallied with Seymour continued to attend the Lords without molestation.[241]

Surprisingly, Northumberland's supremacy was not marked by a stricter parliamentary discipline and a tighter control over attendance. In later years the earl of Derby was to recall 'that he, with the lord Windsor and lord Dacres, with one more, whose name I have forgotten, did not consent to those acts [of the Edwardian Reformation]; and that the nay of them four would be to be seen, as long as the parliament house stood.'[242] The journal record bears him out. Conservative peers were permitted to attend regularly and resist the two uniformity bills, clerical marriage, Tunstall's deprivation, the suppression of Latin primers, and other measures.[243] If Northumberland desired them out of the way, it was more than he chose or dared to attempt.

Despite their declining prestige and status, and their new subordination to the State, the Edwardian bishops provide the most dramatic evidence of both the Crown's impotence (or tolerance) and the Lords' independent temper. The more conservative of them resisted every step in the Edwardian Reformation,[244] only giving way as they were constantly outvoted in the house (Table 1).

Until the government took the drastic step of depriving several conservative bishops and compelling two others to resign, it made no attempt to exclude them. Not only did they continue to attend the Lords until they were deprived, but they did so with remarkable regularity (Table 2).

Mary's rapid purge of the episcopate forestalled any repetition of the parliamentary resistance which had characterised Edward's reign. The focus of opposition to official policies shifted instead to the peers. However, after their giddy politicking in the first parliament of 1554, their resistance was tempered with caution and refined with subtlety. Prominent peers preferred to withdraw discreetly, leaving their clients and allies in the Commons to serve as their front-line infantry.[246] Although this blunted effective

Table 1. Dissenting votes of the conservative bishops in the Edwardian parliaments.

	1547		1548/9			1549/50		1552	Total
	I	II	III	IV	V	VI	VII	VIII	
Aldrich			*	*	*	*	*	*	6
Day	*	*	*	*	*	*	*		7
Sampson			*			*			2
Tunstall	*		*	*	*	*	*		6
Skip	*	*	*	*					4
Kitchin			*		*				2
Bonner	*	*	*	*	*				5
Repps	*	*	*	*	*				5
Thirlby			*	*		*	*	*	5
Heath	*	*	*	*	*	*	*		7
	6	5	10	8	7	6	5	2	

I	Dissolution of chantries
II	Bill for the sacrament of the altar
III	Debate on the sacrament
IV	First bill of uniformity
V	Clerical marriage
VI	Abolition of sundry books and images
VII	Ordering of ecclesiastical ministers
VIII	Second bill of uniformity

Table 2. Attendance record of the conservative bishops in the Edwardian parliaments.

	1547	1548/9	1549/50	1552	1553
Aldrich	87%[245]	96%	96%	80%	92%
Day	100%	96%	96%	deprived 10 Oct, 1551	
Sampson	29%	90%	79%	sessional absentee	sessional absentee
Tunstall	97%	95%	94%	In Tower – deprived 14 Oct. 1552	
Skip	71%	93%	96%	52%	died 28 March1552
Kitchin	11%	93%	sessional absentee	sessional absentee	sessional absentee
Bonner	94%	96%	deprived 1 Oct, 1549		
Repps	63%	90%	resigned *ante* 26 Jan, 1550		
Thirlby	sessional absentee	97%	100%	98%	100%
Heath	69%	97%	100%	deprived Oct, 1551	

opposition in the Lords, the Crown did not contribute to the process and old Edwardians, such as Hereford and Bray, were free to attend if they chose so to do.

It can be plausibly argued that the Crown preferred to concentrate on its second line of defence, by granting licences of absence on request, and ensuring that proxy votes were assigned to councillors or other reliable members. The figures certainly support this argument, because privy councillors were named as sole or first proxies to 111 of the 168 licensees between 1547 and 1558.[247] Nor was the choice of proctors always a free one. The bishop of Peterborough was pardoned from the second Edwardian parliament 'so as he make out his sufficient proxy to some discreet personage of the State';[248] and when, in 1555, Sir William Petre despatched a licence to the earl of Shrewsbury, who had been 'lately evil vexed', he directed him to name two reliable Marians, Viscount Montagu and the bishop of Ely, as his proctors.[249] Prominent officials made a rich haul of proxies: Northumberland held six in 1552, Arundel twelve and Gardiner 18 in the parliaments of 1554 and 1555.[250] At the end of the day, however, what matters is whether these proxy votes were cast in the Lords, and there is no evidence that they were.[251]

When the Crown sought to tamper with the Lords' membership, it resorted to alternative techniques. Imprisonment during royal pleasure was not unknown, though even then exclusion from parliament was usually incidental and not the cause. Stephen Gardiner was the sole (but very important) Edwardian exception. He was in the Fleet from 25 September 1547 until 8 January 1548, a fortnight after parliament had risen.[252] By the time parliament reassembled in the following November, he was back in prison, where he remained until the end of the reign. Gardiner at least had no illusions about the reason for his prolonged detention: that he headed a parliamentary faction, and that an opposition would polarise around him if he was free to attend the Lords.[253] Similar treatment, prompted by similar fears, was meted out to Edward Courtenay, earl of Devon, in Mary's reign.[254] However, these were isolated cases. Perhaps the Crown drew back from actions which infringed the rights of membership of the House of Lords and might produce a parliamentary backlash. It was one thing to mask its wish to exclude dangerous opponents, by punishing them for another, extra-parliamentary offence; but to tamper directly with the right of a lord of parliament to receive and act upon his writ would have been a clumsy and even pyrrhic act.

The Crown displayed a similar reluctance to exploit the licensing procedure. Or perhaps it attached no political importance to it. Licences were of more practical value to would-be absentees than to the government. They enabled them to avoid parliamentary service, whilst proxies confirmed their continuing right to a voice in the House. Yet licencees were equally oblivious to their political significance.[255] Proctorial representation was symptomatic of a two-way social process: absentees normally and naturally nominated as proctors the more influential members of the House, whilst the accumulation of proxies confirmed the eminence and satisfied the ego of the proctor. In so far as the government used licences to serve political ends, it regulated attendance in a positive rather than a negative way. Its prime concern was to include, not exclude, to ensure a sufficient presence for the efficient conduct of business.[256] The frequency of unlicensed absenteeism suggests that the Crown tackled the problem with only limited efficiency and little success.[257] Cromwell's careful scrutiny of applications in the thirties[258] contrasts with the next two decades, when the incidence of both licensees and unauthorised truants rose,[259] and for which only one refusal has survived.[260]

Nevertheless the mid-Tudor governments displayed a continuing concern that the Upper House should have a sufficiency of members. Reminders were sent out before each meeting of multi-sessional parliaments. Bishops and peers were warned when a new parliament was pending.[261] Royal officials were summoned to Westminster and instructed to appoint deputies to fill their rooms in their absence: when Cobham and Stourton were called over from Calais and Newhaven in 1547, the lord protector even took the trouble to arrange the former's accommodation.[262] Prominent royal servants might be recalled for consultations in the parliament time, so enabling them to advise the government and, at the same time, attend the Lords. Mary's deputy in Ireland, Thomas third earl of Sussex, was licensed to repair to her in both January and November 1558, in order 'to confer upon the state and affairs of that realm'.[263] Shortly before the second session of 1558, she also directed eight senior peers to leave their charges and 'repayre hither w[ith] all the diligence you may' to advise on urgent and important matters.[264]

The government's energies were therefore consistently focussed on attendance rather than absenteeism, and it usually displayed an enlightened tolerance of criticism and opposition. There was no systematic attempt to exclude opponents *en masse*, even when Seymour and his following attempted a parliamentary stir, when conservative bishops resisted the Edwardian Reformation, when Gardiner and Pembroke canvassed Courtenay's suit to Mary, or when Paget contested the bishop of Winchester in April 1554 and sank some of the queen's bills in the process. The explanation is simple enough: that Tudor politicians thought in terms of consensus and quality, rather than of mere numbers. In this climate, the arithmetical management of parliament was utterly alien. Managerial politicians were not accustomed to devising lists of possible 'ayes' and 'noes', totting up votes, or building majorities. Nor did they endeavour to demolish opposition and silence criticism by sweeping large numbers into prison or coercing them into parliamentary exile with private letters or unsolicited licences. Quality – leadership – was what mattered. That priority was expressed in two forms of action: first, by the selective removal of potential opposition leaders; and secondly, by ensuring an effective 'front bench' in each House. The vanguard of that leadership was the privy council. With unusual (and perhaps accidental) insight, the imperial ambassador recognised this when, on 7 November 1549, he reported that 'parliament opened last Monday, but business is sluggish because of the . . . Councillors' indisposition'.[265] Effective management of the Upper House was not to be achieved by the manipulation of attendance or by a whipped majority, but by the parliamentary skills of the official leadership. The new bishops and peers of April 1554 were not intended to swamp the chamber with official battalions, wheeling and turning at the Crown's command, but to strengthen that leadership. In the same way Habsburg patronage in 1554 was not a device to pack the House with clients who were politically bonded with the golden cords of patronage. Most of the gifts and grants went to the same group of favoured men who were already high in the queen's favour and service.[266] The object – to bind Mary's leading servants in parliament to Catholic–Habsburg interests – was nowhere more clearly stated than in Simon Renard's letter to Prince Philip: 'Your Highness will also do well to make presents to the Councillors . . . thus ransoming their hearts and obliging them to remain faithful.'[267] Calculated and cynical this may have been. Nevertheless Renard, well versed in the arts of patronage-politics, divined an essential truth: that political success depended upon reliable and effective leadership. Yet even this was unable to transform the mid-Tudor House of Lords into a compliant assembly directed by official creatures.

5

COHESION AND DIVISION

To those contemporaries who were outside the charmed circle of the well born and personally unacquainted with the governing elite in Church and State, the peers and bishops of the Upper House may have projected a public image of cohesion and homogeneity. The seventy or eighty members were not strangers to one another but familiars, in many cases even intimates. The peers belonged to a legally defined status group, a tiny social elite, within which they became personally associated in their social lives, whilst they were thrown together, in close acquaintanceship, in the business of governing the realm under the prince. The bishops constituted a separate, office-holding elite, engaged in ecclesiastical administration, but they shared with the peers the contemporary ideals of fidelity and obedience to the Crown and service to the commonwealth.

The peers in particular were bound together by the social cement of blood and marriage. Nevill(e)s held the earldom of Westmorland and the baronies of Bergavenny and Latimer.[1] Viscount Bindon and William Lord Howard of Effingham were sons of Thomas Howard, duke of Norfolk.[2] The ramifications of the Howard clan spread their tentacles through much of the peerage. Thus the third duke's grandchildren married into the FitzAlan, Neville, Berkeley and Scrope families, which in turn established marital links with Lumleys, Greys and Cliffords.[3] Marriages with the children of Henry and Edward Stafford, second and third dukes of Buckingham, forged kinship connections between the Percy, Radcliffe, Hastings, Stafford, Neville and Manners families as well as, of course, with the ubiquitous Howards. Whilst there was a natural tendency towards regional groupings it was not exclusive. Henry fifth earl of Westmorland, William third Lord Dacre, John third Lord Conyers, the first

Lord Wharton and, more distantly, Edward third earl of Derby, Henry second earl of Cumberland and Thomas sixth earl of Northumberland were related to the Talbot family; but so too were the third duke of Norfolk, the earls of Bath, Rutland, Southampton, Sussex and Worcester, Viscount Montagu and Lords Bergavenny, Bray, Chandos and Sandys.

The mid-Tudor peerage was therefore a lattice of kinship connections. Intermarriage was such an important expression of their social affinity that 60 of the 114 marriages contracted by peers before Elizabeth's accession were to members of other noble families.[4] It might also be consciously employed to establish advantageous social alliances with powerful noble houses – perhaps the purpose of the multiple marriage, celebrated on 3 July 1536, between heirs and daughters of the three earls of Oxford, Rutland and Westmorland.[5] And in the hands of the ambitious it could become a political weapon, designed to build up a connection or, in one case, to bring the Crown into his family: on 25 May 1553 the duke of Suffolk's daughter, Lady Jane Gray, was wedded to Guilford Dudley, his sister Katherine to Henry Lord Hastings, the earl of Huntingdon's heir, and Jane's sister to Henry Lord Herbert, whose father was the earl of Pembroke and whose uncle was the marquess of Northampton. The political alliance headed by the duke of Northumberland, and including Suffolk, Northampton, Huntingdon and Pembroke, was thereby underpinned by marriage.[6] Whatever the motive of such marriages, the general effect was to interlace the peerage – the lay majority in the Upper House – with a network of familial ties.

Matrimonial alliances, however, were not sufficient in themselves to guarantee the social and political harmony of the peers. Nor did common ideals, political responsibilities and elitist attitudes create an identity of interests, either amongst themselves or with the bishops. Consequently the lords temporal and spiritual did not coalesce into a cohesive assembly in the parliament chamber. Forces of equal and often greater strength acted in a reverse and centrifugal direction.

The bishops constituted a separate order, socially apart from the peers and inferior to them. Reginald Cardinal Pole, Mary's choice as successor to Thomas Cranmer, was intimately connected with several noble families: Henry Lord Stafford was his brother-in-law and the second earl of Huntingdon was married to his niece Catherine Pole.[7] But then Pole was of noble status and royal blood; his maternal grandfather was George duke of Clarence, Edward IV's brother, and his father, Sir Richard Pole, was Henry VII's cousin.[8] No other bishop could claim such noble antecedents, status or connections. Ties of kinship were few and tenuous. Apart from Huntingdon and Thomas Wriothesley, who married the half-sister of Bishop Gardiner's nephew,[9] none of the Edwardian or Marian nobility established links with the episcopate by marriage, whilst none of those bishops who ventured into matrimony (nor the two who actually repeated the experiment) took a wife of noble rank.[10]

This social separateness, coupled with the inferior origins of the bishops, did nothing to discourage and indeed may have strengthened the peers' latent antipathy towards them which sometimes broke surface during sittings of the Upper House. If so it did no more than sharpen an aversion compounded chiefly of anti-clericalism, a prejudice against ecclesiastical authority, and the distasteful memory of the abuse of that authority in pre-Reformation England. Whether the memory was real or imagined and the abuse was genuine or apocryphal matters little. The prejudice was real enough. Henry VIII's lord chancellor, Thomas Lord Audley, had given voice to it when he pointed out to Bishop Gardiner, in the course of a debate in the Lords,

looke the Act of Supremacy, and there the Kings doinges be restrayned to spiritual jurisdiction; and in a nother acte it is provided that no Spirituall Lawe shall have place contrary to a Common Lawe or Acte of Parliament. And this wer not . . . you bishops would enter in with the Kinge and, by meanes of his supremacie, order the layty as ye listed. But we wil provide . . . that the premunire shall ever hang over your heads, and so we lay men shalbe sure to enjoye our inheritaunce by the Common Lawes and acts of Parliament.[11]

During Edward VI's reign the nobility was firmly in the saddle in both government and parliament. They had no reason to fear episcopal power and their self-confidence expressed itself in a scornful, even intimidatory, treatment of the bishops. This is illustrated in the public disputation on the first Prayer Book and in Northumberland's outburst against them during the second Edwardian parliament.[12] Mary's accession, however, was accompanied by a resurgence of the politically active bishops who had been deprived in the previous reign. They were restored and

raised to high office. The Marian purge removed religious
division from the body of lords spiritual. Bishop Gardiner, who
became their effective political leader, also presided over the
House of Lords in his capacity as lord chancellor. The nobles'
fears revived: fears of the bishops' augmented authority, a papal
restoration which would threaten their continued possession of
monastic property, and an increase in the spiritual membership
of the Lords if the parliamentary abbots and priors returned in
force. These issues, complicated by Mary's Spanish marriage,
served only to exacerbate relations between the temporal and
spiritual orders in the Upper House. Friction came to a head in
Mary's second parliament when Gardiner's personal legislative
programme produced a confrontation with the majority of peers.
The central and crucial issue was the fate of secularised lands.
And the insistence of Mary's third parliament on a papal and
parliamentary confirmation of the laity's possession of expropriated monastic property unmistakably reflects the acute
concern of the landed classes about this question. The political
temperature of the Upper House dropped in 1555, especially
after Gardiner's death in November of that year. Nevertheless, the
anti-clerical fear and prejudice of the lords temporal were
amongst the chief sources of conflict in the House for most of this
period.[13]

The peers' anti-clericalism was genuine enough, but their
fears of a revival of episcopal power were, at the least, exaggerated. The spiritual order of bishops in the Lords was in a
weak, divided and socially depressed condition, and consciously
on the defensive. The dissolution of the monasteries, accompanied
by the disappearance of the regulars from the Upper House, had
reduced the lords spiritual from a substantial minority of the
assembly in the 1530s[14] to about one-third of the actual membership in the mid-Tudor parliaments.[15] Their prestige had likewise
diminished. The Henrician bishops had become the subordinates
of a supreme head who was also king. Their autonomy vanished
and their freedom of action shrank. In 1547 the decline accelerated. The decision of the Edwardian privy council, that the
bishops should sue out new commissions, rested on the assumption
that their spiritual jurisdiction had lapsed, like the authority of
any royal servant, on the death of the previous monarch.[16] In
Edward VI's first parliament, later that year, the king was

empowered to appoint bishops by letters patent 'as thoughe conge deslier had been given, thelection duelie made and the same confirmed'.[17] Although the government's view – that the bishops' jurisdiction was merely delegated and that the council had authority in ecclesiastical matters – met with resistance from the conservative Gardiner, its actions in 1547 had effectively transformed them into Erastian civil servants.[18] The papal restoration in 1554 made little real difference, because Mary maintained a firm control over their appointment and conduct and they remained, in practice, bureaucrats in royal service.

The bishops even lacked the exalted social status and origins which might otherwise have compensated, in some degree, for the declining prestige of the episcopal office. The families and social rank of only 25 of the 52 mid-Tudor bishops have been identified, but it is a large enough sample to enable meaningful observations to be made about the social complexion of them as a whole. Reginald Pole apart, the nobility provided no recruits to the episcopal bench. The gentry, however, contributed 16 bishops (or just under two-thirds of the sample). Thus William Barlow came from a landed family of Essex and Hertfordshire.[19] John Bird was possibly a member of a prominent and powerful Cheshire family, and Edmund Bonner was (supposedly) the bastard of a Cheshire priest, George Savage, and so related to the Bulkeleys of Anglesey.[20] Gilbert Bourne was the nephew of Sir John Bourne, Mary's principal secretary of State.[21] Arthur Bulkeley was descended from an ancient gentry family in Anglesey or from a cadet line of the Bulkeleys of Cheshire.[22] As for Cranmer, his secretary recorded that he was 'the sonne of one Thomas Cranmer, gentilman, descending of an aunciente and famous famylie and progeny' in Aslacton, Nottinghamshire. The archbishop himself professed humbler origins, however, when he said to his fellow commissioners for the cathedral school at Canterbury, 'I take it that none of us here being gentilmen borne (as I thinke) but hadd our begynnyng that way from a lowe and base parentage.' It could have been false modesty, but it was, most probably, an attempt to counter the move made by some of the commissioners to 'have none admitted but younger brethren and gentilmenys sonnes'. Whatever the motive, Cranmer was denying his gentle origins.[23] Two fellow reformers, Robert Ferrar and Robert Holgate, and a Marian, John Hopton, hailed from landed

gentry in Yorkshire, adjacent to Cranmer's home county.[24] Six
other prelates were members of gentry families scattered about
the country from Dorset to Lincolnshire.[25] And Nicholas Ridley's
relatives were gentry of some importance in Northumberland,
where the head of the family lived in Willimotiswick Castle.[26]

Charity might prompt the addition of Cuthbert Tunstall's
name to this list, for if, as was alleged, he was the bastard son of
Thomas Tunstall, then he belonged to the armigerous and
worshipful Tunstall family of Thurland Castle in Lancashire, and
his legitimate brother Brian was a squire.[27] Socially, however, the
rest must have been of little account to the nobles who faced
them from their benches on the other side of the House. John
Taylor may have been the son of a master of the rolls, William
Glynn's father was possibly a Welsh rector, and Robert King was
undoubtedly from yeoman stock (albeit related by marriage to
Lord Williams of Thame).[28] Thomas Thirlby's maternal grandfather was a London gentleman, William Campion, but his
father was further down the social scale, serving as town clerk,
scrivener and treasurer of Cambridge.[29] As for those prominent
Henricians, Stephen Gardiner and Nicholas Heath, whose day
came again in Mary's reign, they too were of urban origins though,
unlike Thirlby, they came from trading families. Gardiner was
the son of a clothworker of 'substance and standing' in Bury St
Edmunds, and Nicholas Heath was born to a 'citizen and cutler
of London'.[30] The overwhelming impression is of an episcopal
bench recruited from lower-middle-class families. Even the 16
bishops whose origins were landed and gentle did not come from
families which were numbered amongst the county elite: in
February 1554, for example, only two of them, the Bournes of
Worcestershire and the Ridleys of Northumberland, were
represented on the commission of the peace.[31] The handicap of
social inferiority, added to the declining prestige of their office
and the anti-clerical prejudice of the lay majority, must have
further weakened their political position in the mid-Tudor
Lords.

Coming from such a diversity of backgrounds, the bishops
lacked the social homogeneity of the peers and their sense of
identity with a small close-knit social elite. Nor could they look to
marriage, either to provide that cohesion or to bridge the social
and political gulf between themselves and the lords temporal.

They laboured under a serious disadvantage because, until Edward VI's reign, clerical marriage was not permitted by law. This did not deter Cranmer, Coverdale and Hooper, all of whom married before Henry VIII's death.[32]

In Edward's reign, however, the legal obstacles were rapidly removed. Convocation sanctioned clerical marriage in 1547; parliament did so in 1549, and three years later it legitimised the offspring of such unions.[33] If the opportunity now existed, it does not appear that a general inclination did. William Barlow wedded an ex-nun, Agatha Welsborne, over-indulged himself and acquired two sons and five daughters.[34] Seven other bishops contracted marriages.[35] And for them, as for Cranmer, Coverdale and Hooper, marriage became a demonstration of their reformed religious opinions. John Bird protested, after Mary's accession, that he had taken a wife against his will and 'for bearing with the time', whilst Robert Holgate protested to Sir Richard Southwell (in 1554 or 1555) that he had only married 'by the councell of Edwarde then the Duke of Somersett and for feare of the laite Duke of Northumberlande using to call him papiste'.[36] These were by way of apologies for having offended Mary's strong views on clerical celibacy; nevertheless there may have been some truth in their assertions that, in Edward's reign, marriage had become a test of their religious position. After all, every married prelate was a reformer. The Henrician conservatives remained celibate in Edward's reign; not only the leading critics and opponents of reformation, Gardiner, Bonner, Day, Heath and Tunstall, but the conforming bishops too.[37] Nor, it would seem, did all the reformers risk wedlock. There is no record of marriages contracted by Goodrich, Harley, Ridley and Taylor. Even in the parliament of March 1553, when clerical marriage had been legalised for several years, less than half of the eligible bishops – ten out of 22 – were married.

For most of them it was, in any case, their last appearance in the Upper House. Mary's accession was followed by the repeal of the acts permitting clerical marriage.[38] In a flurry of new-found chastity Bird and Scory repudiated their wives.[39] Bird was nevertheless deprived for his offence; Scory was displaced by the automatic restoration of George Day to Chichester in August 1553 and shortly afterwards he withdrew to the Continent.[40] Holgate, Ferrar and Bush were deprived at the same time as

Bird, because they too had contracted marriage 'to the grave scandal of all orders clerical and lay'.[41] The other married bishops were not deprived specifically for this offence. Nevertheless they, too, rapidly departed the parliamentary scene: Barlow hastily resigned Bath and Wells,[42] Ponet was displaced in August 1553 and Coverdale in September, by the restitution of Gardiner and Veysey.[43] Hooper was removed to the Fleet prison on 1 September, ostensibly for debts owed to the Crown;[44] a fortnight later Cranmer went to the Tower for his published declaration against the Mass.[45] They remained in prison until they were burnt for heresy, Hooper in 1555, Cranmer in 1556. When Mary's first parliament met, only two married bishops, Bird and Bush, remained in possession of their sees, their liberty and writs of summons to the Lords.[46] By April 1554 they too had gone.

Naturally the bishops appointed or restored by Mary were not married and did not marry. Altogether only eleven of the 52 mid-Tudor bishops took wives, in stark contrast with the 91 Edwardian and Marian peers, of whom eight married thrice, 38 twice, and all but two of the remainder once. Despite the Edwardian relaxation of the laws against clerical marriage, the pre-Elizabethan episcopate remained a largely celibate minority in the Upper House. If anything the legalisation of marriage had been a political encumbrance with no accompanying advantage. As the bishops who ventured into matrimony took wives from outside the peerage, even in some cases from outside the gentry too,[47] clerical marriage failed to establish a closer affinity with the peers, and, therefore, to diminish the social separateness of their order. Instead it became one of the issues which widened the division between conservative and reformer. The sordid wrangles arising from the marriage of the aged Archbishop Holgate to Barbara Wentworth and the scandal of Ponet's illegal contract with the wife of a Nottingham butcher enabled conservatives to vent their ridicule, scorn or moral indignation.[48] Such episodes not only served to discredit clerical marriage; they may also have contributed to the decline in prestige and dignity of the episcopal office.

Even without the additional provocation of clerical marriage the lords spiritual would have been a deeply divided body in the Lords. Their divided opinions on doctrine and the order of worship were free to come to the surface after Henry VIII's death. The

Edwardian government's sponsorship of a reformation effected by statute meant that these divisions were carried into the Upper House. The issue of reformation rent the unity of the lords spiritual, and prevented them from offering a united front in defence of their property and the privileges of their order.[49] The public disputation on the first Prayer Book in December 1548 revealed considerable conservative opposition to change. A minority of the bishops cast its votes against every reformation measure. And though the number of recorded parliamentary dissenters steadily declined during the reign, this was the consequence, not of a change of heart on their part, but of the deprivation of staunch conservatives and the public conformity of the less intransigent.[50] It was not until the Marian purge of 1553–4 that a genuine religious unity prevailed amongst the lords spiritual: when the reformers were deprived, the Henricians were restored, and those bishops who remained conservative in religion (and unmarried) were left in possession of their offices, despite their conformity in the previous reign.[51]

The picture presented thus far may convey the impression of a dominant and united lay majority cracking the whip over a dispirited and disarrayed minority of bishops. If so it must be corrected in several important particulars. The inferior attendance record of the peers made their numerical preponderance less impressive and important than it might otherwise have been. And, in so far as the majority of them were anti-clerical in temper, it was one of the few matters on which they were in general accord. The lords temporal, who gathered together in the parliament chamber for solemn deliberations in the service of Crown and commonweal, were also members of a competitive, thrusting aristocracy which was shot through with political rivalries, personal antipathies and family feuds. In March 1552 a matter of contention led Baron Bergavenny to strike the earl of Oxford in the presence chamber, an offence for which he was committed to ward.[52] Two months before this incident a fierce jurisdictional dispute between Lord Willoughby, the deputy of Calais, and Sir Andrew Dudley, who was captain of Guisnes, was brought before the council by Northumberland, Dudley's brother. The outcome was the removal of both men from their offices, later in the year.[53] Neither of these episodes had parliamentary repercussions of any kind; yet they are symptomatic of the fact that the peerage was not an elite living in a state of harmony induced by common ideals and personal ties.

Personal antagonisms might be set aside during a parliamentary session or rather occasions did not arise for their expression. But the avoidance of conflict over such public issues as established religion was more difficult, especially when they were directly touched upon by measures before the House. The Edwardian parliaments, for example, revealed that the peers were no more immune than the clergy from the disruptive effects of the Reformation. Conservative peers firmly rejected the radical Protestantism associated with Northumberland's regime, as Derby did when he declared to the Lords in 1550 'that the Holy Sacrament should be publicly revered and worshipped, and told the marquess of Northampton that he would lay down his life for it'.[54] He joined with Lords Dacre, Stourton and Windsor to vote against the Edwardian innovations; so too, though with less consistency, did the tenth Lord Morley and Thomas Lord Wharton.[55] Arrayed against them, amongst the advocates of religious change, were the earl of Pembroke and Lord Darcy of Chiche, new recruits to the House, and the marquess of Dorset, recently created duke of Suffolk, all of whom had been raised in rank as a reward for their loyalty to Northumberland. The conflict between reformer and conservative, confused as it was with political ambition and personal rivalry, cut across the division between lords spiritual and temporal to create disunity within each of the two groups.

Politics and religion are difficult, if not impossible, to separate in Reformation England. There is, nonetheless, an unmistakably secular vein of political activity in Edwardian faction politics when one of the chief prizes was control of the regency government with the attendant prospects of profit and power. Even in the first three parliaments of Mary's reign, when religious issues were so prominent, we can detect a personal rivalry between Gardiner and Paget which stemmed from political ambition and temperamental antipathy, as much as from conflicting priorities and positions in religion.[56] Political ambition, with its disruptive parliamentary consequences, manifested itself very early on, in the protectorate parliaments of 1547 and 1548/9. Thomas Lord Seymour of Sudeley was driven on by envy of his brother Edward duke of Somerset. Ambitious to remove him from the office of lord protector, he intrigued against him ceaselessly, in and out of parliament. Without tact, discretion or moderation, Seymour's political imbecility is even more impressive than that of Henry earl of Surrey or Robert earl of Essex. His bid for power ended ignominiously when he was arrested and sent to the Tower in January 1549. Amongst the charges drawn up against him was his intention to make 'a broile or tumulte and uprore' in parliament,[57] to set noblemen one against the other, and to exploit parliament for his own ends. As he had attempted to stir up a parliamentary 'tumult', so he was, appropriately enough, dealt with in a parliamentary way: he was condemned by an act of attainder, and executed in March 1549.

Seymour's wish was posthumously granted when Somerset was ousted in October 1549 at the instigation of the earl of Warwick, in combination with the conservative earls of Arundel and Southampton, and with the assistance or acquiescence of Lord Russell, Sir William Herbert and other councillors. The October coup, however, did nothing to heal the rifts in the nobility. Once he had unseated the protector, Warwick had to overcome a threatened Catholic takeover in a struggle which extended from November 1549 to the end of January in the following year. Although the ex-protector was spared, his considerable support in the council and parliament eventually prompted Northumberland to destroy him by a rigged trial in December 1551 and his execution took place on the day before the 1552 session of parliament began. Despite these precautions, his regime did not survive without challenge. Conservative peers had already expressed their disapproval of religious innovations during Somerset's protectorate and they disliked even more the radical Protestantism associated with Northumberland's regime. If the imperial ambassador, Johan Scheyfve, is to be believed, the earls of Derby and Shrewsbury, in particular, struck up hostile attitudes towards the new government. On 1 September 1550 Scheyfve predicted trouble in the next parliamentary session, because the two earls had quarrelled with William Lord Paget[58] over county boundaries. Together with Arundel, they intended to cause trouble in the Lords.[59] The ambassador continued to pick up rumours about Derby and Shrewsbury, though it is not possible to discover what substance there was in the stories which he retailed.[60] In any case nothing seems to have eventuated, and Derby's appointment to the privy council in August 1551 suggests that a *rapprochement* may have occurred.[61]

Not even the ruling clique, however, was free from such tensions during the latter years of Edward's reign. In December 1551 Scheyfve reported that the earl of Pembroke had fallen out with Warwick (recently promoted to the dukedom of Northumberland), because he had been over-attentive to Somerset.[62] When, in July 1552, Northumberland took Pembroke northwards with him on business, 'some say it is because [one] does not trust the other'.[63] Three months later, when Pembroke delayed his response to a summons to Court, rumour had it that he had quarrelled with the duke.[64] Edward VI confirmed the persistence of these rumours when he wrote in his journal that an Irishman had been imprisoned for spreading 'ill bruits . . . how the Duke of Northumberland and the Earl of Pembroke were fallen out, and one against another in the field'.[65] In the following February Scheyfve was assured 'that there is no good intelligence between [them], but the times are not ripe yet'.[66] The imperial ambassador did not have entrée to the governing circle as his Marian successor, Renard, did and for this reason his reports must be treated with caution. It is difficult to believe, however, that there was no truth in them, especially as rumours of this kind had even reached the king's ears. And Northumberland had a special talent for making enemies: Arundel and Southampton, whom he drove from the government after his successful *coup d'état* in 1549; Paget and Grey de Wilton who endured lengthy spells in prison for their part in Somerset's supposed plot against the government in 1551; conservative peers who were fearful of the religious direction of Northumberland's government; and perhaps Pembroke too, for he assumed a leading role in the council's desertion of Northumberland in July 1553.

By no stretch of the imagination could we regard the Edwardian lords temporal as a body united in either politics or religion. But at least the conflicts of competing factions had been worked out, for the most part, in the council chamber and elsewhere, not in parliament. In the first two years of Mary's reign this was not the case. The personal collisions between Bishop Gardiner and Lord Paget, and their different positions on such matters as the Spanish marriage, the reunification with Rome, and the

thorny issue of secularised property, were transferred to the
Lords. There, in Mary's first two parliaments, the bishop's plans
were eventually thwarted.[67] In the summer of 1554 Philip
arrived in England and Mary's marriage was consummated.
During her third parliament England was reunited with Rome.
Most of the great issues of the past 18 months lost some of their
significance, and the sources of conflict in the Lords diminished.
Yet the Upper House was not to be trusted. In her first parliament Mary's own lord chancellor, Gardiner, aided by Pembroke,
had mounted a parliamentary campaign in both Houses with the
object of persuading her to marry an English suitor, Edward
Courtenay; in her second, Pembroke had joined Paget and other
nobles to oppose Gardiner, sabotaging in the process some of the
queen's most cherished measures; and in the parliament which
met in November 1554 a disturbingly large group of nobles had
withdrawn, rather than give their approval to Philip's appointment as regent in the event of her pre-deceasing him during the
minority of their child.[68] Some – Suffolk, Devon, Oxford, the
fifth earl of Westmorland, the eighth Lord Audley, Bray and the
ninth Lord Cobham among them – were prepared to resort to
treason, or at least were suspected of doing so, whilst Thomas
Lord Darcy of Chiche and others could never be trusted because
of their past record and present attitude.[69] In Mary's reign, no
less than in Edward's, the lords temporal were a politically
volatile and deeply divided order.

Political competition need not surprise us; nor religious conflict, in the Reformation crises of the forties and fifties. But even
those very characteristics of a noble elite which might be expected
to promote cohesion and unity were themselves productive of
friction and division; and amongst these must be numbered such
considerations as noble lineage, possession of hereditary title and
social status. The particular *bêtes noires* here were age of title and
social origins. Any discussion about the antiquity of a particular
pedigree or title must be to some degree relative, that it is older
or newer than another. If we take 1558 as our year of reference,
can we treat Lord Windsor as a new peer when he was the third
of the family to hold the title? Yet as it was only created in 1529
it can hardly be termed old. However, this does not alter the fact
that, whilst Henry twelfth earl of Arundel, for example, was
indisputably of ancient pedigree, peers of the first generation

were obviously new, and that significant social attitudes distinguished the old and the *nouveau*.

Some 22 of the mid-Tudor peers could claim a lineage stretching back to the fourteenth century.[70] A larger number – 32 – held titles created in or after 1529 and, except for the third Lord Windsor, they were all of the first or second generation.[71] As none of them were scions of old noble houses, they could not lay claim to the ancient pedigree which might have compensated for the rawness of their titles and so diminished the scorn in which they were held by the possessors of ancient title. For many of the old peers regarded the new recruits, particularly those of inferior social origins, with suspicion and even hostility. The third duke of Norfolk had conspired to bring down Thomas Cromwell, whose description as 'a person of poor and low degree, as few be within this your realm' in the act which attainted him in 1540, may be attributed to the duke.[72] When Lord Paget was victimised by Northumberland for his loyalty to Somerset, he was degraded from the order of the garter 'chiefly because he was no gentleman of blood, neither of father's side nor mother's side'.[73] Their origins were undoubtedly modest, even humble. Cromwell was the son of a rural craftsman. Paget's father, who was described in the Staffordshire Visitations of 1583 as *mediocris fortunae vir*, was recorded variously as a barber (in 1502) and a clothworker (in 1530) in London.[74]

Cromwell and Paget were not alone. Edward North and Richard Rich also rose from an urban and trading environment to seats in the Lords.[75] Their social origins contrasted with those of Thomas Wharton, member of a family of minor gentry who for long had been Clifford dependents. Yet their rise was no more dramatic than his, because he had achieved the remarkable transformation from a position of social dependence into a peer rivalling the old families for office and regional influence in the far north.[76] Both peers and gentlemen of respectable pedigree were affronted by the rise of these men to power, title and profit in the king's service. During the pilgrimage of grace, one of the complaints forwarded by the conservative leadership to Henry VIII was that he 'takes of his Council and has about him, persons of low birth and small reputation . . . whom we suspect to be lord Cromwell and sir Ric[hard] Rich'.[77] It made no difference that Rich's family had been Hampshire landowners for several generations,[78] nor for that matter that Wharton was of gentle status. They were sufficiently parvenu to arouse the resentment of old-established families, especially those whom they were displacing, and their rise contributed to the disunity which afflicted the peerage. New peers such as Thomas Cromwell and William Paget became victims to the contempt and bitterness of the old. Some of the antique peers – Norfolk in 1547, Arundel in 1550 – became sacrifices to the ambitions of the new.

The intruding influence of the new men was experienced no less in the countryside than in Whitehall and Westminster – hence the antipathy of Lord Stourton to the earl of Pembroke's acquisition of estates in Wiltshire.[79] Nowhere was resentment so intense and serious as in the north where Lord Wharton, ennobled and enriched by the Crown, challenged the social pre-eminence and traditional monopoly of marcher offices enjoyed by the Clifford, Dacre and Percy families. Wharton's advancement was an integral part of the Henrician policy of enhancing royal authority at the expense of the old-established northern magnates.[80] Although their power was already in decline without the king's assistance,[81] Henry VIII accelerated the process. He achieved this effect partly by the temporary destruction of Percy power[82] and partly by the promotion of new men who, as owners of extensive properties granted by the Crown and as representatives of royal authority, could challenge their former superiors and masters.[83]

As the most successful of the parvenu peers, Wharton was also the most hated. In 1538 he complained to Cromwell of the enmity of the earl of Cumberland and Lord Dacre towards him.[84] The bishop of Llandaff sympathised with him when he wrote in praise of his services to the Crown and added 'it were pity that the disdain of his neighbours should discourage him'.[85] What else could Llandaff expect but disdain from the second earl of Cumberland, head of the ancient noble family of Clifford? Wharton was risen from clientage to the position of interloper in Clifford country and a successful competitor who, in 1544, secured the wardenship of the west marches over his head. Disputes inevitably occurred between the aggressive Wharton and the tetchy Cumberland. In 1548 there was a 'varience' between them 'for the grounde whereon the Faire of Kerkeby Steeven was wunte to be kepte'. It reached the ears of the privy

council which acted promptly to prevent the situation getting out
of hand. On 27 April they were accordingly instructed to 'for-
beare' and Cumberland was promised that 'at his next repaire
hether to the Parleament order should be taken'.[86]

Whether the council fulfilled its promise we do not know, but it
certainly failed to reconcile the antagonists or impose a lasting
truce. In 1549 Richard Musgrave, acting on Wharton's behalf,
brought a bill into parliament to deprive Cumberland of his
hereditary shrievalty.[87] During September the feud threatened
to flare into violence, when some Clifford servants, despatched to
Mallerstang Forest 'ther to hunt and kylle redde dere', were
confronted by Sir Henry Wharton, one of Lord Wharton's sons,
'with many others to the nomber of three hundred persons of
the household, servents and adherents of the seid Lord Wharton'.
Sir Henry's followers, who had been 'unlawfully assembled and
getheried together by procurement and comaundmente' of Lord
Wharton, 'sore manassed and thretyned to bayte' Cumberland's
servants who sensibly 'gave place unto the seid offenders' and
hurried on their way to Mallerstang Forest, with Wharton's
armed band in hot pursuit. Lord Wharton himself now entered
the scene. He kept his adherents 'assembled together at Wharton
all that day lokyng for the returne' of Cumberland's servants
who (improbably) 'for the preservacyon of your peace' and
(undoubtedly) for the 'savegard of their own lyves' shivered
their way through a night in the forest. Only when some of the
Westmorland magistrates had dispersed Wharton's armed band
did they dare to return home. As the sole source of evidence for
this episode is a petition to Star Chamber,[88] and as the tale is
related by those discomforted Clifford retainers, we should not be
too hasty in assigning to them the role of poor innocents and
casting the Whartons in the role of unmitigated villains. It is
not necessary to treat too seriously the petitioners' protestations
that they were particularly anxious to preserve the king's peace.
There is no doubt, however, that a confrontation had occurred,
and that behind the baron's son and the earl's servants were the
two nobles themselves.

The feud dragged on into Mary's reign. On 20 June 1554 the
privy council had to instruct Shrewsbury and the council in the
north to see the peace kept between Cumberland and Wharton,
and their servants and tenants, in a dispute over 'the building of

a wall of a parke'.[89] When this too failed to achieve a settlement the matter was deferred until Cumberland and Wharton came south for Mary's third parliament. The council then imposed upon them a public reconciliation.[90] A public demonstration of goodwill, performed under compulsion, was a popular Tudor device, but it naturally failed to mitigate the mutual hostility which continued unabated. On 3 February 1558 it even carried over into parliament, when a bill was introduced into the Lords for punishing the 'lewd misdemeanours' of the earl of Cumberland's servants and tenants towards Wharton.[91] Its failure to progress beyond a first reading may indicate the successful opposition of the earl's friends in the House or, as seems most probable, prompt council action in securing its suppression or withdrawal. By its very nature the bill could have had a disruptive effect, forcing the lords temporal to side with one or other of the parties to the dispute; therefore the council preferred to settle the matter without recourse to parliament. This is confirmed by a council minute of March 1558, just a fortnight after the session had ended. The council noted Wharton's complaint of 'sundry heinous and grevious disorders' committed by Cumberland against him and his tenants. As England was at war with France, however, there was a constant danger that the Scots might take advantage of this to raid or invade the border counties. National security naturally took precedence over local feuds and the council decided 'having respect to the present time of service' not to call them away from the marcher counties. Instead it deferred a hearing of their dispute until parliament reassembled 'in wynter nexte', and in the meantime it admonished them both – but particularly Cumberland – to refrain from molesting each other.[92] Although Wharton attended parliament in November 1558,[93] Cumberland did not. And so the unresolved conflict was bequeathed to the next reign, one of the minor Marian legacies.

Wharton's rise posed a particular threat to the Dacre family. In the past they had been one of the Crown's natural choices for service in marcher offices. William Dacre therefore followed the traditional pattern when he was appointed to the wardenry of the west march in 1527, two years after he had succeeded his father as third Lord Dacre of Gilsland. But this is where the traditional pattern ended. He occupied the office for only seven years until his opposition to the breach with Rome led to his dismissal and imprisonment. On 9 July 1534 he was acquitted of high treason in a trial before his peers,[94] but he was not re-appointed to office. Henry VIII's suspicion of Dacre was just one example of the mistrust in which he held the northern families. Their political unreliability was particularly dangerous in the 1530s, when there were recurrent fears of foreign invasion and domestic rebellion in reaction to his revolutionary policies. Cumberland's equivocal conduct during the pilgrimage of grace can hardly have reassured him.[95]

It was in these circumstances that the king adopted the deliberate policy of extending effective royal authority into the far north. Every opportunity was seized to diminish the authority of the old families. To judge by the results, the most effective technique was to elevate members of the local gentry to peerages, appoint them to marcher offices, and endow them with sufficient estates for the maintenance of the dignity and the expense of their offices. In this way clients of the Cliffords and Percies could be transformed into fee'd men of the king. Sir William Eure was raised to a barony in 1544 and for ten years served in old Percy territory as warden of the east march and captain of Berwick Castle.[96] In the west Sir Thomas Wharton was similarly advanced at a time when the Dacre family was under a cloud; from 1537 to 1544 he served as deputy warden of the west march to which was added the governorship of Carlisle in 1541; and in March 1544 he received the king's letters patent creating him a baron and his commission as warden,[97] the office which had been the traditional preserve of the Dacres until the third Lord's dismissal ten years before.

Dacre's resentment at the intrusion of Wharton into the wardenry of the west march resulted in a permanent condition of hostility. This state of affairs was viewed with grave concern by both the Edwardian and Marian privy councils: constant feuding which involved royal officials would weaken the Crown's authority in the far north, and endanger border security. In the parliament time it might result in broils in the Upper House where, of course, both Dacre and Wharton sat. This fear of parliamentary disruption accounts for the council's firm action in the closing months of 1551. The government was in the throes of a political crisis as Northumberland engineered the final downfall of Somerset, who was imprisoned in mid-October and convicted of felony on 1 December. Parliament did not meet until 23 January 1552, but, as early as the previous November, Dacre had already arrived at Court, whither he had been summoned by the privy council. He had been involved in a clash with Wharton's supporters, the Musgraves, and, when the council received reports of it, the lord chancellor had been instructed to send for the antagonists.[98] The council clearly preferred the Musgraves' version of what had happened, because, on 25 November, Dacre was ordered to prison. Doubtless this was intended by the council as no more than a warning for the future because, on 19 December, less than four weeks later, Sir Robert Bowes was instructed to 'enlarge the Lord Dacres of imprisonment'.[99] With parliament due to assemble in a month's time, however, and with Wharton on his way south to attend, it was a very timely warning, designed to discourage them from continuing their feud in the House of Lords.

Nor did the council let matters rest there. On 8 March 1552, half-way through the session, it enforced on them a public reconciliation.[100] The possible parliamentary repercussions of these aristocratic feuds had to be avoided at all costs and this concern is reflected in the council's stated motive for its actions: 'considering how perilous a thing [their quarrels] were, aswell for this troublesome season as in this tyme of Parlyament and assemble of the nobles of the realme'.[101] Wharton's attendance record in the Lords is also revealing. He was present every day from the opening until 8 March, when the public reconciliation took place; thereafter he did not make a single appearance.[102] It looks as though Wharton had been called south for the sole purpose of participating in the reconciliation ceremony. Perhaps, however, the council did not have sufficient faith in the efficacy of such public demonstrations and preferred to keep the combatants apart by ordering Wharton home. If so, its decision was a wise one. Although the reconciliation 'so well ended with the great rejoysing of all their Lordships',[103] the feuding continued unbated.

Mary's reign saw a revival of Dacre fortunes. Wharton had been one of Northumberland's supporters, and from July 1552 onwards, when the duke was warden general of the entire border, he had been deputy-warden of all three marches[104] – a record not guaranteed to inspire Mary's confidence. In December 1553, Lord Conyers was appointed to the east march and, in the following month, Dacre displaced Wharton in both the middle and west marches.[105] Dacre was riding high. Perhaps, in his exuberance, he could not resist the temptation to needle his ousted rival, or to use his authority as warden to harrass him. Whatever the reason, by April 1554 the ex-warden was complaining of 'certayne wronges doone unto hym by the Lorde Dacres'.[106] The council responded by instructing the earl of Shrewsbury to examine and resolve their differences.[107] When Cumberland, rejuvenated by the Lord Dacre's reinstatement as warden, actively renewed his perpetual feud with Wharton, the privy council seized the opportunity of their presence at the third Marian parliament to effect another public reconciliation. Cumberland and Dacre 'betwene whom and the Lorde Wharton muche variaunce and strife hath of long time depended'[108] swore undying love and devotion to each other – and carried on quarrelling. During 1555 Wharton's fortunes took an upward turn when, in July, he displaced Dacre in the middle march and in December acquired the eastern wardenship as well.[109] Every shift in marcher power was accompanied by renewed conflict – and 1555 was no exception.[110] The perpetual feuds and rivalries of the far north just could not be assuaged by the admonitions of the privy council. Nevertheless, in its pursuit of the thankless task of keeping the peace, its actions were motivated by political common sense, because conflicts of this kind might disrupt marcher government and weaken the border defences. They might also be transmitted to the floor of the parliament chamber, where the Lords could be thrown into disarray and the business of the House neglected.

Intermarriage proved to be no more effective as a cohesive force than common membership of a legal status group resting upon hereditary noble title. It too could work in a reverse and centrifugal direction. Most noble marriages were launched for social and economic – and less frequently political – reasons, and they were the end-product of lengthy negotiations and elaborate marriage contracts which sought to take into account all future financial contingencies. Personal compatibility, however, was the unknown factor. It was an unexplored sea for which there were no navigational charts, with the result that many marriages

foundered on the reefs of personal antipathy or simple absence
of affection, sometimes with harmful effects on family relation-
ships. This had already been demonstrated in bizarre fashion in
Henry VIII's reign. In 1533, after twenty years of marriage, the
third duke of Norfolk separated from his second wife, Elizabeth,
daughter of the duke of Buckingham.[111] Five years later the earl
of Surrey, Norfolk's heir, resisted his sister's proposed marriage to
Thomas Seymour. With a characteristic mixture of tactlessness
and high aristocratic disdain, he scorned an alliance with the
newly risen Seymours and recommended instead that she warmed
the king's bed.[112] In the last months of Henry VIII's reign the
indiscretions of father and son proved almost fatal to the Howard
house. Even Norfolk's mistress testified against him to the privy
council, whilst the testimony of Surrey's sister helped to procure
his condemnation and death.[113]

The mid-Tudor peerage had its share of marital disharmony
too. Sometimes it is impossible to discover, through the meagre
evidence, why marriages broke down. The estrangement of
John second Lord Bray from his wife Anne, daughter of the
fifth earl of Shrewsbury, may have occurred because the conservative Talbots and Anne herself disapproved of his radical
religious opinions; yet it is possible that the explanation lies in
some insurmountable personal antipathy.[114] Sometimes, however,
it is not necessary to hunt for the answer in politics and religion:
when, for example, three peers were driven into drastic courses
by the infidelity of their wives. Edward Lord Grey of Powis, who
died in 1551, divorced Anne, the legitimised daughter of Charles
Brandon duke of Suffolk, at some time prior to Thomas Cromwell's fall.[115] William marquess of Northampton took the same
step when Anne – daughter of Henry Bourchier second earl of
Essex – 'elowped' in or about 1542.[116] And Henry second earl
of Sussex was provoked to divorce his 'unkind' wife Anne, the
daughter of Sir Philip Calthorp, who left him, committed
adultery, and was even imprisoned in 1552 on charges of sor-
cery.[117]

The marital indiscretions of Grey's wife did not have any
parliamentary repercussions though when her transgressions
became legal as well as moral the law was forced to take a hand.[118]
In contrast the breakdown of Sussex's marriage did become a
parliamentary matter because, with the assistance of his friends

in the Lords, he attempted to take revenge on his wife. In 1555 a bill 'to debar Ann the late divorced wife of Henry Earl of Sussex, of her Jointure and Dower' was introduced into the Upper House, obviously on his behalf, though not by him because he was absent from the entire session. The House was not in unanimous agreement, because, when it was passed, the bishops of Bangor and St David's dissented. The bill was not in any case destined to become law, because the Commons rejected it in a division on the third reading.[119]

Northampton's case, which is well documented because it raised important theological questions concerning the law of marriage, did not have the same obvious parliamentary repercussions, and yet it must have introduced once more enmity into a House whose membership was already riven with differences of many kinds.[120] He had obtained a divorce *a mensa et thoro*[121] (but not *a vincula*) in the ecclesiastical courts, on the grounds of his wife's adultery. When he wished to remarry he petitioned the king for a commission to determine whether he could do so whilst his first wife was still alive. The commission was appointed in April 1547 and the outcome of its deliberations was eventually favourable to Northampton. But it took a year to reach its decision, during which time his patience expired and he married Elizabeth Brooke, daughter of the ninth Lord Cobham. The council took a stern view of his 'misconduct', summoned him to appear before it, and ordered him to separate from her until the commission had arrived at its decision. To ensure that its order was carried out it placed Elizabeth in the custody of Queen Katherine Parr. Nearly a month later Van der Delft, the imperial ambassador, wrote of Northampton that 'He is only spoken of secretly and does not show himself at Court.' The dilatory proceedings of the commission together with the personal humiliation heaped upon him turned him into one of Somerset's bitterest enemies.[122] In their different ways Northampton's case and Sussex's bill hint at the disruptive parliamentary effects of marital failures.

Even (perhaps especially) when adultery was not the reason, the dissolution of a marriage may have engendered yet another enmity between noble families: for example, when the unconsummated wedding of the eleven-year-old heir of William Eure to the three- (or four-)year-old daughter of Lord Darcy of

Darcy (Aston) in 1541 was dissolved fifteen years later;[123] or when the third marquess of Dorset (elevated in 1551 to the dukedom of Suffolk) dissolved his marriage to Katherine, daughter of the eleventh earl of Arundel, and married Francis Brandon in 1533 whilst his first wife was still alive.[124] Twenty years later Katherine Grey, one of the children sired by Suffolk in his second marriage, was wedded to Henry Herbert, heir of the first earl of Pembroke. When Suffolk's treason ruined the family fortunes in Mary's reign, however, Pembroke contrived to secure the dissolution of the marriage.[125]

The severance of marital links between noble families was certainly not guaranteed to improve relations between them and was more likely to leave a legacy of ill will, although it is usually incapable of proof. It may have contributed to the antipathy between the twelfth earl of Arundel and Northumberland's regime in which Suffolk, who had repudiated Arundel's sister, occupied a prominent place. It is possible that the sixteenth earl of Oxford's projected marital adventure in 1547, less than 18 months after the death of his first wife, the fourth earl of Westmorland's sister, had a similar effect. The banns for his marriage to a 'gentlewoman . . . Mistress Dorothy late woman to my Lady Katherine his daughter' had already been twice called when Sir Thomas Darcy, his brother-in-law, intervened to prevent it. Darcy appears to have succeeded, because, in the following year, Oxford married Margery Golding. Oxford did not pine for long when his intentions were frustrated. One suspects, however, that he would have been resentful rather than grateful for the interference of Darcy, who was, incidentally, elevated to the peerage and therefore to the Upper House in 1551.[126]

Even those marriages which endured could be politically disruptive. The duke of Somerset's second wife, Anne Stanhope, niece of John earl of Bath, was by all accounts imperious, sensitive of both her lineage and her precedence as the protector's wife, and a political meddler. Her jealousy of the precedence accorded to the queen-dowager was inflamed when Katherine Parr married Lord Seymour, her brother-in-law. The marriage was impolitic, even dangerous. It aroused Somerset's anger, provoked disputes between the wives, and contributed to the deteriorating relations between the two men.[127] When, during the troubled summer of 1549, Van der Delft expressed the opinion that the

protector 'would certainly never do any good', Sir William
Paget's terse comment, that 'he has a bad wife', served as the
explanation for Somerset's failure. It also expressed his disapproval
of her unwanted intrusion into politics and her baleful influence
on the protectorate.[128] It is of course impossible to gauge the
disharmony, even enmity, caused by unpopular wives and
broken marriages. They cannot be dismissed, however, as of no
consequence. Norfolk's downfall, Northampton's antagonism
towards Somerset (and perhaps to Cranmer too) and Arundel's
hostility towards the regime of Somerset's successor, the protector's
fratricidal conflict with Thomas; all resulted partly from marriages which were personal failures or political blunders.

Obviously we should not assume any natural unity of opinion or
harmony of interest in the mid-Tudor Lords. It was not the
assembly of one homogeneous class but of two orders, spiritual
and temporal, which were set apart by social differences, an
absence of familial and marital connections, and the presence of
conflicting interests. Even among the lords temporal, the competition of factions, the personality conflicts, the antipathy
between the families of antique pedigree and the new men of
humbler origins who were displacing them from office – all
served to weaken and undermine the theoretical unity of the
social elite. The religious conflict aggravated these divisions,
cutting across them and dividing the house into two parties,
which crystallised around the opposing banners of Catholicism
and Protestantism. At times it subsumed all other causes of
disunity in the one process of religious polarisation.

Such divisive forces cannot be ignored in any study of the
mid-Tudor Lords. Their detrimental – and occasionally disastrous – effects on the business of the House will be considered
in due course. At the same time they ought not to be exaggerated.
Intermarriage could act as a social cement as well as a disruptive
force. Service to the prince, as an ideal, must have tempered the
self-interested competition of peers for office. And in one respect
at least, as elites in State and Church, the peerage must have
shared with the bishops certain common attitudes, such as
political responsibility and deference to the Crown. Disagreement,
heated debate and conflict were common enough occurrences in
the mid-Tudor parliaments. This cannot be denied. But it would
be false and misleading to suggest that this was the normal state of

affairs. For much, indeed most, of the time, the members of the House, temporal and spiritual, worked constructively and co-operatively to scrutinise and enact a formidable volume of legislation, the bulk of which was technical, complex and often tedious in nature, and not in any way productive of conflict. The machinery which was at the disposal of the House for the fulfil-ment of this legislative function was elaborate, sophisticated and efficient. And it is to this that attention must next be turned.

6

THE LORDS' INHERITANCE: CLERKS AND ASSISTANTS TO THE HOUSE

The clerical organisation of the Upper House and the presence of a professional corps of judges and lawyers, on whose advice and assistance the lords spiritual and temporal could call, must be counted amongst the most important assets of the mid-Tudor House of Lords. In these respects it may even have been more adequately equipped than the Commons to fulfil the parliamentary functions of deliberation and legislation. This would not be surprising. The Lords was the historic nucleus of parliament, a fact reflected in its membership and in the very arrangement of the parliament chamber. The judges, king's serjeants-at-law, law officers of the Crown and masters of chancery together occupied the woolsacks in the middle of the chamber and were the official members of the king's continual or permanent council, his legal councillors. The lords spiritual and temporal represented the medieval great council, transformed by the growth of a theory of lay peerage which equated peers with lords of parliament, confined the temporal element of the *magnum concilium* to nobles, and yet enlarged it to comprehend the entire nobility. The throne was the perpetual reminder that parliament had originated as a royal assembly, an afforced meeting of the king's council. And there were also present, on the wool-sacks, the lord chancellor and his chancery clerks, who had nurtured parliament from its medieval origins. As parliament evolved into separate Houses, the great council ceased to be the nucleus, the essence, of parliament and became instead just one of the two Houses. As the descendant of that medieval nucleus, however, it retained many of its attributes and amenities, in particular a clerical organisation endowed with the long experience and professional expertise of chancery and the assistance of the legal members of the permanent council.

The retention of the title 'clerk of the parliaments' by the Lords' clerk underlines the Lords' fortunate position as the beneficiary of the medieval parliament, in which chancery was the core. The clerk had always been, and in the sixteenth century continued to be, recruited from chancery.[1] He brought to his parliamentary office the necessary qualifications of all clerks in the lord chancellor's department: a competence in written and oral Latin, French and English. Combined with his professional expertise was a new-found independence from chancery itself. 'The clerk of the parliaments and his assistants were acquiring *circa* 1500 an independent status as a department immediately responsible to Parliament.' This development was demonstrated by the retention of the original acts by the clerk instead of their transmission to chancery, which had been the recognised procedure until 1497.[2] Thus the mid-Tudor Lords enjoyed the benefits of a clerk who, with his assistants, was professionally trained and fluent in the three essential languages of parliamentary and diplomatic procedure, and who was the custodian of the separate developing parliamentary archives.

The efficiency of the Upper House must have rested to a considerable extent on his competence and conscientiousness, because his duties were significant, multifarious, and not restricted in time to the duration of a parliamentary session. They began with the scrutiny of the writs of summons when they were despatched, and amendments to the list of eligible members caused by deaths and creations. He drew up, on instruction, the lists of receivers and triers of petitions, and at the opening ceremony read them out 'in *French*, according to the Ancient and unusual manner'; he filed the petitions received, 'called every Lord in the House by his Name, that so it might be seen, who were present', compiled the attendance lists, listed the readings on the dorse of the engrossed bills, registered proxies and sometimes 'drew' them, and regularly kept a record of bill proceedings which was, in the course of the century, transformed into the official journal of the House.[3] He read aloud to the House the text of each bill in what was literally the first reading, and he or his subordinates engrossed bills and endorsed successful measures 'soit baille aux Communs' before their despatch to the Lower House, transcribed amendments, and supplied copies of bills to interested members.

The range of the clerk's activities during the session is betrayed in his own jottings. At the end of the Edwardian journal for 1548–9 is a sheet of his scribbled remembrances: a note 'to searche out the Acte for thuse of handgonnes', a reminder to deliver the 'boke of the merchentes that traffique to Island' to a legal assistant, and a record of those to whom bills had been committed. He appears to have been responsible not only for the custody of bills between readings but also for passing them on to the convenors of committees and for locating old acts which were pertinent to a committee's work.[4] He could not even relax during the closing ceremony, for then it was his duty, in response to the clerk of the Crown's reading of the title, to intone the monarch's assent or veto of each bill passed by the two Houses and inscribe the formula of assent on it.[5] When the members of the Lords and Commons dispersed at the conclusions of a session, however, the clerk of the parliaments remained. He had to decide which acts were to be published by the king's printer, whom he supplied with copies and even, on occasion, with the originals themselves. Presumably he also supervised his subordinates in the enrolment of statutes on the parliament roll.[6]

The clerk served parliament in general then, but during the session he served the House of Lords in particular, at the head of an expert and experienced clerical organisation provided by chancery. Eulogies about its efficiency and adequacy, however, ought not to trip too lightly off the tongue. An examination of the two Lords' Journals kept by deputy clerks for the 1542 session, for example, must cast doubts on the accuracy of the journal, especially as a record of attendance.[7] And a letter from Protector Somerset to Sir Edward North attests to the haphazard fashion in which the parliamentary archives were managed in the mid-sixteenth century. North had surrendered the clerkship of the parliaments in 1540; yet Somerset was compelled to write to him eight years later, on 6 November 1548, 'to delyver to Sir John Masone knighte all suche Actes of Parlement and other writings touching the same as sythen the tyme you were Clercke of the Parlement have out of their place remayned in your Custodie'.[8] Moreover the present clerk was Sir William Paget who had replaced North, not Mason who only succeeded to the office 20 months later. Mason may have already taken over the duties of clerk of the parliaments. Nevertheless it was a strange bureaucratic situation when Mason, who was not yet officially clerk, was to receive parliamentary records from North, who had not occupied the office for the past eight years.[9]

The clerk of the parliaments and his subordinates were managed and directed by the lord chancellor, who sat in the Lords *ex officio* and without a writ of summons, whether or not he was a commoner – originally in his capacity as a judge or councillor, eventually because he was prolocutor of the House and head of chancery which issued the writs of summons.[10] The first officer of State in precedence, invariably a member of the privy council, the autocratic head of chancery, and the effective head of the system of equitable and prerogative jurisdiction, he was at once adviser, administrator and judge. In the Lords he served in a fourfold capacity: as 'ye principall clerke of the higher house',[11] presiding officer, an adviser to the House and a leading royal servant. On the one hand he was 'the mouth of the . . . house' and on the other 'the voyce and orator of the prince'.[12] He provided a degree of co-ordination between the government and the House of Lords, and between the members of the House and the legal assistants (amongst whom he might also be classified).[13]

Under the direction of king and council the lord chancellor and his chancery clerks were responsible for the organising of a parliamentary session, in particular the issue of writs to bishops and peers, assistants to the Upper House, and sheriffs.[14] He stage-managed the opening ceremonies, delivering what was the descendant of the fifteenth-century parliamentary sermon and the ancestor of the speech from the throne, and replying to the speaker on the prince's behalf. In 1547 Richard Lord Rich opened proceedings with 'a great proposition for the assembly of the parliament'. Bishop Gardiner's peroration in November 1554 'dealt mainly with the religious question' though 'it also contained much other matter'. This is hardly surprising as it 'lasted a good two hours'.[15] The lord chancellor's speech was no mere ceremonial exercise. On his skilful presentation of the government's record and its financial and legislative needs may have depended to some extent the willingness of parliament to satisfy the wishes of the prince.

Nor did the lord chancellor's parliamentary duties end with his central role in the opening ceremonies. They were time-consuming, onerous, and continuous throughout the session until he delivered the closing address and declared the prorogation or dissolution of parliament. As speaker of the House his daily presence was required and certainly the mid-Tudor chancellors lived up to their responsibilities. Rich attended 94% of the sittings in 1547, 88% in 1548/9 and 97% in 1549/50. Goodrich did not miss a single day of the last two Edwardian sessions; nor did Gardiner during the two parliaments of 1554, although he died during the following parliament in 1555, after attending only two days. Archbishop Heath's record – 100% in the two sessions of 1558 – was also one of exemplary regularity. Doubtless this was expected of them. Before parliament assembled the chancellor was usually appointed to the privy council committee entrusted with the devising of an official legislative programme,[16] and he must have been expected to keep a weather-eye on its passage through the Lords. On occasions he played a prominent part in the drafting of bills during the session. Gardiner for example, had a hand in the measures for Philip's security and the reunion with Rome in Mary's third parliament.[17] The chancellor was not frequently appointed to committees, presumably because of his other commitments which must have kept him fully occupied: he received all bills presented to the House, ensured that the correct legislative procedures were observed in their enactment, and chose the legal assistants who were to carry successful bills down to the Commons. It was also his duty to ensure that amendments to a bill by the Lords were duly incorporated in it. When, in Mary's third parliament, the Commons returned the bill to reunite England with Rome, recommending that 19 lines concerning ex-episcopal properties should be 'razed' and 'taken out of the act', the Upper House concurred. Whereupon 'the Chancellor, in the Sight of all the Lords, with a Knife, cut them, saying these Words, "I now do rightly the Office of a Chancellor." '[18]

It was the lord chancellor's duty to manage and discipline the Lords. When the House assembled at the beginning of a session he ought 'to call by name all ye Lords of ye parliament and likewise at other times as he seeth occasion'. If, during the session, 'anie disorder . . . be amonge the lords, and they will not be reformed, then he must forthwith advise the king'.[19] The object of such discipline and control was efficiency, regular attendance and orderly conduct. There is no evidence that the Crown attempted to use or indeed was capable of using the chancellor to force the House into compliancy with its policies. Nevertheless the chancellor was of crucial importance, both to the Crown whose spokesman he was and to the efficiency of the Upper House whose speaker he was. To his parliamentary functions he might bring a prestige augmented by other offices in his possession or by sheer force of personality. The Venetian ambassador, Michiel, writing a week after Bishop Gardiner's death, described the late chancellor as having been 'feared and respected in an extraordinary degree by everybody. . . . It seems . . . as though there remains no longer any one who knows how to exercise authority in such a way as he did, nor with the knowledge so extensive and minute, both of the business and of all the persons of any account in this kingdom, and also of the time and means by which to please or flatter, or to overawe and punish them.'[20]

The chief source of the lord chancellor's parliamentary influence, however, was not his personality but his cancellarial office which gave him considerable authority in both government and parliament, in the counsels of the king and the deliberations of the Lords. It must have benefited the Upper House too. In contrast with the formal request of the Commons' speaker for liberty of access to the monarch's presence 'upon all Urgent and Necessary Occasions',[21] the lord chancellor enjoyed a natural and continuous access, by virtue of his office and his seat at the council board.

The presence of assistants to the House, seated on the woolsacks in the centre of the chamber, is yet another reminder that the Tudor House of Lords, now only one member of a bicameral institution, was nonetheless the legatee of the medieval parliament and the beneficiary of its assets. Five classes of royal servants were summoned to the House on writs of assistance and were duly enrolled on the parliament pawn:[22] the judges, the king's serjeants, the master of the rolls, the king's legal counsel – the attorney- and solicitor-general – and the secretaries of State. The masters of chancery also attended the Lords but, with the exception of the master of the rolls, they were not enrolled and so presumably did not receive writs. The fact that all the assistants were royal servants is indicative of the origins of writs of assistance, because they had originally been members of the permanent council summoned to advise the Crown. The judges and the law officers of the Crown had been an integral part, indeed the nucleus, of the earlier medieval parliament. But they had long since ceased to be part of the active membership of the Lords and by the sixteenth century they had been transformed into mere advisers and assistants. They rendered invaluable services, both in an advisory and legislative capacity, but they possessed neither voice (unless their advice was sought) nor vote.

In 1539 Henry VIII attempted to strengthen the conciliar element in the Lords by the retention of privy councillors there too. The act 'For placing of the Lords in Parliament' determined the place and precedence of Henry VIII's vicegerent, and the order in which the archbishops and bishops should sit. It placed 'the great officers of the Realme' above the peerage,[23] with the exception of the king's close relatives, and it gave precedence to his chief secretary 'being of the degree of a Baron [or Bishop] . . . above all Barons [or Bishops]' who did not occupy any of the great offices of State specified in the act. If any commoner held the office of lord chancellor, lord treasurer, lord president of the council, lord privy seal or chief secretary 'by reason whereof they can have noe interest to give any assent or dissent in the said House, that then in every such case [he] shall sit and be placed at the uppermost part of the sacks in the midst of the said parliament chamber'.[24]

The object of this act was not to strengthen royal control of the House by augmenting the conciliar element within it. Those peers and bishops who were officers of State were entitled to a writ of summons and a voice in the House in any case, by virtue of their peerage or episcopal status, whilst commoners occupying high office could only attend as assistants without voice or vote. The prime purpose of the act was probably to give statutory recognition to the right of the king's council, as the historic nucleus of parliament, to be represented in the parliament chamber, and, with the division of parliament into two Houses and the growth of the concept of peerage, to safeguard their places there. When Lord Chancellor Audley introduced the bill into the Upper House 'he stated that His Majesty had commanded [it] to be made, so that thereby the said magnates, knowing their places, might avoid contention in the future'.[25] It

may also have been designed to furnish the Lords with administrative and diplomatic experts in much the same way that
the judges and law officers advised the House on legal and
legislative matters. Sir Thomas Smith, himself an Edwardian
secretary, wrote that the secretaries sat in the Upper House 'to
aunswere of such letters or thinges passed in counsell whereof
they have the custodie and knowledge'.[26]

Apart from reorganising the precedence of the House in favour
of noble and episcopal officers of State, however, the practical
effects of the act were very limited. The clause which placed
certain office-holding commoners in the Lords as assistants was
in most cases inapplicable. The Edwardian and Marian chancellors, treasurers, lords president of the council, keepers of the
privy seal, great chamberlains, marshals and admirals were
bishops or peers.[27] Only the secretaryship, divided into two after
Thomas Cromwell's surrender of the office in 1540, was held by
royal servants 'under the degree of a Baron of the Parliament'.[28]
Altogether seven commoners held secretaryships during one or
more parliamentary sessions in the reigns of Edward VI and
Mary: Sir William Petre (during nine sessions), Sir John Bourne
(six), Sir William Cecil and Dr John Boxall (two apiece), and
Sir Thomas Smith, Sir John Cheke and Dr Nicholas Wotton
(one each).[29] On all but three occasions they certainly received
writs of assistance to the Upper House. The possible exceptions
were Sir Thomas Smith (in 1548/9), Dr Nicholas Wotton (in
1549/50) and Sir William Cecil (in 1552). As they were appointed
to secretaryships at various times after the first session of Edward
VI's first parliament, they are naturally not enrolled as assistants
on the pawn for that parliament. The pawn, it must be remembered, was devised as the master record for the issue of
writs to the opening session of a parliament, and was not amended
to take into account changes in personnel which had occurred by
the time succeeding sessions of the same parliament were held.
Therefore the absence of these men from the pawn does not
preclude the possibility of their summons and attendance in the
second, third and fourth sessions of this parliament, during their
tenure of the secretarial office.

Apart from two secretaries, Doctors Wotton and Boxall, who
were ineligible to sit in the Commons, all the mid-Tudor secretaries were members of the Lower House in those sessions for

which they also received writs of assistance to the Lords. The question arises, in which House did they actually sit? G. R. Elton argues that none of them attended the Lords, and the fact that 'many of them came to seek election to the House of Commons . . . amply illustrates the new position of that body where the presence of leading ministers came to be common practice and (from the Crown's point of view) essential'.[30] Elton's assertion is really a twofold one: the fact that no secretaries sat in the Lords but most of them were present in the Commons; and the conclusion which he draws from this fact about the relative importance of the two Houses. His facts are, with one exception, indisputably correct. An examination of the journals for the two Houses reveals that, on almost every occasion on which they were both elected and summoned, they were active in the Commons: Petre in eight sessions, Bourne in four, Cecil in two[31] and Smith in one. There is no reference to Sir John Cheke in the Commons' Journal of March 1553, nor to Sir John Bourne in April–May 1554 and November 1558. As they are not mentioned in the Lords' Journal either, however, it cannot be determined in which House (if any) they sat. The solitary exception to the secretaries' preference for the Commons occurred in 1547: on 26 November a bill before the Upper House was committed to five bishops, four peers, 'Magno Secretario, Judicibus, et aliis Domini Regis a Consiliis Juris-peritis'.[32] There is a variety of possible explanations for this isolated appearance of Petre in the Lords' Journal. It may be a clerical error. Perhaps the sparseness of the early Commons' Journal and the fuller but still terse record of the Lords' proceed-ings obscure the real relationship of the secretaries to the two Houses. Or Petre may have been alternating weekly between the two Houses, in accordance with a royal order of 1540[33] – hence his election to the Commons, as well as his receipt of a writ of assistance. Whatever the explanation, Petre's recorded presence in the Lords does not seriously detract from the general factual accuracy of Elton's comments.

Moreover, at first sight the regularity with which the mid-Tudor secretaries served the Crown in the Lower House appears to confirm Elton's conclusion, that it reflected the growing power of the Commons. It was necessary for the monarch to devote more attention to that House. Thus when Henry VIII appointed two secretaries in 1540, he modified the act of the previous year, for the placing of lords, and ordered that 'considering the good service that [they] may do him in the Nether Nouse . . . the one of them [was] to be one week in the High House and the other in the Low House, and so that he that was in the Lower House to be the next week in the Higher House, changing their places by course, unless it be upon some special day for matters to be treated in the Nether House, at which time they shall both be present there accordingly'.[34] Yet it has already been observed that both secretaries almost invariably sat in the Commons in mid-Tudor sessions. Furthermore the secretary had ceased to be merely 'a confidential servant employed about the king's correspondence'. During his tenure of the office from 1534 to 1540 Cromwell had transformed it into the lynch-pin of government, with a 'universal hold on the affairs of the realm' and with a precedence second only to the great offices of State and household.[35] For the Crown to ensure the presence of the powerful royal secretaries in the Commons in the mid-Tudor period might well be taken as a signal mark of its respect for the growing self-confidence and importance of the Lower House.

To arrive at this conclusion, however, is to misread the political situation in the mid-sixteenth century. As Elton himself points out, when Cromwell gave up the secretaryship in 1540 'it dropped in standing below the second rank of Household officers and below all peers'.[36] Apart from Cecil, whose tenure of office was brief (1550–3), the mid-Tudor secretaries were of lesser calibre than Cromwell, and none of them was a politician of the first rank. Not until Elizabeth's reign did the Cecils, father and son, and Sir Francis Walsingham restore the office to its former Cromwellian status and greatness. When the Crown ensured the secretaries' presence in the Commons, it was not directing its most important and influential servants there. Under both Edward VI and Mary every great officer of State sat in the Lords by virtue of episcopal office or noble status; so did every lord steward or great master and all but one (Sir John Gage, 1553–6) of the lords chamberlain of the household. Peers such as Somerset, Northumberland, Suffolk, Winchester, Northampton, Arundel, Bedford, Pembroke, Darcy of Chiche and Paget dominated the aristocratic regimes which governed for Edward VI. In Marian politics Archbishops Pole and Heath, Bishop Gardiner, the earls of Arundel and Pembroke, and William Lord

Paget were pre-eminent, whilst Howard of Effingham, Hastings of Loughborough and Viscount Montagu enjoyed authority and influence to a lesser degree. The privy council too was aristocratic in complexion. Prelates and peers constituted 48% of its membership in 1547, 61% in 1551 and 57% in 1558.[37] A preponderance of officers of State and a majority of privy councillors and prominent politicians sat in the mid-Tudor House of Lords. In these circumstances, therefore, it became increasingly necessary to guarantee that at least one leading royal servant represented its interests in the Commons. The Crown's action in ensuring this was probably the consequence, not of any shift in the distribution of power within the parliamentary trinity from Lords to Commons, but of the creation of a new peerage from prominent royal servants between 1529 and 1558[38] and of the clerical resurgence under Mary,[39] which together deprived the Crown of adequate ministerial representation in the Lower House.

The presence of the secretaries in the Commons could hardly have detracted from the efficiency of the Lords where the majority of prominent Crown servants attended and could furnish the House with such information as it required about matters of government, administration and diplomacy. More valuable to the Lords in its parliamentary business were the other classes of assistants who had for long represented the king's permanent council in parliament: the judges of king's bench, common pleas and exchequer, the king's serjeants, the master of the rolls, the attorney- and solicitor-general, and the masters of chancery (the last class not receiving writs of assistance but attending nevertheless). Few of them seem to have sought election to the Commons.[40] The incompleteness of the *Official Returns* prevents a complete survey but the absence of nearly all the assistants from the election returns does suggest that they did not normally secure seats in the Lower House rather than the Lords, either of their own free will or at the Crown's command. On only six occasions did this occur.[41] Four – James Dyer, a king's serjeant, and Robert Bowes, master of the rolls, in March 1553, William Cordell, master of the rolls, and Clement Higham, chief baron of the exchequer, in 1558 – took their seats in the Lower House. But of these Dyer and Cordell were exceptional cases, having been chosen by the Crown as speaker of the Commons in their respective parliaments. Two others, Robert Southwell (master of the rolls) in 1547 and Edward Saunders (a king's serjeant) in March 1553 disregarded their election and duly took their seats in the Lords.[42]

There may be other cases in which legal assistants were returned to the Commons, but which are concealed by the deficiencies of the evidence. It is improbable, however, that a few additions will alter the general impression: that assistants did not usually seek election to the Lower House and that, even when they did so, they were sometimes required to respond to their writs of assistance and serve the Lords instead. Unlike the secretaries, whose services could be spared because of the presence of an abundance of officers of State and privy councillors in the Upper House, the judges and law officers of the Crown were needed to assist the Lords in the business of drafting, revising and amending legislation, and in practice a writ of assistance took precedence over election to the Commons. The election of many of the privy councillors who did not hold great offices of State may have been, as A. F. Pollard asserted, 'a recognition of the growing weight of the house of commons and of the popular element in the constitution'.[43] But the act of 1539 and the fact that those who were summoned as legal assistants were normally not diverted to the Commons suggest that the Crown was equally aware of the importance of the Lords and concerned with its legislative efficiency. The care taken to ensure the presence of some prominent royal servants in the Lords and others in the Commons betokens the Crown's awareness of the importance of parliament, rather than of one House within it.

The presence of the legal assistants was of particular value to the Upper House which leant heavily on them, not only for their expertise in legislation but for their general fund of knowledge on matters of law. Sir Thomas Smith described them as those who 'sit there to aunswere their knowledge in the law, when they be asked if any doubt arise among the Lordes'.[44] That the assistants' place in parliament was no sinecure is evinced by the handsome payments which they received for their parliamentary services.[45] When in doubt the government turned to the judges for advice in point of law: whether, for example, the decisions of the impending parliament of March 1553 would be valid in the absence of the sick king; or again, in 1559, when Elizabeth adjourned the opening of the session for two days 'by the advice of her Privy-

Council, and of her Justices of both her Benches, and other of her Council Learned'.[46] The Lords, too, freely resorted to its assistants for advice: in 1555 its reply to the Commons in a case of privilege rested upon the opinion of the judges, master of the rolls and serjeants; and in 1572 they were consulted when the privileges of one of the members, Henry Lord Cromwell, were impugned.[47]

Valuable though their services were in this respect, the prime function of the legal assistants was to guide and assist the Lords in the legislative business of a parliamentary session. Throughout the legislative process their learning and expertise were prominent, even the pre-eminent, formative influences. The judges pronounced that the assent of the Commons, but not of the spiritual lords, was required to make an act valid;[48] they discussed the legal principles of bills which were to be introduced into either House; and together with learned counsel they were placed on conciliar committees entrusted with the task of preparing the official legislative programme for the next parliamentary session: for example in February 1554, when Nicholas Hare, master of the rolls, was included, and on 23 December 1558 when not only the lord keeper, judges and attorney- and solicitor-general but also the queen's serjeants were appointed to a large committee 'for consideration of all things necessary' for the first Elizabethan parliament.[49]

The judges and learned counsel must have framed much of the legislation which the government was anxious to enact, though evidence of a direct kind is unfortunately occasional and fragmentary. Even so, when Edward VI noted in his journal, during the month before the 1552 session, that 'there were certain devices for laws delivered to my learned Council to pen',[50] there is little doubt that they were being entrusted with the initial drawing of bills. They participated too in the framing of measures during parliamentary sessions. In an anonymous letter written during Mary's third parliament, it was observed that:

Yesterday, the same lords and judges returned and with much difficulty it was at length settled that all the laws made at the time of the schism against the papal authority should be abrogated thus: that in the Act of Parliament, all those [laws] which they have been able to collect are to be specified, and to remove all difficulty, they have placed at the end of a general repeal . . . [an acknowledgement] that the Church property is to remain in the hands of its present English possessors.[51]

In any case the legislative duties of the assistants extended beyond the drafting of official bills to encompass any measures which were not of official provenance and might impinge upon the interests of Crown or commonwealth. According to Robert Aske, at his examination in 1537,

Lord Darcy said that in any matter touching the King's prerogative the custom of the Lords' house was that they should have, upon their request, a copy of the bill to be scanned by their learned counsel in case they could perceive anything prejudicial to the prerogative or, if it were between party and party, if the bill were not prejudicial to the commonwealth.[52]

The legislative services described so far were rendered by legal assistants to the Crown. This is not surprising because they were, after all, royal servants. But as legal assistants, summoned by writ to the Upper House, they also served the House of Lords. The fact that they possessed neither voice nor vote did not diminish their influence or render nugatory their role in the legislative process. They were called upon to perform a variety of services ranging from the merely mechanical – such as the custody of bills, their engrossment on parchment, and the carrying of completed bills down to the Commons – to the quintessential, perhaps the drafting and certainly the revision of measures under consideration. They came into their own when the committee stage was reached, usually though not invariably after the second reading. At this point a bill might be immediately engrossed at the direction of the House, put into a nominated *ad hoc* committee for revision and amendment, or simply referred to one or two members for examination. Whichever procedure the House chose to adopt, it remained to a great extent dependent upon the services of the judges, law officers of the Crown and king's serjeants.

If immediate engrossment was ordered, then it was frequently a legal assistant to whom the task was entrusted, as on 12 January 1555, when the bill 'for the reformacon of excesses in apparaile' was referred to one of the queen's serjeants, James Dyer, 'ut ingrossaretur' [*sic*].[53] And when the House chose instead to put a bill into committee it often appointed one or more of the assistants to sit with the nominated bishops and peers.[54] Sometimes the committee was composed solely of the assistants, and with even greater frequency a measure was referred to one judge, the attorney- or solicitor-general or a serjeant, for revision, scrutiny or custody. In the five parliamentary sessions of Edward VI's reign the assistants were co-opted onto 17 committees for the examination and revision of bills, whilst on 18 occasions they comprised the entire committee.[55] In the Marian sessions the totals fall to one and three respectively, but this is symptomatic of a deterioration in the quality of the journals, not of a decline in the assistants' activity, for few committals of any kind are recorded by the clerk.

The number appointed to sit with the prelates and peers usually ranged from one to four, though occasional entries in the journal suggest that sometimes even more may have participated: the bill for the erection of a new court for ecclesiastical and civil causes was committed on 30 November 1547 to five bishops, four peers, the principal secretary, the judges 'et aliis Domini Regis a Consiliis Jurisperitis'.[56] The size of the committees which the assistants monopolised also varied, two being the commonest but rising to as many as five.[57] When they constituted the entire committee their legislative competence appears to have been in no way restricted. Their task remained one of revision and amendment (which they would then offer to the House for its assent), as in 1552 when the bills 'for the Pricing of Wools' and 'for the relief of the Poor and Impotent' were committed to two serjeants-at-law, Edward Saunders and David Broke, 'ut in formam Actus redigatur'.[58]

If the admittedly capricious recording of the clerk of the parliaments is a reliable guide, it seems that the Upper House referred bills to a single legal assistant with much greater frequency than to committees: altogether 47 Edwardian and five Marian bills were thus assigned.[59] Regrettably the clerk more often than not confined his terse journal entry to the fact that a bill had been referred without explaining why the House had taken this action. Nonetheless, the few occasions on which he has enlightened us reveal why the Lords sometimes opted for reference to a single assistant. The explanation is to be found in the degree and nature of revision which a bill might require after its second reading. An important public bill or a contentious measure might require drastic amendment, a task which would be entrusted to a committee. In contrast, a relatively innocuous bill might be left in the hands of a judge, a serjeant or one of the Crown's law officers whose task would be to peruse its contents and phrasing, perhaps consider the legal principles which it embodied, and if necessary recommend amendments.

Sir Simonds D'Ewes noted the purpose of referring a bill to a single assistant when he described the enactment of the bill for the recognition of Elizabeth's title to the imperial crown in 1559. It was referred to the queen's attorney '(who, as is most likely, with the residue of the Queen's Learned Council, did at first draw it) that so upon further perusal thereof, he might again bring it into the House and Certifie the Lords, if any thing were to be altered or reformed in it'.[60] The House might also instruct an assistant to effect minor amendments or devise a proviso in accordance with decisions taken in the debate on the bill: so on 10 December 1554, the bill 'for the Punishment of seditious Words and Rumours' was referred to William Sta(u)nford, one of the justices of common pleas, 'for the making of a proviso unto it'.[61] Other bills, however, were simply 'committed' into the custody of a serjeant, law officer or master of chancery for the time being, or were delivered to one for engrossment, whilst on 22 February 1558 a measure 'for the bringing in of Armour and Bowstaves' was committed to the attorney-general 'to move the Queen's Highness therein' – a useful illustration of the value to the House of assistants who were not only learned in the law but also had direct access to the monarch.[62]

One particular service which was rendered by the law officers of the Crown and which sheds some light on their significance in legislative business would escape detection if attention was confined to the Lords' journal alone. Thirty-two original acts of parliament of Edward VI's reign were endorsed by the king, privy councillors and other royal servants.[63] Endorsements by others than the monarch did not occur in Mary's reign, nor in the second Edwardian parliament (1553). They were therefore limited in time to four sessions: one in 1547, eleven in 1548/9, eight in 1549/50 and four in 1552. Seventeen acts in this parliament were endorsed by the king, four by the lord protector and twelve by Sir John Mason, nine by privy councillors and eight by one or both of the law officers. The monarch's signature acknowledging his approval of a bill before its entry into parliament was not unusual nor was it confined to this reign. But Edward was a minor, hence, perhaps, the duke of Somerset's occasional endorsement in 1547 and 1548/9, as the effective head of State, lord protector and governor of the king's person. Mason presumably signed ten acts in 1548/9 and two in 1549/50 in his capacity as acting clerk of the parliaments *vice* Sir William Paget. He was appointed to the clerkship on 11 July 1550 and thereafter his signature was no longer appended to any acts.

With one exception, in 1547, the endorsements by privy councillors are confined to the third and fourth sessions of Edward's first parliament, both of which were held in the shadow of Warwick's coups against Somerset. This may explain the presence of their signatures on certain acts. It is noteworthy that of the seven acts endorsed by them in 1549/50 four were concerned with the consequences of the past conduct of the Seymour family.[64] Perhaps Warwick, aware that his position was as yet insecure, sought to involve his accomplices in the coup, the privy councillors, in a collective responsibility for the removal of Somerset and the legitimacy of the new regime.

There is an alternative explanation: that, as the king was a minor, the council gave its prior consideration and approval to any document which required his signature. So a bill in the interest of John Seymour first appeared on a council agenda before it entered parliament bearing the sign manual. A petition for the assurance of lands sold by the Crown to the City of London was endorsed by six councillors before it was submitted to the Lords, and later seven endorsed the king's signature on the engrossed bill. However, this argument is flawed by the fact that, whereas Edward signed 17 acts, the protector endorsed only four and the councillors nine. Whilst it may be the consequence of a characteristic administrative inconsistency, the political explanation offered above is the likeliest one.[65]

Similarly the endorsements by the attorney- and solicitor-general, Henry Bradshaw and Edward Gryffyn, were confined to the same sessions, 1549/50 and 1552, and their signatures too may have been the consequence of political circumstances. But they are also indicative of another legislative function rendered by these particular legal assistants. In each case in the earlier session their names were preceded by the abbreviated legend *Ex. per nos* [examined by us]. In 1552 Edward Gryffyn alone endorsed three acts, prefixing his signature again with *Ex per*.[66] It is clear that Bradshaw and Gryffyn did not inscribe bills in this fashion merely after the House had committed the measures to them. The restitutions of Sir William Hussey and Thomas Isley were both referred to the attorney-general alone, whereas the original acts are endorsed as 'examined by us' Henry Bradshaw and Edward Gryffyn. This discrepancy suggests that their joint examination of these bills was not a record of their commitment by the House, but yet another scrutiny of them, perhaps before they were even entered into the Lords. Every one of the eight bills so endorsed by the law officers in the first Edwardian parliament were put into the Upper House first,[67] a fact which suggests that their examination of them was a recognised legislative procedure of the Lords, albeit an infrequent and exceptional one. If so, it is an instance of the care and responsibility which it displayed in the transaction of legislative business.

The committee work of the legal assistants was not limited to scrutiny and revision. When a dispute between the fallen lord protector and John eighth Lord Audley was brought to the attention of the House, it nominated a committee consisting of the chief justice and two justices of the common pleas to consider the matter; a second committee, appointed five days later, substituted the chief baron of the exchequer for one of the justices.[68] They even participated in joint-committees of the two Houses, as on 16 December 1547 when a committee to consider the repeal of 'certain Statutes for treasons and felonyes' included 'certain of the Kinges learned Counseil'.[69]

There remains one other significant service which the legal assistants performed: as members of the panels of receivers of petitions.[70] The two panels of receivers in each parliament – for England, Ireland, Wales and Scotland, and for Gascon and other foreign petitions – were composed of common-law judges and masters of chancery (including the master of the rolls) in roughly equal proportions.[71] The original function of the receivers that of receiving, sifting and 'digesting' of petitions, had progressively declined because of the increasing control of the Lower House over private petitions. Yet their offices did not become sinecures: 'other functions were found to justify their existence, though not their name'. Those receivers who were common-law judges were in any case summoned on writs of assistance and, as already observed, performed other valuable legislative services. Pollard was specifically referring to the masters of chancery who, apart from the master of the rolls, were not legal assistants in receipt of writs yet sat with him as receivers on the panels. Although their original function of receiving petitions was now defunct, they continued to attend the Lords and provided an additional pool of legal experience and knowledge on which the House could call. As civilians they were especially useful in advising Lords' committees on problems outside the compass of the common law.[72]

Useful the masters of chancery might be, but their status was generally recognised as inferior and subordinate to that of assistants in receipt of writs.[73] They might be attendant on committees to explain legal niceties, but they were not once appointed as members of a committee to scrutinise and revise bills. They sat on the lower woolsack, silent onlookers unless their opinions were sought. Indeed in 1576 one Dr Barkley was severely reprimanded when he 'rashly and indecently opened his mouth without waiting to be called upon by the lords'.[74] Apart from their usefulness as civilians, their duties were confined to the mechanical and routine, providing the members of the House with copies of bills before they were entered into the Lower House,[75] carrying bills down to the Commons, and acting as *nuntii* from the Upper House. In 1554 Sir Richard Rede and Dr Armstede went down with a subpoena that Mr Beamond of the Commons and his wife had caused to be served upon the earl of Huntingdon during the session, 'and prayen the Order of this House for that Offence'. A fortnight later the master of the rolls and Rede 'declared from the Lords, that Serving-men attendant upon this House shall not suffer their Servants to make Frays in Smythfield; for so the Lords have done'.[76] Passing to and fro between the parliament chamber and St Stephen's Chapel with bills and messages was a useful but uninspiring and probably tedious duty, and doubtless it was not their capacity for exercise but their training in civil law which enabled them to make a valuable contribution to the work of the Upper House.

Although the parliamentary burdens of the assistants were heavy, the nature of the duties which each performed and the frequency with which the House demanded their services varied considerably. The judges and the attorney- and solicitor-general were deeply involved in the framing of legislative measures. The burden of committee membership in the mid-Tudor Lords fell, in roughly equal proportions, on these same men afforced by the king's serjeants, but there were significant variations in individual records of service.[77] Whereas the House of Lords was served by as many as nine judges and four serjeants in each session, there were only two law officers. Apart from Sir Edward Montague, chief justice of common pleas, who was named to thirteen committees in the mid-Tudor parliaments, the judges only sat on two apiece; in contrast Edward Gryffyn, first as solicitor- and then as attorney-general (throughout the period 1547–58) and Henry Bradshaw (attorney-general in the first Edwardian parliament) were appointed to 21 committees between them. The demands on the law officers, who were learned in the law and who, as the Crown's legal advisers, safeguarded its interests, were particularly heavy. They received no less than 62% of all bills referred to a single assistant for scrutiny, revision or engrossment, whereas the judges' and serjeants' shares were a modest 18% each.

The attorney- and solicitor-general also shouldered a disproportionately large share of the routine duties, carrying down to the Commons more than one-third of all bills which passed the Lords during the two reigns. Sometimes they were required to transmit the opinions or wishes of the Upper House with respect to the bill they carried: a request 'that these Words "And for as much as divers of the same Traitors", being 17 lines from the nether End, with all the whole Words following to the latter End, might wholly and clearly be put out' of the confirmation of Suffolk's and Sir Thomas Wyatt's attainder; or the delivery of a bill 'with a new Proviso added by the Lords, and a Request to the Commons to take away the two Provisoes annexed by them'.[78] They served as *nuntii* in other matters too, seeking an answer whether the Commons would pass Thomas Lord Seymour's attainder 'in such Order as was passed in the Higher House', requesting a joint-conference of the two Houses 'for Parliament Matters', or declaring 'that divers of the Lords will come down, to confer with this House, for weighty Affairs of this Realm'.[79] The law officers of the Crown were unquestionably the busiest, and perhaps the most important, of the legal assistants to the Lords.

Of the other assistants little remains to be said. With the exception of the judges,[80] the work of carrying bills and conveying messages to the Commons was distributed albeit unequally amongst all of those who were attendant on the House. The master of the rolls and other masters of chancery carried more than two-fifths and the serjeants just over one-fifth of bills into the Commons. As for the conveyance of messages to the Lower House, the distribution of the work-load followed a similar pattern: the masters of chancery and the law officers each accounted for 34.5% and the serjeants for a little less, 31%. Although at one time or another each class of legal assistants engaged in most of the multifarious activities which have been examined, it is clear that each had certain primary functions to perform: the judges, law officers and serjeants to assist in the legislative business with their specialist skill and learning in the common law; the common-law judges and civilians to man the panels of receivers; and, with the exception of the judges, a general participation in the more routine functions. The burden of mere mechanical work, however, fell chiefly upon two classes of assistant: the masters of chancery, and the law officers, those maids-of-all-work of the House of Lords.

It would be difficult to exaggerate the value and importance of the assets which the medieval parliament bequeathed to the Tudor House of Lords. The legal assistants provided a professional stiffening to an assembly of amateur legislators. The expertise which they placed at the disposal of the Lords, and its willingness to utilise it, made of it a critical, efficient and responsible chamber, in contrast to the Commons which remained 'a rather easy-going assembly'.[81] That this was so is surely no matter for exclamation. For the Upper House had inherited the assistance of the king's permanent council and the clerical organisation of chancery, which together had constituted the very essence of the medieval parliament. Together they armed it with inestimable advantages in the business of legislation. Occupant of the parliament chamber, heir of the medieval parliaments, with its complement of judges, learned counsel and trained clerks, the House of Lords was the assembly which regulated and ensured the high quality of Tudor legislation.

7

THE RULES OF BUSINESS:
PROCEDURE

In the wake of W. Notestein[1] it has become a *sine qua non* of
Tudor parliamentary history that procedures were political
weapons in a power-struggle between Crown and Commons. If
actual confrontations and crises were relatively few, especially
in contrast to the early seventeenth century, conflict was always
inherent in a situation in which the monarch was on the defensive
and the Lower House was probing and exploring new and
enlarged frontiers of independence and authority. Moreover in
this political treatment of parliamentary procedure it is not
necessary to look beyond the House of Commons. The way in
which a compliant upper chamber conducted its affairs is of
little moment.

However, if the recent admixture of modest revision[2] and
more trenchant criticism[3] is a reliable barometer, then the
historical climate is changing. There is a dawning realisation
that parliament was neither intended to be, nor was it in practice,
a political arena and the occasion for a gladiatorial encounter
between Crown and Commons. Rather it was, both in purpose
and actuality, a market place for the transaction of an infinite
variety of legislative business. It was not generally regarded as an
opportunity to flex political muscle against the Crown, to indulge
in opposition or to engage in blind political conflict. Instead,
Tudor parliaments continued to be responsible assemblies
characterised by co-operation between the monarch and the
governing class. Naturally the relationship was not devoid of
stress, especially during the 1530s, the Edwardian Reformation,
the fulfilment of the Marian programme in 1553–5, Elizabeth's
reluctance to resolve the Succession problem, and the government's failure to rectify the grievance of monopolies in 1597–1601.
In all but the last of these episodes the Lords played a prominent,

and sometimes the leading, part.[4] Such political encounters, however, were the exception and not the rule. In so far as there was a regular conflict of interests, it cannot be expressed in terms of a power-struggle, but rather as a conflict of priorities. The Crown was anxious to secure the enactment of desirable legislation and the grant of revenue, whereas local communities, economic lobbies and individual members of both Houses seized the chance to promote their interests by the passage of beneficial acts. Chapuys wrote of parliament in 1531 that 'they are discussing the enactment of the sumptuary laws and the prohibition of the pastime of cross bows and hand guns, especially to foreigners . . . Nearly the whole time of Parliament has been occupied with these petty matters, and with complaints between different towns and villages.' Fifty years later the problem had not changed. In 1581 a member of the Commons advised a councillor how to keep sessions short and, at the same time, to push through government business. He identified two problems: the excessive number of private bills 'of singuler persons' and 'bills of occupation . . . speciallie the bylles of London'.[5] The constant clutter of private bills could hamper, obstruct and even thwart more general measures which were designed to facilitate good governance. It remained a problem throughout the remainder of the sixteenth century.

The Crown held the whip-hand, because it controlled the tempo and duration of each session. On the other hand, the two Houses ensured that due attention was given to private bills. Thus, by an unwritten compact, and in what seems to have been an unsystematic manner, parliament fulfilled the expectations and needs of both Crown and governing class. It was also a process in which both Houses participated and, more often than not, collaborated. This is scarcely surprising since the assent of all parts of the parliamentary trinity was required in order to translate bills into acts.[6] These are obvious and elementary facts of parliamentary practice which contemporaries at least chose not to ignore. Their reiteration here may seem superfluous, except that historians of the Tudor parliaments have so frequently brushed them aside, preferring to represent the institution in terms of six-gun politics rather than of the tedious business of legislation. Ironically the mid-Tudor reigns which are the subject of this volume experienced more frequent parlia-

mentary clashes between the government and *some* members
than at any other time during the sixteenth century. But even
then co-operation not conflict was the predominant theme.

When procedure is considered in this context, it ceases to be a
mere managerial device wielded by privy councillors to head off
or neutralise nascent opposition. Nor was it just a weapon exploited by opposition politicians to promote their policies and
outflank the government. Again there were exceptions, but they
were few and far between. Procedure should not be associated
with this kind of political objective, especially in a century when
criticism and complaint seldom moved on to actual confrontation
and conflict in parliament. Instead the corpus of rules, resolutions
and practices evolving into conventions, which together constituted parliamentary procedure, should be seen for what it
was: a means to the more efficient and rapid despatch of business
by both Houses, in the usually compatible interest but often
competing priorities of Crown and governing class.

Such a proposition is clean contrary to the tradition handed
down, like the keys of the kingdom, from A. F. Pollard to Notestein, Conyers Read and J. E. Neale.[7] Notestein in particular
argued that procedures were instruments for control of an ob-
streperous Commons,[8] whilst some of the Commons' procedural
innovations were intended to liberate it from official control.[9] To
do him justice it must be admitted that certain procedures had
become acknowledged weapons in the Crown's managerial
arsenal.[10] With few exceptions, however, they were intended to
promote the efficient transaction of business, rather than to
forestall or muzzle opposition politicians (who, in any case, did
not exist as a recognisable species in most Tudor parliaments, but
merely drift, phantom-like, through the writings of the 'orthodox'
interpretation).[11]

The onus of proof inevitably, and rightly, rests upon those who
would challenge such a well-entrenched interpretation. As
always the problem is one of sources. The patchy – at times
fragmentary – evidence has for long permitted the grand assumption that the Lords' procedure generally followed that of the
Commons, albeit in a more informal and less rigorous manner.[12]
The Upper House is airily dismissed because nothing is apparently
known about its rules of business.[13] On all counts such charges
are, at the best, unrealistic and, at the worst, patently absurd.

The Upper House was, after all, the older chamber and so it is improbable that it trailed behind the Commons in the evolution of procedures which met its legislative requirements. This is incapable of comparative proof before 1547, because of the absence of a Commons' Journal until then. In contrast traces of the Lords' Journals survive from the mid-fifteenth century onwards. They reveal that, early in Henry VIII's reign, the House was groping its way towards the three-reading procedure, which has been the norm for the past four hundred years. If conjecture must serve for want of evidence, then it is more realistic to assume an initial lead for the Lords, rather than its slavish willingness to model its rules on those of the younger chamber. When it is argued that the Commons 'caught up' in Elizabeth's reign,[14] this is in itself an admission that it had a considerable leeway to make up in the first place.

The journals of the two Houses, which constitute the record of parliamentary business, are both terse and sparse. They are confined to the readings of bills, a few details on committees, the occasional tantalising hint of 'arguments' upon a bill[15] and (in the case of the Lords) a daily attendance record. In addition, privilege cases and the quasi-judicial proceedings of both Houses in private bills[16] receive some notice. What becomes plain from a reading of the journals is not only the attention to business and the bicameral co-operation, but also the probability that the two Houses advanced by a process of procedural cross-fertilisation – another expression of the collaborative bicameral tradition. This is most clearly demonstrated in the better-documented reign of Elizabeth, when Thomas Norton proposed that joint-conferences should be regularised and formalised, and when the Lords' pressure compelled the Lower House to appoint a committee for sifting bills into an order of priority. The purpose of both innovations was the same: to get through the essential business of the session as quickly and efficiently as possible. The Lords was no laggard in the process of procedural refinement. Even in the early seventeenth century the Commons could learn lessons from it. Hakewil praised its committee which, in 18 James I, collected all the existing rules and orders which were then engrossed and ordered to be read at the beginning of each parliament. 'It were (in my poore opinion) to be wisht, that the same course were taken by the house of Commons.' Likewise he lauded the Lords' order for a committee to 'peruse and perfect the Clerkes notes' weekly and, at the end of each session, to arrange for them to be engrossed 'and fairly bound up'. He lamented the Commons' laxity: 'If . . . there were some provision made . . . for the safe preserving of [the Commons' Journals] the . . . Records of the Commons house would not (as they now may) . . . bee removed to and fro in hazard of being lost, as corrupted and defiled.'[17]

The cursory descriptions and even peremptory dismissals of the Lords' procedures, characteristic of the 'orthodox' interpretation, seem to derive from a confusion between lack of organisation and lack of formality. The actual membership of the Upper House reached a maximum of only 79 under the mid-Tudors. During the same period the Commons rapidly grew from 343 to 400 members. Mere size must have imposed upon it a need for strict rules of debate and voting, simply in order to wrest order out of chaos. This was particularly pressing when, for example, about half (and sometimes more) of the Commons' members in every Elizabethan parliament were novices in need of guidance and instruction.[18] It also had its fair share of praters and babblers, as Thomas Cromwell had observed as long ago as 1523.[19] The choir of noisy debaters lampooned in a 'lewd pasquil' in 1566, Elizabeth's irritation with meddlesome, 'frivolous and superfluous speech' in 1571, and William Fleetwood's confident response to an amused House, that 'I think you would be content to hear me these two hours', all testify to the continuing addiction to loquacity.[20] The only way to counter the threat of interminable debate – and so the obstruction of business – was by the formulation of constraining rules. By the 1560s at the latest each knight and burgess could only speak once to a bill on any one day 'for else one or two with altercation woulde speack all the time'.[21]

The Upper House was, in contrast, a small, even intimate, assembly whose average daily attendance was only 41 in the Edwardian parliaments and even less, 36, in those of Mary. Furthermore, as most of its members enjoyed life-tenure, they became experienced parliament men who knew the ropes and required fewer rules to guide and direct them in their deliberations. The House could afford to be more indulgent towards speakers in debate, and to make regular use of a voting procedure which was not only certain and precise but also time-consuming.[22] The smallness of the assembly made for greater flexibility and freedom from constraint, but hardly informality – not in a body of men who were so concerned with precedence and protocol, and whose sense of rank and degree was visibly reflected in both the seating arrangements[23] and the order of voting in the House.[24]

Likewise it is possible to exaggerate the poverty of evidence on the Lords' procedure. Certainly it is not necessary to depend solely on common sense, conjecture and calculated guesswork. In spite of their deficiencies the pre-Elizabethan journals of both Houses *do* provide a record of business, and the original acts fill out some flesh on the bones. So too do the treatises of political commentators and lawyers. Of course most of them have only a limited value because they derive from a later age. When the early Stuart lawyers, antiquaries and parliamentary bureau-crats[25] wrote, many of the embryonic mid-Tudor procedures had been systematised and formalised. Sometimes they cite sixteenth-century precedents, and for that one must be grateful[26] but, for the most part, their Stuart observations cannot be taken as pertinent to Edwardian and Marian practice. Nevertheless the needs of the Tudor investigator are surprisingly well served by the official parliamentary records, together with a select band of pre-Stuart commentaries and law books. William Lambarde, Edmund Plowden, Richard Robinson, Sir Thomas Smith and John Hooker (*alias* Vowell) all possessed some knowledge or experience of the mid-Tudor parliaments or at least of their Elizabethan successors. Plowden was a contemporary. Lambarde's *Archeion* was completed by 1591. Robinson's manuscript on Elizabethan courts was dated 10 July 1592 on the title page, and 1602 on the cover; Sir Thomas Smith drafted *De Republica Anglorum* whilst serving as ambassador in France during the 1560s; and Vowell's treatise on parliament must have been based on his experience as burgess for Exeter in 1571.[27]

However, the political realities of parliaments may not be discernible through records of business and formal descriptions of procedure. The only reason for summoning a parliament was the enactment of royal business, and the first priority of many in both Houses was to secure acts for themselves or others; so the purpose of procedure was to satisfy the expectations of both Crown and governing class by maximising efficiency and therefore productivity. It served a nice compromise of competing interests and priorities. Procedure was not an uncomplicated creature, prodded and pushed in one direction solely by the need for efficiency. It also reflected and was influenced by other considerations, such as the importance attached to rank and precedence and a predilection for solemn ceremony. Above all else, however, it was efficiency which dictated procedural development. The novel volume and range of legislation entered into parliament from the 1530s on; the growth in the Commons' size; the often-competing legislative priorities of Crown and governing class: together they stimulated a search for more effective methods of transacting business.

An added spur was the pressure of time imposed by short sessions, which both Mary and Elizabeth preferred. Privy councillors shared their preference. During the 1548/9 session Sir William Paget had complained to Protector Somerset that a subsidy bill had not been introduced nearly five weeks after parliament had assembled, although 'indede . . . it was the onelie cause why the parliament was called before Christmas'. He pointed out that the Commons had expected it to be 'the furst thinge that shuld have come in parliament'. In fact Somerset prolonged it until mid-March in order to secure the parliamentary attainder of his brother. By then Paget was wringing his hands because 'both houses saye [they stay] only upon your graces pleaser'. He pleaded 'for gods sake to end the parlyament'. Short sessions were the ideal.[28] Moreover sittings were traditionally confined to the mornings. Gradually, and in a halting fashion, the Lords wilted under the twin pressures of too much business and too little time. It began to experiment with extended hours of sitting. Although the experiments varied, a pattern of sorts becomes apparent. So in 1547 and 1548/9 the House first met at 9 a.m., but the adoption of an earlier hour, eight o'clock, became more frequent as the session progressed. However, the second session was more erratic, fluctuating between the alternatives of eight and nine, *inter octavam em nonam*, and even, on four occasions (when no business is recorded), as late as ten o'clock. In 1549/50 the house reverted to a more or less consistent practice, assembling at nine o'clock on 80% of the days for which a time of commencement is recorded. A preference or need for an earlier hour, however, could not be stifled. In 1552 and March 1553 the incidence leapt from

20% first to 37% and then to 46%. Despite the scrappiness of the Marian record, the continuous upward trend is unmistakable: to 50% and 70% in the two parliaments of 1554.[29]

As business piled up during the session, the House was obliged to extend its activities into the afternoons. The practice was not yet a frequent one, fluctuating between solitary occasions in 1547 and 1554/5 and five afternoons in 1552. Nevertheless neither the deficiencies of the record nor the inconsistency of the various experiments can entirely conceal what was happening. In 1566 the House opted for the later hour of nine a.m. but sat on seven afternoons. The one o'clock starting time on these occasions suggests a sense of urgency and must have denied their lordships the time to dine at leisure. Five years later the pressure is even more evident: eleven afternoon sessions, 23 morning sittings which began at eight and only 13 at nine.[30] Richard Bagot's report on the earl of Essex's parliamentary activity in 1593 illustrates the continuous and increasing burden of business on the Upper House: 'every forenoon, between seven and eight, his Lordship is in the higher Parliament House, and in the afternoon upon committees for the better hearing and amendment of matter in bills of importance'.[31] The experiments with extended hours do not accord with a diminishing volume of business or a declining legislative role, even if the House occasionally found itself without bills to consider.[32]

Although the Lower House always handled more bills, this was the consequence of its size and representative nature rather than a register of its importance. The mid-Tudor Lords received a share of the increased volume of business resulting from the enlarged competence of parliament in the 1530s. It also enjoyed a special prestige derived from the fact that it was the legatee of three hundred years of parliamentary history. Its place as the original nucleus of parliament was duly reflected in the physical structure of the House. John Hooker, member for Exeter in 1571, sketched a contemporary picture:

The house is much more in length than it is in breadth, and the higher end thereof in the middle is the kinges seate, or throne hanged richly with cloath of estate, and there the kinge sitteth allwaies alone. On his right hand there is a long bench next to the wall of the house which reacheth not so farr up as the kinges seate, and upon this sitteth the Archbishops and Bishopes, everie one in his degree. On his left hand there are two like benches, upon the Inner sittes the Duks, Marquesses, Earles, and Viscountes. On the other which is hindermost and next unto the wall, sit all the Barons, everie man in his degree. In the middle of the house betweene the Archbishops & the Dukes seat, sitteth the speaker, who commonly is Lord Chancellor . . . and he hath below him his two clerkes sitting at a table before them upon which they doe wright & lay their bookes. In the middle of ye rome beneath them, sit . . . all such as be of the kinges learned counsell . . . and all those sit upon great woll sackes, covered with red cloath. At the lower end of these seates is a barre or raile, betweene which, and the lower end of ye house is a voyde roome serving for the lower house and for all sutors that shall have cause & occasion, to repair to the kinge or the Lordes.[33]

Changes in precedence were effected by the act 'for placing of the Lords in Parliament' (1539)[34] and the commission of 1547 which allocated the protector a special seat 'nexte on the right hand of our siege reall'.[35] However the effect of the former on seating arrangements was nominal and the latter was short lived.[36] Nor did they touch procedural development which continued to be determined primarily by the need for efficiency in the face of insufficient time and excessive business.

That business was legislation, and the Lords' procedures were designed to fulfil its role in the legislative process.[37] The classic three-reading process for the enactment of bills was in essence already in being by 1547[38] – so much so that Edwardian clerks sometimes endeavoured to conceal variations from the norm and create the illusion of conformity. Thus in 1547 the act 'for the Declaration of Tenures in Capite' had two 'second' readings.[39] So did the confirmation of Sir William Sharington's attainder, the acts to repeal the act of precontracts, 'for Fines to be levied in the County Palatine', to punish buggery, and to pave Calais, all in 1548/9. These and other measures went to more than three readings, and the clerk was fertile in the devices which he employed to keep the record straight. Sometimes he did not number a fourth reading, simply evading the issue with the formula *lecta est*. In other instances he stuck doggedly to the fiction that the last reading was the third, even when it was patently not.

It would be too much to expect consistency in this practice. The vagabondage act of 1549/50 had four readings which were recorded as such; the same is true of the act 'against Hunters'; and the bill 'against the Rising of the Common People' went to six readings, all of which were correctly and honestly numbered.

Nevertheless the tendency towards bureaucratic tidiness, which was an expression of the growing lip-service to the three-reading procedure, is unmistakable. In the same session a restitution bill had three 'second' readings before passing on the third;[40] nor was this the only occasion on which he employed such fictions, either then or in the remaining years of Edward VI's reign, although the inconsistencies had by no means disappeared by 1553.

In one respect this picture of evolving clerical practice may have to be modified: when two recorded second or third readings faithfully described a debate overlapping from one day to the next. Sometimes it is possible to demonstrate that this is what actually happened. So 'upon the reading and debating' of a cloth bill on 5 April 1552, the Lords 'for certain Doubts found in the same' appointed a committee 'to meet and talk with certain of the Lower House . . . for the better understanding of the said Bill, and for their full instruction therein'. On the following day the House resumed and completed the third reading and finally passed the bill. The two second readings of a bill concerning the king's revenues, recorded on 15 and 16 March 1553, may also refer to a debate which commenced on one day and resumed the next. On the other hand successive second readings, recorded days or even weeks apart (as frequently occurs in the mid-Tudor journals), are probably bureaucratic devices rather than two instalments of one debate.[41]

In the Marian parliaments the clerks continued to doctor the Lords' record in much the same fashion. Furthermore the Commons was no nearer a standardised and inflexible three-reading procedure[42] and its clerks too restored to fictions in order to mask the truth.[43] What we are observing is a tortuous process of procedural evolution. In spite of the aberrations, the two Houses were moving towards a bicameral standardisation, in which there was an increasing correspondence between actual procedural practice and the clerks' version of events. This is confirmed by the record of the first session of 1558, when 16 acts were passed.[44] Thirteen of them had three readings in the Lords and twelve did so in the Commons. In each of the three exceptional cases in the Lords, the clerk of the parliaments recorded the last reading as the third, even though the bill for the 'Taking of soldiers' went to five readings. The Commons' clerk preferred the device of repeating the second- or third-reading entries, even when, in one instance, they occurred a week apart.[45] Lip-service to the three-reading norm and its increasing adoption in practice were characteristic of the mid-Tudor parliaments, and the Lords did not lag behind the Commons in the process.

No particular sanctity should be attached to the three-reading procedure. It evolved simply as the most practical and effective way of making statute law, because it satisfied the requirements of contemporary legislators. First, it informed members, in an age when they were not supplied with the printed text of bills; then it permitted discussion of the principles and substance of the measure before them; and finally it provided an opportunity to ensure textual precision and clarity. Translated into practical terms, sound law could only be made if members were well informed, able to discuss it, amend it, hone and temper its language and even, at the end, reject it. In this way the rights of all parties to the legislative process were taken into account, even if they were not always preserved intact. Thus the process ensured that a bill did not trench upon the royal prerogative, contravene common law principles, offend the general interests of the governing class or harm the commonweal (at least as parliament interpreted it).

The procedure which met these requirements was hammered out in the course of the sixteenth century and, as we have seen, the process was already well advanced in the Edwardian and Marian parliaments. The lack of a surviving Commons' Journal before 1547 may have created an illusion of novelty about procedural developments, especially in the Lower House. Nevertheless Sir John Neale was correct when he contrasted the flexible, variable and even casual way in which the mid-Tudor Commons managed its affairs with the more 'critical and responsible' conduct of the Lords.[46] Far from slavish imitation of the other House, the Lords probably had the edge on it in procedural matters. As they both advanced along parallel lines towards a uniform three-reading process, the Lords' use of the legal assistants enabled it to be more thorough in the scrutiny of bills. However, thoroughness did not necessarily mean uniformity. The rules of business were still flexibly and loosely applied and inconsistencies abounded. Henry Elsynge observed this in his study of legislation, written in the next century: 'even in the dayes of H.8, E.6 and Q.Mary Bills were no oftener read then till the

Lords were satisfied either to allowe or deny the same, many being then read but twice and many about 3 or 4 tymes'.[47] When he discovered that many mid-Tudor bills were not committed during their passage,[48] he may have been guilty of exaggeration in his conclusion that parliament was in a primitive stage of procedural evolution. It looks now as if clerical errors and omissions, especially in the inferior Marian journals, account for some of the apparent variations in practice. Yet even when this allowance has been made, one must concede that he was substantially right. Almost 40% of all bills which completed their passage through the Lords in 1547 had more or less than three readings. By 1558 the proportion had slowly declined to 32%. With figures of 31% and 41% in the same two sessions, the Commons' record was no better.[49] The record of the second Edwardian parliament, midway through the period, confirms that the move towards uniformity was steady but slow.[50] These were early days.

On the other hand, parliamentary practice was less erratic than these figures suggest. Certain classes of bill which regularly featured in parliaments were normally passed in less than three readings. Whilst they constituted a departure from what was to become the three-reading norm, they had acquired a procedural consistency of their own. Some grace bills, bearing the sign manual,[51] together with general pardons and subsidies, both clerical and lay, fell into this category. Even this process was by no means complete by 1558. Although the Lords usually passed the general pardon in one reading, in 1548/9 it went to three. The Commons fluctuated between one and three readings too.[52] Elsynge clearly ante-dated the process when he wrote that 'The Subsidy Bill, and the King's general Pardon, were used to be read but once, and so were expedited', citing 3 Edward VI to support his case.[53] The state of affairs when the general pardon 'hath but one reading in the Lords house, and one below'[54] certainly had not yet been reached. But once again the movement towards uniformity was unmistakable. It was also relentless because it was necessary in order to meet the demands of efficiency, limited time and a large number of bills. The four sessions of Edward VI's first parliament averaged no more than 86 days, just over twelve weeks apiece. His second parliament lasted a mere month, whilst Mary's parliaments emulated its brevity — even if we exclude the November 1558 session, cut short by her death, they averaged a mere 52 days. These totals included Sundays, which were naturally parliamentary rest-days, whilst Star Chamber and convocation days made further inroads on the time available to the Lords – in 1548/9, for example, the Lords held only 73 business sessions during the 111 days between the assembly and prorogation of parliament. In this short span of time it considered over 90 bills.[55] Simply knowing what to do next (and how to go about it) was conducive to a faster and more efficient transaction of business.

The initial steps in the legislative process were the drafting of a bill and its introduction into parliament. It is now clear that most bills were not official in origin – in other words they were not drawn and handed in by the government – although it might put the weight of its sympathy and support behind other measures which were not of its devising. Bills originated in a variety of ways, but most of them can be assigned to one or other of three categories: those of official provenance; measures introduced by members of either House for themselves, or on behalf of friends or relatives, patrons or clients, sectional interests, economic lobbies or communities which they represented; and bills drafted by order of the Lords or Commons. Official legislative programmes were of much more modest proportions than was once supposed. Nevertheless the government paid scrupulous attention to its request for a subsidy, which usually headed its list of priorities, especially in Edward VI's reign[56] – hence Paget's reminder to Somerset to 'Resolve upon your procedinges in the parliament for money', the king's question before the 1553 parliament 'What kind of ayde or subsidie' should be sought, and Northumberland's advice that the council should not feel obliged to provide the Commons with an account of official expenditure. The council's role in such preparations was much less than in the flanking reigns of Henry VIII and Mary, simply because both Somerset and Northumberland preferred to circumvent it and retain important business in their own hands, consulting only a few trusted lieutenants. The end result, so far as parliament was concerned, however, was the same: that the government busied itself with preparations for an approaching session. Moreover the government certainly took the opportunity to promote other desirable measures as well as those for which parliament had been specifically called. So Edward noted, in

December 1551, that certain laws proposed by the privy council had been 'delivered to my learned Council to pen, as by a schedule appeareth'. The official programme was certainly a mixed bag. The council was prepared to respond to lobbies, pressure groups and private petitions by sponsoring bills on their behalf; and it initiated bills for the commonweal. (Is this what Edward was referring to when he asked, before his second parliament, 'What nombre of actes are thought best to passe this parliement and which'?) The variety of the council's legislative interests is illustrated by the earl of Shrewsbury's memorandum 'of suche things as have been consyderyd by him most necessarye to be preferryd' in the approaching session.[57]

Finally the council approved and ordered the drafting of measures, and (under Edward) it scrutinised countersigned bills which were of grace or touched the king's prerogative in any way. These tasks were assigned to a council sub-committee appointed on 23 February 1554. Undoubtedly there were similar preparations before other parliaments.[58]

Official programmes accounted for only a small proportion of the total volume of bills submitted to parliament. By far the largest number belonged to the second category. In contrast, the measures drafted by parliamentary committees constituted the smallest group, although they were often general in scope and therefore of some national significance.[59] Obviously bills devised by one House were first read there. However the official and private sponsors had to decide whether Lords or Commons was the more appropriate point of entry, and their motives for choosing one rather than the other were as many and diverse as the range of bills themselves. Some customarily commenced in one place: the lay subsidy in the Commons, for example, and the confirmation of ecclesiastical taxation in the Lords, where the bishops sat. The decision was sometimes politically motivated.[60] Councillors and other royal servants were approached to sponsor bills, whereupon the choice of house was determined by their presence there. Conversely, elected clients might be expected to promote a patron's interests.[61] It cannot even be assumed that bills for boroughs, ports and other communities would be submitted first to the Commons, just because their elected representatives sat there. The skilled advocate might vary the technique as one of Exeter's burgesses, Geoffrey Tothill, did in

1563 when he explained why he had exhibited one measure for the city in the Lords and another in the Commons: 'Trustyng by that time we have thorolye consydered that byll . . . and redye to be sent offe to the lords, the lords byll wylbe redye to come down . . . If we shuld have putte bothe in at one place then peradventure the howse wold nott be best contentyed with too bylles for our private Cyttye.'[62] Parliamentary tactics thus guaranteed the Lords at least a small share of bills which were local in scope and economic in nature.

The legislative process could often be accelerated and streamlined if the initial scrutiny took place behind the scenes and outside the parliament house – that is before a bill was actually handed in. Here the Lords could once again call upon the services of the monarch's legal counsel and the judges in their capacity as legal assistants to the House. The particular concern of this preliminary scrutiny was to ensure that a bill did not harm the interests of either the Crown or the common law. How regular was the practice is uncertain, but it was not a recent innovation. Nor did it apply only to bills originating in the Upper House but also to those coming up from below.

The legal assistants were always in the thick of it, not merely scrutinising but also drafting and revising. When William Petyt described how the judges and other of Mary's learned counsel 'consulted and advised upon the penning and drawing up of' the ratification of Mary's marriage and the act for treasons and the government of the king's and queen's issue in the 1554 parliaments, it was all of a piece with his interpretation of the judges' constitutional duty: that they, 'being of the Queen's learned Counsel, were obliged, *ratione Officii*, to give their mature deliberation in forming of such Bills'. The importance of the legal assistants' parliamentary 'Travail and Pains' was acknowledged by the substantial payments made to them at the end of each session. Although the Commons' speaker received an 'accustomed fee and rewarde' of £100, there was no fixed fee for the legal assistants. The judges received £20 to £30 each after Edward VI's first session, £35 to £40 in 1552 and £30 to £33. 6s. 8d. after Mary's second parliament. The attorney and solicitor were paid £13. 6s. 8d. each for their services in Henry VIII's last session, but this had risen to £30 apiece a year later. The serjeants' fee fluctuated from £13. 6s. 8d. (in January 1547) to £10 (1 Ed.

VI), £40 (5/6 Ed. VI), and £26. 13s. 4d. (1 Mary, 1554). The variations in amount must have been determined by such considerations as rank, importance, length of session and services rendered, but no clear pattern emerges. However one trend is clear: that the most important legal assistants were gradually overhauling the Commons' speaker. Thus the chief justices received £30 apiece in 1 Ed. VI and £100 each in 5/6 Ed. VI; after the short session of April 1554 the chief justice of king's bench was paid £80, although the head of common pleas was gifted only half that amount. Likewise the payments of £13. 6s. 8d. and £30 to the attorney and solicitor for their services in the two sessions of 1547 were augmented, to £60 in 5/6 Ed. VI and £40 in 1 Mary (1554). It is a mark of the parliamentary work-load of the Crown's legal counsel that the attorney's and solicitor's clerks were also rewarded with sums ranging from £4 each in 5/6 Ed. VI to £10 in 1 Ed. VI and 1 Mary (1554). Neither speaker nor legal assistants, however, could match the lord chancellor's handsome emolument: in January 1550 it amounted to £800 'for his attendaunce thies thre last Sessions of Parliament'.[63]

No matter when a bill was subjected to the scrutiny of the legal assistants, the House only took cognizance of it at its first reading. This was a literal reading, a recital of the text which, in the absence of printed copies, was the only way to inform members of its contents. Manuscript copies could be purchased. The clerk of the parliaments and his subordinates were obliged to 'give and deliver the copies of all such bills their read, to such as demand for ye same'.[64] However, such services could tax members' purses when for every private bill 'wherof he giveth a copie [the clerk] hath for everie tenne lines a pennye'.[65] Apart from those bills which personally touched a bishop or peer, who in consequence might have been tempted to purchase copies, the literal reading must have sufficed.

Each bill introduced into the Lords, regardless of its provenance,[66] was given into the hands of the lord chancellor. He 'forthwith delivereth [it] to the Clarkes to be safly kept'.[67] From this point on, the first-reading procedure is uncertain. So is the process by which bills were arranged in order of priority. It must be assumed, especially as the procedure of the two Houses so often paralleled each other, that the lord chancellor was paramount in the business of ordering bills.[68] Elsynge's description of

Stuart practice was probably applicable to the mid-sixteenth century too; certainly it closely corresponds with the procedure of the Elizabethan Commons: 'The Clerk reads the Bill, standing at the Table, and then delivers the same, kneeling unto the Lord Chancellor, together with a Brief of the Bill.' The Chancellor reads the title of the bill, then reports the effect of the same, out of the brief and concludes, 'This is the first Time of the Reading of this Bill.'[69]

With the exception of grace bills, written on parchment and bearing the sign manual, bills were drafted on paper. So the measure which the clerk held as he intoned the text might have been drawn on vellum and oversigned *Edward R.* or *mary the quene* – a physical manifestation of the Crown's powerful and persuasive support which must have inhibited criticism. More frequently, however, it was a paper draft, lacking that endorsement and so a likelier subject and even victim of a critical assembly. Whichever form bills assumed, first readings were becoming merely informative exercises, which were not accompanied by debate, followed by committal or concluded by rejection. According to Scobell, bills were normally heard for the first time 'without being spoken unto, unless it were for the rejection of it'.[70] However, he was writing in a later age, when many procedural irregularities had been tidied up. It was Elsynge who drew attention to the contrast between Stuart uniformity and mid-Tudor inconsistency. Whereas '[a]t the first Reading, the Bill is seldom now spoken against', this had not always been the practice, and he cited the measure *pro Jurisdictione Episcoporum* as proof. In November 1549 it was rejected on its first reading and a committee was appointed 'to draw a new Bill'. Furthermore 'there are very many Precedents that Bills have been committed at the first Reading, in the Times of Henry the Eighth, and Edward the Sixth'.[71]

It is difficult to test the general validity of Elsynge's comments, because debate is rarely recorded in the journals, but it can be safely assumed that rejection at the first reading was preceded by some discussion. Yet we should not be misled by the example singled out by Elsynge, for it was one of the very few cases in which, so far as we can tell, a bill was either debated or rejected at this early stage in its passage. The remaining bills dashed by the mid-Tudor Lords reached the third reading

before they received the 'thumbs down'.[72] Furthermore the one
exception which he cited touched a particularly sensitive spot
in the anti-clerical lay majority in the Lords. In this respect at
least the House had already become consistent in its procedure.
Not so, however, with committals after the first reading when, in
1547, 30% of all first readings ended in this way.[73] If this session
is considered in isolation, it might appear to confirm Elsynge in
his verdict that the three-reading procedure was still at a primitive stage in its evolution. Yet two sessions later the picture had
dramatically altered: only six bills were committed and one
rejected (just under 15%) after their first reading in the Lords.
The trend continued. In 1555, 12% were referred to a committee
or dashed,[74] and in 1558 the figure shrank to 11 then 7%.[75] The
move to procedural uniformity was eliminating irregularities[76]
and the unchallenged first reading was fast becoming the rule. A
similar trend is observable in the Commons: in 1548/9 19 bills
were committed after the first reading and 17 after the second; by
April 1554 the totals were three and 16.

The second reading was the crucial stage. The initial moves may
have been those later described by Henry Elsynge: that the clerk
read the bill and delivered it to the lord chancellor (this time
without a brief), whereupon he simply recited the title and
declared 'This is the second Reading'.[77] The House then proceeded to debate the substance of the bill. When it did so it
enjoyed a natural advantage which derived from its very size. In
a small assembly members were able to indulge their natural
loquaciousness and, probably, to speak more than once to a bill
on the same day.[78] It was a significant advantage, because
adequate time for the airing of views, as well as freedom from
severe constraints on what they wished to say, were prerequisites
of the effective scrutiny of bills. The first condition was fully
satisfied: 'he that will, riseth up and speaketh with or against it;
and so one after another as long as they shall think good'.[79]

Debate was required to be orderly and anyone addressing the
House was expected to conduct himself respectfully and with
moderation: 'when he speaketh, he must stand bare headed
and speake his minde plainely, sensiblie & in decent order'.[80]
However, the duke of Northumberland's angry outburst against
Cranmer in March 1553 suggests that the rules and conventions
of parliamentary etiquette were not always honoured. Perhaps it

was just that those in power enjoyed a certain licence in speech which was denied the rest. In any case, whilst debate in the mid-Tudor Lords was undoubtedly heated on occasions, there is no evidence of the kind of unruly conduct which, according to Arthur Hall, typified the Elizabethan Commons: 'once an auncient gentleman and grave councellor told me he had seene some doe, which was, so intemperately, rudely, rashly and malitiously to use some in that place as he assured hymselfe he thought they durst not doe in an Ale-house, for feare of a knock with a pot'.[81]

On one matter there is no doubt: that the second condition for effective scrutiny – freedom from constraint – was not permitted in any subject which touched the royal interest. Contemporaries might claim that there was free speech in the Lords: from Stephen Gardiner, reminiscing about Henry VIII's reign,[82] to Richard Robinson who wrote of the Elizabethan Upper House that 'They have also freedom of speeche graunted everyone of them to speake his minde baudly.' But Robinson added that characteristic qualification which, in practice, could so severely restrict free opinion in debate: 'so it bee with observing Decorum of Dutifull Obedience to the Prince and the Supreme Authoritie'.[83] In practice the restraints on debate were numerous and intimidating, especially on matters of general and public importance such as the prerogative, royal policy, and religion. Gardiner recalled 'the case of her that we called Quene Anne; where all suche as spoke agaynst her in the Parliament Howse, all though they ded it by speciall commaundement of the Kynge, and spake that was truth, yet they were fayne to have a pardon, by cause that speakinge was ageynst an acte of Parliament'.[84] The threat of royal reprisals was particularly inhibiting. Although Gardiner insisted that there had been 'free spech without daungier' in the Henrician Lords, even the redoubtable bishop curbed his tongue after a warning from Chancellor Audeley that 'we wyl provide . . . that the premunire shal never goo of your hedes. This I bare awaye there and held my pease.'[85] The threat of praemunire must have persuaded many of the prelates to exercise discretion in debate.

Despite W. K. Jordan's belief[86] in the liberalisation of the parliamentary climate during the protectorate, the government remained willing to pressure and coerce its critics in the Upper

House. The Prayer Book disputation of December 1548 was not an ordinary Lords' debate, but a carefully staged public show piece. Nevertheless the hectoring and interruption by Warwick and Sir Thomas Smith, as the conservatives strove to present their case, was all too characteristic of official impatience with publicly voiced criticism.[87] In this respect there was little to choose between the regimes of Somerset and Northumberland.[88] Mary too could react sharply to parliamentary 'misconduct' – hence Lord Paget's disgrace because of his activity in the Lords in April 1554.[89] It required courage (or at least a commendable foolhardiness) to stand up and be counted amongst the parliamentary critics of official policies and bills. Yet such men were never lacking in either reign.[90] As a result the House of Lords never sank to a state of abject compliance, even when it was considering measures dear to the monarch. There is evidence enough that second-reading debates were often lively and even critical of the government. However, official bills, especially those which were liable to be contentious, constituted only a very small proportion of the legislation before the House. Most bills concerned commonweal matters, sectional or economic interests, localities and individuals. It can only be assumed that, when these were before the House, Stephen Gardiner was correct: there was 'free spech without daungier'.

At the end of the second-reading debate a bill might be rejected. However, this was already becoming a rare event[91] and its more frequent fate was committal for amendment[92] or engrossment.[93] Frequency did not yet mean regularity, because, once again, the ordered certainties of Stuart procedure were built on the fumblings of earlier Tudor experimentation. In the first Edwardian session in 1547, for example, only 15 of the 26 bills which reached a third reading in the Lords (and so were the only bills to proceed beyond what later became the normal point of committal) were referred – and one of these was simply assigned to the lord chancellor for safe keeping. Thus almost half of these bills were not recorded as being committed for either engrossment or amendment after the second reading. In 1549/50 the proportion escalated to just over 70% and in 1555 it rose even further to 79% . Although the figure dropped to 40% in 1558[94] the picture bears no obvious relationship to the Stuart world of Henry Elsynge. It still required Elizabeth's reign to iron out the wrinkles and systematise many of the procedures of the mid-Tudor Lords. The truth may be distorted by the deficiences of the journals, especially those of the Marian parliaments. The frequent omission of the adjournment formula and even, on occasions, the absence of a record of business means that some committals may have gone unrecorded too.[95] Furthermore those bills which were not referred included some up from the Commons. These were already engrossed and less likely to require amendment. Such qualifications notwithstanding, it does look as if the Lords (and the Commons too) was still a long way from the procedural uniformity of the early seventeenth century.

This leaves an unresolved question: how else were bills revised if they were not referred to committees? The only answer, excusably an unsatisfactory one, is that as yet there was no automatic assignment of them to committees. Only those in which the House sought change during the second reading were so committed. Members were then named to draw up recommended changes and to pen provisos where necessary. Stuart commentators shed little light on the earlier procedure for such appointments. Hakewil only describes the noisy hit-or-miss practice for the nomination of Commons' committees.[96] 'Everyone of the house that list may call upon the name of any one of the house to be a committee.' The clerk was expected to write in his journal 'the name of every one so called upon, at leastwise of such whose names (in that confusion) he can distinctly heare'. At least Elsynge does examine the Lords, but he is recording the well-rounded practice of the Stuart House: that it decided first 'how many of each Bench shall be of the committees'. Once this had been agreed 'they are named, *promiscue*, by any of the Lords, but the Clerk is careful to set down those whom he hears first named'. If he wrote down more than the number agreed upon, 'it is the Liberty of the House to take out the latter'. The Lords might add legal assistants to the committee and finally it would appoint a time and place of meeting.[97] Any member 'that speaketh directly against the body of the Bill' was disbarred, because 'he that wold totally destroy will not amend'.[98]

The extent to which mid-Tudor practice conformed to this is not entirely clear. Hooker's Elizabethan description – 'that the lord chancellor must choose a certaine number of [that] house as he shall think good, and to them commit the bill, to be reformed and amended'[99] – credited him with an improbably decisive authority. Perhaps what he was describing was the chancellor's exercise of a supervisory role in calling for nominations from the floor, ensuring the exclusion of absentee lords and those who had spoken against the substance of the bill, and the inclusion of legal assistants where necessary. He also kept an eye on the right apportionment of places to the lords spiritual and temporal. The early Stuart Lords displayed a particular concern to achieve an equitable representation from both the smaller orders of prelates and senior peers and from the larger number of barons: 'if there be five Earls then five Bishops and ten Barons'.[100] Elsynge noted that, in contrast, the mid-Tudor House had often departed from the strict application of this practice; for example in 1549/50, one committee consisted of an earl, four bishops and two barons, and another increased the number of lords spiritual to five.[101] It was not until the later parliaments of James I that an order was observed 'to name a set Number of each Bench, or to double the Number of Barons'.[102] Once more he was right about the flexibility of the mid-Tudor Lords. Some bills were assigned to neatly symmetrical committees of two senior peers, two prelates and two barons; others varied the mixture[103] and, in some cases, included (or consisted entirely of) legal assistants.[104]

Committee proceedings in both Houses remain one of the darker aspects of parliamentary activity, only rarely illuminated by Tudor accounts, such as Hooker's in 1571,[105] the retrospective comments of Elsynge and Scobell, and some clues in the original acts. Committees of the Lords normally met in the Painted Chamber or 'the little Room adjoyning'.[106] The order and conduct of their business is not known. Both Tudor and Stuart commentators exemplified the contemporary concern with protocol and precedence and confined themselves to such matters. So we know that any who spoke did so uncovered, although he 'might sit still if he please';[107] that other members might be present but not vote, and they had to 'give Place to all of the Committes & sit below them'.[108] When judges or other learned counsel were appointed to attend, 'they were not to sit or be covered . . . unless it was out of favour for infirmity sake, in which case sometimes such Judge had a stool set behind, but uncovered'.[109] There is no reason to think that in an elitist assembly, so much given to the burning considerations of rank, degree and etiquette, these practices significantly changed in the sixty years after Edward VI's accession.

Unfortunately this gets us no nearer to an understanding of how a mid-Tudor committee operated. Elsynge provides a clue when he describes Stuart practice: an 'attendant' read the bill to the committee and wrote any emendation 'in paper with directions as to places to be amended', and likewise with provisos.[110] Attendants – that is legal assistants – were not invariably named to committees. Presumably a bishop or peer was often appointed to perform this task. Whoever did so recorded on a paper billet the minor changes, a mixture of interlineations, deletions and corrections. They testify to the conscientious, painstaking and precise manner in which at least some committees went about their business.[111]

When it had completed its task of revision, the committee had to report back to the house with its recommended alterations. The Tudor commentators are, as usual, silent on the subject, whilst their Stuart successors bent themselves to a study of forms. So, the 'first of the Committees that was present' stood bare-headed to make his report,[112] before delivering the bill, provisos, and other amendments to the lord chancellor via the clerk. However, the crucial part of the process, as described by Henry Elsynge, can be verified from the mid-Tudor journals. When the amendments had been read out by the committee spokesman (and endorsed '1ª vice lecta'), they were read again. This brought them up to the same number of readings as the bill itself.[113]

Once the committee's recommendations had been accepted, the House ordered the bill to be written out in fair copy on parchment. Sometimes, however, a bill produced no demand for revision at the second reading. When that occurred it was straightway committed for engrossment. Once again mid-Tudor procedure was variable. Bills were engrossed after the third and even fourth readings. The journal entries reveal a significant gap between reality and Sir Thomas Smith's idealised description.[114] Whenever engrossment occurred the bill, now neatly written out on vellum, was duly returned to the House for its third and final reading and its approval (or rejection). D'Ewes was confident 'that the Form used at this day, is one and the same with that which was observed [in 1559] and the rest ensuing of her Majesties

Reign'. He observed that, when the bill for the restitution of first
fruits to the Crown came up for its final reading:

Francis Spilman Clerk of the House, standing by the Table at the nether
Woolsack, read the same Bill, and then indorsed upon it, being fairly
ingrossed in Parchment, these words, 3 *vice lecta*, and then delivered the
same, kneeling to the Lord Keeper, without any Brief of the Bill, who
thereupon, repeating the Title only of the Bill, said, This is the third
Reading of the Bill.

Thereupon the House proceeded to the question,[115] or so he
would have us believe. He may have been right on that particular
bill, but his account of what happened was an idealised version of
the practice in the two previous reigns and even later.[116] Debate
was still possible at the third reading.[117] So was committal for
revision.[118] On the other hand it was becoming common practice,
if not yet the norm, for members to confine themselves to the
refinement of wording at that stage. The original acts bear
many signs of this continued watchfulness and attention to
detail.[119]

At the end the Lords proceeded to a vote. Herein lies one of the
most important differences between the two Houses. The Commons proceeded orally and collectively, by acclamation. Only if
that was disputed did it move on to a division by counting of
heads.[120] Not so the Lords, as Sir Thomas Smith confirms. When
the third-reading discussion had run its course, the lord chancellor
asked the House if it would go to the question, 'and if they agree
. . . then he sayth, here is such a lawe or act concerning such a
matter which hath been thrise read here . . . are ye content that
it be enacted or no?' The lords spiritual and temporal 'give their
assent and dissent ech man severallie and by himselfe . . . saying
only content or not content, without further reasoning or replying'.[121] The voting proceeded in accordance with an inverted
order of precedence, the most junior barons first and then ascend-
ing to the senior members of the same rank, through the bishops
and archbishops to the senior peers and ending with the premier
duke or marquess.[122] '[A]s the more number doeth agree, so it
is agreed on, or dashed.'[123]

The procedure was not as simple as appears at first sight.
Hooker described a second and alternative method of voting to
which the house could resort if no clear-cut result had emerged.
The lord chancellor 'must cause the house to be divided, [and]

then judge of the bill according to the greater number'. Stuart commentators disagreed with Hooker. Hakewil acknowledged the 'the triall thereof is by saying content or not content', but he continued 'if that be doubtfull, then [to proceed] by telling the Poles, without dividing the house'.[124] Elsynge offered a more elaborate version. The lord chancellor addressed the house: 'The Question is thus "Such of your Lordships, as are of Opinion, that this Bill is fit to pass, or shall pass, say Content. They, which are of another Opinion, say, Not content."' He then repeats Smith's description in which each member answered individually from the newest baron to the premier duke or (failing that) marquess. If the first declaration of opinions was inconclusive[125] 'then, one Lord who said Content, and another Lord, who said, Not content, are appointed to number them by the Poll. They go together to the Barons Bench, and every Lord, who said, Content, stands up.' They moved on to the bishops' and earls' benches, and then round again totting up the 'not contents'.[126] Smith makes no mention of this alternative procedure. As for Hooker, he frequently writes less from knowledge than from the assumption that the upper house conducted its affairs in the same way as the Commons. Whoever was right about the alternative, there is a general consensus that the mid-Tudor Lords' voting procedure was, in the first instance, more sophisticated and reliable than that of the Lower House. Edmund Plowden confirmed the fact: 'As in Parliament the majority of voices in the Upper House may be easily known, because they are demanded severally and the Clerk of the House reckons them, but in the Lower House of Parliament it is otherwise, for there the assent is tried by the voices sounding all at one time.'[127] The method of voting employed by the two Houses may have been appropriate to their respective sizes. Nevertheless it remains true that the Commons' initial and primitive method of acclamation contrasted unfavourably with the Lords' practice, which possessed the virtues of immediate certainty and accuracy, and enabled the clerk to register dissenters, by name, in his journal.

At this stage in the legislative process, the Upper House presents us with a paradox. Although its clerk 'recordeth . . . each particular man's severall consent or not consent', it had a preference for consensus politics,[128] and unanimity remained the ideal. It is difficult to believe that, in the case of most bills which passed the

House, the formula *communi omnium Procerum Assensu conclusa est* truly reflected universal agreement. Certainly unanimity was not invariable. Sometimes only a majority assented,[129] and dissenters' names were entered in the journal. The 'not contents' are named in the Edwardian record on 51 occasions (ten per session) dropping to 39 in the Marian journals, or a sessional average of just under eight. The fall is accounted for partly by the lack of a journal for the first parliament and the brevity of the last session.[130] On other occasions the greater part voted 'not content' (whereupon individual dissenters were not identified).[131] Nevertheless the majority of bills put to the question were approved by the whole House,[132] even though it used a voting technique which made it much easier for an opponent to register his disapproval – literally to stand up and be counted.

Rejected bills could not be reintroduced in the same session.[133] As for those which had successfully charted a course through the shoals and reefs of the Upper House, it only remained for the clerk to subscribe them with the requisite formula in the top or bottom right hand corner: *Soit baille aux communs* if it had commenced in the Lords, or *A ceste bille les Seigneurs sont assentus* to a Commons' bill. He did the same with any proviso, adding *avecque un Provision annexe* to the standard formula.[134] Once the lord chancellor had assigned a bill to legal assistants for despatch to the Commons,[135] that was the last which the Lords saw of it until it was returned. It might return with the unqualified blessing of the Lower House or, alternatively, with amendments or even in redrafted form. It might be a bill which had first passed the Commons and was entering the House for the first time. Whichever was the case, it was carried up with solemn ritual by a deputation from the other House.[136]

Nevertheless, in practical terms of time and labour there was a significant distinction between measures which had commenced in the Lords and those which it received from the Commons. Bills which had been altered or redrawn in the second House obviously required to be sent back to the House of origin for its consent. More than this, however, the initiating chamber had to effect the actual changes. The reason for this lies in its proprietary rights. Bills were always on parchment by the time they had completed their passage through it. If the second House chose to alter a bill in certain particulars, it returned it along with recommended corrections. Scobell described the Lords' practice, which the Commons also observed:

> If upon the second reading the same were committed, the Amendments were to be set down in paper by the Committee, with reference to the Line and the Words between which it is to be inserted, and to be reported to the House, and if the House approve them, or make any alterations in them, then the same Amendments as they are agreed, are to be sent with the Bill to the Commons, to be accordingly by them amended, if they think good.

He later repeated the description but added, with emphasis, that 'the Bill itself is not to be amended'. His commentary was supported by the mid-Tudor journals: when, on 11 February 1552, the Lords sent down the bill to deprive 'divers Offenders' of benefit of clergy 'with Request, that certain Words, which were amiss there, and lacked for the making of the Sentence perfect, might be amended and put in'; and later, in the same session, when the Upper House sent down a proviso to a Commons' cloth bill and a request that, if they liked it, they should pass it, and annex it to 'the book'. Sometimes the recommended alteration was a deletion, as on 4 May 1554, when the Lords requested the removal of the last 17 lines from the confirmation of the duke of Suffolk's attainder. No matter whether the amendment was substantial or trifling, it was always couched in the form of a recommendation, with the decision and action left to the House of origin.[137]

Scobell's observation, that recommended alterations were set down on paper, requires modification in one particular. When a bill which had passed one House was actually redrawn by the other, the latter assumed proprietary rights over the *nova billa* and engrossed it. In 1552 a Lords' bill 'for buying of wools' was replaced by the Commons which wrote it on parchment before delivering it 'upstairs'; in March 1553 the Commons scrutinised a Lords' measure for the king's revenues, devised a new book and engrossed it. When, in 1552, the Commons redrafted an Upper House bill concerned with the buying and selling of offices, roles were reversed so that, when the Lords wanted to amend the measure, it could only make a recommendation which the other House, in this case, rejected. This journal evidence is reinforced by the fortunate survival of the Lords' original and engrossed chantries bill of 1547. It is subscribed *Soit baille aux communs* but with no corresponding Commons' assent because it was replaced there. The new bill also survives, engrossed and endorsed before its return to the Lords and the successful completion of its parliamentary passage there. It should be added that when one House redrafted the other's measure it returned the discarded bill along with the new one – hence the survival of the Lords' chantries bill.[138]

Although a redrafted bill altered the relationship between the two chambers, in all other cases the House of origin retained its proprietary rights and the responsibility to approve and effect amendments on its parchment bill: 'amendments ought alwaies to bee in that house from whence the thing to bee amended originally proceedeth, though the directions for the amendments came from the other house'. The House of origin was free to accept or reject recommended changes. Rejection might result in an impasse, as it did when the Commons refused to accept the Lords' request to excise, from the confirmation of Suffolk's attainder, a clause on entailed lands and the bill failed. However, the verdict of the House of origin was usually accepted as final. In March 1553 the Lords gave a third reading to two provisos on a Commons' schedule attached to a bill for the reformation of financial courts. The general consensus of opinion was that the second of these might prejudice the king's interests. So the House set it aside, redrafted the other and returned it to the Commons 'to the intent, in case that they should so agree, the bill might pass in that sort'. On 7 March 1558 the House agreed to the two Commons' provisos to the bill for continuance of acts, but rejected a third touching the purchase of Leadenhall in London, 'and therefore required . . . that it be quite taken away from the said book'. Bishop Gardiner brought a touch of drama to the tedious but necessary business of revision and refinement. The Marian bill reuniting England with Rome was drawn by a joint-committee of the two Houses, but it was technically a Lords' measure because it was first read there. During its parliamentary passage, the inclusion of a general exemption to holders of expropriated Church property rendered redundant a nineteen-line clause protecting the rights of three peers. The Commons returned the bill with two provisos and a request that this specific exempting clause should be deleted. The Lords acted on the provisos, and redrafted one which it disliked. The Lower House duly agreed and the bill was returned. However, it was accompanied with a reminder that the nineteen lines had not been removed. Gardiner personally assumed responsibility when he slashed the offending lines with a knife. The defaced parchment in the House of Lords Record Office bears physical witness to his flamboyance.[139]

All procedural rules in the Tudor parliaments were inevitably and frequently honoured in the breach. Sometimes the second chamber devised a proviso and engrossed it, as occurred in 1581: 'A bill that came from the Lords was amended, and a scroll of addition in parchment, put unto it, and sent to the Lords, without any indorsement, *Soit baille aux Seigneurs*; and for want thereof they would not proceed, but remanded it to pass the bill, and withdraw that addition, or else to indorse it, and thereupon it was indorsed.'[140]

It is of some technical interest that the Lords was concerned about the lack of endorsement and not the fact of engrossment. More significant, however, is the consistent observance of the rule that the House of origin alone could affirm and attach provisos which had been devised and even engrossed by the other chamber.

It is understandable that the House of origin should retain such proprietary rights. Usually it had invested more hours and labour in the bill which came before it first. It had knocked it into shape, revised and engrossed it, honed and tempered it. More often than not the other House approved it without alteration, or merely suggested provisos or further polishing of the text. If it redrafted a bill, it might well redress the balance of the work-load between the two Houses, but this kind of drastic action was exceptional.[141] The legislative (and sometimes political) significance of the House of origin in the parliamentary passage of bills will become more apparent in the following chapter. Its relationship with the other House, however, also raises a question of procedural importance which warrants an examination here. Bicameral co-operation was essential in order to ensure the smooth operation of the law-making process, especially when bills offended or dis-satisfied members of the second House to receive them. It would be wrong to assume that revision, redrafting or rejection were provocative acts, intended as political snubs or designed to cause political confrontations with the House of origin. With few exceptions,[142] such actions stemmed from a response to bills which were judged on their merits and found wanting. Nevertheless disagreement between the two Houses could endanger desirable bills, and this they worked hard to avoid. A classic example occurred in 1571. The Commons resolved 'That certain Words required by the Lords to be put out, should stand qualified with other Words, with condition that if the Lords should not agree to the said qualification, the Commons would not be bound by that resolution, which was done of purpose to avoid the hazard of the Bill, in case the Lords should not agree thereto'.[143] So they both made use of a number of procedural devices, in order to keep open the channels of communication and negotiation and thereby lessen the chances of friction and misunderstanding: notably messages, deputations, and joint-conferences.

Messages were employed to transmit or request information. So in 1548/9 the Lords sent down the master of the rolls, two serjeants and the king's solicitor to learn the Commons' pleasure about attainder proceedings against Thomas Lord Seymour. The two legal assistants who brought down a restitution bill on 8 March 1552 also conveyed a message to hurry their business along because of the impending dissolution. Two years later messages included a protest against a subpoena, which a member had caused to be served on the earl of Huntingdon, and an instruction that serving-men attendant upon members should not permit their servants 'to make frays in Smithfield, for so the Lords have done.'[144]

The Lords made particular use of deputations in order to urge, exhort and apply pressure to the other House, especially on money matters. On 14 November 1558 the queen's attorney and solicitor bore down to the Commons not only a bill but also a declaration 'that divers of the Lords will come down, to confer with this House, for weighty Affairs of this Realm; and therefore require this House to tarry their Coming'. The deputation duly appeared, led by Lord Chancellor Heath and consisting of seven peers and four bishops. Once they were seated, where the privy councillors 'use to sit', their spokesman, Heath, demanded 'that by Necessity, for the Safeguard of this Realm from the French and Scots, a Subsidy must be had; Mr Speaker, and the Privy Council, then sitting from them on the lowest Benches'.[145] Their mission completed, the chancellor and those accompanying him swept forth from the chamber. The occasion illustrated the prestige and dignity of the Upper House and the Commons' deference before such a prestigious delegation. Messages could be used to reverse the process and call up members of the Lower House to hear what their superiors had to say. On 24 January 1558 the speaker and ten or twelve members were summoned to the Lords, where they were informed 'that it was meet to seek for the sure Defense of the Realm, and a Relief for the same'.[146]

The third and most effective mechanism for preventing or ironing out differences over bills was the joint-conference. It was not put on a regular and formal footing until a Commons' resolution of 1571 and the motion of the great parliament-man Thomas Norton, ten years later.[147] Nonetheless it was already being employed to good effect in the Edwardian and Marian parliaments. Joint-conferences figure in the journals,[148] and Sir Thomas Smith was not describing a post-Marian development when he wrote,

If they cannot agree, the two houses . . . if it be understode that there is any sticking, sometimes the Lordes to the Commons, sometimes the Commons to the Lordes doe require that a certaine of each house may meete together, and so ech part to be enformed of others meaning, and this is alwaies graunted. After which meeting for the most part, not alwaies, either parte agrees to the others billes.[149]

The importance of the joint-conference confirms the contemporary priority of co-operation in the cause of successful legislation. It also placed the Lords at a distinct psychological advantage in its relations with the Commons. This is suggested by Scobell's description:

[Such as were sent from the Lower House] being come Hither . . . at the time and place appointed by the Lords . . . the Lords come to them all at once, and not scatteringly, which might take from their gravity, and prevent their places. The Lords did sit there covered, the Commons did stand bare during the time of the Conference.[150]

One Elizabethan, writing in 1581, recognised the Lords' advantage:

I must confesse the [Joint] Conference may doe and doth good, but mutch of it sometimes doth more hurte, and there is noo one thinge that hathe soe shaken the true libertie of the howse as oftene conferences . . . sometimes by teriefienge of men's opinions. I meane not that the Lordes doe teriefie men, but men of the Common howse cominge up amonge them at conferences espie their inclinations and knowinge that in the common hose nothing is secret, they gather other advisements.[151]

The *hauteur* which invested the Lords' dealings with the Lower House was also expressed in its instruction that members of the Commons 'be sent for',[152] as occurred on the death of Queen Mary.[153] On these occasions the purpose was not to confer but to instruct or inform. It was conduct befitting a House which was the ancient nucleus of parliament and which combined, in a strange way, the independence and lofty bearing of a social elite and the panoply of government.

There remains one further point to consider. So far bills have been examined generally and generically, without bothering to distinguish between those which were public and those designated 'private'. Yet the distinction is an important one. Although the preceding description of the Lords' procedures is, by and large, equally applicable to both classes of bills, it ignores and omits practices peculiar to private-bill legislation. The classification of such private measures was determined, not by scope, but by fees. Public bills proceeded without the payment of fees to the speaker, clerks, and other members of the parliamentary bureaucracy, whereas private bills did not.[154] In practice most (but not all) of the former were of general application, 'concerned with the common interest', and the latter were usually beneficial measures for local, sectional, or individual interests.[155] In seeking to advance their own causes through legislation, such interests often posed a threat to the well-being of others who naturally challenged their bills and sought to air their grievances. So these, rather than public bills, were liable to provoke criticism, obstruction and conflict. Parliaments provided such opponents with both the opportunity and the machinery to state their case. And on these occasions the Lords and the Commons conducted themselves in a quasi-judicial manner. They summoned interested parties with counsel to committees and to the bar of the House, and they made copies of the bill and other pertinent evidence available to them.[156] In this, as in all other matters, the Upper House did not lag behind the Commons in the use and development of appropriate procedures.

THE LEGISLATIVE RECORD OF
THE MID-TUDOR LORDS

Behind the formal institutional facade of parliament lay the reality of political activity. Although such activity was normally positive and constructive, it could assume a negative, obstructive, even destructive, character. Whatever form it took at a given moment, its end was usually a legislative one – politics and legislation were but two faces of the same process. The enactment or frustration of a bill was not a simple mechanical process, isolated from the mixture of high idealism and self-interest, hostility and alliance, competition and collaboration, which inevitably characterise any assembly of men. In this respect the Lords was probably the more important House. Its lay majority stood at the centre of a web of social connections which included the membership of the Commons. Many of the knights and burgesses were attached to peers by bonds of friendship, kinship, deference and clientage;[1] and frequently their election was guaranteed or assisted by the support of a duke of Norfolk, an earl of Bedford or Pembroke,[2] or other powerful regional magnates. Although political parties did not exist, it would not be fanciful to imagine that sometimes the lords temporal – and the occasional bishop – utilised the services of relatives and clients in the Lower House in order to advance their own measures and obstruct others.[3] It proved also to be a more convenient and safe course of action to resist the Crown by proxy, through the Commons, than to engage in open confrontation in the Lords.[4] However, politicking did not commonly carry with it the more sinister political implications of conflict, deadlock and the threat of addled parliaments. It was simply a part of the eternal parliamentary game, in which just as much energy could be expended over personal or private bills as on matters of great and urgent national concern.[5]

Nevertheless, in certain circumstances political activity within parliament could adversely affect its performance and diminish the business efficiency and productivity of both Houses.[6] When politicking and lobbying were taken beyond their normal limits they had seriously disruptive consequences: divisions within one House (or both), bicameral conflict, confrontation between the government and its critics, and, worst of all, the sabotage or defeat of official measures. This is no mere hypothetical proposition, because that is precisely what happened in the early Marian parliaments. In 1553/4 the divisive politics of Court and council invaded the House of Lords, and the councillors who sat there deserted their managerial duties.[7] The political circumstances were unusual and the blinkered irresponsibility of members marked a dramatic departure from the Tudor norm. Yet it does underline the need to pay due attention to politics, if only for their role in both the furtherance and the hindrance of parliamentary business.

That business was legislation. The productivity – and therefore the success – of parliaments can only be measured by the enactment of statute. Not, of course, in a simple and crude quantitative way, by the number of acts resulting from each session; nor solely in terms of the Crown's ability to extract the money and measures for which it had summoned parliament, though naturally this would have been the government's gauge of success. As the governing class was a vital party to the legislative process, only a parliament which satisfied at least some of its expectations as well could have been greeted with general satisfaction. Similarly the role of the House of Lords can only be evaluated in terms of its productivity: the part which it played in translating royal and governing-class wishes into the practical form of statute.

Any attempt to demonstrate this with precision is beset with problems and is bound to fall far short of complete success. Apart from the fact that arithmetical measurements are by themselves unsatisfactory, because some bills were more equal than others in scope and importance, there are the difficulties caused by their broad contemporary classification as either public or private. The distinction was a purely technical one and was not determined by scope and content,[8] even though most public measures were of general application and the majority of private ones were not. Furthermore it is often impossible to identify unsuccessful bills as either one or the other. More often than not their text has not survived, and the clerks' descriptions of them (in lieu of official titles) are variable and often misleading.[9] For these same reasons any attempt to reclassify acts and bills, in accordance with the criteria of scope and content, founders, not only because of ignorance about many of them, but also because any attempt at a content-classification – even of acts (for which at least the text usually exists)[10] – simply spawns a large and rather meaningless set of categories. At the end, and in the absence of a satisfactory alternative, one is forced to fall back on the contemporary twofold classification. However, within these two broad classes it is possible to identify certain sub-species which shared common characteristics: acts of grace, restitutions,[11] attainders (and confirmations thereof), general pardons and clerical subsidies. In most cases their passage was a formality. Consequently they were exceptions to the general rule that, unless a bill was redrafted or drastically revised in the other chamber, the House of origin was the chief formative influence on its final shape.[12] As most bills of this exceptional kind commenced in the Upper House, they deserve due consideration in any assessment of its legislative role.

Between Edward VI's accession and Mary's death, 747[13] bills were submitted to parliament or devised[14] by it. Only a minority of them (264, or 35%) began their parliamentary passage in the House of Lords. Furthermore 41 of them were restitutions, attainders, pardons and clerical subsidies which sped through parliament with a minimum of fuss and time.[15] These bills ought to be subtracted from the Lords' share, if we are to arrive at a realistic and reasonably accurate assessment of its initiating role in the legislative process.[16] The results of such an adjustment are set forth in Table 3.[17]

The Commons enjoyed a clear-cut arithmetical superiority. However, parliament's record of productivity, which is after all what really matters, presents a dramatically different picture. Only 277,[18] or 37%, of the 747[19] Edwardian and Marian bills passed into law. These were the tangible fruits of parliament's labours and it is significant that, whilst the Lords initiated a much smaller number of all bills, it struck a much higher success rate. Well over half (57%) or 157 of the 277 acts began there. Even when no account is taken of those measures which usually had an uncontested passage, its record as an initiating chamber was scarcely inferior to that of the Commons (Table 4).

Table 3

		House of Lords		House of Commons	
		Number of bills	Percentage of all bills	Number of bills	Percentage of all bills
Bills originating in each house	Ed. VI	192	41	281	59
	Mary	72	26	202	74
Subtract bills whose passage was usually a formality	Ed. VI	22	—	0	—
	Mary	19	—	0	—
Amended totals	Ed. VI	170	38	281	62
	Mary	53	21	202	79
	1547–58	223	32	483	68

Table 4

	House of Lords		House of Commons	
	Number	Percentage	Number	Percentage
Acts originating in each house	157	57	120	43
Subtract acts whose passage was usually a formality	41	—	0	—
Amended totals	116	49	120	51

The Lords' achievement can be spelt out in simple quantitative terms of productivity: that 157 (59.5%) of the 264 bills introduced or drawn there became acts. Even when we set aside the crop of grace bills and other uncontested measures, some 52% of Lords' bills still became law. The Commons' harvest was, in contrast, a meagre one: only 120 (or 25%) out of 483. The reason is not hard to find. In short sessions[20] the Lower House had to cope with a spate of measures handed in by gentlemen, burgesses and lawyers. Some concerned local administration, others up-dated the law and overhauled the judicial process, and many more advanced local and sectional economic interests. Together they imposed a burden of business so heavy that a failure rate of as much as 3 to 1 was almost inevitable.[21]

The House of Commons alone exercised the right to initiate lay taxation: subsidies, fifteenths and tenths and, in the first parlia-

ment of each reign, a grant of tunnage and poundage for life. Yet
even this did not give it an automatic and unchallenged primacy.
It enjoyed no monopoly in grants of revenue, nor was it immune
from pressures applied by the Lords when it initiated them.
Clerical subsidies were voted by convocation and confirmed, *first*
by the Upper House and only then by the Lower. Not that every
mid-Tudor parliament voted lay or clerical taxation to the Crown,
which made no requests for aid in 1547, 1552, and the first three
Marian parliaments.[22] When the Crown did, the Lords carefully
scrutinised each grant up from the Commons and frequently
amended it: as in 1547 when it added a proviso for the Steelyard
to the tunnage and poundage grant; and in 1548/9 and March
1553 when it returned the subsidy bill with additions.[23] During
Mary's war with France it went further and intruded itself into the
initiating process. On 14 November 1558 a delegation headed by
Lord Chancellor Heath entered St Stephen's Chapel, displaced
the speaker and privy councillors from their customary seats and
demanded a subsidy. The very next day the Commons lent consideration to the matter.[24] In the previous session the Lords had
similarly impressed on it the need for financial aid. A joint-
committee of the two Houses had thereupon appointed three sub-
committees or 'Councells' to examine the problem 'that no way or
polliceye shall be undevysed or not thought upon'. They met
separately for three days, before coming together to draw up the
terms of the grant and recommend them to both Houses.[25] Even
in matters financial, the Lords was far from being a cypher.[26]

In non-financial matters the Upper House had a distinct
advantage, at least so far as efficiency and productivity were concerned. It initiated a much smaller volume of business. It was also
an assembly of more manageable size; it had a higher proportion
of experienced members; and the legal assistants were at its beck
and call. In these circumstances it is no surprise that the mid-
Tudor Lords performed more efficiently and successfully. Em-
bedded and concealed in this general analysis, however, are
significant regnal differences. First, there was a dramatic deterioration in the 'quality' of parliament under Mary. It manifested
itself in a variety of ways: in briefer sessions, fewer statutes,
inferior standards of recording,[27] and declining attendance;[28]
above all, in the case of the Lords, in the shrinkage of its business
and the decline of its initiating role. Whereas 192 bills – 41% of

all those before the Edwardian parliaments – had originated there,[29] the share of the Marian Upper House was only 26% (72).[30] Likewise the proportion of acts which it initiated fell from 64% to 45%:[31] a clear shift of emphasis in the bicameral relationship.[32]

There is evidence too of a more fractious, or at least critical, spirit in Mary's House of Lords. More bills were rejected.[33] And although recorded dissenting votes declined[34] in the parliament of April–May 1554, the session was a short one, with the House sitting on only 20 mornings to transact business. Even then the Lords chalked up an impressive tally, with four bills thrown out and members voting against five others: 30% of all measures before the House.[35] Where the precise point of change occurred can only be discovered by a closer look at each session, but everything points to the years 1553/4. It was certainly not in the previous reign, when the Lords had played a vigorous part in the making of law. Fewer bills had come before it and fewer had originated there than in the Commons but its success rate had been invariably higher. Despite a number of sessional variations, the pattern had been a strikingly consistent one: in five sessions the proportion of all bills commencing in the Lords fluctuated within the narrow range of 33–44%; and apart from 1549/50 – when the total fell to 52% – the house initiated 65–76% of all acts.[36]

The Lords' part in the enactment of major pieces of Edwardian legislation endorses this more general impression. In 1547 it initiated all but one of the Reformation measures. It gave nine readings to the bill for the sacrament of the altar, and even then added a proviso; it also read a measure for the election of bishops five times and amended it, whereas the bill had a straightforward passage through the other House. Admittedly its chantries bill, which replaced two before the Commons, was in turn superseded by a *nova billa* in the Lower House. On the other hand, a Commons' bill – 'for benefices with cure, common preachers, and residence' – went no further than a second reading in the Lords. As for the repeal of some of Henry VIII's treason legislation, it was a model example of bicameral co-operation. It passed the Lords, but only after a thorough scrutiny and five readings. Even then the House felt compelled to add a proviso. Although the Commons replaced it with a new bill of its own devising, the

Lords called for a joint-conference and thereafter added amendments which the Lower House accepted.

In the following session the acts for uniformity in religion and 'the abstaining from flesh on certain days' were submitted first to the Lords, which also redrafted the Commons' bill for the marriage of priests. And it continued to be an active agent in the enactment of important public acts. In 1549/50 it was the first to consider the proposed revision of the canon law, and it amended the Commons' measure to suppress Catholic books and images. On the debit side the Lords' bill for the ordering of ecclesiastical ministers was replaced by the other House, and although the House backed a bishops' bill in support of their jurisdiction it failed to complete its parliamentary passage. Against these, however, must be set the Commons' enclosure bill which it redrafted. Furthermore its thoroughness did not slacken. It only assented to a draconian measure dealing with risings of the common people after six readings – though, on this occasion, the Commons went one better, redrafting it and giving it *eight* readings. In the last session (1552) of Edward's first parliament, the Lords sustained its customary vigour. It was the first to treat the second uniformity act and a measure to punish brawling and fighting in churches. If its bill against excessive wool prices was redrafted by the Commons, this must be set against its amendment of one measure for industrial regulation and its replacement of another for 'the maintenance of tillage'. When a new parliament assembled in March of the following year, there was no significant departure from the established pattern. The overriding impression is of parliaments in which both Houses were active and co-operative – with the Lords having the edge as a formative influence in the enactment of major public measures. It would be easy to point the finger at the Lords and accuse it of procedural sloppiness because it subjected some of these important bills to more than three readings. However, at a stage of procedural development when the three-reading procedure was not yet an inflexible norm, four, five or six readings were at least an indication of thoroughness.

Mary's reign stands in stark contrast. The ratification of her marriage, the confirmation of her authority, and the restitution of the bishopric of Durham, all in 1553/4, had a more-or-less straightforward passage through the Lords.[37] However, a considerable number of important measures fell foul of the Upper

House after negotiating the Commons. In April 1554 two bills – one against heresy, the other concerning the possessors of secularised Church lands – proceeded no further than a second reading in the Lords. During the same parliament another heresy bill was rejected on the third reading, and a treason bill to protect Mary's husband was so emasculated as to render it useless. Nor did it end there. The Lords' unacceptable demand for deletions in the confirmation of the duke of Suffolk's attainder resulted in a stalemate. Although the House at first adopted a low profile in November 1554, its mood quickly changed. In December and January it provided the dynamic of parliamentary criticism and opposition to the unpopular features of official measures, especially in the reunion with Rome, the heresy laws, and the revived (and revised) treasons bill.[38] However, in Mary's fourth parliament the Lords surrendered the critical initiative to the Commons. It assented to the bills to restore first fruits and tenths and to penalise exiles, but the first was thereafter amended and the second was dashed in the Lower House. Nor, in 1558, did it regain the initiative.[39]

Therefore the point of change in the Lords' initiating role can be traced to the first two years and three parliaments of Mary's reign. We must search out the reason. It cannot be explained away by a sudden inundation of bills which dented efficiency and impaired productivity. Quite the contrary. The volume of legislation before the Edwardian Commons had been 44% over and above that handled by the Lords. In Mary's reign it rose to 61%. It simply will not do to argue the case for inefficiency in terms of a novel and insupportable volume of business. Instead it was the Commons which had to square up to a problem which must have caused the failure of many bills through sheer lack of time.[40] Nor can it be argued that there were institutional or procedural changes which carried with them harmful effects. The legal assistants continued to serve in their vital role. Procedures were being refined and standardised. All the signs point to institutional progress, not decline.

The answer must be sought elsewhere: in the parliamentary consequences of a disturbed political climate. Conflict and confrontation between the Crown and some members of each House were uncommon occurrences. Yet they did happen, and with greater frequency under the mid-Tudors than at any other time during the century.[41] However, such phenomena posed no threat to government legislation in Edward VI's reign. Conservative bishops and peers might resist (with varying degrees of strictness it is true) every major piece of Reformation legislation,[42] but there was never much likelihood of their becoming an effective voting majority. Instead their ranks were thinned as obdurate prelates were deprived and Stephen Gardiner, the one man who might have welded them into a formidable force, was kept out of harm's way, first by imprisonment and then by deprivation.[43] Similarly, whilst Edwardian Court politics and aristocratic rivalries sometimes rippled over into parliament, their effects were minimal. Neither official bills nor other business were endangered, even by Thomas Lord Seymour's attempt to exploit the Lords and Commons against his brother.[44] When, in 1549/50 and 1552, parliament assembled after Northumberland's coups against Somerset, faction conflicts were either stilled or worked out in Court and council, not in Lords and Commons. Parliament's only involvement was to give statutory sanction to measures which consolidated the victor's position, rewarded his supporters and penalised his opponents.[45]

Occasionally the power struggles at the centre had parliamentary reverberations. In 1552, for example, they broke surface when Northumberland sought to deprive Bishop Tunstall and attaint him for misprision of treason. Archbishop Cranmer 'spoke freely' against the bill, 'not satisfied, it seems, with the charge laid against him'.[46] The measure was finally dropped when the government refused the Commons' demand to hear both Tunstall and his accessories.[47] As always, and for a variety of reasons, public and private bills were obstructed and opposed, shelved and even defeated.[48] The many divisions, hostilities and rivalries within the membership of the Upper House could also have disruptive parliamentary effects.[49] With few exceptions these were no more than the natural hazards of the parliamentary game. Rarely did they divert parliament's attention from its main task or jeopardise official business. Furthermore the very nature of Edwardian government – an aristocratic regency – caused a resurgence of noble power, wedded the House of Lords to the council, and magnified its prestige and political authority.

Of course it is possible to focus attention on contentious measures, especially the pieces of commonwealth and Reformation legislation. Together with those bills which were dashed, or failed in other ways, they can be applied to paint a picture of parliament in which strife was the natural order of things. However, it would be a false picture. The purpose of parliament was to enact 'rounded' and effective laws. This could only be achieved by a good deal of hard work and a willingness to work together. Frequently it also necessitated the reconciliation of conflicting interests and the protection of those who might be unjustly affected by new laws. A classic case is the passage of the chantries bill of 1547. The clause for the surrender of guildable lands to the king prompted the burgesses for Lynn and Coventry to criticise the bill. They even introduced bills designed to protect guild lands in their own boroughs. The privy council was quick to see the danger because their action 'might have ministred occacion to others to have labored for the like'. It was also prompt to act. It persuaded the promoters of the bills that 'if they medeled no furder' against the chantries bill, the king 'ones having the guyldable landes graunted unto him by thact as it was penned unto him, shuld make them over a newe graunt of the landes pertaining then unto their Guyldes & co., to be had and used to them as afore'.[50]

The session of 1549/50 admirably illustrates the same point. By a selective process it can be portrayed as a fractious assembly: when, for example, the Lords registered a sizeable dissenting vote against three bills on religion;[51] and when two more, on enclosures and 'unlawful hunting' (a subject which naturally exercised the minds of their lordships) were subjected to extended debate and extensive revision before passing into law.[52] There were also protracted proceedings over the bill for 'the Fine and Ransom' of the duke of Somerset. The House of Lords insisted on satisfying itself that the fallen protector's confession had been volunteered and not 'enforced'; it examined a controversy between Lord Audley and Somerset; and finally it despatched the bill to the other House, accompanied by articles of submission. By the time it passed into law it had received further amendments from both Houses.[53]

Thus far the impression conveyed is that of a parliament hag-ridden by division and dispute between the members of the parliamentary trinity – worse still, that it provided the occasion for powermongers like Northumberland to pursue their vendettas.

Yet what we are actually looking at, in the case of the Lords, is a House scrupulously carrying out its legislative responsibilities. In any case these more contentious measures must be set in their proper parliamentary context. Twenty-four other acts were passed, most of them without evidence of friction or dissent.[54] Parliament also considered 50 bills which did not become law. Their failure, however, was not the consequence of conflict. Often they were the victims of time, or rather lack of it. The Lords' share was a small one. Twenty-six Commons' bills did not proceed beyond a second reading in the House of origin; two were rejected and six more were redrafted without proceeding to the other House. In contrast the Lords shelved only six of its own bills and rejected one. Six more completed their passage through one house, only to expire for lack of time in the other. Of the remainder, one bill received the royal veto and another stuck on the unacceptability of a Lords' amendment to a Commons' measure. Neither event was in itself startling or indicative of bitter conflict. They were simply instances when it proved impossible to arrive at a formula satisfactory to all parties. The loss of some bills was inevitable and there is nothing to suggest that, on these occasions, failure ruffled tempers. The sole exception may have been the abortive bill on episcopal jurisdiction, but this was a highly sensitive subject to both orders in the Upper House.[55] Even when it is added to the seven contentious measures which became acts, just over 90% of the bills entered into parliament have no record of protracted debate, heated opposition or public dissent. The characteristics of this session are common to the parliamentary history of the entire reign. Contentious bills were the exception, not the rule, and the impact of religious divisions, personal enmities and faction politics at Court was limited and ephemeral.

Mary's accession was accompanied by a religious volte-face and a peculiar set of political circumstances. Her policies were controversial and, in combination, they guaranteed opposition within (but not necessarily by) the two Houses: in particular the restoration of both Catholicism *and* papal supremacy, the concomitant and vexed problem of secularised property, the queen's Habsburg fixation, the persecution of heresy (with its implied threat to owners of lands once belonging to the Church), and the future authority of the queen's Spanish consort. Her parliamentary programme in 1553/4 was designed to fulfil these objectives. It also contained within it fuel enough to stoke the fires of parliamentary opposition. Mary's attempt to implement that programme consequently endowed her first three parliaments with a kind of political unity.

Inseparable from the queen's aims was the alignment of factions which she created at Court by her very choice of councillors. The inflated size of her council, which A. F. Pollard so severely criticised, was not in itself of particular importance. Many of its members were sleeping partners, whose appointment was a reward for past loyalty rather than in expectation of future service. To all intents and purposes, advice and administration were the preserve of an inner ring of councillors, and in this respect the Marian system was a reversion to the pre-Cromwellian council. Nevertheless the divisions within that group were many, varied, and posed a serious threat to both effective government and efficient parliamentary management.[56] They polarised around the temperamental antipathy, policy conflicts, and bitterness derived from their different experiences, between Stephen Gardiner and William Paget. Gardiner had spent most of the previous reign in prison, before Mary promptly released him and restored him to the bishopric of Winchester. Until 1553 his erstwhile protégé, Paget, had fared rather better. In the declining years of Henry VIII Gardiner incurred his disfavour, whilst Paget became his confidant. In Edward VI's reign the bishop was kept under lock and key, but his rival served as Somerset's lieutenant and then received a peerage for deserting him. Paget too eventually suffered imprisonment under Northumberland, but he remained an Edwardian, sympathetic to the Reformation and upholding the view (anathema to Gardiner) that bishops were Erastian civil servants.[57]

When Mary became queen she appointed them both to the privy council and named Gardiner to be her lord chancellor. As her programme unfolded, they became diametrically opposed. The restored bishop desired the queen to wed and bed an Englishman, preferably his own nominee Edward Courtenay. He sought statutory powers for the persecution of heresy. And when he belatedly accepted Mary's choice of a Spanish husband, he actively worked for a time-table which provided for the restoration of the pope as head of the English church before she married — otherwise the reunion with Rome would be widely and unpopularly regarded as a Spanish project. Paget, either on principle or with a weather-eye to his own future, enthusiastically promoted the queen's marriage to Philip. According to his time-table it should have been contracted and consummated before England re-entered the Roman Catholic fold. So Paget hitched his star to the Habsburg chariot. However, the antipathy was a fundamental one, and not confined merely to policy disagreements. As the owner of secularised property, a prominent Edwardian, and a layman touched with the common suspicion of clerical pretensions, Paget opposed all that the bishop represented.[58]

The division at the centre of power cannot be explained in the simplistic terms of a Gardiner–Paget confrontation. There was much more to it than that. Sir Henry Jerningham, Sir Francis Englefield, Sir Robert Rochester, and other of Mary's household servants, some of whom had suffered for their faith in the previous reign, resented the profit and power now enjoyed by prominent members of the Edwardian establishment. Religious opinion on the council ranged from convinced papalism, through conservatism, to reforming sympathies. A traditional anti-clericalism was sharpened by the appointment of four bishops to the council, Gardiner's installation as lord chancellor, and the fear that regulars would reappear in the House of Lords. This confusion of antagonisms and loyalties was further complicated by a political fluidity. Alliances were ephemeral and positions frequently shifted. So Bishop Thirlby lent a general support to Gardiner but disapproved of his precipitate conduct in religious matters. And Pembroke, who supported the chancellor in Mary's first parliament, was aligned with Paget against him in her second.[59]

In this mosaic of political disagreement two facts were of crucial importance: that, as in Edward VI's reign, the hard-core of the government sat in the Lords, but that, in contrast, the disputants were willing to carry their antagonisms into parliament. This cannot be condemned out-of-hand as an irresponsible act. Mary's objectives – and the lord chancellor's too – could only be fulfilled through statute. When Gardiner acted unilaterally to push his own policies through parliament, politicians who opposed him had to resist him there – and most of them sat in the Lords. Furthermore some aspects of Mary's programme were unpopular in certain quarters – in particular the reversal of the Edwardian Reformation, the restoration of papal supremacy,[60] and the implicit threat to secularised lands. Councillors were tempted to exploit such fears and antagonisms in order to thwart Gardiner's parliamentary designs. It was not just a cynical exercise. The widespread concern of many members about the revival of religious persecution and the security of their property was genuine enough.[61] Nevertheless prominent politicians, some of whom were councillors, did use parliament to coerce the queen and defeat her chancellor. They even trampled underfoot some of her more important measures in the pursuit of their own faction fights. It is difficult to avoid the conclusion that councillors such as Gardiner, Paget, and those who supported them, were guilty of gross negligence and dereliction of duty. It was their responsibility, as the queen's councillors, to manage parliament in her interest. Almost to a man they reneged on their duty.

There were few hints of what was to come when Mary's first parliament met. Although fears and doubts about her political intentions were already being voiced, she had governed with a studied moderation until then. She had not conducted a pogrom against those involved in the duke of Northumberland's attempted coup. In a proclamation of 18 August she had reaffirmed her own religious position, but declared her intention not to coerce her subjects until 'such time as further order by common assent may be taken therein'. In the interest of law and order she even imposed an impartial ban on preaching by both reformers and conservatives.[62] A fortnight later Mary publicly promised to honour Edward VI's debts and remitted the outstanding instalment of the subsidy granted by his last parliament.[63] These popular moves were followed a month later by a third proclamation which set forth the queen's titles, including that of Supreme Head of the Church of England and Ireland.[64] Despite her personal loathing of it, she exercised public restraint. Its inclusion in her official styling must have reassured some of those who feared a precipitate restoration of the pope.

Mary's first parliament assembled on 5 October. Her cautious and calculated public conduct, coupled with the euphoric hangover from her coronation just four days before, may have contributed to a quiet start. By 21 October the repeal of all treasons (except those specified in the 1352 act) and all praemunires made since 1509 had passed both Houses. On that day Mary took the unusual step of giving her assent to it during the session. She also approved the two restitutions for Edward Courtenay and his mother, the Lady Marquess Gertrude. It was a curiously mixed bag which hardly seemed to justify such prompt action. Yet, in this event, we are treated to the first glimpse of managerial politicking which was to be so damaging to the performance of parliament, and especially of the Lords, in 1553/4.

Courtenay and his mother were survivors of the 'white rose' party which had been destroyed by Henry VIII in 1538. They had spent 15 years in the Tower where, since June 1548, their fellow prisoners had included Stephen Gardiner. Mary's accession dramatically reversed their fortunes: Gardiner became lord chancellor, Gertrude a companion of the queen, and Edward earl of Devon.[65] Courtenay himself was of little significance. He was politically naive, spineless and morally vicious. His importance derives from the design of some leading politicians that Mary should take unto herself an English husband. Mary thought differently and negotiations were already in hand for a match with Emperor Charles V's son, Philip. This did not deter Gardiner. He promoted Courtenay as a rival and native candidate and he even duped the queen into serving as accomplice to his designs. If Courtenay was to be an eligible suitor, the stigma of corrupt blood consequent upon his father's attainder had to be removed. Hence the speed with which restitution bills were rushed through parliament. When the imperial ambassador, Simon Renard, asked Mary who had advised her to assent to them during the session, she named her lord chancellor.[66]

Soon after parliament reassembled on 24 October, it became clear that the honeymoon was over, if indeed it had not evaporated earlier.[67] The repeal of the Edwardian Reformation statutes ran into stiff opposition in the Commons, where debate extended over five days[68] and 80 voted against it.[69] It was a signal to the queen that she had no hope of restoring papal supremacy in this parliament.[70] At the same time she came under pressure from politicians who, for a variety of reasons, feared the consequences of a Spanish alliance. Whether or not criticism of the bill repealing the Edwardian Reformation extended to the Lords,[71] the campaign to promote Courtenay's marriage suit was certainly devised by councillors who sat there. Bishop Gardiner was the architect. With a motley collection of aides and politicians of like sympathies, ranging from the queen's household servants to the reforming earl of Pembroke and the Catholic Derby, he organised parliamentary support for his protégé in both Houses. There emerged a loose, ephemeral connection of peers and bishops, knights and burgesses, who followed Gardiner's lead because of their hostility to a foreign marriage.[72] Therefore it is not too fanciful to suspect that when, at the end of October, the Commons determined to petition the queen to marry an Englishman, the hands of the lord chancellor were pulling the strings.[73]

Mary stalled with excuses and pretexts until she had agreed to a formal acceptance of Philip's suit. On 8 November her council endorsed her decision, with Gardiner's rivals, Paget and Arundel, hot in her support.[74] Now she could present parliament with a *fait accompli*. So, eight days later, she finally agreed to hear its petition. Her peremptory rejection of it, in the typically grand Tudor manner, effectively marked the end of the campaign to promote Courtenay. She even accused Gardiner of inciting the Commons to resist her wishes. Some of the nobles and councillors in his following deserted to her side.[75] In December the bishop himself recognised the inevitable and, in a lightning reversal of his position, he proceeded to sell the Spanish marriage to the governing class.[76] Although parliament was prolonged by protracted debates and quasi-judicial proceedings on a bill to invalidate the duke of Norfolk's attainder and restore his confiscated property, it was dissolved early in the same month.[77]

Early signs of the disruptive parliamentary effects of Court politics are discernible in the legislative record of this parliament. As 34 acts were passed in a mere two months, and 22 of them originated in the Lords, the first impression is one of continuity with the Edwardian parliaments. However appearances are deceptive. The first parliament of a new monarch, especially one whose policies represented an about-turn from the two previous reigns, naturally extended a merciful hand to their victims: ten acts, almost one-third of the entire legislative output, consisted of restitutions in blood. They all commenced in the Lords and their passage was probably a formality.[78] The confirmation of the attainder of Northumberland, Cranmer and others, a bill for the continuance of acts, and another for the denization of specified individuals, all started there too and had a rapid unhindered passage through parliament.[79] In contrast, two of the more important public bills originated in the Upper House,[80] but four[81] did not. Behind the facade of the Lords' continued arithmetical superiority as an initiating House the reality was quite different. Of course each parliament was a different creature. No two sessions were the same, either in the relative importance of Lords and Commons or in the distribution of the workload between them. Nor would it be wise to assume, at this stage, a direct causal relationship between the eruption of Court politics into parliament and the diminishing role of the Lords. Nevertheless the drift ought to be noted, especially in the light of events in the two parliaments of 1554.

By then the political temperature in Court and council had risen dramatically, as personal rivalries and policy disagreements intensified and an acidic bitterness poisoned relations within the ruling clique. Stephen Gardiner continued to be the catalyst of this political in-fighting. In a long political career spanning more than 20 years he had displayed driving energy and considerable skill, flawed by an irascible temper and arrogance. He readily created intense loyalty[82] or fierce hostility in those around him and he was seldom far from the centre of controversy: as Thomas Cromwell's opponent in the thirties, as the conservatives' leader in their power-struggle with the reformers in the twilight years of Henry VIII, and as the symbol of resistance to the Edwardian Reformation. Henry excluded him from his son's regency council which he believed – with some justice – would not be able to control him.[83] The Edwardian council feared that, because of his formidable personality and managerial talents, his parliamentary presence would imperil the religious Reformation on which it had embarked. So it felt obliged to adopt draconian measures, imprisoning him during three parliamentary sessions and finally depriving him of his bishopric.[84]

When Mary made him lord chancellor in the summer of 1553, Gardiner obtained, at long last, the power which had eluded him for so long. With characteristic energy he threw himself into the preparations for Mary's first parliament.[85] By the time it assembled he had secured the election of a sizeable following of servants and clients,[86] many of whom sat in successive assemblies until his death.[87] In the previous reign he had strenuously denied the existence of a parliamentary following – 'Winchester's faction, as som terme it'. Yet in the same breath he tacitly admitted as much when he threatened the privy council which had imprisoned him:

> If it should be of anye man through polecy to kepe me from the Parliament, it were good to be remembred whether mine absence from the upper house, with the absence of those I have used to name in the nether house, wil not engender more cause of objection, if oportunitye serve hereafter, then my presence with such as I should appoynte, were there.[88]

So far as Mary's prospects of parliamentary success were concerned, Gardiner was a potent force for good or ill. His experience as an electoral[89] and managerial politician, his parliamentary following in both Commons[90] and Lords,[91] and his influence as presiding officer in the Upper House made him a formidable parliamentary figure. He brought to his duties the authority of a commanding presence, a driving energy, and a conscientious attention to business. His addresses at the opening and concluding ceremonies of parliament received extravagant praise from eyewitnesses.[92] He put his arts of persuasion and stage-management at Mary's disposal, accusing himself and the rest of parliament as guilty of the schism, and confessing that, when he sued at Rome for the dissolution of Henry VIII's first marriage, 'he did wrong in obedience to the King's orders out of a hope to please him'.[93] Moreover he was present at every daily sitting of the second and third of the queen's parliaments. The last public service which he rendered before his death was the opening of her fourth.[94] Gardiner's role was central to the parliamentary drama of 1554.

The prologue to that drama – Wyatt's abortive rebellion – augured well for Mary's second parliament, which had been summoned to ratify the Spanish marriage. By the time it met, opposition to the match had become indelibly associated with treason. However, the government took no chances. It appointed a sub-committee of the privy council to draft its legislative programme.[95] Courtenay's imprisonment denied a rallying-point to opponents of the Spanish marriage. New peers were created and episcopal vacancies were filled.[96] On this occasion there was also a novel supplement to the traditional managerial resources. The imperial ambassador recommended that, as parliament had been summoned, the peers should be 'conciliated by pensions and liberalities'. His advice was heeded. By the time it met, gold chains, pensions, benefices, and offices in Philip's household had been given or held out as alluring promises to almost one-third of the Lords.[97]

Yet all came to nought, because at the very heart of power there was no unity of purpose. The queen and two of the most influential men in her government had divergent, even conflicting, policies. The relationship between the three principal actors was a complex one. Paget's support of Mary's intention to marry a Spaniard was genuine, albeit self-interested, whereas Gardiner was a belated fellow traveller. The queen and her chancellor favoured a papal restoration and the renewal of the laws against heresy, whilst Paget shuddered for the fate of secularised lands. Gardiner schemed to exclude Elizabeth from the succession, but his rival was anxious to protect her rights. As we have already seen, there were also disagreements about the time-table to be adopted. The consequence was a confused conflict of policy and personality within official circles. Gardiner was undeterred by his failure to call parliament at Oxford, as a punishment for London's luke-warmness during Wyatt's rebellion. He proceeded to graft his own measures on to the official Marian programme. When the council agreed that only a few measures, dear to Mary, should be placed before parliament – in particular ratification of her marriage, and extension of the treason laws to protect her husband – Gardiner went his own way. He ignored the council's decision and devised other controversial measures of his own: a renewal of the heresy laws, the strengthening of ecclesiastical jurisdiction, the restitution of the see of Durham and its tem-poralities, and Elizabeth's exclusion from the succession. He may have contemplated, too, the restoration of papal authority – or at least a statute enabling Mary to drop the odious title of supreme head.[98] His was a programme which would introduce into the Lords the sensitive subjects of religion, secularised property and the succession. Disaffection and disarray were bound to follow.

To give the bishop his due, Gardiner was not entirely devoid of tact or discretion. On 5 April 1554 he wrote to Cardinal Pole, the pope's legate entrusted with the mission to reunite England with Rome. His letter was an advice to Pole to write to parliament, and to confirm landowners in their continued possession of secularised property.[99] He also nipped in the bud a Court con-spiracy, which was designed to persuade Mary to assume a novel authority and 'do what she liste', and he hurried a bill through parliament in order to thwart the conspirators. The evidence of this episode derives from William Fleetwood, London's recorder, in 1575. The conspirators had argued that, as Mary was not a king, her power was indeterminate and undefined. Therefore she was not bound by the restraints imposed upon past kings. Their argument was drawn up in 'platt forme' and secretly presented to the queen, who strongly disapproved and promptly consulted Gardiner. He condemned such 'pernitious devises' which were 'most horrible to be thought of'. Although Mary concurred, and cast the offending book into the fire, Gardiner took the precaution of drawing a bill to confirm that the queen enjoyed the same authority as her male progenitors. This astute move forestalled a change of heart by the queen and stopped 'the mouthes of them that were then musing of mischeifes'. Even so the bill did not pass without question. One member in the Commons questioned its necessity and suspected a sinister motive.

If we be a Lawe do allowe unto her majestie all such preheminencies and authorities in all thinges, as any of her most noble progenitors kinges of England, ever had . . . Then do we give to her majestie the same power that her most noble progenitor William the Conqueror had, who seized the landes of the English people and did give the same unto strangers.

Ironically this member suspected Gardiner of pro-Spanish sympathies. Despite his doubts the bill was eventually passed, after amendment in committee. Fleetwood's tale is incorrect in certain aspects: in particular the measure did not commence in the Lords, as he claimed, but in the Commons. Nevertheless there is no reason to dismiss out of hand the essentials of Fleetwood's surprisingly favourable account of Gardiner's conduct.[100] On the other hand none of this alters the fact that Gardiner's personal legislative programme threatened disruption in parliament and spelt trouble for the queen. Events turned out that way. Councillors polarised around Gardiner and Paget and worked out their quarrels in parliament. They did so in a political climate in which widespread fears about the future made both Houses a fertile recruiting ground for those who would oppose the government's programme or Gardiner's designs.

The result was disastrous for both Mary and her chancellor. The ratification of the Spanish marriage sailed through smoothly enough. That is hardly surprising because it embodied a cherished desire of the queen and that was usually sufficient to guarantee an easy parliamentary passage. Although the House of Lords was to display an uncommon disrespect for her wishes in this parliament, it must be viewed in the context of the continuing loyalty of the governing class to the Tudor dynasty. Despite the stresses of her reign, that loyalty survived more or less intact into the next. The parliamentary disruption of 1554 must be seen in this light. When it is, the extraordinary delinquency of the Upper House becomes a disturbing phenomenon which must have shaken the queen's confidence in it.

The first signs of trouble were not long in coming. The bill for the restitution of Durham eventually became an act, but only after lengthy proceedings in the Commons over property rights.[101] The rest of the legislation sought by Mary and Gardiner stuck fast or failed in the Lords. The bill to extend the protection of the treason laws to Philip was rendered so ineffective by a bill committee that, once it had passed the House, it did not proceed to the Commons.[102] One measure against heresy went no further than a second reading in the Lords, after a safe passage through the Lower House,[103] and another was actually rejected – again after the Commons had approved it.[104] Gardiner did not even risk the introduction of his bills for reunion with Rome and the settlement of the succession. By the end of the session his programme lay in ruins, and his royal mistress fared little better. The architect of their mutual discomfort was Lord Paget. On the committee to scrutinise and reform the treasons bill he, together with Arundel, Shrewsbury and Rich, outnumbered Gardiner's supporters.[105] When the chancellor approached him with a proposal to introduce a bill disinheriting Elizabeth, he turned it down. In a scribbled note to Renard, Paget implored him to persuade Mary to dissolve parliament. Otherwise the bishop's 'private leanings will cause him to bring forward proposals that will heat the people altogether too much'.[106] He then proceeded to organise opposition, both to a lesser Gardiner measure which terminated pensions to married priests and to the heresy bills.[107]

Paget's conduct is something of an enigma. He favoured the Spanish marriage yet, as Mary later explained to Renard, he opposed the treasons bill more stubbornly than anyone else.[108] His behaviour can only be attributed to pique and an irresponsible obstruction of his rival. Renard, who was always prone to panic, feared that Paget might even abandon his pro-Habsburg position 'out of spite in order to cross the designs of the Chancellor, who never consults him about Parliament'.[109] Nevertheless this does not explain why he was able to command such widespread support in the Upper House. Certainly religion did not determine behaviour, because he could call upon conservatives, such as Arundel, Shrewsbury and Sussex, as well as trimmers[110] and reformers.[111] Nor is hostility to Gardiner an adequate explanation. It required another issue to align a majority (which included some of the chancellor's usual allies) against his legislative proposals and even some of the queen's as well. That issue was the fate of secularised property. Early in the session Lord Rich had cast the sole dissenting vote against the bill to restore the bishopric of Durham and its temporalities – probably a gesture of resistance to the principle of restoring expropriated lands to the Church. Paget later claimed that Rich had been instrumental in spreading disaffection in the Lords by playing on the peers' concern for the fate of their ex-monastic property.[112] In the hectic scramble to ingratiate themselves with the queen when the session was over, the air was filled with charge and counter-charge. Pembroke and others blamed Paget whose opinion, 'that it was proposed to take away the Church property from them', provoked them to act.[113] Paget placed the responsibility squarely on the shoulders of Rich, who had convinced him with the same argument.[114]

Whatever the motives of these troubled peers, the effect of their resistance was to frustrate both Mary and Gardiner in many of the measures most precious to them. The disturbed political climate of the Lords was expressed in other ways too. Apart from the spare harvest of 15 acts passed by this parliament, the House considered another 15 bills, of which eleven had originated in the Commons. Five of them proceeded no further than a second reading,[115] one slept in committee,[116] and four were rejected.[117] The Lords also redrafted a Commons' bill against excess in apparel; it required the deletion of the last 17 lines of the confirmation of the duke of Suffolk's attainder, which the Lower House could not accept;[118] and of course it excised from the treasons bill the vital clause which made it a treasonable offence to take up arms against Philip.[119] The legislative record of the Upper House was a sorry one and accurately reflected its fractious mood.[120] Moreover it was a depleted House. Apart from the brief session in the closing days of Mary's life, it was the only mid-Tudor parliament to register an average daily attendance of less than half the eligible members.[121] Although, once the session had ended, Mary vented her spleen on Paget in particular, she must have been disillusioned by the Upper House in general, where her councillors had sacrificed her wishes to their internecine quarrels and the rest had fallen away from their usual standard of responsibility.[122]

The queen's shaken confidence was not restored by the time parliament met again in November of the same year. Inevitably the restitution of Cardinal Pole began in the Lords. So did the 'great Bill touching the Repeal of Acts against the See of Rome'.[123] That is not surprising. It was drawn by a joint-committee of the two Houses, with the judges prominent in its work. Therefore it was natural that it should first pass the scrutiny of the Lords, where the judges sat as legal assistants.[124] However, seven of the other nine measures which were probably officially inspired began in the Commons.[125] The two exceptions were renewed attempts to enact the confirmation of the duke of Suffolk's attainder and the extension of the treason laws to protect Philip. Furthermore the second of these was redrafted, enlarged and, in the process, transformed by the Commons. Public confidence, as well as the queen's, had been shaken by the Lords' uncharacteristic fractiousness and irresponsibility in the previous April. Whereas two-fifths of all bills in the Edwardian parliaments had been submitted first to the Upper House, that proportion was now halved.

The Lords' temper in this session was a volatile one. It may have assembled in chastened mood, after its flurry of heady opposition in the last parliament, and certainly the opening days of the session were quiet. On the other hand ominous signs of future trouble were once again present from the beginning. Dissenters always had two courses of action open to them, whenever they were faced with objectionable government policies and bills. They could confront the Crown, or they could resort to self-effacing absenteeism which acquired a particular edge if they departed without a royal licence. The fact that 18 bishops and peers (or 24% of the eligible membership) chose to stay away from the entire session[126] is not in itself a mark of disaffection but, as we shall see, when it is combined with the incidence of departures during the session, absenteeism does, for once take on a more sinister political aspect. Those who remained found themselves in a dilemma, because the defeated official measures of the previous parliament were inevitably revived. However, the House was still in a critical mood. So it passed the treasons bill, but debated ecclesiastical authority at some length before re-enacting the heresy laws. It also spearheaded parliament's pressure on the papal legate, Cardinal Pole, in order to secure the inclusion of the papal dispensation on secularised property in the reunion bill.[127]

It was the treasons bill, however, which spawned conflict and crystallised opposition. When it was introduced into the Lords, it was no more than the original measure of April 1554. As such it received the Lords' assent and went down to the Commons on 6 December.[128] Prompted perhaps by one of Gardiner's clients,[129] it was thrown out and redrawn, between 17 and 20 December, on the grounds that it supplied inadequate protection of Philip's interests and security. Not only was he to enjoy the full protection of the treason laws. He was also to be protector and guardian of any issue from his marriage, if Mary predeceased him during the heir's minority. A regency council, consisting of six bishops, six senior peers and six barons, was to assist him in governing the realm. Its consent would also be necessary to summon a parliament, declare war, and permit the heir's marriage. The terms of the bill appeared to touch the peers upon a most sensitive point of privilege. Whilst they would bear the main burden of responsibility on the regency council, they were to be denied what they regarded as their traditional right to appoint a protector during a minority. During the Christmas recess several of them warned Renard that the House would throw the bill out, because it gave the Commons the right to participate in a decision which was traditionally the concern of the privy council. Although the regency council was eventually removed from the bill, Philip was left as the effective head of State in the event of a regency.

The alteration did nothing to appease aristocratic resentment but Renard, the usual source of our information, was misinformed about its causes. After all it was no novelty to use statute for this purpose. Perhaps he was deliberately misinformed by peers who sought a pretext to conceal their real concern about Philip's future authority. There was widespread hostility to proposals for his coronation (which might enlarge his power). There were rumours that he sought only to involve England in war with France, and that he would appoint Spaniards to high office during his protectorate. Indeed on the penultimate day of this parliament an address was presented to Philip and Mary seeking confirmation that he would not employ foreigners. Peers who were high in the king's favour but fearful for the future were liable to mask their real motives behind an explanation which would not be offensive to him. However, some may have been piqued as well by the Commons' effrontery in drafting such a measure (or by the chancellor's hand therein). At the moment of decision, however, the peers chose discretion rather than valour. Between 27 December and 12 January, whilst the regency bill was agonising its way through the Commons, eight peers including Arundel, Cumberland, Pembroke and Sussex quietly withdrew from parliament – all but two of them without the queen's permission.[130] The keeper of the privy seal, Bedford, sued out a licence, naming Arundel and Pembroke as his proxies. However he stayed his hand, absenting himself when the regency bill was before the Lords on 14–16 January, before returning for the closing ceremonies on the afternoon of the 16th.[131] All the evidence points to a delicate, tactful, and well-timed withdrawal.

Historians have customarily focussed their attention on the mass secession of 106 knights and burgesses from the Commons during the last week of the parliament.[132] Although there are alternative explanations[133] of their action, it is probable that they were politically motivated. Like their social superiors in the other place, they staged a protest against the regency bill. Furthermore the odds are in favour of a collaboration between the seceders from the two Houses. Managerial politics, after all, were not unknown. Gardiner practised them and Paget had done so in April 1554. Would it be so surprising that Bedford, Pembroke and others, who had seen fingers burnt in the previous parliament, should practise the politics of discretion and at the same time serve as puppet masters, using members of the Commons to sing their song of protest for them? Amongst those who walked out of the Commons were between ten and twenty from constituencies where the Bedford interest was strong. The possibility of such a political connection ought not to be dismissed out of hand.[134]

In his recent study of Mary's reign D. M. Loades discounted the possibility that prominent peers either opposed the regency bill or absented themselves in protest. He drew attention to Philip's shrewd and successful policy of conciliation towards Paget, Arundel and Pembroke during the autumn of 1554. On this account he dismissed Renard's report that several peers had stayed away to avoid giving their approval to the bill: partly because the ambassador's list included Arundel and Pembroke, but also because he was well wide of the mark when he explained their conduct. Renard was certainly guilty of bad history when he wrote that they were offended because it was the Lords' traditional right to name a protector. As we have seen, however (and as Loades himself acknowledged), there were other real and substantial fears about the future which were sufficient to drive peers to protest. The fact that Renard misunderstood (or was misled about) their motives does not negate the fact that Arundel, Pembroke and others did withdraw as the regency bill ground its way through parliament. In this at least he was right. Furthermore the past record of these men should not be forgotten. Pembroke had backed Courtenay against Philip. Paget and Arundel had sat on the committee which, in April 1554, rendered useless the bill to extend the protection of the treason laws to Philip. They, together with Pembroke, were in disgrace after that parliament. Now Arundel and Pembroke quietly withdrew. When Loades writes that the intense feelings generated by the regency bill 'were contained in committee and in debate' was it not because nobles chose to be absentees rather than the spokesmen of parliamentary discontent? The conduct of Bedford, an Edwardian who, like the marquess of Winchester, had skilfully changed horses several times since his career began in Henry VIII's reign, reinforces this possibility. So too does their attendance record, and the affiliations of many of the 106 unlicensed absentees from the Commons. Loades discounts any political motive for their withdrawal, and it is true that the evidence for such prompting is only circumstantial. Nevertheless it cannot be discounted, because managerial politicians did practise in the mid-Tudor parliaments. Moreover the wish of men, high in office and with much to lose, to protest without consequent pains or penalties is both reasonable and understandable.[135]

By the time the Lords reassembled in 1555, Mary's patience may have been sorely tried. In her first parliament Gardiner and Pembroke had manipulated a pressure group on the subject of marriage; in her second the Lords had sabotaged official measures; and in her third the peers had mixed critical scrutiny and pressure tactics with discreet absenteeism which could be just as detrimental to efficiency as direct confrontation. In fact the Commons was the focal point of opposition to Marian policies in this parliament. The act to restore first fruits and tenths to the papacy had a rough passage there, whilst the bill to penalise exiles was actually defeated.[136] The shift in emphasis and activity may have been caused by Gardiner's death, three weeks after parliament met. The event had several immediate and significant consequences. The removal of Paget's rival naturally damped down faction politics and lowered the temperature in the Lords. On the other hand the absence of the late chancellor's commanding authority and assiduous attention to business caused discipline to slacken and gave advantage to hot spirits in the Lower House.[137] At the same time privy councillors in the Commons may have filled the managerial vacuum left by Gardiner's departure.[138]

Neale and Notestein remained mesmerised by their Commons fixation and true to the strange misconception that an ability and willingness to oppose the Crown were marks of political success. The former in particular almost venerated the unruly behaviour of the Lower House in 1555 as the parliamentary pinnacle of the reign. Of course it was quite the reverse. Conflict and opposition were harmful to efficiency and productivity and undermined the very function and purpose of parliament. The year 1555 marked the parliamentary nadir of the reign; and to some extent this state of affairs resulted from the Lords' recent unreliability. Although on this occasion it seems to have conducted itself with more of its customary moderation and responsibility, it paid the penalty for its past indiscretions. Its business shrank: only 18% of all the bills before parliament began there and its share in the initiation of acts suffered another drop from 43% to 29%. Two of the government's most important measures were submitted to the Lords first, because it was worried about the reception which they would receive in the Commons. It must have been aware that the surrender of first fruits to the papacy, coupled with a request for a subsidy, would provoke criticism; similarly that its bill to penalise exiles would touch very few members of the Upper House. Tactics therefore determined the choice of initiating House, because bills might stand a better chance of success in the Commons if they were already endorsed with the Lords' assent. Events justified the government's fears. First fruits were only restored after 'long arguments', amendment, and a division in which 126 knights and burgesses voted against the bill. The penal measure against exiles survived the Lords, though even there it had five readings and underwent revision. However, the assent of the Upper House could not prevent it from being dashed in the Commons.[139] Both the critical initiative and the bulk of business now belonged to the Lower House, and the House of Lords was but a pale shadow of its vigorous Edwardian predecessor.

A revival might have been expected in 1558, when so many bills were concerned with war, which was the traditional preserve of the nobility. Its pressure-tactics and intimate involvement in the voting of a subsidy amply demonstrated that it still had considerable parliamentary muscle, which it was willing to use when the occasion demanded.[140] Nevertheless its legislative record continued to be unimpressive. It initiated two acts, for the provision of armour and the prevention of abuses in the recruiting system, but six other military bills began in the Commons; so did three of the four xenophobic and penal measures directed against the French. The Lords' share in the initiation of bills (28%) and acts (38%) actually increased, but its performance remained inferior to that of the Commons and, indeed, to its own in the previous reign. Nor did the brief addled session of November 1558 do anything to suggest a dramatic recovery, when it initiated only four of the 14 bills before parliament. It had not lost its power to intimidate the Commons, as it showed when once again it demanded a grant of revenue. Nevertheless its legislative role had diminished. It had become less productive and the sponsors of bills now preferred to submit them to the other House first. The aberrant behaviour of the Lords in 1553–4 had much to do with this, even though it is impossible to measure precisely its effect. Its erratic conduct was, in turn, the result of the 'overspill' of Court politics into parliament. The extent of the decline must not be exaggerated, nor should its permanence be assumed. The causes were short term and the effects immediate, but they may have been ephemeral. It cannot be taken for granted that the House thereafter slithered into the obscurity to which it was so conveniently assigned by Neale and Notestein. In Elizabeth's reign it was still capable of matching and even excelling the Lower

House in its share of the legislative initiative and output.[141] Yet it cannot be denied that, despite such variations, the Commons' share of business and productivity inexorably increased in the second half of the sixteenth century and that its advance can be traced back to the parliaments of 1553–4.[142]

Epilogue

Of course the last word has not been said on the role of the mid-Tudor House of Lords. It is to be hoped, however, that future parliamentary studies cannot be confined to a study of Crown and Commons, with a casual nod in the direction of the other House. In a parliamentary trinity all parties to the legislative process warrant a thorough scrutiny. If it is realistic to focus attention on the heartland of power, then it is the Crown which should enjoy precedence over both of its parliamentary partners. It was, after all, the motivating force of parliament, determining its life and death, or the limbo of prorogation. It remained the dynamic force, the initiator of major bills, the seeker after money, and the managerial expert. In any case parliaments ought to be seen in their right perspective. They were occasions, interludes, and not a continuing part of the machine of government. However, there is another face to the coin. When they did meet, the government had to persuade *both* chambers to accede to its requests, because the Upper House, no less than the Commons, was essential to the fulfilment of its parliamentary objectives. Secondly, the Lords enjoyed a particular prestige derived from its position as the original nucleus of parliament, the older House, and the assembly of an elite in Church and State.[143] Moreover in normal circumstances it was, for a variety of reasons, the more efficient and productive legislative body: its size was more manageable; its membership was more experienced; its volume of business was not so large as to become unwieldy; and it enjoyed the inestimable benefits of its legal assistants, entrée at Court, and therefore easy access to the monarch. These institutional advantages were reinforced by the informal authority which individual peers and bishops exercised as managerial politicians. The Musgraves working on Lord Wharton's behalf, the silent manipulations of Arundel, Bedford and Pembroke in protest at the regency bill, the latter's sponsorship of Courtenay – even

Thomas Seymour's clumsy parliamentary stirs – demonstrate the fact well enough. Small matter for surprise, therefore, that the Edwardian council feared 'Winchester's faction' and preferred to keep the bishop shut up in the Tower.

In spite of all these advantages, the reputation and reliability of the House of Lords sagged during the early Marian parliaments. The sense of responsibility which invested its proceedings and its greater institutional efficiency were the two vital and customary contributions which it made to the success of parliaments. When its members reneged on the first, they impaired the second. They also provoked an immediate loss of royal and public confidence, starkly demonstrated by the dramatic fall in the number and proportion of bills introduced there in preference to the Commons. However, a new reign brought with it fresh opportunities and the chance to wipe the slate clean. Only a thorough and systematic examination of the Elizabethan parliaments will prove the point, but it does look as if the Lords recovered some of the ground lost in Mary's reign. In any case it continued to be a vital parliamentary force. Sir Edward Coke, writing early in the next century, could make the observation

that Parliaments have not succeeded well in five Cases. First when the king hath been in displeasure with his Lords or with his Commons. 2. When any of the Great Lords were at variance between themselves. 3. When there is no good correspondence between the Lords and the Commons. 4. When there was no unitie between the Commons themselves. 5. When there was no preparation for the Parliament before it began.[144]

In the first three points Coke put his finger on some of the problems in the early Marian parliaments. He also acknowledged the continuing importance of the House of Lords, even when Tudor England was no more than a memory.

ABBREVIATIONS

A.J.L.H.	American Journal of Legal History
A.P.C.	Acts of the Privy Council
B.I.H.R.	Bulletin of the Institute of Historical Research
B.J.R.L.	Bulletin of the John Rylands Library
C.P.R.	Calendar of the Patent Rolls
Cal.S.P.Dom.	Calendar of State Papers Domestic
Cal.S.P.For.	Calendar of State Papers Foreign
Cal.S.P.Span.	Calendar of State Papers Spanish
Cal.S.P.Ven.	Calendar of State Papers Venetian
C.H.J.	Cambridge Historical Journal
C.J.	Journals of the House of Commons (manuscript)
C.J.	Journals of the House of Commons (printed)
D.N.B.	Dictionary of National Biography
E.H.R.	English Historical Review
G.E.C.	G. E. Cokayne, The Complete Peerage
H.J.	Historical Journal
H.L.R.O.	House of Lords Record Office
H.L.Q.	Huntington Library Quarterly
H.M.C.	Historical Manuscripts Commission Reports
H.P.T.Biogs	History of Parliament Trust Biographies
J.M.H.	Journal of Modern History
L.J.	Journals of the House of Lords (manuscript)
L.J.	Journals of the House of Lords (printed)
L.P.	Letters and Papers, Foreign and Domestic, of the Reign of Henry VIII
PP.	Past and Present
T.R.H.S.	Transactions of the Royal Historical Society
V.C.H.	Victoria County Histories

APPENDIX A: COMPOSITION

The distinction between *nominal* and *actual* membership adopted in the text is also used here. Any bishop or peer qualifies as a nominal member, but only if he received a writ of summons and was still eligible to attend when the parliament met was he an actual member. Whether he turned up or not is irrelevant.

I. The lords spiritual

	Edward VI					I Mary (Oct.)	Philip and Mary				
	1	2/3	3/4	5/6	7		I Mary (April)	I & 2	2 & 3	4 & 5 (Jan.)	5 & 6 (Nov.)
A. *Number of Sees* at time of each parliamentary session	27	27	27	26	25	25	26	26	26	26	26
B. *Bishops: Nominal Membership* at time of each parliamentary session	26	27	26	23	22	23	22	22	26	23	21
C. *Ineligible Bishops* at time of each parliamentary session:											
1. royal detention	1	1	1	1	0	6	1	1	1	0	0
2. royal service overseas	0	0	0	0	0	0	1	0	1	0	0
D. *Actual Membership* eligible lords spiritual at time of each parliamentary session:											
1. bishops	25	26	25	22	22	17	20	21	24	23	21
2. abbot of Westminster	0	0	0	0	0	0	0	0	0	1	1
Total eligible (i.e. actual											

II. The lords temporal

A. Peerage: Nominal Membership at time of each parliamentary session:

dukes	2	2	2	2	2	2	2	1	1	1	1	1
marquesses	2	2	2	2	2	1	2	1	1	1	1	1
earls	14	13	13	14	14	15	14	15	15	15	15	15
viscounts	0	0	0	1	1	1	1	1	2	2	2	2
barons	36	38	39	36	36	36	36	40	39	39	38	38
Total	54	55	56	55	55	55	55	58	58	58	57	57

B. Ineligible Peers at time of each parliamentary session:

1. minority	6	7	8	7	7	6	6	7	5	5	5	5
2. royal detention	0	0	1	3	0	0	1	1	0	0	0	0
3. royal service	0	0	0	0	0	0	0	0	0	2	2	2
4. exile	0	0	0	0	0	0	0	0	1	0	0	0
5. poverty	1	1	1	1	1	1	1	0	0	0	0	0
6. reason not known	0	0	0	1	1	0	0	0	0	0	0	0
Total	7	8	10	12	9	7	8	8	6	7	7	7

C. Actual Membership eligible peers at time of each session:

dukes	1	1	0	2	2	2	1	0	0	0	1	1
marquesses	2	2	2	2	2	1	1	1	1	1	1	1
earls	13	13	13	12	13	13	14	13	13	13	14	14
viscounts	0	0	0	1	1	1	1	2	2	2	2	1
barons	31	31	31	26	28	30	34	34	36	33	33	

APPENDIX A—*(contd)*

	Edward VI					1 Mary (Oct.)	1 Mary (April)	Philip and Mary			
	1	2/3	3/4	5/6	7			1 & 2	2 & 3	4 & 5 (Jan.)	5 & 6 (Nov.)
eldest sons summoned v.p.	0	0	0	0	3	2	2	3	3	2	2
Total eligible (i.e. actual membership)	47	47	46	43	49	50	52	53	55	52	52

III. Total actual membership of the mid-Tudor Lords

72	73	71	65	68	65	70	71	76	74	72

APPENDIX B: ROLL OF THE 'ACTUAL' MEMBERS OF THE HOUSE OF LORDS, 1547–58

I. The lords spiritual

Name	See occupied at time of meeting of Edward VI's first parliament, Nov. 1547	Consecrations, promotions, resignations, deprivations and deaths between 4 Nov. 1547 and end of Mary's last parliament on 17 Nov. 1558
Robert Aldrich (Aldridge)	Carlisle	d. 5 March 1556
William Barlow	St David's	transl. to Bath and Wells, Feb. 1548; res. *ante* 4 Oct. 1553
Ralph Baynes	—	cons. bp of Coventry and Lichfield, 18 Nov. 1554
John Bird (Byrd)	Chester	depr. March 1554
Edmund Bonner	London	depr. 1 Oct. 1549; rest. 5 Sept. 1553 and restoration ratified, 2 March 1554[1]
Gilbert Bourne	—	cons. bp of Bath and Wells, 1 April 1554
James Brooks	—	cons. bp of Gloucester, 1 April 1554
Arthur Bulkeley	Bangor	d. 14 March 1553
Paul Bush	Bristol	depr. March 1554[2]
John Chambers	Peterborough	d. 7 Feb. 1556
John Christopherson	—	cons. bp of Chichester, 21 Nov. 1557; d. *ante* 28 Dec. 1558
George Cotes (Coates)	—	cons. bp of Chester, 1 April 1554; d. Dec. 1555
Miles Coverdale	—	nom. bp of Exeter, 2 Aug. 1551; cons. 30 Aug. 1551; depr. Sept. 1553

[1] *C.P.R., Ph. & Mary*, I, 74–5, 121–2; Strype, *Eccl. Mems*, III (I), 35.
[2] Not June 1554, as in *H.B.C.*, p. 207. See *C.P.R., Ph. & Mary*, I, 175; *D.N.B.*, *sub* Paul Bush.

APPENDIX B—*(contd)*

Name	See occupied at time of meeting of Edward VI's first parliament, Nov. 1547	Consecrations, promotions, resignations, deprivations and deaths between 4 Nov. 1547 and end of Mary's last parliament on 17 Nov. 1558
Thomas Cranmer	Canterbury	depr. 11 Dec. 1555; d. 21 March 1556
George Day	Chichester	depr. 10 Oct. 1551; rest. Aug. 1553; d. 2 Aug. 1556
Robert Ferrar	—	cons. bp. of St David's 9 Sept. 1548; depr. March 1554[3]
Stephen Gardiner	Winchester	depr. 14 Feb. 1551; rest. Aug. 1553; d. 12 Nov. 1555
William Glyn(n)	—	cons. bp of Bangor, 8 Sept. 1553; d. 21 May 1558
Thomas Goldwell	—	cons. bp of St Asaph, Aug./Sept. 1555
Thomas Goodrich (Goodricke)	Ely	d. 10 May 1554
Maurice Griffith (Griffin)	—	nom. bp of Rochester, 19 March 1554; cons. 1 April 1554
John Harley	—	nom. bp of Hereford, 26 March and cons. 26 May 1553; depr. 15 March 1554
Nicholas Heath	Worcester	depr. 9[4] or 10[5] Oct. 1551; rest. Aug. 1553;[6] nom. to York, 19 Feb. and conf. 21 June 1555
Henry Holbeach (alias Rands)	Lincoln	d. 6 Aug. 1551
Robert Holgate	York	depr. March 1554
John Holyman	—	cons. bp of Bristol, 18 Nov. 1554
John Hooper	—	nom. bp of Gloucester, 3 July 1550 and cons. 8 March 1551; res. 26 April 1552; nom. bp of Worcester and Gloucester, 20 May 1552;[7] automatically depr. of Worcester by Heath's

[3] *C.P.R., Ph. & Mary*, I, 175; *Machyn*, p. 58.　　[4] *Grey Friars' Chron.*, p. 71.　　[5] *H.B.C.*, p. 262.

[6] Not 1554 as in *H.B.C.*, p. 262. See P.R.O., Parl. Pawns, Petty Bag, C.218, Pt I, No. 7, and *C.P.R., Ph. & Mary*, I, 75.

[7] The united bishopric of Worcester and Gloucester was granted to Hooper on 8 December 1552. *C.P.R., Ed. VI*, IV, p. 231.

Name	See	Notes
John Hopton	—	restoration in Aug. 1553; depr. of Gloucester, 15 March 1554[8] nom. bp of Norwich, 4 Sept. and cons. 28 Oct. 1554; d. *post* 24 Aug. 1558
Robert King	Oxford	d. 4 Dec. 1557
Anthony Kitchin (alias Dunstan)	Llandaff	
Henry Morgan	—	cons. bp of St David's, 1 April 1554
Owen Oglethorpe	—	cons. bp of Carlisle, 15 Aug. 1556
Richard Pate(s)	—	nom. bp of Worcester *ante* 5 March 1555
David Pole	—	cons. bp of Peterborough, 15 Aug. 1557
Reginald Pole	—	cons. archbp of Canterbury, 22 March 1556; d. 17 Nov. 1558
John Ponet	—	nom. bp of Rochester, 8 March and cons. 29 June 1550; transl. to Winchester, 23 March 1551; depr. Aug. 1553
William Repps (alias Rugg(e))	Norwich	res. *c.* Christmas 1549 and certainly *ante* 26 Jan. 1550[9]
Nicholas Ridley	Rochester	transl. to London, April 1550; depr. 5 Sept. 1553 (See Edmund Bonner above)
John Salcot (alias Capon)	Salisbury	d. 6 Oct. 1557
Richard Sampson	Coventry and Lichfield	d. 25 Sept. 1554
John Scory	—	nom. bp of Rochester, 26 April and cons. 30 Aug. 1551; transl. to Chichester, 23 May 1552; depr. Aug. 1553
Cuthbert Scott (Scot)	—	nom. bp of Chester *ante* 24 April and prov. 6 July 1556
John Skip (Skyppe)	Hereford	d. 28 March 1552
John Taylor	—	nom. bp of Lincoln, 18 June and cons. 26 June 1552; depr. March 1554

[8] 17 March according to *Machyn*, p. 58. *C.P.R., Ph. & Mary,* I, 175–6.
[9] *D.N.B.,* *sub* William Rugg, *H.B.C.*, p. 243.

Name	See occupied at time of meeting of Edward VI's first parliament, Nov. 1547	Consecrations, promotions, resignations, deprivations and deaths between 4 Nov. 1547 and end of Mary's last parliament on 17 Nov. 1558
Thomas Thirlby	Westminster	res. 29 March 1550 when see suppressed and absorbed into London; transl. to Norwich, 1 April 1550; transl. to Ely, 10 July 1554
Cuthbert Tunstall	Durham	depr. 14 Oct. 1552; rest. Aug. 1553[10]
James Turberville	—	cons. bp of Exeter, 8 Sept. 1555
John Veysey (Voysey alias Harman)	Exeter	res. 1 Aug. 1551; rest. 28 Sept. 1553; d. 23 Oct. 1554
John Wakeman (alias Wiche)	Gloucester	d. ante 6 Dec. 1549
Robert W(h)arton (or Warblington, alias Parfew, Purefoy)	St Asaph	transl. to Hereford 1554[11]; d. 22 Sept. 1557
Thomas Watson	—	cons. bp of Lincoln, 1 Aug. 1557
John White	—	cons. bp of Lincoln, 1 April 1554; nom. to Winchester 16 May and prov. 6 July 1556
John de Feckenham (Fecknam, alias Howman)	—	cons. and installed as abbot of Westminster, Nov. 1556[12]
Sir Thomas Tresham	—	appointed grand prior of order of St John of Jerusalem, 2 April 1557[13]

[10] Although the commission appointed by Mary did not restore Durham and declare Tunstall's deprivation invalid until 18 January 1554, a writ of summons to Mary's first parliament was despatched to him in mid-August. P.R.O., Parl. Pawns, Petty Bag, C.218, Pt 1, No. 7.

[11] In March (as in *Machyn*, p. 58 and *D.N.B., sub* Robert Warton), not July as in *H.B.C.*, p. 278. In the Lords' Journal of April 1554, he is described as bishop of St Asaph until 10 April and thereafter as bishop of Hereford. L.J., iii, 9–10.

[12] *Machyn*, pp. 118–20; *Wriothesley's Chron.*, ii, 136.   [13] *C.P.R., Ph. & Mary*, iv, 313.

Sources

H.B.C.; D.N.B.; P.R.O., Parl. Pawns, Petty Bag, C.218, Pt I, Nos 4–11; C.P.R., Ed. VI; ibid., Ph. & Mary; Machyn; Grey Friars' Chron.; Wriothesley's Chron.; Strype, Eccl. Mems; L.J., ii, iii.

'Nominal' members who do not qualify for inclusion in the above list

Maurice Clynnog   nom. bp of Bangor in 1558 but withdrew[14]

Thomas Reynolds   nom. bp of Hereford *ante* 7 Nov. 1558, but not cons.[15]

William Peto (Petow, Peytoo)   prov. to Salisbury in 1557, but declined the appointment 'on account of his age, and for other reasons'[16]

Francis Mallett   Mary's chaplain, recommended by the king and queen to Paul IV for the bishopric of Salisbury after William Peto's refusal, 31 Oct. 1558. Mary's death occurred before Mallet could be cons.[17]

William Knight   bp of Bath and Wells at the beginning of Edward VI's reign: in August 1547 he received a writ of summons to Edward's first parliament, but died before it met on 4 Nov. 1547[18]

Abbreviations

bp bishop. conf. confirmed. cons. consecrated. d. died. depr. deprived. nom. nominated. prov. provided. res. resigned. rest. restored. transl. translated.

[14] *H.B.C.*, p. 275.

[15] *C.P.R., Ph. & Mary*, iv, 469

[16] *H.M.C.*, Portland MSS, ii, 11.

[17] *Ibid.*

[18] P.R.O., Parl. Pawns, Petty Bag, C.218, Pt 1, No. 4; *H.M.C.*, Dean and Chapter of Wells MSS, ii, 275.

APPENDIX B—(contd)

II. The lords temporal

Title held on 4 Nov. 1547, when Edward VI's 1st parl. assembled	Name	Creations, promotions, forfeitures and deaths between 4 Nov. 1547 and end of Mary's last parl. on 17 Nov. 1558	Dates of birth and death
A. Senior Peers			
3rd Duke of Norfolk, att. and all hons forf., Jan. 1547	Thomas Howard	rest. 3rd duke, 3 Aug. 1553.[19] Att. reversed in Oct. 1553 parl.[20]; d. 25 Aug. 1554	1473–25 Aug. 1554
—	Thomas Howard	Succ. grandfather as 4th duke of Norfolk, 25 Aug. 1554, when still a minor	12 March 1537–1572
1st earl of Warwick	John Dudley	cr. duke of Northumberland, 11 Oct. 1551; att. and hons forf, 18 Aug. 1553; exec. 23 Aug. 1553	1502–53
1st duke of Somerset	Edward Seymour	exec. for felony, 22 Jan. 1552; att. posthumously by statute and hons forf.	c. 1500–52
3rd marquess of Dorset	Henry Grey	cr. duke of Suffolk, 11 Oct. 1551; att. and hons forf, 17 Feb, and exec. 23 Feb. 1554	17 Feb. 1517–54
1st marquess of Northampton	William Parr	att. and hons forf, 18 Aug. 1553; rest. in blood, not hons, 1554	1513–71
1st Baron St John	William Paulet	cr. earl of Wiltshire, 19 Jan. 1550; cr. marq. of Winchester, 11 Oct. 1551	c. 1483–1572
12th earl of Arundel	Henry FitzAlan		23 April 1512–80
2nd earl of Bath	John Bourchier		1499–1561
1st Baron Russell	John Russell	cr. earl of Bedford, 19 Jan. 1550; d. 14 March 1555	c. 1485–1555
—	Francis Russell	summ. *v.p.* in paternal barony of Russell, March 1553; succ. father, 14 March 1555	1527–85

19 C.E.C. IX 618–19.

20 H.L.R.O. Orig. Acts Mary I st 1 & 2, 37.

Earldom	Notes	Name	Dates
1st earl of Bridgewater	d. 12 April 1548	Henry Daubeney	Dec. 1493–12 April 1548
2nd earl of Cumberland 3rd earl of Derby —	cr. earl of Devon, 3 Sept. 1553, with warrant of precedence[21], d. 18 Sept. 1556	Henry Clifford Edward Stanley Edward Courtenay	c. 1517–70 1509–72 1526–18 Sept. 1556
2nd earl of Huntingdon —	nephew of 6th earl of Northumberland who d. 1537 and son/heir of Sir Thomas Percy, att. and exec. 1537. Cr. earl of Northumberland with precedence of ancestors, 1 May 1557.[22]	Francis Hastings Thomas Percy	c. 1514–60 1528–72
16th earl of Oxford —	cr. Baron Herbert of Cardiff, 10 Oct, and earl of Pembroke, 11 Oct. 1551	John de Vere William Herbert	c. 1516–62 1501/6–70
2nd earl of Rutland 5th earl of Shrewsbury 1st earl of Southampton	d. 30 July 1550	Henry Manners Francis Talbot Thomas Wriothesley	23 Sept. 1526–63 1500–60 21 Dec. 1505–30 July 1550
2nd earl of Sussex —	d. 17 Feb. 1557 summ. v.p. in paternal barony of FitzWalter, Oct. 1553, April 1554, 1554/5, 1555; succ. father as 3rd earl of Sussex, 17 Feb 1557	Henry Radcliffe Thomas Radcliffe	c. 1506/7–17 Feb. 1557 c. 1525/6–83
4th earl of Westmorland —	d. 24 April 1549 succ. father as 5th earl of Westmorland, 24 April 1549	Ralph Neville Henry Neville	21 Feb. 1498–24 April 1549 1524/5–64

21 *C.P.R., Ph. & Mary*, 1, 70.   22 *C.P.R., Ph. & Mary*, III, 495.

APPENDIX B—(contd)

Title held on 4 Nov. 1547, when Edward VI's 1st parl. assembled	Creations, promotions, forfeitures and deaths between 4 Nov. 1547 and end of Mary's last parl. on 17 Nov. 1558	Name	Dates of birth and death
2nd earl of Worcester	d. 26 Nov. 1549	Henry Somerset	c. 1499-1549
—	succ. father as 3rd earl of Worcester, 26 Nov. 1549	William Somerset	1526/7-89
3rd Baron Ferrers	cr. Viscount Hereford, 2 Feb, 1550	Walter Devereux	c. 1488/9 or c. 1491- 17 Sept. 1558
	cr. Viscount Montagu, 2 Sept. 1554	Anthony Browne	29 Nov. 1528/9-92
B. Junior Peers			
6th Baron Bergavenny		Henry Nevill	26 Nov. 1527-87
8th Baron Audley	d. *ante* 20 Jan. 1558	John Tuchet (Touchet or Tucket)	c. 1483-1558
—	succ. father as 9th Baron Audley after 6 Dec. 1557 but *ante* 20 Jan. 1558	George Tuchet	*ante* 20 Jan. 1537-60
7th Baron Berkeley	posthumous son and heir, succ. to barony at birth 26 Nov. 1534	Henry Berkeley	26 Nov. 1534-1613
2nd Baron Bray(e)	d. 18 or 19 Nov. 1557	John Bray(e)	?-18/19 Nov. 1557
3rd Baron Burgh (Borough)	d. 28 Feb. 1550	Thomas Burgh	1488 or earlier-1550
—	succ. father as 4th Baron Burgh, 28 Feb. 1550, when a minor[23]	William Burgh	c. 1530/1-84
—	cr. Baron Chandos of Sudeley, 8 April 1554	John Bridges (Brydges, Bruges)	9 March 1492- 12 April 1557
—	succ. father as 2nd Baron Chandos, 12 April 1557	Edmund Bridges	c. 1522 or earlier-1573
9th Baron Clinton and Saye		Edward Fiennes Clinton	1512-85

Title	Notes	Name	Dates
9th Baron Cobham	d. 29 Sept. 1558	George Brooke	c. 1497–1558
—	succ. father as 10th Baron Cobham, 29 Sept. 1558	William Brooke	1 Nov. 1527–97
3rd Baron Conyers	d. June 1557	John Conyers	c. 1524–57
1st Baron Cromwell	d. 4 July 1551	Gregory Cromwell	c. 1514–51
3rd Baron Dacre(s) of Gilsland		William Dacre(s)	29 April 1500–63
—	rest. in blood/hons by act of parliament, 1549[24] to barony of Darcy of Darcy (Aston), after att./forf. of hons by father, Thomas Lord Darcy, in 1537; d. 28 Aug 1558	George Darcy	?–28 Aug. 1558
—	succ. father as 2nd Baron Darcy of Darcy, 28 Aug. 1558	John Darcy	c. 1530–1602
—	cr. Baron Darcy of Chiche, 5 April 1551; d. 28 June 1558	Thomas Darcy	1506–58
—	succ. father as 2nd Baron Darcy of Chiche, 28 June 1558	John Darcy	c. 1532–81
9th Baron De la Warr	d. 25 Sept. 1554	Thomas West	1472?–1554
—	succ. father, 3rd Baron Dudley, who was never summ., as 4th Baron in Sept. 1553	Edward Dudley (alias Sutton)	?–1586
1st Baron Eure	d. 15 March 1548	William Eure	c. 1483–1548
—	succ. grandfather as 2nd Baron Eure, 15 March 1548, when still a minor	William Eure	10 May 1529–94
4th Baron Grey of Powis	d. 2 July 1551	Edward Grey	?–1551
13th Baron Grey de Wilton		William Grey	c. 1509–62
—	cr. Baron Hastings of Loughborough, 19 Jan. 1558	Edward Hastings	c. 1520–72
—	cr. Baron Howard of Effingham, 11 March 1554	William Howard	1510–73
4th Baron Latimer		John Nevill	c. 1520–77

[24] H.L.R.O., Orig. Acts, 2/3 Ed. VI, no. 41. Title treated as a new creation until Lords resolved in 1559 that it was a restoration. L.J., iii, 133–67, 173–87.

APPENDIX B—(*contd*)

Title held on 4 Nov. 1547, when Edward VI's 1st parl. assembled	Creations, promotions, forfeitures and deaths between 4 Nov. 1547 and end of Mary's last parl. on 17 Nov. 1558	Name	Dates of birth and death
—	father exec. in 1537 for treason; rest. in blood/hons as 5th Baron by act of parl., 1547,[25] when still a minor	John Lumley	1533/4–1609
2nd Baron Monteagle		Thomas Stanley	25 May 1507–1560
1st Baron Mordaunt		John Mordaunt	c. 1480/5 or 1490[26]–1562
10th Baron Morley	d. 27 Nov. 1556	Henry Parker	ante 1486–1556
	succ. grandfather as 11th Baron Morley, 27 Nov. 1556	Henry Parker	1531/2–77
6th Baron Mountjoy		James Blount	c. 1533–81
—	cr. Baron North by writ of summons, April 1554	Edward North	c. 1504–64
6th Baron Ogle		Robert Ogle	30 May 1529–62
—	cr. Baron Paget of Beaudesert, 3 Dec. 1549	William Paget	c. 1506–63
1st Baron Rich		Richard Rich	c. 1496–1567
2nd Baron Sandys of the Vyne		Thomas Sandys	?–6 Feb. 1560
8th Baron Scrope of Bolton	d. 22 Jan. 1549	John Scrope	?–1549
—	succ. father as 9th Baron Scrope, 22 June 1549, when still a minor	Henry Scrope	c. 1534–92
1st Baron Seymour of Sudeley	cr. Baron Seymour of Sudeley att. by act of parl. and all hons forf.; exec., 20 March 1549	Thomas Seymour	c. 1508–49
1st Baron Sheffield of Butterwick	d. 31 July 1549	Edmund Sheffield	22 Nov. 1521–49
—	rest. in blood and cr. Baron Stafford by act of parl. 1547.[27]	Henry Stafford	18 Sept. 1501–63

[25] H.L.R.O., Orig. Acts, 1 Ed. VI, no. 17.

[26] *G.E.C.*, ix, 193; *D.N.B.*, *sub* John 1st Lord Mordaunt.

7th Baron Stourton	William Stourton	c. 1500–16 Sept. 1548	d. 16 Sept. 1548
—	Charles Stourton	1518/24–57	succ. father as 8th Baron Stourton, 16 Sept. 1548; att. for felony; exec. 6 March 1557
2nd Baron Vaux of Harrowden	Thomas Vaux	24 April 1509–56	d. Oct. 1556
—	William Vaux	Aug. 1535–95	succ. father as 3rd Baron Vaux, Oct. 1556
1st Baron Wentworth of Nettlestead	Thomas Wentworth	1501–51	d. 3 March 1551
—	Thomas Wentworth	1525–84	succ. father as 2nd Baron Wentworth, 3 March 1551
1st Baron Wharton	Thomas Wharton	c. 1495–1568	
—	John Williams	c. 1496–1559	cr. Baron Williams of Thame by write of summons to parl. (April 1554)
1st Baron Willoughby of Parham	William Willoughby	c. 1515–70 or 1574	
2nd Baron Windsor of Stanwell	William Windsor	1498–1558	d. 20 Aug. 1558
—	Edward Windsor	1532–75	succ. father as 3rd Baron Windsor, 20 Aug. 1558
8th Baron Zouche of Harringworth	John Zouche	c. 1486–1550	d. 10 Aug. 1550
—	Richard Zouche	c. 1510–22 July 1552	succ. father as 9th Baron Zouche, 10 Aug. 1550
—	George Zouche	c. 1526–69	succ. father as 10th Baron Zouche, 22 July 1552

C. Heirs Apparent summoned v.p. in junior dignity of father

earl of Warwick (b. *ante* 1528; d. 21 Oct. 1554)	John Dudley, 3rd but eldest surviving son and heir of John duke of Northumberland. Summ. to March 1553 parliament *v.p.* in paternal earldom of Warwick
Lord St John (c. 1510–76)	John Paulet, son and heir of 1st marq. of Winchester. Summ. *v.p.* in paternal barony of St John in 1554/5, 1555, Jan. 1558
Lord Talbot (c. 1528–90)	George Talbot, son and heir of Francis, 5th earl of Shrewsbury. Summ. *v.p.* in paternal barony of Talbot in March 1553, Oct. 1553, April 1554, 1554/5, 1555, Jan. 1558.

'Nominal' members who do not qualify for inclusion in the above list

Henry Brandon, 2nd Duke of Suffolk: b. 18 Sept. 1535; d. 14 July 1551 before attaining his majority.[28] Charles Brandon, 3rd duke of Suffolk; b. in 1537/8; d. same place and day (though half-an-hour later) as his brother.[29]

Henry Wriothesley, 2nd earl of Southampton: b. 1545; succ. father 30 July 1550; did not attain majority until Elizabeth's reign.[30]

Walter Devereux, 2nd Viscount Hereford, b. 1541 (?); succ. grandfather on 17 Sept. 1558; did not attain majority before Mary's death.[31]

Henry 2nd Baron Cromwell (b. c. 1538 and succ. father 4 July 1551), John 2nd Baron Sheffield (b. c. 1538 and succ. father 31 July 1549), and John 9th Baron Stourton (b. Jan. 1553 and succ. father 6 March 1557); did not attain majority until Elizabeth's reign.[32]

John 3rd Baron Dudley, who succ. father in 1532 and d. in Sept. 1553, was never summ. because of his poverty and/or lunacy.[33]

William Parr, cr. Baron Parr of Horton, 23 Dec. 1543, was summ. to Edward VI's first parliament but d. before he could attend.[34]

Abbreviations

att. attainted. b. born. cr. created. exec. executed. forf. forfeited. hons honours. marq. marquess. rest. restored.
succ. succeeded. summ. summoned. *v.p. vita patris.*

[28] *G.E.C.*, XII(1), 461.
[29] *Ibid.*; *D.N.B.*, *sub* Henry and Charles Brandon.
[30] *G.E.C.*, XII(1), 125–7.
[31] *D.N.B.*, *sub* Walter Devereux, 1st earl of Essex; *G.E.C.*, VI, 479.
[32] Stone, *Crisis*, p. 805; *G.E.C.*, III, 558; *ibid*, XI, 662–3; *ibid.*, XII(1), 308–9.
[33] *G.E.C.*, IV, 481 and n; *D.N.B.*, *sub* John (Sutton) de Dudley; *Maclyn*, p. 44; *L.P.*, Henry VIII, v, No. 1727; *ibid*, XII(1), No. 1263.
[34] *G.E.C.*, v, 910+11; P.R.O., Parl Pawns Petty Bag C218 Pt1 No 4

APPENDIX C: ATTENDANCE

Entries marked with an asterisk indicate a single appearance during the session and may be clerical errors.

When a member was disabled and therefore ineligible for an entire session, the space has been left blank; if he was eligible but sessionally absent o has been recorded against his name.

Bishops are recorded under their sees and peers under their current titles. Therefore many of them appear more than once in the Attendance Tables: e.g. Nicholas Heath under Worcester and York, and Henry Grey as marquess of Dorset and duke of Suffolk.

If a member succeeded to a title or died during a session, his attendance record has been calculated as a percentage only of those sittings for which he was eligible.

I. Daily attendance record of lords spiritual, 1547–58

(Each member's record is calculated as a percentage of the daily sessions for which attendance is recorded in the journals.)

	Edward VI					1 Mary	Philip and Mary			
	1	2/3	3/4	5/6	7	(April)	1 & 2	2 & 3	4 & 5	5 & 6
Bangor										
Bulkeley	3	0	0	0	0					
Glynn								100	62	0
Bath and Wells										
Barlow		99	100	67	92					
Bourne						83	91	80	71	0
Bristol										
Bush	100	99	0	97	84					
Holyman							57	63	3*	0

APPENDIX C—*(contd)*

| | Edward VI | | | | | 1 Mary (April) | Philip and Mary | | | |
	1	2/3	3/4	5/6	7		1 & 2	2 & 3	4 & 5	5 & 6
Canterbury										
Cranmer	94	93	92	100	100					
R. Pole								61[1]	18	0
Carlisle										
Aldrich	89	96	96	80	92	0	83	49	79	100
Oglethorpe										100
Chester										
Bird	29	0	0	97	0					
Co(a)tes						100	80	0		
Scott									74	33
Chichester										
Day	100	96	96			88	52	91	68	67
Scory					92					
Christopherson										
Coventry and Lichfield										
Sampson	29	90	79	0	0	0	80	60	0	89
Baynes										
Durham										
Tunstall	97	95	94	100		96	85	66	0	0
Ely										
Goodrich	100	97	100	100	100	0	80	97	88	0
Thirlby										

See / Bishop	1	2	3	4	5	6	7	8	9	10
Exeter										
Veysey	0	7	0			0				
Coverdale				95	96					
Turberville								91	77	100
Gloucester										
Wakeman	3*	18								
Hooper			0	90						
Brooks						83	72	60	85	0
Hereford										
Skip	71	93	96	52						
Harley						2*				
Warton/Parfew							88	63		
Llandaff										
Kitchin	11	93	0	0	0	0	0	0	44	0
Lincoln										
Holbeach	100	96	100							
Taylor				92						
White					96	92				
Watson							96	89	74	44
London										
Bonner	94	96				63	91	80	82	100
Ridley			88	96						
Norwich										
Repps/Rugge	63	90	0²							
Thirlby				98	94					
Hopton							100	69	97	

Harley: Eligible only for 1 Mary (1553), from which he was excluded on the first day.

² He resigned during the session.

APPENDIX C—(*contd.*)

	Edward VI					1 Mary (April)	Philip and Mary			
	1	2/3	3/4	5/6	7		1 & 2	2 & 3	4 & 5	5 & 6
Oxford										
King	0	1*	5	0	0	0	0	0		
Peterborough										
Chambers	57	41	0	2*	0	0	0	0		0
D. Pole							0	0	82	
Rochester										
Ridley	97	97	97							
Scory				22						
Griffith						96	0	97	88	
St Asaph										
Warton	63	18	82	78	84					
Goldwell								0	62	100
St David's										
Barlow	94									
Ferrar		97	99	87	88					
Morgan						96	67	71	74	0
Salisbury										
Salcot	91	99	3	0	0	0	0	0		
Westminster										
Thirlby	0	97	100							
Winchester										
Gardiner						100	100	14[3]		
Ponet				98	100					
White									88	89

Lords spiritual (continued):

Member								
Worcester								
Heath	69	97	100	89	88	98	88	71	100
Hooper								
Pates								
York								
Holgate	54	80	2*	97	68			0
Heath								
Prior of St John								
Tresham							21	0
Abbot of Westminster							88	0

II. Daily attendance record of lords temporal, 1547–58

(Each member's record is calculated as a percentage of the daily sessions for which attendance is recorded in the journals.)

Member									
Dukes									
3rd Norfolk						96			
4th Norfolk									78
Northumberland	100				72				
Somerset		66	68	72					
Suffolk			83	76					
Marquesses									
Dorset	91	92	97	52	72				
Northampton	60	70	76	92	100				
Winchester			92	92	54	83	100	53	56
Earls									
Arundel	66	92	3	60	88	92	48	71	68	0
Bath	71	100	89	60	92	0	91	86	38	0

APPENDIX C—(contd)

	Edward VI					1 Mary (April)	Philip and Mary			
	1	2/3	3/4	5/6	7		1 & 2	2 & 3	4 & 5	5 & 6
1st Bedford						0	70	0		
2nd Bedford					32				85	78
Bridgewater	17									
Cumberland	0	4	2*	0	0	0		0	0	0
Derby	66	89	89	90	92	54	37	60	74	11*
Devon	(Probably present in Mary's 1st parl. for which there is no extant journal)									
Huntingdon	63	82	32	0	80	63	70	63	77	22
Northumberland									0	0
Oxford	77	36	85	72	92	96	0	83	56	56
Pembroke		95	0	22	44	58	30	46	9	22
Rutland			26	83	92	67	72	89	53	56
Shrewsbury	97	84	14	83	60	88	80	0	91	89
Southampton	94	84	14							
2nd Sussex	94	93	14	78	20	63	37	0		
3rd Sussex								0	74	
Warwick (Snr)	0	82	14							0
4th Westmorland	0	3								
5th Westmorland			64	28	92		63			
2nd Worcester	0	4	0[4]		92	0	0	0	9	0
3rd Worcester			33[5]	82	92	0	0	83	71	78

[4] He died during the session.   [5] He succeeded during the session.

Viscounts										
1st Hereford				92	92	0	48	97	0	
1st Montagu							85	97	97	78
Barons										
Bergavenny	0		24	50	48					
8th Audley		0	86	88	80	0	4	0	0	0
9th Audley		0				88	0	0	77	67
Berkeley									62	0
Bray(e)	57		65	28	68	54	15	49		
3rd Burgh	11		46	73	76	75	74	54	53	
4th Burgh						54	94	91		44
1st Chandos										
2nd Chandos									56	
Clinton	94	96	0	20	80	88	70	91	68	44
9th Cobham	74	52	20	77	80	88	11	77	65	56
10th Cobham										0
Conyers	63	96	76	30	96	0	0	57		
1st Cromwell	94	95	97*	80	88	0	33	0	0	89
Dacre of the North	94	97	2*	0	0	0	0	0	68	
1st Darcy of Darcy			5							
2nd Darcy of Darcy										0
1st Darcy of Chiche				63	92	83	67	54	59	44
2nd Darcy of Chiche										
De la Warr	0	6	35	0	0	0	0	0	35	
4th Dudley							91	83		
1st Eure	89			88	0	92	76	80	0	0
2nd Eure		96	86							
Ferrers	40									

APPENDIX C—(contd)

	Edward VI					1 Mary (April)	Philip and Mary			
	1	2/3	3/4	5/6	7		1 & 2	2 & 3	4 & 5	5 & 6
Grey de Powis	60	92	85							
Grey de Wilton	0	53	14		0	0	13	34		
Hastings of Loughborough										
Howard of Effingham	77	90	88	70	88	13	54	89	65	67
Latimer	60	0	0	63	96	50	80	66	77	67
Lumley						88	78	83	82	0
Monteagle						92	94	74	3*	67
Mordaunt	0	1*	0	0	0	25	0	0	0	0
10th Morley	66	93	97	20	52					
11th Morley						83	0	0	85	67
Mounjoy						4*	98	0	62	89
North							78	80	68	56
Ogle							63	0	0	0
Paget			62[6]		100	75	11	80	38	0
Rich	94	88	97		52	88		77	56	56
Russell	100	97	80	0						
St John (cr. earl of Wiltshire nr end of 1549/50)	89	80	77							

[6] He was called to the Lords during the session – only eligible for 47 days.

	1	2	3	4	5	6	7	8	9	10
Sandys	31	0	0	85	72	13	2*	74	0	0
8th Scrope	71	30	86	15	0	83	61	46	62	67
9th Scrope	69		94	65	72		59	80	56	
Seymour of Sudeley	80	91[7]								
1st Sheffield	63	95	0	0	0	58	39	0	24	0
Stafford		93	82	90	56		0	37		
7th Stourton	3*	96	100	43			100	0		78
8th Stourton	63	0	70	93	96	88	74	0	91	44
2nd Vaux	0	97	97	83	88	92	91	69	74	89
3rd Vaux		97	0	72	0	79	70	97	85	
1st Wentworth	83	96			92	92	4	80	77	0
2nd Wentworth	94	92			92	75		31		
Wharton	0	4			92	0	0	80	18	0
Williams of Thame							65	89	44	22
Willoughby of Parham							46	74	3*	0
2nd Windsor										
3rd Windsor										
8th Zouche										
9th Zouche										
10th Zouche										
Warwick (jnr)										
Talbot										
St John (jnr)										
FitzWalter										
Russell (jnr)										

[7] Seymour was eligible for only 33 sittings, being arrested part-way through the session, on 17 January 1549.

APPENDIX D: LEGISLATION

Parliamentary Session	Number of bills			House of origin of bills		House of origin of acts	
	Before Lords	Before Commons	Before parl.	House of Lords	House of Commons	House of Lords	House of Commons
1547 (1 Ed. VI)	46	68	84	32	52	16	5
1548/9 (2/3 Ed. VI)	93	131	151	65	86	39	21
1549/50 (3/4 Ed. VI)	46	74	81	27	54	16	15
1552 (5/6 Ed. VI)	74	99	118	51	67	24	13
March 1553 (7 Ed. VI)	25	36	39	17	22	12	5
1554 (1 Mary)	30	48	49	9	40	6	9
1554/5 (1 & 2 Ph. & Mary)	29	59	61	12	49	9	12
1555 (2 & 3 Ph. & Mary)	41	72	73	13	60	7	18
Jan. 1558 (4 & 5 Ph. & Mary)	27	41	43	12	31	6	10
Nov. 1558 (5 & 6 Ph. & Mary)	4	11	14	4	10	—	—
Total: Edward VI	284	408	473	192	281	107	59
Total: Philip and Mary	131	231	240	50	190	28	49
Total: 1547–58	415	639	713	242	471	135	108

N.B. The calculations in the text (see above, pp. 175–8) include the acts for Mary's first parliament, but they have been omitted here.

Parliamentary Session	Percentage of bills before Lords	Percentage of bills before Commons	Percentage of bills originating in House of Lords	Percentage of bills originating in House of Commons	Percentage of acts originating in House of Lords	Percentage of acts originating in House of Commons
1547 (1 Ed. VI)	55	81	38	62	76	24
1548/9 (2/3 Ed. VI)	62	87	43	57	65	35
1549/50 (3/4 Ed. VI)	57	91	33	67	52	48
1552 (5/6 Ed. VI)	63	84	43	57	65	35
March 1553 (7 Ed. VI)	64	92	44	56	71	29
1554 (1 Mary)	61	98	18	82	40	60
1554/5 (1 & 2 Ph. & Mary)	48	97	20	80	43	57
1555 (2 & 3 Ph. & Mary)	56	99	18	81	28	72
Jan. 1558 (4 & 5 Ph. & Mary)	63	95	28	72	37.5	62.5
Nov. 1558 (5 & 6 Ph. & Mary)	29	79	29	71	—	—
Average: Edward VI	60	86	41	59	64	36
Average: Philip and Mary	55	96	21	79	36	64
Average: 1547–1558	58	90	34	66	56	44

NOTES

Chapter 1: Introduction

1 S. E. Lehmberg, *The Reformation Parliament, 1529–36* (Cambridge, 1970).

2 *Ibid.*, chapter 4 and pp. 76ff.

3 J. E. Neale, *Elizabeth I and her Parliaments* (hereafter cited as Neale, *Elizabethan Parliaments*, I and II), 2 vols (London, 1953–7), I, 28–9.

4 However, bishops were not required to be present when any bill passed the House.

5 C. C. Weston, *English Constitutional Theory and the House of Lords, 1556–1832* (London, 1965), p. 1.

6 L. O. Pike, *A Constitutional History of the House of Lords* (London, 1894).

7 J. H. Round, *Studies in Peerage and Family History* (London, 1901) and *Peerage and Pedigree, Studies in Peerage Law and Family History*, 2 vols (London, 1910).

8 E. R. Adair and F. M. Greir Evans, 'Writs of Assistance from 1558 to 1700', *E.H.R.*, 36 (July 1921), 356–72; A. F. Pollard, 'The Authenticity of the "Lords' Journals" in the Sixteenth Century', *T.R.H.S.*, 3rd ser., 8 (1914), 17–39; 'The Clerical Organisation of Parliament', *E.H.R.*, 57 (January 1942), 31–58; 'Receivers of Petitions and Clerks of Parliament', *E.H.R.*, 57 (April 1942), 202–26; 'The Clerk of the Crown', *E.H.R.*, 57 (July 1942), 312–33.

9 E.g. in A. F. Pollard, *The Evolution of Parliament*, 2nd edn (London, 1964)

10 *Ibid.*, pp. 160, 215, 277.

11 E.g. W. Notestein, 'The Winning of the Initiative by the House of Commons', *Proceedings of the British Academy*, 11 (1926, reprint 1959); Neale, *Elizabethan Parliaments*, I and II; C. Read, *Lord Burghley and Queen Elizabeth* (London, 1960).

12 Neale, *Elizabethan Parliaments*, I, 11, 28, 420–1 and II, 435–7.

13 *Ibid.*, I, 20, 40–1; Neale's thesis is succinctly expressed in *The Elizabethan House of Commons* (London, 1961), pp. 15–16: 'By Elizabeth's reign, a balanced history of parliament would be almost as predominantly a history of the House of Commons as it is in early Stuart times.' This dismissive view won wide acceptance, e.g. C. Read, *Burghley*, p. 34; Notestein, pp. 22–4; G. R. Elton, *The Tudor Constitution* (Cambridge, 1960), pp. 242–4, 254–61, 282, 302, 303.

14 Neale, *Elizabethan Parliaments*, 1, 23–6, 91ff.

15 J. S. Roskell, 'Perspectives in English Parliamentary History', *B.J.R.L.*, 46, 2 (March 1964), 448–75.

16 J. E. Powell and K. Wallis, *The House of Lords in the Middle Ages* (London, 1968).

17 V. F. Snow, 'Proctorial Representation and Conciliar Management during the Reign of Henry VIII', *H.J.*, 9, 1 (1966), 1–26; 'Proctorial Representation in the House of Lords during the Reign of Edward VI', *J.B.S.*, 7, 2 (May 1969), 1–27; 'A Rejoinder to Mr Graves' Reassessment of Proctorial Representation', *J.B.S.*, 10, 2 (May 1971), 36–46.

18 See pp. 63–4 of the present volume.

19 H. Miller, 'Attendance in the House of Lords during the Reign of Henry VIII', *H.J.*, 10, 4 (1967), 325–51; M. A. R. Graves, 'Proctorial Representation in the House of Lords during Edward VI's Reign: A Reassessment', *J.B.S.*, 10, 2 (May 1971), 17–35.

20 S. E. Lehmberg, *Reformation Parliament*, pp. 76ff.

21 G. R. Elton, 'Studying the History of Parliament', *British Studies Monitor*, 2, 1 (1971), 4–14; 'The Body of the Whole Realm: Parliament and Representation in Medieval and Tudor England', in A. E. Dick Howard (ed.), *Jamestown Essays on Representation* (Charlottesville, 1969); 'Tudor Government: The Points of Contact: 1. Parliament', *T.R.H.S.*, 5th ser., 24 (1974), 183–200; 'The Early Journals of the House of Lords', *E.H.R.*, 89 (July 1974), 481–512; 'Parliament in the Sixteenth Century: Functions and Fortunes', *H.J.*, 22, 2 (1979), 255–78.

22 See J. E. Neale's cursory dismissal of the Lords in *Elizabethan Parliaments*, 1, 40–1. His observation that its proceedings were not sufficiently interesting 'to excite much comment from foreign ambassadors or from letter-writers' perfectly illustrates his priorities. Ambassadors were chiefly interested in political issues which might affect their own nations; gossips were naturally attracted by crisis and high drama. But none of these shed much light on parliament's real and continuing value and significance to the Crown, the governing class and the commonwealth.

23 House of Lords Record Office, Journals of the House of Lords, i–iii; Journals of the House of Commons, i. 1 Edward VI–9 Elizabeth; Original Acts, 1 Edward VI–4/5 Philip and Mary; P.R.O., Parliament Pawns, Petty Bag, C. 218.

24 The Lords' Journal for the first Marian parliament is missing; so are three original acts: 2/3 Edward VI: For Gavell kynde; and 1 Mary: The restitution in blood of Sir William Parr and the heirs of Henry Pole, Lord Montagu. The text of the two Marian acts, however, survives on the parliament roll. Parl. Roll. 1 Mary. C.65/162, Nos 25 (22) and 47. The parliament pawns are complete for the period 1547–58. Their solitary serious shortcoming is that they are an accurate guide only to the initial membership of single-session parliaments or the first session of multi-sessional parliaments. New pawns

were not issued for succeeding sessions and so, as time passed, the changes in personnel rendered the original pawn less and less reliable as a guide to membership.

25 The adjournments are frequently missing from the Marian journals; even the business is not recorded on 13 days. L.J., iii, 6, 7, 17, 20, 26, 37–9, 44–5, 48–9, 51, 55–83, 91–124, 133–66, 174–82. The original acts are clean parchment copies of the original paper bills, most of which have not survived. As the paper bills bore all the evidence of revision during the formative second-reading and committee stages in the House of origin, the loss is a serious one; but at least the original acts incorporate all the evidence of amendment from that point on.

26 Thus he left out speeches and debates because they served no useful purpose; and although he registered proxies, for which he received fees, we remain ignorant about many aspects of the operation of licensed absenteeism and proctorial representation.

27 For a full discussion of these, see M. A. R. Graves, 'The Tudor House of Lords in the Reigns of Edward VI and Mary I: A Study of Composition, Quality, and Attendance', 2 vols (unpublished dissertation, Otago, New Zealand, 1974), I(I), 50–2.

28 See M. A. R. Graves, 'The Two Lords' Journals of 1542', *B.I.H.R.*, 43 (November 1970), 182–9.

29 See chapter 4, *passim*.

30 Neale, *Elizabethan Parliaments*, I, 41.

31 N. H. Nicolas, *Memoirs of the Life and Times of Sir Christopher Hatton, K.G.* (London, 1847), p. 482.

32 E. R. Foster, *Proceedings in Parliament, 1610*, Yale Historical Publications, Manuscripts and Edited Texts, vols 22, 23 (New Haven and London, 1966), I, 92–3.

33 Calculated from L.J., iv, 65–131; C.J., i, 216–52b; and H.L.R.O., Orig. Acts, 5 Eliz., no. 1.

34 I am indebted to David Dean for this information.

35 The earliest known reference to the 'House of Lords' was as recent as 1544. Before and after that date contemporaries also described it in a variety of other ways: as 'the Lords', the 'Upper House', 'Higher House', 'the Lords' House', 'parliament house', *domus procerum*, 'Head House' and 'parliament chamber'. They could with equal facility refer to the physical venue or to the assembly of lords spiritual and temporal. However, for convenience's sake the assembly has been described as the 'House of Lords', 'Upper House' or simply 'the Lords'. 'Parliament house' and 'parliament chamber' have been used to identify the actual place of meeting. A. F. Pollard, *The Reign of Henry VII from Contemporary Sources*, University of London Historical Series, no. 1, 3 vols (London, 1913–14), I, xxxiii.

Chapter 2: The Composition of the House

[1] With one exception, the bishopric of Sodor and Man which was a family preserve of the earls of Derby. By an act of 1542 the diocese was 'annexed adjoyned and united to the saide province and metropoliticall jurisdiction of York in all poyntz and all purposes and effects'. H.L.R.O., Orig. Acts, 33 Henry VIII, no. 29. Yet it remained under Stanley control, with its own convocation and without a seat in the Lords.

[2] The abbot of Westminster and the lay prior of the order of St John of Jerusalem were summoned to the last Marian parliament and the first of Elizabeth's reign.

[3] H. Miller, 'The Early Tudor Peerage, 1485–1547', unpub. M.A. thesis, University of London, 1950, fo.3. Henry VIII's creation of Lord Monteagle in 1514 marked a 'complete divorce from territorial notions'. Powell and Wallis, pp. 552–3.

[4] Hence a bishop was not summoned to parliament until he had received the temporalities of his see – it was a reflection of the tenurial origin of his right of membership. Pike, pp. 162, 165, 327.

[5] W. Lambarde, *Archeion* (London, 1635, repr. Cambridge, Mass., 1957), p. 123.

[6] The new sees were Bristol, Chester, Gloucester, Oxford, Peterborough and Westminster. T. Rymer and R. Sanderson (eds), *Foedera, Conventiones Litterae* . . . 20 vols (London, 1727–35), xiv, 718, 724, 731, 754, 758; *Reports from the Lords' Committees Touching the Dignity of a Peer of the Realm*, 5 vols (London, 1820–9), i, 373.

[7] Elton, *Tudor Constitution*, p. 230; Sir Thomas Smith, *De Republica Anglorum*, ed. L. Alston (Cambridge, 1906), p. 48.

[8] See App. A: Composition.

[9] Much of the information on this and the following pages is derived from G. E. Cokayne, *The Complete Peerage*, ed. V. Gibbs, 13 vols in 14 (London, 1910–59).

[10] In August 1553 Northampton was attainted and his honours forfeited. He too was not executed and in the following year he was pardoned and restored but only in blood not in honours. It was not until 1559 that he was re-created marquess. *G.E.C.*, ix, 671.

[11] H.L.R.O., Orig. Acts, 3/4 Ed. VI, no. 28.

[12] C. Wriothesley, *A Chronicle of England*, ed. W. D. Hamilton, 2 vols, Camden Soc., new ser. xi, 2 pts (1875–7), ii, 135.

[13] H.L.R.O., Orig. Acts, 5 Eliz., no. 41; *G.E.C.*, iv, 158, 159 and n. (a).

[14] J. R. Dasent (ed.), *Acts of the Privy Council of England*, 32 vols (London, 1890–1907), ii, 16.

[15] *Ibid.*, 16–18.

[16] E. Coke, *The Institutes of the Laws of England*, 4 pts (London, 1628–1644), iii, 106, cit. F. B. Palmer, *Peerage Law in England* (London, 1907), pp. 216, 220–4.

[17] *G.E.C.*, IV, 332.

[18] See p. 231, n.24.

[19] The fathers of Lumley and Darcy had been attainted in 1537 for their part in the pilgrimage of grace. Stafford was the heir of the third duke of Buckingham who had been executed in 1521.

[20] H.L.R.O., Orig. Acts, 1 Ed. VI, nos 17 (Lumley) and 18 (Stafford), 2/3 Ed. VI, no. 41 (Darcy).

[21] L.J., ii, 49ff., 140ff., and *ibid.*, iii, 6ff.

[22] L.J., iii, 148–9.

[23] L.J., iv, 3–60.

[24] H.L.R.O., Orig. Acts, 37 Henry VIII, no. 32.

[25] *Ibid.*, 1 Mary, st. 2, no. 27.

[26] *Ibid.*, 1 Mary, st. 2, no. 19.

[27] The earls of Hertford and Essex, Viscount Lisle and Lord Wriothesley became respectively the duke of Somerset, marquess of Northampton, and earls of Warwick and Southampton.

[28] In 1550 Baron Ferrers became Viscount Hereford, Russell was raised to the earldom of Bedford and St John received the earldom of Wiltshire. In 1551 Wiltshire became marquess of Winchester, Warwick was made duke of Northumberland, and the marquess of Dorset was raised to the dukedom of Suffolk.

[29] Somerset (1552), Northumberland (1553) and Suffolk (1554) were executed and Northampton (1553) was deprived.

[30] *C.P.R., Ed. VI*, IV, 225, 231.

[31] H.L.R.O., Orig. Acts, 7 Ed. VI, no. 17.

[32] *C.P.R., Ph. & Mary*, I, 377–8; H.L.R.O., Orig. Acts, 1 Mary (1554), no. 3.

[33] Mary chose to disregard both Heath's deprivation and Hooper's appointment to Worcester in the previous reign. Heath was automatically reinstated without formal process. When the summonses for Mary's first parliament were despatched in August 1553, Worcester's writ was addressed to Nicholas, not John. P.R.O., Parl. Pawns, Petty Bag, C.218, Pt I, No. 7. The commission to deprive Hooper referred to him only as bishop of Gloucester. *C.P.R., Ph. & Mary*, I, 175–6.

[34] For the number of dioceses at the time of each parliament, see App. A: Composition.

[35] Edmund Bonner, sole episcopal victim of the protectorate, and Thomas Cranmer who was not deprived until December 1555.

[36] George Day (Chichester), Stephen Gardiner (Winchester) and Nicholas Heath of Worcester (all in 1551), and Cuthbert Tunstall (Durham) in 1552.

[37] The government dressed up its real motives in acceptable garb. Thus Veysey resigned because of his 'extreme old age' and Repps was obliged to step down because of his financial malpractices. Whilst there was truth enough in these explanations, they were both religious conservatives and Repps was one of Somerset's sympathisers.

C.P.R., *Ed. VI*, II, 385; *ibid.*, IV, 14, 36; W. K. Jordan, *Edward VI. The Young King* (London, 1968), p. 325.

[38] Mary differentiated between the three Henrician and eight Edwardian appointments. The former – Holgate (York), Bird (Chester) and Bush (Bristol) – together with one Edwardian, Robert Ferrar of St David's, were deprived for clerical marriage. The remainder – Coverdale (Exeter), Harley (Hereford), Hooper (Worcester–Gloucester), Ponet (Winchester), Ridley (London), Scory (Chichester) and Taylor (Lincoln) – forfeited their offices primarily because their original appointments were held to be invalid. *C.P.R.*, *Ph. & Mary*, I, 175–6.

[39] *H.M.C.*, *The Manuscripts of the Dean and Chapter of Wells*, 2 vols (London, 1914), II, 276–7.

[40] Chester, Gloucester, Hereford, Lincoln and St David's.

[41] George Cotes (Chester), James Brooks (Gloucester), John White (Lincoln) and Henry Morgan (St David's) replaced deprived reformers, Gilbert Bourne (Bath and Wells) succeeded William Barlow who had resigned, and Maurice Griffith (Rochester) ended a vacancy which had lasted since May 1552.

[42] Reduced to four when John Holyman and Ralph Baynes were consecrated bishops of Bristol and of Coventry and Lichfield on 18 November and lodged their writs two days later. *L.J.*, iii, 42.

[43] The sole – and important – exception was Cranmer who was not deprived until two days after the dissolution of this parliament.

[44] See p. 233, n.2, in the present volume.

[45] *L.J.*, XIV, 10.

[46] According to D'Ewes it was still being applied in a flexible manner, and at the royal discretion, in the early seventeenth century: 'no peer is called to sit as a Member ... or to have his free voice, until he have accomplished his full Age, unless by the special grace of the Prince, and that very rarely, unless they be near upon the Age of twenty at the least'. Sir Simonds D'Ewes, *The Journals of All the Parliaments during the Reign of Queen Elizabeth* (London, 1682), p. 11.

[47] *G.E.C.*, XII (1), 461.

[48] D'Ewes, p. 96.

[49] *C.P.R.*, *Ed. VI*, III., 167.

[50] *A.P.C.*, III, 262; *G.E.C.*, X, 35.

[51] P.R.O., Parl. Pawns, Petty Bag, C.218, Pt 1, Nos 6, 7.

[52] Poverty may have contributed to Ogle's disqualification. His father, the fifth lord, did not lodge his writ or take his seat in 1539, the first session after the termination of his minority. In 1542 his name did not even appear on the close roll as one of those entitled to a summons. It suggests a continuing family problem such as financial embarrassment. When Robert was appointed to the middle march in April 1551, he protested to William Cecil that 'it is well known that my living is very small, not the twentieth part fitting for a man in that room'. Perhaps this should not be taken too seriously; it smacks of the wheedling and begging posture assumed by so many Tudor

servants. In any case why did Mary summon him to parliament if poverty had previously disabled him? *G.E.C.*, x, 34; P.R.O., Close Rolls, C.54, No. 426; *Cal.S.P.Dom.*, Add., 1547–65, p. 409.

[53] *G.E.C.*, VII, 169.

[54] *Ibid.*, 170–1. It was not until 1571 that he successfully petitioned for recognition as the earl of Kent. P.R.O., S.P. 12/77, fo. 107; *ibid.*, 12/78, fo. 254.

[55] *D.N.B.*, *sub* John Dudley (Sutton) 1st Baron Dudley; *G.E.C.*, IV, 481.

[56] Edward 2nd Lord Burgh was declared a lunatic in 1510. From then until his death 18 years later he was not summoned to parliament because he was 'distracted of memorie'. *G.E.C.*, II, 422–3.

[57] Miller, 'Attendance', 329 and n. 25.

[58] Graves, 'The Mid-Tudor House of Lords', 1(1), 74–6. He displayed a genius for invention and fabrication, devising a list of summonses for the second session of the 1558 parliament, in which he included two Lords Windsor, William and Thomas. In fact there was only one and he was named Edward. W. Dugdale (ed.), *A Perfect Copy of all Summons . . . to the . . . Parliaments* (London, 1685), p. 519.

[59] Lehmberg, *Reformation Parliament*, p. 47.

[60] *G.E.C.*, IV, 481.

[61] *L.P.*, Henry VIII, XII (1), No. 1263; *C.P.R.*, *Ph. & Mary*, II, 22–3; *ibid.*, III, 34–8; L.J., iii, 37; Miller, 'Attendance', 328; *G.E.C.*, IV, 481 n.

[62] P.R.O., Parl. Pawns, Petty Bag, C.218, Pt. 1, Nos 1–5; Rymer, *Foedora*, XIV, 738; *G.E.C.*, I, 342; *ibid.*, IV, 156; *L.P.*, Henry VIII, V, Nos 612, 873–5, 1720; *ibid.*, XVI, No. 1369; Miller, 'Attendance', 328–9, 340.

[63] Miller, 'Attendance', 328.

[64] Grey de Wilton, Thomas 2nd Lord Wentworth and Edward Lord Dudley.

[65] P.R.O., Parl. Pawns, Petty Bag, C.218, Pt 1, Nos 5, 7–11; *H.M.C.*, Frederick Peake, Neville of Holt MSS., 2nd Report, App. (London, 1871), 96; M. A. S. Hume and R. Tyler (eds), *Calendar of State Papers Spanish*, 13 vols (London, 1862–1954), XII, 145, 149, 172–3, 177, 205, 246, 249, 286–8; W. B. Turnbull (ed.), *Calendar of State Papers Foreign, Edward VI and Mary*, 2 vols (London, 1861), II, 84–5; *C.P.R., Ph. & Mary*, IV, 2; Strype, *Eccl. Mems*, III, Pt II, 110; *G.E.C.*, XII (1), 521–3; *ibid.*, XII (II), 500; Grey and Wentworth surrendered to the French in January and spent the last year of Mary's reign in captivity. Dudley managed to return to England where he attended the Lords. All three had received writs.

[66] C. H. Garrett, *The Marian Exiles* (Cambridge, 1966), pp. 130–1; P.R.O., Parl. Pawns, Petty Bag, C.218, Pt 1, No. 10; James Basset to earl of Devon, 17/18 Oct. 1555, R. Brown, C. Bentinck and H. Brown, *Calendar of State Papers Venetian*, 9 vols (London, 1864–98), VI, Pt 1, No. 249; same to same, 22 Nov. 1555, *ibid.*, No. 286; *G.E.C.*, IV, 331; *D.N.B. sub* Edward Courtenay.

[67] Francis did not succeed to the earldom until 14 March 1555.

[68] Garrett, pp. 275-7.

[69] P.R.O., Parl. Pawns, Petty Bag, C. 218, Pt 1, No. 10.

[70] *Ibid.*, No. 7; *Wriothesley's Chron.*, II, 91-2; C. L. Kingsford (ed.), *Two London Chronicles*, Camden Miscellany, XII, 3rd ser., xviii (London, 1910), p. 28; J. G. Nichols (ed.), *The Diary of Henry Machyn*, Camden Society, old ser., xlii (London, 1848), p. 38; *Cal.S.P.Span.*, XI, 133, 366.

[71] J. G. Nichols (ed.), *The Chronicle of Queen Jane*, Camden Society, old ser., xlviii (London, 1850), pp. 60-1; P.R.O., Parl. Pawns, Petty Bag, C.218, Pt 1, No. 7; J. G. Nichols (ed.), *Grey Friars of London Chronicle*, Camden Society, old ser., liii (London, 1852), p. 88.

[72] P.R.O., Parl. Pawns, Petty Bag, C.218, Pt 1, No. 8.

[73] D. M. Loades, *Two Tudor Conspiracies* (Cambridge, 1965), pp. 19, 89-95; *Cal.S.P.Span.*, XII, 16, 139.

[74] *Ibid.*, 94, 142, 160, 197, 233.

[75] *Ibid.*, 82, 151, 230, 252.

[76] P.R.O., Parl. Pawns, Petty Bag, C.218, Pt 1, Nos. 8, 9; *Queen Jane*, pp. 59, 76; Robert Swift to earl of Shrewsbury, E. Lodge (ed.), *Illustrations of British History, Biography, and Manners*, 3 vols (London, 1838), I, 235; *Wriothesley's Chron.*, II, 116; Michiel to doge and senate, 8 April 1555, *Cal.S.P.Ven.*, VI, Pt 1, No. 49 (pp. 44-5).

[77] The Limitation was endorsed by 26 peers, twelve of whom also signed the Engagement. *Queen Jane*, pp. 91, 99-100. A dozen also put their hands to the letter of 9 July 1553, exhorting Mary to obey Queen Jane. Foxe, VI, 386.

[78] Nine peers were present at the proclamation. *Wriothesley's Chron.*, II, 89; *Machyn*, p. 37.

[79] *Machyn*, pp. 37-9, 43; *Wriothesley's Chron.*, II, 91, 103; *Grey Friars' Chron.*, p. 81; *Two London Chrons.*, p. 28; R. Holinshed, *Chronicles*, ed. H. Ellis, 6 vols (London, 1807-8), IV, 1; *Queen Jane*, pp. 15, 26-7; *A.P.C.*, IV, 304, 307-8, 311-12, 342, 356, 416, 425; Foxe, VI, 537; *Cal.S.P.Span.*, XI, 116; J. G. Nichols (ed.), *Narratives of the Days of the Reformation*, Camden Society, old ser., lxxvii (London, 1859), pp. 134-5, 138.

[80] *Queen Jane*, pp. 15, 26; *Wriothesley's Chron.*, II, 103; *Machyn*, pp. 38-9; *A.P.C.*, IV, 311-12, 342, 356, 359-60, 416, 425; *Cal.S.P.Span.*, XI, 236, 255, 307; Foxe, VI, 537, 541; *C.P.R., Ph. & Mary*, I, 457, 466; *Narratives of Reformation*, pp. 134-5, 138; W. C. Metcalfe, *A Book of Knights Banneret, Knights of the Bath, and Knights Bachelor* (London, 1885), p. 106.

[81] *A.P.C.*, IV, 307; *Queen Jane*, p. 15; *Cal.S.P.Span.*, XI, 205; *C.P.R., Ph. & Mary*, I, 457.

[82] P.R.O., Parl. Pawns, Petty Bag, C.218, Pt. 1, No. 7.

[83] E.g. Suffolk, Huntingdon, Rutland.

[84] *Cal.S.P.Span.*, XI, 366, 395.

[85] *G.E.C.*, IV, 10; *ibid.*, XII (1), 308; Foxe, VI, 293.

[86] See chapter 5, pp. 98-9, of the present volume.

[87] *A.P.C.*, II, 131-2, 157-8, 208-10; *ibid.*, III, 213-14; *Wriothesley's*

Chron., II, 3, 46, 97; *Grey Friars' Chron.*, pp. 56, 68, 82; Foxe, VI, 264–5, 537; *Cal.S.P.For.*, Ed. VI, 73.

88 R. R. Reid, *The King's Council in the North* (London, 1921), pp. 173–5; *Grey Friars' Chron.*, p. 73; *Wriothesley's Chron.*, II, 65, 96; *A.P.C.*, III, 448–9; *Machyn*, p. 26; *D.N.B.*, *sub* Cuthbert Tunstall; D. E. Hoak, *The King's Council in the Reign of Edward VI* (Cambridge, 1976), pp. 71–2.

89 Hooper was imprisoned on 1 September, Cranmer a fortnight later, and Holgate on 4 October, the very eve of parliament. *A.P.C.*, IV, 337, 347, 354; *Grey Friars' Chron.*, p. 84; *Queen Jane*, p. 27; *Machyn*, p. 46. Uncertainty surrounds the date of Ferrar's arrest. In Foxe's account he was continuously in prison from about 1551, as a result of 'the importunate suit of his adversaries'. These were members of his chapter with whom he was involved in a lengthy dispute. Nor had it been resolved when Mary became queen. Yet he was free to attend parliament in 1552 and March 1553 and he did so regularly. Therefore the probable date of his arrest lies somewhere between Mary's succession and the meeting of her first parliament. Foxe, VII, 21; *A.P.C.*, III, 318; *H.M.C.*, Calendar of the Manuscripts of the Marquess of Salisbury (London 1883), XIII, 32; L.J., ii, 209–301.

90 Foxe, VI, 394; *Grey Friars' Chron.*, pp. 84–5.

91 Foxe attributed his exclusion and later deprivation to the specific offence of clerical marriage. Foxe, VI, 394.

92 *Ibid.*, 541; Julius Terentianus to John ab Ulmis, 20 Nov. 1553, H. Robinson (ed.), *Original Letters relative to the English Reformation*, 2 vols, Parker Society (Cambridge, 1846–7), I, 372. In the same letter Terentianus mistakenly assigned Coverdale (Exeter) to the Tower and he may have been incorrect about Goodrich's fate as well. Foxe and the *Grey Friars' Chronicle* agree on the removal of Taylor and Harley, but they make no mention of Goodrich. *Grey Friars' Chron.*, p. 85.

93 However Cranmer was attainted for treason on 13 Nov. 1553 and this must have provided sufficient grounds for withholding his writ.

94 *Cal.S.P.Ven.*, VI, Pt I, Nos 276 (p. 247), 322 and 327 (p. 293); L.J., iii, 91–125; *D.N.B.*, *sub* Thomas Goldwell.

95 Thirlby's record is a permutation of the various courses adopted by the Crown towards episcopal absentees abroad; in 1547, when he was at Charles V's Court, he received a writ followed by a licence of absence; when Mary's first parliament was called he was again abroad and his summons was duly despatched to his custodian, but he was later recalled, and during the second session of the 1558 parliament, when his writ was still operative, he was required to give priority to the peace negotiations with France at Cercamp. L.J., ii, 126; *D.N.B.*, *sub* Thomas Thirlby; *Cal.S.P.Span.*, XI, 255, 258–9; *Cal.S.P.For.*, II, Nos 849, 854. P.R.O., Parl. Pawns, Petty Bag, C.218, Pt I, Nos 4, 7, 11.

96 See App. A: Composition.

97 Pike, p. 273 and n. 2.

⁹⁸ P.R.O., S.P. 10/18, fo. 8.

⁹⁹ *Ibid.*, fo. 6.

¹⁰⁰ P.R.O., Parl. Pawns, Petty Bag, C.218, Pt I, Nos 5, 7, 9.

¹⁰¹ Nor was their loyalty always certain, although some of the current fears and suspicions sprang from Renard's phobia. *Cal.S.P.Span.*, XI, 441.

¹⁰² *L.J.*, III, 544; Pike, pp. 238–9.

¹⁰³ J. G. Nichols (ed.), *The Chronicle of Calais*, Camden Society, XXXI (London, 1846), p. 166.

¹⁰⁴ *Cal.S.P.Dom.*, 1547–80, Eliz., I, No. 52.

¹⁰⁵ P.R.O., Parl. Pawns, Petty Bag, C.218, Pt I, No. 4; *A.P.C.*, II, 131–2; J. A. Muller, *The Letters of Stephen Gardiner* (Cambridge, 1933), pp. 410, 443.

¹⁰⁶ Neale, *Elizabethan Commons*, pp. 140–1.

¹⁰⁷ See App. A: Composition and App. B: Actual Membership.

Chapter 3: The quality of the House

¹ T. F. T. Plucknett, 'Some Proposed Legislation of Henry VIII', *T.R.H.S.*, 4th ser., 19 (1936), 121–5; J. Simon, *Education and Society in Tudor England* (Cambridge, 1979), p. 337; L. Stone, *The Crisis of the Aristocracy, 1558–1641* (Oxford, 1965), p. 97; see also p. 48 of the present volume.

² Viscounts Beauchamp and Lisle (later dukes of Somerset and Northumberland), and Barons Bray, Parr (later marquess of Northampton) and Seymour of Sudeley, Elizabeth, however, restored Parr to his marquessate and made Somerset's son earl of Hertford.

³ Two recipients of new titles – Bray and Windsor – had been succeeded by their heirs before Edward VI's reign began.

⁴ Viscount Montagu, the earls of Bedford, Pembroke and Southampton, the marquesses of Northampton and Winchester, and the dukes of Northumberland and Somerset.

⁵ He was not created by writ of summons to the parliamentary session of 1539; nor was he summoned before his creation in the following year as J. H. Round maintains in his *Studies in Peerage and Family History*, p. 355. Only Thomas, his father, is named on the parliament pawn for 1539. P.R.O., Parl. Pawns, Petty Bag, C.218, Pt I, No. 2. However he *was* called in 1542 and in the Lords' Journal he is entered as the most junior baron. P.R.O., Close Rolls, C.54, No. 426; L.J., i, 503. Richard Hilles was mistaken when he wrote of the king's artifice in conferring Thomas Cromwell's title 'while he was yet in prison upon his son Gregory in order that he might more readily confess his offences', *Original Letters of the Reformation*, I, 202–3. In fact Gregory was created baron in December 1540. Corrigenda to *D.N.B.*, v, 201b.

⁶ See chapter 2, pp. 11–12, of the present volume.

⁷ *Ibid.*, p. 12.

8 He had been 'of the Chamber' since 1544 and an esquire of the body since 1545. *G.E.C.*, xii (i), 702.

9 See pp. 50–1 of the present volume.

10 See chapter 5, pp. 108–14.

11 W. K. Jordan, *The Chronicle and Political Papers of King Edward VI* (London, 1966), pp. 19–20; Jordan, *Edward VI. The Young King*, pp. 100–1, 516–17, 520–22; L.J., ii, 150; *C.P.R., Ed. VI*, iii, 162; *ibid.*, iv, 128.

12 *Ed. VI's Chron.*, p. 20; *A.P.C.*, ii, 371; *C.P.R., Ed. VI*, 138.

13 *Queen Jane*, pp. 9, 44, 51–2, 63.

14 Hastings's involvement in the crisis of July 1553 was limited to a bout of fisticuffs with Francis Lord Russell in which, according to his supporters, the Catholic champion prevailed. Imperial ambassadors to Charles V, 19 July 1553, *Cal.S.P.Span.*, xi, 94.

15 *Ibid.*, xiii, 140, 144; D'Ewes, pp. 23, 28(2), 30, 31.

16 *Narratives of Reformation*, pp. 136–7.

17 *C.P.R., Ed. VI*, i, 138; *A.P.C.*, iv, 422; *G.E.C.*, iii, 126; P.R.O., Lists and Indexes, No. ix, List of Sheriffs (London, 1898), pp. 51, 154.

18 *C.P.R., Ed. VI*, iv, 258; *A.P.C.*, iv, 197; *Ed. VI's Chron.*, p. 155; *G.E.C.*, v, 180–1; *ibid.*, xii (ii), 595–7; Reid, *King's Council in North*, p. 490.

19 *G.E.C.*, v, 180; M. E. James, 'Change and Continuity in the Tudor North: The Rise of Thomas First Lord Wharton', *Borthwick Papers*, No. 27 (York, 1965), p. 30.

20 *G.E.C.*, xii (ii), 595–7.

21 *Ibid.*, x, 276–7; N. H. Nicolas (ed.), *Proceedings and Ordinances of the Privy Council of England, 1386–1542*, 7 vols (London, 1834–7), vii, 4; *A.P.C.*, i, 118.

22 *Ibid.*, ii, 16. No-one contested Paget's personal testimony. Certainly he, more than anyone else, enjoyed the king's confidence in the drafting of his will and the compilation of the board of executors.

23 Edward VI to Charles V, 10 June 1549, *Cal.S.P.Span.*, ix, 387; *A.P.C.*, iii, 419; *G.E.C.*, x, 277.

24 G. R. Elton, *The Tudor Revolution in Government* (Cambridge, 1962), p. 100 and n. 1; *G.E.C.*, xii (ii), 650–1.

25 He was born in *c.* 1483. *Ibid.*, 757.

26 In February 1550 he replaced the fallen protector.

27 And as president of the council *c.* 1545–50.

28 *G.E.C.*, xii (ii), 757–62; *Wriothesley's Chron.*, i, 183, 186–7; *C.P.R., Ed. VI*, i, 177, 326; *Cal.S.P.Dom.*, 1547–80, Mary, xiii, No. 10.

29 *G.E.C.*, x, 775; *C.P.R., Ed. VI*, i, 76; *History of Parliament Trust Biographies; L.P.*, Henry VIII, xix (2), No. 384.

30 *G.E.C.*, ix, 650 and n. (c); Foxe, vi, 386; *C.P.R., Ed. VI*, i, 78; P.R.O., List of Sheriffs, p. 14.

31 *G.E.C.*, v, 9; *C.P.R., Ed. VI*, iv, 259; *A.P.C.*, iv, 382. However, his ennoblement was not a recognition of past services, but a politically inspired creation consequent upon his appointment as lord admiral. The decision to elevate him must have been influenced by the fact

that his first assignment would be to escort Mary's consort, Philip, from Spain. *A.P.C.*, iv, 359–60; *C.P.R.*, *Ph. & Mary*, i, 148–50, 262. The imperial ambassadors had already acknowledged the value of his goodwill by granting him a pension.

32 *G.E.C.*, ix, 193–5.

33 Even this solitary appearance could have been a clerical error, because he had a licence to be absent from that particular session. L.J., ii, 51.

34 Eventually it gained him a seat at the council board in March 1544. *L.P.*, Henry VIII, xix(1), No. 182. One wonders about Henry's supposed talent for choosing able men to serve him, especially when the following examples are taken into account.

35 A. F. Pollard, *England under Protector Somerset* (London, 1900), pp. 177–80.

36 See chapter 8, pp. 88–9, 104–5, of the present volume.

37 So was Sheffield. One can only echo Pollard's query: why did Henry recommend him for a barony? Apart from his military service in France in 1544, and his attachment to Lisle's French embassy two years later, his career remains a curious blank until he was ignominiously clubbed to death by a butcher during the fiasco of Northampton's 1549 expedition against the East Anglian rebels. *G.E.C.*, xi, 661–2; *Wriothesley's Chron.*, ii, 19; W. Dugdale, *The Baronage of England*, 2 vols (London, 1675), ii, 336. The promotion of Wentworth, who figures only on occasional military service before 1529, is puzzling too. *G.E.C.*, xii (ii), 497.

38 *L.P.*, Henry VIII, xix(1), Nos. 1 and (g) 80(i); *C.P.R.*, *Ed. VI*, i, 174.

39 N. Pocock (ed.), *Troubles connected with the Prayer Book of 1549*, Camden Soc., new ser., xxxvii (London, 1884), pp. 23, 25–7, 29, 30–3, 35–6, 40–1, 44–5; Jordan, *Edward VI. The Young King*, p. 468.

40 *G.E.C.*, x, 405–8; *C.P.R.*, *Ed. VI*, ii, 368; *ibid.*, iii, 329; *ibid.*, iv, 12; *ibid.*, v, 276; *ibid.*, *Ph. & Mary*, iii, 556; *ibid.*, iv, 93; *Cal.S.P.Dom.*, 1547–80, Mary, xiv, p. 108; *A.P.C.*, iv, 48, 277–8; R. Somerville, *History of the Duchy of Lancaster*, i, *1265–1603* (London, 1953), pp. 632, 633, 649; P. Williams, *The Council in the Marches of Wales under Elizabeth I* (Cardiff, 1958), pp. 36–7.

41 *Cal.S.P.Dom.*, 1547–80, Mary, xiii, No. 63.

42 John Dudley, whose mother was *suo jure* Baroness Lisle, was entitled to the viscountcy of Lisle on the death of his stepfather, Arthur Plantagenet, on 3 March 1542. Instead Henry VIII ennobled him afresh as Viscount Lisle nine days later. It was in a sense, therefore, an artificial creation. *G.E.C.*, ix, 722–3.

43 However, the protector's expensive and unsuccessful garrison-fixation, during his war on the Scots, reveals his serious deficiencies as a strategist. M. L. Bush demonstrated this in his examination of *The Government Policy of Protector Somerset* (London, 1975).

44 *C.P.R.*, *Ed. VI*, iii, 425; Scheyfve to Charles V, 1 Sept. 1550, *Cal.S.P. Span.*, x, 167; Somerville, *Duchy of Lancaster*, i, 424; *G.E.C.*, xii(ii), 702–3; *Cal.S.P.Dom.*, 1547–80, Mary, xiv, p. 108.

45 *G.E.C.*, x, 405 and n. (f), 406–8; *C.P.R., Ph. & Mary*, III, 556; *H.M.C.*, F. J. Savile Foljambe MSS., 15th Report, App. v (London, 1897), pp. 2–4; *P.R.O.*, S.P. 11/11, fo. 7.

46 *G.E.C.*, XII(I), 123.

47 Another new peer, Gregory Lord Cromwell, displayed no talent whatsoever, but at least he assiduously attended the Edwardian Lords: 94 per cent of sittings in 1547, 95 per cent in 1548/9, and 97 per cent in 1549/50.

48 Neale, *Elizabethan Commons*, p. 302.

49 J. H. Hexter, 'The Education of the Aristocracy in the Renaissance', *J.M.H.*, 22 (1950), 1–20; Stone, *Crisis*, chapter XII; L. Stone, 'The Educational Revolution in England, 1560–1640', *PP.*, 28 (1964), 41–80; M. H. Curtis, *Oxford and Cambridge in Transition, 1558–1642* (Oxford, 1959), pp. 60–3; see also K. Charlton, *Education in Renaissance England* (London, 1965), p. 135, and W. Prest, 'Legal Education of the Gentry at the Inns of Court, 1560–1640', *PP.*, 38 (1967), 21–3.

50 Stone, 'Educational Revolution', *passim* and *Crisis*, chapter XII.

51 Edmund Dudley, *The Tree of Commonwealth*, ed. D. M. Brodie (Cambridge, 1948), p. 45.

52 D. Lloyd, *The Statesmen and Favourites of England since the Reformation*, 2 vols (London, 1766), I, 148.

53 Amongst the articles of complaint forwarded by Robert Aske (himself of gentle birth) to Henry VIII in 1536 was one that the king was taking into his service and employing as counsellors men 'of low birth and small reputation'. *L.P.*, Henry VIII, XI, No. 705. See also Paget's degradation. *Ed. VI's Chron.*, p. 119.

54 Charlton, *Renaissance Education*, p. 186; cf. Prest, 21–2.

55 Neale, *Elizabethan Commons*, pp. 302–5, 307–8.

56 Graves, 'The Mid-Tudor House of Lords', II, App. Education I–v.

57 J. and J. A. Venn, *Alumni Cantabrigienses*, 10 vols (Cambridge, 1922–1954), Pt I, I, 187, 250, 355; II, 328; III, 499.

58 *Ibid.*, II, 356.

59 W. H. Cooke (ed.), *Students Admitted to the Inner Temple, 1547–1660* (London, 1878), p. 42; Venn and Venn, *Alumni Cantab.*, Pt I, IV, 55–6, 148, 367, 423, 495; J. Foster (ed.), *The Register of Admissions to Gray's Inn, 1521–1889* (London, 1889), p. 45.

60 *Inner Temple Adm.*, p. 48; Foster, *Gray's Reg.*, pp. 14, 29–30; Venn and Venn, *Alumni Cantab.*, Pt I, I, 313; Stone, *Crisis*, p. 679.

61 E.g. the households of the earls of Derby and Southampton, William Lord St John and Henry Stafford.

62 Charlton, *Renaissance Education*, chapter V, espec. pp. 137–9, and chapter VI, espec. pp. 194–5; Prest, 25–9, 38.

63 Anthony à Wood, *Athenae Oxonienses*, 2 vols (London, 1691–2), I, 45–6.

64 Venn and Venn, *Alumni Cantab.*, Pt I, I, 422; III, 499; *G.E.C.*, III, 557 n. (c).

65 Curtis, p. 131.

66 *G.E.C.*, VIII, 269–77; *ibid.*, IX, 211; *ibid.*, XII(I), 173, 182–3; Stone, *Crisis*, pp. 706, 714, 716; W. H. Welply, 'John Baron Lumley, 1534?–1609', *Notes and Queries*, 181 (Aug. 1941), 87; Venn and Venn, *Alumni Cantab.*, Pt I, IV, 142; S. Jayne, *Library Catalogues of the English Renaissance* (Berkeley, 1956), pp. 106, 109, 140; *Athenae Oxonienses*, I, 45–6; Foster, *Gray's Reg.*, p. 6; A. H. Anderson, 'The Books and Interests of Henry, Lord Stafford (1501–1563)', *The Library*, 5th ser., 21, 2 (June 1966), 87–114.

67 Only six of them were university students in the forties and fifties: (4th) Norfolk, (2nd) Bedford, Devon, Lumley, (2nd) Wentworth, and (10th) Cobham.

68 *Cal.S.P.Span.*, X, 62; *H.P.T.Biogs*; A. L. Rowse, 'Thomas Wriothesley, First Earl of Southampton', *H.L.Q.*, 28 (Feb. 1965), 107; *Cal.S.P.Ven.*, VI, Pt III, App. 115; *Athenae Oxonienses*, I, 89; *D.N.B.*, *sub* John Lumley.

69 The first earl of Southampton, Barons Bergavenny, (4th) Burgh, De la Warr, Dudley, Grey of Powis, Mordaunt, North, Paget, Rich, Stafford, (2nd) Wentworth, (2nd and 3rd) Windsor.

70 Charlton, *Renaissance Education*, pp. 177–81, 186; Stone, *Crisis*, pp. 690–1. Although some of the features of this decay have been questioned – e.g. in Prest, 21, and Simon, *Tudor Education*, p. 355 – Prest ultimately arrived at the same conclusion: that 'judging by the quality of the legal instruction they provided, the Inns of Court were as educationally moribund as the Elizabethan and early Stuart universities'. To some extent this conclusion is applicable to the forties and fifties.

71 'The inns came closest to fulfilling the role of humanistic academies.' Prest, 38–9.

72 Mordaunt, North, Paget, Rich, Stafford, Wriothesley.

73 *G.E.C.*, XII (II), 794–7.

74 *Ibid.*, 499.

75 In 1534 he wrote to Cromwell of his ineffectiveness in the Lords. 'I ame noe man mete to reson noe mater there, but to say ye or nay, for the impedyment that God hays geve me in my tonge, whiche I can not remedy.' P.R.O., S.P. 1/82, fo. 10.

76 W. Roper, 'The Life of Sir Thomas More', in *Two Early Tudor Lives*, ed. R. S. Sylvester and D. P. Harding (New Haven and London, 1962), p. 246.

77 'Few persons who have held a prominent position in the state have had so little said to their credit.' Wriothesley had but 'scanty legal learning' and proved to be 'very inadequate to the discharge of the judicial duties of his office'. He endured two terms in chancery where he was 'pelted by motions which he knew not how to dispose of, and puzzled by causes the bearings of which he could hardly be made to understand'. Henceforth he delegated his duties there to the master of the rolls and others. E. Foss, *A Biographical Dictionary of the Judges of England* (London, 1870), p. 767; John Lord Campbell, *Lives of the Lord Chancellors*, 10 vols (London, 1856–7), II, 117–18.

78 *A.P.C.*, II, 48–55; A. J. Slavin, 'The Fall of Lord Chancellor

Wriothesley: A Study in the Politics of Conspiracy', *Albion*, 7 (1975), 268, 271, 285; and A. J. Slavin, 'Lord Chancellor Wriothesley and Reform of Augmentations. New Light on an Old Court', in A. J. Slavin (ed.), *Tudor Men and Institutions* (Baton Rouge, 1972), pp. 61, 63.

79 This total may be an underestimate. Six other peers – Somerset, Suffolk, (3rd) Sussex, and Lords (8th) Audley, Clinton and (2nd) Vaux – may have attended universities, but the evidence is inconclusive. Graves, 'The Mid-Tudor House of Lords', ii, App. Education, i–iv.

80 E.g. William 10th Lord Cobham at Padua.

81 T. Starkey, *A Dialogue between Reginald Pole and Thomas Lupset*, ed. K. M. Burton (London, 1948), pp. 120, 196; Richard Mulcaster, *Positions*, cit. Charlton, *Renaissance Education*, p. 215.

82 Starkey, *Pole and Lupset*, p. 169.

83 Curtis, pp. 67–9; Simon, *Tudor Education*, pp. 341–3.

84 See also Neale, *Elizabethan Commons*, p. 307; *Narratives of Reformation*, p. 273.

85 Curtis, pp. 65–6; Sir Thomas Elyot, *The Book named the Governor*, ed. S. E. Lehmberg (London, 1962), pp. 19, 35, 39, 44–5, 52.

86 *Athenae Oxonienses*, i, 583; *L.P.*, Henry VIII, iv(2), Nos 4560, 4916; *ibid.*, v, No. 926; *ibid.*, vii, No. 1135; *ibid.*, xiii(1), Nos 183, g.(190(1)), 1409, 1410; *ibid.*, xvi, No. 1011 (p. 483); *ibid.*, xxi(1), No. 9; *Cal. S.P.Span.*, xii, 96; *G.E.C.*, iii, 557 n. (c); Simon, *Tudor Education*, pp. 155–6; H. Ellis (ed.), *Original Letters, Illustrative of English History*, 11 vols in 3 series (London, 1824–46), 3rd ser., i, 341–5. Cobham and Cromwell, however, also attended universities.

87 N. Williams, *Thomas Howard, Fourth Duke of Norfolk* (London, 1964), pp. 6, 24–5, 29–31.

88 Graves, 'The Mid-Tudor House of Lords', i(1), p. 332.

89 Anderson, 'Stafford's Books', p. 92.

90 J. G. Nichols (ed.), *Literary Remains of King Edward VI*, 2 vols (New York, n.d., first published London, 1857), i, lvii, lxiv.

91 E.g. Gregory Cromwell's elaborate programme. See n. 86 above, and pp. 45, 49 of the present volume.

92 T. Fuller, *The Worthies of England* (London, 1684), p. 465: Stone, *Crisis*, pp. 715–16.

93 *D.N.B.*, *sub* John Russell, 1st earl of Bedford; J. H. Wiffen, *Historical Memoirs of the House of Russell*, 2 vols (London, 1833), i, 181.

94 The statutes devised for Lord Wharton's new free grammar school at Kirkby Stephen, however, required that Latin and 'other humane doctrine' should be taught, and they hint at a growing acceptance of humanism even in the far north. James, 'Change and Continuity', pp. 41–2.

95 *A.P.C.*, iii, 409. This may be a reference to his calligraphy rather than his literacy.

96 E. Casady, *Henry Howard, Earl of Surrey* (New York, 1938), p. 84; Jordan, *Edward VI. The Young King*, p. 86; *Cal.S.P.Span.*, x, 19.

97 Williams, *Norfolk*, p. 7; *Cal.S.P.Span.*, XI, 327.

98 *L.P.*, Henry VIII, VII, No. 1135; *ibid.*, XVI, No. 578 (p. 270).

99 E.g. Northampton, Arundel, Cumberland, Lumley, (10th) Morley, Stafford and (2nd) Vaux.

100 In particular (1st) Bedford, Viscount Montagu, North, Paget, Rich and William (2nd) Windsor.

101 See chapter 6 of the present volume.

102 Twenty-five to forty-seven in 1547 and twenty-five to fifty-two in January 1558.

103 *Narratives of Reformation*, pp. 238–40.

104 William Barlow and the lay prior of St John.

105 Twenty-five at Oxford, twenty-two at Cambridge, and five at both. Nine also studied at continental universities.

106 *Narratives of Reformation*, pp. 218–19.

107 Twenty-eight in divinity and nine in canon and/or civil law. In addition twelve others had become bachelors of divinity, one a bachelor of divinity and one a bachelor of canon and/or civil law. Only Reginald Pole and John Hooper did not progress beyond a B.A., but the former was a scholar of European repute and the latter both a dedicated reformer and a vigorous member of the Lords in 1552 and March 1553.

108 These figures are derived from C. H. and T. Cooper (eds), *Athenae Cantabrigienses*, 3 vols (Cambridge, 1858–1913); *Athenae Oxonienses*; Venn and Venn, *Alumni Cantab.*, Pt 1; J. Foster (ed.), *Alumni Oxonienses*, 4 vols in 2 (London, 1887–8); Fuller, *Worthies*; *D.N.B.*; C. W. Boase and A. Clark (eds), *Register of the University of Oxford* (Oxford, 1885), I.

109 Headmaster of Winchester in 1534 and warden in 1541. J. A. Muller, *Stephen Gardiner and the Tudor Reaction* (London, 1926), p. 252 n. 25.

110 Usher of Magdalen College School, 1542–8; Foster, *Alumni Oxonienses*, II, 651.

111 E.g. Ralph Baynes, who had held the chair of Hebrew at Paris. Also Pate(s), Ridley and Sampson at Paris, Pole and Tunstall at Padua, Coverdale, Hopton and Turberville elsewhere.

112 Also Baynes, Coverdale, Goldwell, Christopherson and Pate(s). W. Schenk, *Reginald Pole, Cardinal of England* (London, 1950), pp. 29–128; Garrett, p. 132; *D.N.B.*, *sub* Thomas Goldwell; *H.M.C.*, MSS. of the Duke of Portland, 13th Report, App. II (London, 1893); L. B. Smith, *Tudor Prelates*, p. 290 and n. 29.

113 F. A. Gasquet and E. Bishop, *Edward VI and the Book of Common Prayer*, 3rd edn (London, 1928), pp. 128–37.

114 Foxe, VI, 396–411; *Grey Friars' Chron.*, p. 85; R. Eden (ed.), *The Examinations and Writings of John Philpot*, Parker Soc. (Cambridge, 1842), pp. 179–214; A. G. Dickens, *The English Reformation* (London, 1968), pp. 300–1.

115 *Cal.S.P.Span.*, XI, 236, 255, 258–9, 423; R. A. Vertot d'Aubeuf and C. Villaret (eds), *Ambassades de Messieurs de Noailles*, 5 vols (Leyden, 1763), II, 223.

116 L.J., ii, 29, 33, 42, 80, 103, 188, 255; Foxe, vi, 126; Gasquet and Bishop, pp. 127–37.

117 J. Strype, *Annals of the Reformation*, 4 vols (Oxford, 1824), i, Pt ii, 399–423, 431–50.

118 John Jewell to Peter Martyr, 20 March 1559. H. Robinson (ed.), *The Zurich Letters*, Parker Soc. (Cambridge, 1842–5, reprint 1966), i, 10.

119 H. C. Porter, *Reformation and Reaction in Tudor Cambridge* (Cambridge, 1958), p. 32; C. Sturge, *Cuthbert Tunstall* (London, 1938), p. 24; L. B. Smith, *Tudor Prelates and Politics, 1536–58* (Princeton, 1953), pp. 31, 56.

120 For details of their diplomatic careers, see *D.N.B.*, *sub* Edmund Bonner, Stephen Gardiner, Richard Sampson, Thomas Thirlby and Cuthbert Tunstall; L. B. Smith, *Tudor Prelates*, p. 75 n. 20; T. F. Shirley, *Thomas Thirlby, Tudor Bishop* (London, 1964), pp. 12, 40–2, 52–95, 119–23, 125–31, 142–52, 192–211.

121 Tunstall served as master of the rolls (1516–22), keeper of the privy seal (1523–30), member of the council in the north (1530–8, 1550–1, 1553–9) and even its president (1530–3, 1537–8). *D.N.B.*, *sub* Tunstall and Veysey; Williams, *Council in the Welsh Marches*, p. xiv; Sturge, pp. 389, 390; Reid, *King's Council in North*, App. ii, pp. 113ff., 487, 490.

122 J. Gillow, *A Literary and Biographical History . . . of the English Catholics*, 5 vols (London, 1885–1903), ii, 32–3, 513; *Athenae Oxonienses*, i, 89–90; *D.N.B.*, *sub* John Ponet and Paul Bush; W. S. Hudson (ed.), *John Ponet (1516?–1556), Advocate of Limited Monarchy* (Chicago, 1942), p. 16 and n. 35; Simon, *Tudor Education*, pp. 252–3.

123 Cranmer, Gardiner, Goodrich, Heath, Thirlby, Tunstall.

124 Goodrich, Gardiner and Heath.

125 Pollard, *Evolution*, pp. 160, 215; Notestein, 17, 22–3, 24; Neale, *Elizabethan Parliaments*, i, pp. 11, 16–29, 40–1, 421; *ibid.*, ii, pp. 334, 435–6; Neale, *Elizabethan Commons*, pp. 15–16, 372–3; Read, *Burghley*, p. 34.

126 Neale, *Elizabethan Commons*, pp. 309–11; Neale, *Elizabethan Parliaments*, i, 91, 406.

127 Neale, *Elizabethan Commons*, p. 309.

128 Calculated from L.J., and *G.E.C.*, *passim*.

129 Possibly 27, if the Thomas Percy who represented Westmorland in 1554–5 was the future 6th (restored) earl. *H.P.T. Biogs.*

130 *G.E.C.*, xii(ii), 497. Pollard stated that William Windsor, who was elected to the same parliament, was replaced by a 'Mr. Bowkleye' after his father was ennobled in December. A. F. Pollard, 'Thomas Cromwell's Parliamentary Lists', *B.I.H.R.*, 9 (June 1931), 39. However, the heirs of barons were not ineligible. William, first surviving son of the 6th Lord Stourton, sat for Somerset from 1529 until his succession in 1535. *G.E.C.*, xii(i), 305. Pollard's alternative explanation, that he 'may have preferred his right, as the eldest son of a peer, to attendance in the house of lords', is strangely confused. Heirs had no right of summons which was entirely a matter of royal grace (and

which in any case was confined to the heirs of senior peerages). He may have strayed into error as a result of his misreading of the Russell test-case. Francis, eldest son of John Lord Russell, was one of the knights for Buckinghamshire when his father was promoted to the earldom of Bedford. The Commons had doubts about the eligibility of an earl's son, but on 21 January 1550 it resolved that 'Francis Russell shall abide in this house in the state he was before'. C.J., i, 29v.

131 William Paulet, John Russell, William Herbert, John Bridges, Thomas Darcy, Edward North and Thomas Wharton.

132 John Dudley, Anthony Browne and John Williams.

133 In contrast members of the Commons had no experience of the Lords, apart from the occasional secretary of State or legal counsel who had sat on the woolsacks, by virtue of a writ of assistance, prior to service in the Lower House. See chapter 6, pp. 127–8, 130–1, of the present volume.

134 *Ibid.*, p. 122.

135 See chapter 1, n. 9.

136 Wriothesley (1544–7) and Rich (1547–51).

137 Goodrich (1552–3), Gardiner (1553–5) and Heath (1556–8).

138 E.g. *L.P.*, Henry VIII, XI, No. 381c; L.J., i, 250.

Chapter 4: Attendance and activity, absenteeism and management

1 Snow, 'Proc. rep. Henry VIII', 1–26; Miller, 'Attendance', 325–51. For a continuation of the debate into Edward VI's reign, see Graves, 'Proc. rep. Edward VI', 17–35: Snow, 'Proc. rep. Edward VI', 1–27; Snow, 'A Rejoinder', 36–46.

2 Snow, 'Proc. rep. Henry VIII', 10, 23, 24–5; Miller, 'Attendance', 350–1.

3 They are calculated as percentages of those summoned because the size of the eligible membership and the length of sessions fluctuated.

4 Miller, 'Attendance', 336.

5 The calculations in this chapter are based upon the attendance registers in L.J., ii, iii. Graves, 'The Mid-Tudor House of Lords', II, App. Attendance I–XVI.

6 The comprehensive sessional attendance figures are as follows: Edward VI, 82%, 89%, 79%, 82%, 76%; Mary, 65%, 80%, 73%, 86%, 54%.

7 The regular attendance figures for each session are as follows: Edward VI, 39%, 66%, 48%, 46%, 56%; Mary, 44%, 34%, 39%, 29%, 23%.

8 Daily attendance figures for each session: Edward VI, 57%, 66%, 51%, 57%, 62%; Mary, 49%, 51%, 53%, 53%, 36%.

9 For the more elaborate and formal features of the Lords' procedures see chapter 7, p. 146 and nn. 23, 24, of the present volume.

10 Average daily attendance totals: Edward VI, 41, 48, 36, 37, 44; Mary, 35, 38, 41, 41, 26.

11 L.J., ii, 49, 70; L.J., iii, 153.

12 L.J., ii, 74, 77, 80.

[13] See chapter 8, pp. 177–8, of the present volume.

[14] See chapter 8, pp. 194–8.

[15] For a more detailed examination see chapter 8, pp. 180–98.

[16] However, the 1547 session is the least impressive.

[17] M. A. R. Graves, 'The House of Lords and the Politics of Opposition, April–May 1554', in G. A. Wood and P. S. O'Connor (eds), *W. P. Morrell: A Tribute* (Dunedin, 1973), *passim.*

[18] *Ibid.*; M. A. R. Graves, 'The Mid-Tudor House of Lords: Forgotten Member of the Parliamentary Trinity' in F. McGregor and N. Wright (eds), *European History and its Historians* (Adelaide, 1977), pp. 25–30.

[19] J. S. Roskell located the first signs of a declining attendance in Edward VI's reign, after an improvement in Henry VIII's later parliaments. However, his figures are misleading, based as they are on only one session, that of 1549/50. How he arrives at his conclusion, that 'only three out of every five lords were present', is a mystery: it is 19% lower than the House record and 25% below the peers' record in the attendance register of the Lords' Journals. J. S. Roskell, 'The Problem of the Attendance of the Lords in Medieval Parliaments', *B.I.H.R.*, 29 (1956), 197. Helen Miller demonstrated that when, between 1536 and 1540, Cromwell's supervision achieved the best attendance record of the reign, general and regular attendance levels were 86% and 55% respectively. The Edwardian averages of 82% and 51% were only slightly inferior and certainly represent a distinct recovery from the declining rates (70% and 29%) in the post-Cromwellian sessions of 1542–47. Miller, 'Attendance', Table 2, 337. Even the Marian record (72% and 34%), whilst no match for the Cromwellian period and Edward's reign, is superior to the late Henrician parliaments. When Roskell claims that, under Elizabeth, 'the lords' attendance seems to have recovered the high level eventually reached under her father' he presents an over-simplified picture. The average general (87%) and regular (40%) attendance record of two sample sessions (1563 and 1571) registered a marked improvement over the late Henrician as well as the Marian parliaments. L.J., iv, 71–131; *ibid.*, v, 6–56. It must be seen rather as a return to the high level of the Cromwellian and Edwardian periods after the interim slumps of the early 1540s and Mary's reign. Roskell, 'Lords' Attendance in Medieval Parliaments', 197.

[20] *Ibid.*, 199.

[21] Miller, 'Attendance', Table 2, 337. In all but two of the last seven sessions, a higher proportion of bishops than peers made an appearance. With one exception – 1545 (when the peers' record equalled that of the prelates) – a considerably higher proportion of the latter were regularly present from June 1536 onwards.

[22] See chapter 5, pp. 98–9, of the present volume.

[23] Graves, 'The Mid-Tudor House of Lords', 1(2), pp. 602–12.

[24] The 1st Lord Wentworth served for only 17 months and Viscount Montagu for a slightly longer period.

[25] E.g. The dukes of Northumberland and Somerset, the marquesses of

Northampton and Winchester, the 1st earl of Bedford, the earl of Southampton, Lords Paget and Rich, Archbishop Cranmer, and Bishops Gardiner, Thirlby and Tunstall.

26 Ralph 4th earl of Westmorland, (10th) Lord Morley and Bishop Sampson.

27 The dukes of Northumberland, Somerset and Suffolk, the marquess of Northampton, the earls of Huntingdon, Southampton and (5th) Westmorland, Viscount Hereford, and the Lords Cobham (9th), Darcy of Chiche, North, Seymour of Sudeley and (1st) Wentworth in Edward's reign; the 3rd duke of Norfolk, the earls of Bath and (2nd) Sussex, Viscount Montagu, and the Lords De la Warr (9th), Hastings of Loughborough, Howard of Effingham, and (2nd) Wentworth under Mary. Eight peers were councillors for at least part of each reign: Winchester, Arundel, (1st) Bedford, Pembroke, Shrewsbury and Lords Clinton, Paget and Rich. For Derby's special and temporary Edwardian commission, see D. E. Hoak, *The King's Council in the Reign of Edward VI* (Cambridge, 1976), pp. 66–9.

28 Cranmer, Goodrich and Ridley were Edwardian councillors; Gardiner, Heath, Thirlby and Reginald Pole were Marians. Tunstall was a councillor in 1547–51 and 1553–8. There are conflicting views on the conciliar role and formal position of Archbishop Pole. According to the council register he did not attend its meetings. *A.P.C.*, v and vi, *passim*. Twice – in August and November 1555 – he refused King Philip's requests that he assume chief responsibility for the government. The Venetian ambassador, however, believed that he was 'both King and Prince, though he exercises [his authority] so graciously and modestly as if he were the least of [the council], not choosing in any way to interfere, not even in public affairs, unless in such as are especially assigned to him'. *Cal.S.P.Ven.*, vi, Pt 2, No. 884 (p. 1070). Although he was not formally appointed to the council, he performed an important function in it as a consequence of Philip's instructions (G. Burnet, *History of the Reformation of the Church of England*, ed. N. Pocock, 7 vols (Oxford, 1865), vi, no. xli) and he directed much conciliar business behind the scenes by advice to the queen. Strype, *Eccl. Mems*, iii, ii, no. lxxx. For these reasons he has been included here amongst the Marian councillors.

29 The comprehensive sessional record of the number of councillors and the proportion of the House which they constituted reads as follows: 1547: 10 (2 bishops + 8 peers) or 14%. 1548/9: 12 (2 + 10) or 16%. 1549/50: 16 (3 + 13) or 22.5%. 1552: 18 (3 + 15) or 28%. March 1553: 18 (2 + 16) or 26.5%. Oct.–Dec. 1553: 17 (3 + 14) or 26%. April 1554: 17 (3 + 14) or 24%. 1554/5: 16 (4 + 12) or 23%. 1555: 15 (4 + 11) or 20%. Jan. 1558: 16 (4 + 12) or 22%. Nov. 1558: 16 (4 + 12) or 22%.

30 Hoak, p. 89.

31 E.g. Norfolk, Northumberland and Somerset, Bedford, Pembroke, Clinton, Howard of Effingham.

32 E.g. Northampton, Arundel, Darcy of Chiche.

[33] E.g. Gardiner, Thirlby.

[34] E.g. Winchester.

[35] E.g. Southampton, Rich.

[36] E.g. (1st) Bedford, Derby, Shrewsbury, De la Warr.

[37] The earls of Cumberland, Northumberland, (4th) Westmorland, Conyers, Dacre of the North, (1st) Eure, Lumley, Talbot, Wharton, Archbishop Holgate and Bishops Thirlby and Tunstall. Holgate and Tunstall had been presidents of the council in the north, and Wharton became vice-president in 1550. Bishops Sampson (1543–8) and Bourne (1558–9) were presidents of the council in the Welsh marches. Councillors included the 3rd earl of Worcester and 1st Viscount Hereford, Lord Grey of Powis, and Bishops Ferrar, Veysey and Warton.

[38] Arundel, (1st) Chandos, Clinton, (9th) Cobham, (4th) Dudley, Grey de Wilton, Howard of Effingham and Willoughby.

[39] Northumberland, Northampton, (the 6th earl of) Northumberland, Rutland, Conyers, Dacre of the North, (1st and 2nd) Eure, Grey de Wilton, Ogle, (8th) Scrope, Wharton.

[40] (3rd) Sussex.

[41] Nor was it confined to the areas already mentioned and which exclude long-serving officials such as John Williams.

[42] Elton, *Tudor Constitution*, p. 286.

[43] For the political and legislative record of the House, see chapter 8 of the present volume.

[44] '[T]he Crown could usually depend upon the privy councillors to be present every day.' Snow, 'Proc. rep. Henry VIII', 23.

[45] Cranmer attended 94% of the sittings in 1547 and 93%, 92%, 100% and 100% in the remaining Edwardian assemblies. Goodrich did not miss a single day between 1549 and March 1553. For Tunstall's record between 1547 and 1549/50 see below, p. 90 of the present volume. These figures, and those in the following paragraphs, are derived from L.J., ii, *passim*.

[46] Warwick was ill and may have had a heart-attack.

[47] L.J., ii, 131–96.

[48] Arundel attended twice and Southampton nine times. For a recent persuasive account of Warwick's successful struggle against the Catholics on the council, which was acted out during this session of parliament, see Hoak, *The King's Council*, pp. 241–58.

[49] Out of 60 days, Pembroke appeared on 13, (5th) Westmorland on 42, Clinton on 12, and Darcy of Chiche on 38. Northumberland himself attended 41 sittings.

[50] Seventy per cent.

[51] Councillors attended 77% of the daily sittings.

[52] Eighty per cent.

[53] See p. 63 and n. 29 of the present volume.

[54] Whether the government went further and sought to transform leadership into a tight disciplined control is considered on p. 63.

[55] However, there were exceptions, e.g. *Cal.S.P.Span.*, XI, 33.

⁵⁶ From the Edwardian range of 65%–86% to one of 60%–74%.

⁵⁷ Eight in 1555, nine in Jan. 1558 and six in Nov. 1558.

⁵⁸ Bath, (1st) Bedford, De la Warr and (2nd) Wentworth in April 1554; (2nd) Wentworth in 1554/5; Shrewsbury, (2nd) Sussex, (2nd) Wentworth and Heath in 1555, and Tunstall in Jan. 1558. The six absentees in Nov. 1558 were Arundel, Bath, Paget, Reginald Pole, Thirlby and Tunstall. Derby's solitary recorded appearance was possibly a clerical error, as he may have been serving as captain of the vanguard in the army of the north. *A.P.C.*, VI, 92; *C.P.R., Ph. & Mary*, IV, 193–4.

⁵⁹ The average Edwardian daily presence was 41, between April 1554 and Jan. 1558 it was 39, and in Nov. 1558 it fell to 26.

⁶⁰ *D.N.B.*, *sub* Thomas 2nd Baron Wentworth.

⁶¹ *Queen Jane*, p. 68; *H.M.C.*, Frederick Peake MSS., 96; *Cal.S.P.Span.*, XII, 149, 173, 177, 205, 286–8, 291, 312.

⁶² Lodge, *Illustrations*, I, 252–3.

⁶³ See chapter 8, pp. 184–6, of the present volume.

⁶⁴ E.g. in Mary's first parliament. See chapter 8, pp. 186–8.

⁶⁵ See chapter 8, pp. 193–4; Graves, 'Forgotten House of Lords', pp. 27–8.

⁶⁶ Especially in 1554/5.

⁶⁷ E.g. in April 1554.

⁶⁸ See chapter 8, p. 199, of the present volume.

⁶⁹ Neale, *Elizabethan Parliaments*, I, 23–6; Notestein, p. 12; *Cal.S.P.Ven.*, VI, Pt I, No. 282 (p. 251).

⁷⁰ The daily attendance of the house averaged 38 in 1554/5 and 41 in 1555.

⁷¹ An average daily attendance of 41 for the whole house and nine for the councillors. An improvement in the bishops' performance (up from 13 to 16 per day) offset the peers' decline from 28 to 25.

⁷² Twenty-six of the whole House, including six members of the privy council, attended each day.

⁷³ Eight (out of 41) in 1547, 10 (48) in 1548/9, 10 (36) in 1549/50, 10 (37) in 1552, 13 (44) in March 1553; 10 (35) in April 1554, 10 (38) in 1554/5, 8 (41) in 1555, 9 (41) in Jan. 1558, 6 (26) in Nov. 1558.

⁷⁴ Bishops Bulkeley, Chambers, King, Reginald Pole, Veysey and Wakeman, the prior of St John (Sir Thomas Tresham), the earls of Bridgewater, Cumberland, Northumberland, (4th) Westmorland and (2nd) Worcester, and Lords (3rd) Burgh, (10th) Cobham, (1st and 2nd) Darcy of Darcy, De la Warr, Mordaunt, (2nd and 3rd) Vaux, (3rd) Windsor, (8th) Zouche.

⁷⁵ Bishop Harley and the earl of Devon who were only eligible in October 1553 (for which there is no surviving journal) must also be discounted.

⁷⁶ For the problems involved in such a classification and a detailed analysis of attendance and committee experience, see Graves, 'The 'Mid-Tudor House of Lords', I (2), pp. 635–43.

⁷⁷ Bonner, Bourne, Bush, Coverdale, Cranmer, Day, Gardiner,

Goodrich, Griffith, Heath, Holbeach, Hooper, Oglethorpe, Pate, D. Pole, Ponet, Ridley, Skip, Thirlby, Tunstall, Watson, White.

[78] For a comparison of their respective performances see Graves, 'The Mid-Tudor House of Lords', 1 (2), pp. 639, 644.

[79] The adoption of a single year as the line of demarcation between the new and old peerage, as W. K. Jordan did, is arbitrary and bears no relation to historical realities. Jordan, *Edward VI. The Young King*, p. 90. Discussion about the antiquity or newness of title must be relative to some degree: that one is older or newer than the other. Nevertheless there were significant social attitudes which tended to separate the old from the new, whilst some individuals were unmistakably one or the other. Whatever dividing line is adopted must be a rather arbitrary and subjective choice. However, it is possible to diminish the artificiality and unreality of Jordan's classification if we do not assume that new nobles withered into antiquity overnight. Therefore only the *arrivistes*, first-generation peers created since *c.* 1529, have been classified as 'new'. Ancient nobility has been restricted to peers of unimpeachable antiquity whose families had originally been ennobled more than a century prior to 1547. This leaves a number of indeterminate nobles in the middle, in transition from the new to the old (and classified as intermediate).

[80] Average daily attendance: 73% of new peers, 66% of intermediate and 65% of old peers. Eleven new peers attended more than 75% of daily sessions, whereas the other two groups mustered only two apiece. Ten of the 15 peers appointed to one or more committees in each session were newly ennobled.

[81] These two groups contributed 43% of the 58 active members.

[82] The proportion of daily sittings attended by the bishops and new peers amongst the actual membership was (with the exception of 1548/9) consistently higher. In 1547 they recorded 81%, the intermediate and old peers 76%. Their performance was more or less equivalent in the next session. Thereafter the prelates and new peers consistently turned in a superior performance: in 1549/50: 80%/50%; 1552: 79%/64%; March 1553: 83%/74%; April 1554: 67%/52%; 1554/5: 75%/54%; 1555: 70%/62%; Jan. 1558: 73%/56%; Nov. 1558: 54%/40%.

[83] The active members were named to committees on 326 occasions. Of these over three-quarters (249) were bishops and new peers.

[84] 71% in 1547, 67% (1548/9), 62% (1549/50), 62% (1552), 60% (March 1553), 62% (April 1554), 63% (1554/5), 64% (1555) and 66% each in January and November 1558.

[85] Bush, Coverdale, Cranmer, Hooper, Ponet and Ridley.

[86] Bourne, Griffith, Oglethorpe, Pate, D. Pole, Watson and White.

[87] Somerset, Suffolk, Northampton, Southampton, (1st) Eure, Sheffield, Seymour and (1st) Wentworth.

[88] (4th) Norfolk, (3rd) Sussex, Montagu, (1st) Chandos, Lumley, Howard of Effingham, North and Williams.

[89] Somerset, Suffolk, Northampton, Arundel, (1st) Bedford, (3rd) Sussex, Montagu, Sheffield and Seymour.

90 Winchester (8 sessions), (1st and 2nd) Bedford (8 and 6 sessions respectively), (1st) Southampton (4), Viscount Montagu (9), (1st) Chandos, (1st) Darcy of Chiche (8 or 11), North (8), Paget (4? +), Rich (14), Seymour of Sudeley (2), (1st) Sheffield (3?), (1st) Wentworth (1), Wharton (8 or 11), Williams of Thame (9), Willoughby (2), (2nd) Windsor (1). There is some doubt whether Darcy of Chiche represented Essex in 1542–4. *H.P.T.Biogs.* Paget may also have been returned to the Reformation Parliament in a by-election. *Ibid.* Stafford may have been elected for Stafford in 1545 and 1547, but it is possible that the returned member was his illegitimate brother or his son. *Ibid.*; *G.E.C.*, XII (I), 183 n. (d) and 185 n. (a). Even the future Lord Stafford's election to the first Edwardian parliament remains doubtful: 'it would have been *infra dignitatem* for the very proud heir of the Staffords to have sat as a burgess for a borough, while the county seats were occupied by a Gryffith and a Fitzherbert'. *H.P.T.Biogs.* Wentworth was elected knight for Suffolk to the parliament which met in November 1529, but by the following month he had been ennobled. *G.E.C.*, XII (II), 497. The Thomas Wharton elected as knight for Cumberland in 1542–4 may have been the 1st Lord Wharton's son. *H.P.T.Biogs.* It is probable that Sir Thomas Percy, the knight for Westmorland in November 1554, was the future 6th earl. If this was so then the total number of peers with Commons' experience rises to 18.

91 Bonner, Gardiner, Thirlby, Tunstall, the marquess of Winchester, Arundel, (1st) Bedford, Southampton, (1st) Darcy of Chiche, North, Paget, Rich and Williams of Thame.

92 Somerset, Clinton, Howard of Effingham, Dacre of the North, (1st) Eure and Wharton.

93 E.g. Shrewsbury and the Bedfords.

94 Jordan, *Edward VI. The Young King*, p. 89.

95 See pp. 71, 79–80 of the present volume.

96 Pollard, *Evolution*, pp. 101–2.

97 Roskell, 'Lords' Attendance in Medieval Parliaments', *passim*.

98 *Ibid.*, 198.

99 Miller, 'Attendance', Table 2, 337; L.J., i, 124.

100 '[It] could only be effective as a short-term policy, and the need even for this was confined to the mid-1530s.' Miller, 'Attendance', 329–35.

101 Roskell, 'Lords' attendance in Medieval Parliaments', 156.

102 Miller, 'Attendance', 335, 339–43.

103 E.g. Cumberland and Westmorland, who were discharged 'of theyre repayre to the Parliament notwithstanding theyre writt receyved to the contrarye' in 1542, and Lord Wharton in November 1547. *L.P.*, Henry VIII, XVI, No. 1464; P.R.O., S.P. 15/1, fos 31, 33, 38.

104 Miller, 'Attendance', 329–35. As late as 1601 Elizabeth directed five peers to stay away after receipt of their writs. Pollard, *Evolution*, p. 306, n. 2.

105 *Ibid.*, p. 273.

106 For a full discussion of the system of licences and proxies, see Graves,

'The Mid-Tudor House of Lords', 1(2), pp. 575–80, 657–65, 667–84.

107 None of the authorised absentees in this period appear to have been granted lifelong exemptions. Snow, 'Proc. rep. Edward VI', 5; Roskell, 'Lords Attendance in Medieval Parliaments', 202–4. Although Henry Elsynge believed that the 'King's verball Licence is sufficient', he acknowledged that sooner or later something was put in writing: a request, a licence or testimonial, an instruction to stay away, or a letter empowering a proctor to act for the absentee. Graves, 'The Mid-Tudor House of Lords', 1(2), p. 659. H. Elsynge, *The Ancient Method and Manner of Holding of Parliaments* (London, 1660), p. 103.

108 For a sample licence, see L.J., iv, 134.

109 D'Ewes, p. 4.

110 Sir Thomas Smith maintained that the registration of proxies was the first business to be transacted in each session. Smith, *De Republica*, p. 50. However, few proxies were submitted at the opening of a parliament, either because of their late arrival, the dilatory conduct of clerks, or the fact that some licences were only granted during the session. E.g. L.J., ii, 126–7, 49–116.

111 E.g. in 1548/9, 1549/50, and 1552. L.J., ii, 49–111, 131–76, 209–46.

112 L.J., ii, 126–7, 272; *ibid.*, iii, 1–2, 33, 87, 129. The 1547 list was displaced, being bound in with the journal for 1549/50. L.J., ii, 126–7.

113 Pollard, 'Clerk of the Crown', 323; Miller, 'Attendance', 349 and n. 151, 345 and n. 124; L.J., i, 698.

114 Miller, 'Attendance', 344.

115 Elsynge, *Ancient Method of Holding Parliaments*, p. 96; D'Ewes, p. 5.

116 '[E]verie Englishman is entended to bee there present, either in person or by procuration and attornies, of what preheminence, state, dignitie, or qualitie soever he be . . . And the consent of the Parliament is taken to be everie man's consent.' Smith, *De Republica*, p. 49.

117 The 123 designated as sessional absentees include a dozen who were recorded, probably in error, as being present on one day.

118 The 5th earl of Westmorland attended three of the four opening days of the first 1558 session. On the fourth day, 25 January, he was appointed lieutenant of the north whereupon his attendance ceased and two days later his proxy was entered. L.J., iii, 129. Graves, 'The Mid-Tudor House of Lords', 1(2), p. 668.

119 This at least is the opinion of V. F. Snow on the Henrician situation. Snow, 'Proc. rep. Henry VIII', 5. The bishops of Bangor and Peterborough and Lords De la Warr and Mordaunt were licensed to be absent from the first Edwardian parliament, but proxies were regularly sent up for each session. On the other hand nine of the ten sessional absentees from the session of January 1558 stayed away in the following November too, yet they did not renew their proxies. Perhaps they just did not bother in the closing days of the reign.

120 Thirteen licensees returned to the House at some time subsequent to the registration of their proxies. Graves, 'The Mid-Tudor House of Lords', ii, App. Attendance xii (ii). In the early seventeenth century,

'a Proxie that is returned becometh void, either when the Peer or Lord that sends the Proxie dies himself, or comes to the House in Person before the end of the Parliament'. D'Ewes, p. 7.

[121] Derby, Lord Vaux's proctor in November 1558, was present on only one day. L.J., iii, 181. Southampton, Bishop Kitchin's proctor in 1549/50, attended 14% of sittings, Arundel with six proxies in 1554/5 and Pembroke, proctor to three peers, managed only 48% and 46% respectively. Graves, 'The Mid-Tudor House of Lords', II, App. Attendance, IV, V, XI, XII.

[122] 'A Proxy cannot be made to a Lord that is absent himself . . . So if the Lord unto whom the proxy is made, be afterwards absent, the Proxy is void.' So in 38 Henry VIII the 4th Lord Latimer sent his proxy 'which the Clerk received, but was repealed by the Lord Chancellor, for that the Lord Latimer's Deputies were not present'. There is, however, no record either of new proctors for Latimer or of replacements for absentee proctors under Edward VI and Mary. Elsynge, *Ancient Method of Holding Parliaments*, p. 104.

[123] Graves, 'Proc. rep. Edward VI', 29–30, 33.

[124] D'Ewes, pp. 3, 5, 7–8; Smith, *De Republica*, p. 50; Miller, 'Attendance', 332, 344; Snow, 'A Rejoinder', 41.

[125] L.J., i, 536, 542; Miller, 'Attendance', 346, n. 127.

[126] Edward VI: 7, 11, 11, 16, 6 (or a sessional average of about 10); Mary: 9, 8, 13, 9, 0 (averaging about 8). Twenty-two are recorded in the first four Elizabethan sessions. L.J., ii, iii, iv, and v.

[127] Over half the mid-Tudor absentees (whose proctors are known) did so. Twenty-eight absentees nominated more than two proctors. D'Ewes, p. 4.

[128] Sir Thomas Smith implied that a proctor cast a vote for each absentee who had nominated him, regardless of whether he was sole or joint proctor, or whatever his precedence was in the list of multiple proctors. Smith, *De Republica*, pp. 51, 56.

[129] Thus, when the archbishop of York named eight proctors in November 1549, he would have created eight additional proxy votes. L.J., ii, 135. A. F. Pollard was operating on this rather naive assumption when he totted up the proxy votes held by the abbots in February 1515 and credited them with this voting power, regardless of whether they were sole or joint proctors. A. F. Pollard, *Wolsey* (London, 1965), p. 43. V. F. Snow stumbled into the same trap when he credited William Repps, abbot of St Benet's, with seven proxy votes, although he was named second to the abbot of Hyde in five cases. Snow, 'Proc. rep. Henry VIII', 20.

[130] Coke, *Institutes*, Pt IV, 12–13.

[131] D'Ewes, pp. 5–6.

[132] L.J., v, 225.

[133] Smith, *De Republica*, pp. 42, 50, 51, 56. It is unlikely that Smith actually took his seat on the woolsacks when he was summoned on a writ of assistance, in his capacity of secretary. See chapter 6, p. 128 of the present volume. Of course one cannot dismiss out of hand his

early Elizabethan account of bishops and peers casting their own votes and those of their proxies 'when it commeth to the question', but he cites no specific examples. Hooker ignores the subject. D'Ewes, Bowyer, Hakewil, Elsynge and Scobell certainly discuss proxy voting, but they were, after all, Stuart commentators, and even their Tudor examples of procedure are often overlaid with later practice. B.L., Harleian MSS., 1178, no. 16, fos 19–27; D'Ewes, pp. 3–9; Petyt MSS., 537/6; W. Hakewil, *The Manner how Statutes are Enacted in Parliament* (London, 1641); H. Scobell, *Remembrances of some Methods, Orders and Proceedings in the House of Lords* (London, 1657).

134 In Edward VI's reign: 7, 6, 8, 1 and 4 (total 26); Mary: 6, 2, 7, 2, 27 (total 44). Twenty were lords spiritual and fifty peers. According to Elsynge, from the later Henrician parliaments on, a written licence was not required as proof of the king's consent, but only so long as the letters of proxy mentioned the licence 'which none will presume on unless he had it'. In the case of a verbal licence the letters of proxy constituted its only record, which fact must have encouraged absentees to send in such letters. Moreover the clerk would hardly have neglected to record them as a register of his due fees. In these circumstances the great majority of licensed members must have received a written licence or produced letters of proxy which were duly registered. Elsynge, *Ancient Method of Holding Parliaments*, pp. 96, 103–4.

135 The sessional figures read as follows: in Edward VI's reign, 22%, 14%, 27%, 20%, 24% (with a regnal average of 21%), and under Mary 36%, 23%, 28%, 20%, 49% (the regnal average being 31% or, if the exceptional November 1558 session is omitted, 27%).

136 For conflicting views on the parliaments of Henry VIII and Edward VI, see Miller, 'Attendance', 350–1, and Snow, 'Proc. rep. Edward VI', 27.

137 The only important public acts were the lay and clerical subsidies and the dissolution of the see of Durham. H.L.R.O., Orig. Acts, 7 Ed. VI, nos 12, 13, 17. Edward VI's note for 'The calling of a Parliament for to get some subsidy . . .', drafted on 13 October 1552, and the inclusion of a lay tax in Shrewsbury's memorandum of proposed measures suggest that this was why it was called. None of the remaining items in Shrewsbury's list, all of which were economic or religious, would in themselves have justified a new parliament. *Ed. VI's Chron.*, p. 178; P.R.O., S.P. 18/1, fo. 13.

138 John Dudley and the heirs of Shrewsbury and (1st) Bedford. P.R.O., Parl. Pawns, Petty Bag, C. 218, Pt I, No. 5; L.J., ii, 275; P.R.O., S.P. 10/18, fo. 8.

139 P.R.O., S.P. 10/18, fo. 6.

140 Strype, *Eccl. Mems*, II, Pt II, 64–6.

141 P.R.O., S.P. 10/18, fo. 6.

142 See chapter 2, pp. 15–16, 28, of the present volume.

143 In January 1558 they were instructed 'to use their best means to procure the election of men of knowledge and experience'. Strype, *Eccl. Mems*, III, Pt I, 245–6; *Cal.S.P.Dom.*, 1547–80, Mary, XII, No. 2;

J. Strype, *Memorials of . . . Thomas Cranmer*, 2 vols (Oxford, 1840), I, 493–4; M. G. Price, 'English Borough Representation, 1509–58', D.Phil. thesis, University of Oxford (1959), fo. 247.

[144] Chandos (created by patent, 8 April), Howard of Effingham (11 March), North (writ entered in journal on 7 April) and Williams (by writ in April). *C.P.R., Ph. & Mary*, I, 175, 266; L.J., iii, 8; *G.E.C.*, XII (II), 652.

[145] Between 15 and 20 March 1554; John Bird (Chester), Paul Bush (Bristol), Robert Ferrar (St David's), John Harley (Hereford), Robert Holgate (York), John Hooper (Gloucester), John Taylor (Lincoln). *Machyn*, p. 58; *C.P.R., Ph. & Mary*, I, 175–6; *D.N.B., sub* Paul Bush; F. M. Powicke and E. B. Fryde, *Handbook of British Chronology*, 2nd edn (London, 1961), p. 236.

[146] On 1 April 1554: Gilbert Bourne (Bath and Wells), James Brooks (Gloucester), George Cotes (Chester), Maurice Griffith (Rochester), Henry Morgan (St David's), John White (Lincoln). In addition Robert Warton was translated from St Asaph to Hereford in March. The new bishops averaged 92% of the sittings and the new peers (with the exception of Lord Howard who departed to take up his duties as lord admiral) 75%. L.J., iii, 5–28; *H.B.C.*, pp. 206, 215, 227, 230, 236, 249, 278–9; *D.N.B., sub* John White.

[147] *Cal.S.P.Span.*, XII, 295.

[148] Graves, 'Politics of Opposition', 7–8, 9.

[149] *Cal.S.P.Span.*, XII, 158–9, 295, 297–9, 315–16; E. H. Harbison, *Rival Ambassadors at the Court of Queen Mary* (London, 1940), App. II, pp. 340–2.

[150] See chapter 8, p. 189, n. 86, of the present volume.

[151] The possible addition was Robert Massey (Flint).

[152] Some of them were also returned in April 1554 and 1554/5, but fewer in 1555 – perhaps a mark of Gardiner's declining energies. Graves, 'The Mid-Tudor House of Lords', II, 200–1. See chapter 8, p. 189, n. 87, of the present volume.

[153] See chapter 8, p. 189, n. 86.

[154] Miller, 'Attendance', 330–5.

[155] L.J., i, 242–695; L.J., ii, 49–272.

[156] Thirty-two were licensed part-way through a session (and were thereafter absent) and thirteen others returned to the Lords after receipt of their licences. Graves, 'The Mid-Tudor House of Lords', II, App. Attendance, XII, XIII.

[157] This gives a grand total of 193 sessional absentees and 45 others, who were licensed for part of a session. This made a considerable inroad on a House whose actual membership never exceeded 80.

[158] Miller, 'Attendance', 329–35.

[159] The following examination of absenteeism has been compiled from *D.N.B., G.E.C., H.P.T.Biogs*, and Graves, 'The Mid-Tudor House of Lords', II, 176–369. The actual record of absences is derived from the attendance register in the Lords' Journals (vols i, ii and iii), which have their fair share of inconsistencies, omissions and errors. Nine

peers and seven bishops are credited with a single appearance during
a session, when in some cases they were demonstrably absent:
Holgate in 1549, when he was on royal business in the north; Dacre
of the North, a licensed absentee serving as warden in the west
marches; and Bedford dissenting from a bill on 5 December 1555
when he was actually in Italy. L.J., ii, 132, 172; *ibid.*, iii, 121. Consequently, solitary appearances have been treated as clerical errors and
those who turned up but once are classified as sessional absentees.
The clerk's record abounds with inconsistencies. He usually prefixed
the names of those present with a 'p', but just to confuse the issue he
employed the variations of 'pp', 'n.p.', 'a' and 'ab'. Occasionally the
lists of members were not annotated at all. E.g. L.J., i, 315, 322, 324,
645, 691–2; *ibid.*, ii, 6, 14, 32, 51–121, 131–96; *ibid.*, iii, 167. Sometimes he simply wrote down the names of those present. L.J., i, 361;
ibid., ii, 49, 50, 70; *ibid.*, iii, 5, 91, 133–4. The cumulative effect of
such variable recording is less to diminish the value of the journals
than to complicate the interpretation of them. A more serious clerical
lapse was the clerk's failure to record the registration dates of proxies
in the second Marian parliament. This renders it difficult – indeed
sometimes even impossible – to discover whether a licence was granted
before or during a session. The binders of the journals created additional hazards, combining the proxies of 38 Henry VIII with the
journal for 1545. See also p. 72 and n. 112, of the present volume. In
spite of this the manuscript record is preferable to the printed
journals, whose editors compounded and multiplied the clerk's errors.
On nearly one hundred occasions they got it wrong, recording absentees as present or vice versa; nor did they rectify the displacement of
the 1547 proxies. L.J., ii, 126–7. The manuscript journals remain the
only worthwhile attendance record and when they can be tested their
accuracy is usually confirmed.

160 Fifteen were unauthorised and eighteen were in receipt of licences:
Bishops Brooks (Nov. 1558), Bush (1549/50), Griffith (1554/5), and
D. Pole (Nov. 1558); Abbot Feckenham and the lay prior of St John,
Sir Thomas Tresham (also Nov. 1558); Huntingdon (1552), 2nd
Sussex (1555), 4th Westmorland (1547), 2nd Worcester (1547), Bray
(1548/9), 10th Cobham, 2nd Darcy of Darcy, 4th Dudley, Monteagle,
Paget, Stafford, 3rd Vaux and 3rd Windsor (all Nov. 1558); 1st
Darcy of Darcy (1552, March 1553, April 1554, 1554/5, 1555),
Mountjoy (1555), Sandys (1548/9, 1549/50, 1554/5, Jan. and Nov.
1558), 8th Stourton (April 1554, 1555), 10th Zouche (March
1553).

161 Many of them were, in any case, supporters, beneficiaries or servants
of the Crown, e.g. Bray (1548/9), 10th Zouche (March 1553), 8th
Stourton (April 1554, 1555), 3rd Vaux (Nov. 1558), Bishops Griffith
(1554/5), Brooks and D. Pole, Abbot Feckenham, Sir Thomas
Tresham, 4th Dudley and Paget (all in 1558).

162 Fifteen bishops (on 44 occasions) and six peers (on 19): Aldrich
(April 1554), Baynes (Jan. 1558), Bird (1548/9, 1549/50, March

1553), Bulkeley (every session of Edward VI's first parliament), Chambers (1549/50–1555), Holyman (Jan. 1558), King (1547, 1548/9, 1552–5), Kitchin (1549/50–1555, November 1558), Morgan and Tunstall (also in Nov. 1558), the aged Salcot (1552–5), Sampson (April 1554), Wakeman (1547), Warton (1554/5) and the ever-reluctant Veysey (1547, 1549/50, April 1554); Viscount Hereford (Jan. 1558), 3rd Burgh (1548/9), De la Warr (1552 and April 1554), 10th Morley (1554/5, 1555), 8th Zouche (1547, 1549/50), and Mordaunt who contrived to stay away from every session – moreover, except for November 1558, he was licensed to do so. *G.E.C.*, ix, 195; L.J., i, 305. The age of the bishops at the time of their first sessional absence ranged from the late fifties (Henry Morgan was about 57–60) to the mid-eighties (Tunstall and Veysey). Many of them occupied distant sees: Bulkeley, Kitchin and Morgan in Wales, Bird (Chester), Holyman (Bristol), Wakeman (Gloucester), Warton (Hereford), Baynes and Sampson (Coventry and Lichfield), not far from the Welsh border, Aldrich (Carlisle) and Tunstall (Durham) in the far north, and Veysey (Exeter) in the remote west. None of them would have smiled on the prospect of dragging their aged bodies to Westminster for a mid-winter or early spring session. The lords temporal in this group were only marginally less decrepit when Edward VI became king: Mordaunt and 8th Zouche were about 60, whilst, at the other end of the spectrum, De la Warr was over 80.

[163] See p. 81, nn. 186–8 of the present volume.

[164] Sturge, pp. 312–15. A ride from Carlisle over the moors to Gretna Green in 1557 had proved almost too much for him. Twice he fell from his horse and at one point his men actually feared for his life.

[165] *D.N.B.*, *sub* Arthur Bulkeley and Robert Warton. Mordaunt's pardon in 1539 'pro eo quod infirmus est' hints at an earlier disability, though it may have been just one of the weapons in his arsenal of excuses; he did not make a single appearance between 1542 and 1547. L.J., i, 305.

[166] Chambers was sessionally absent in 1544 and Jan. 1547 and attended only one-third of the sittings in 1542 and 1543 and one-half in 1545. L.J., i, 503–692. King had a reasonable record in 1543 (48 out of 68 sittings) but was absent in 1544 and Jan. 1547, and he appeared only three times in 1545. Kitchin was away in 1545 and made but one (possible) appearance in Jan. 1547. Veysey made only 12 appearances in the seven sessions between 1539 and 1547. Wakeman's record was more respectable, but even he was absent in 1544 and Jan. 1547. L.J., i, 311–692. All but one of them (i.e. Veysey) were ex-regulars and there is doubtless some truth in V. F. Snow's description of them as 'other worldly in orientation and somewhat averse to secular affairs' preferring 'to reside in their sees rather than a London house'. Snow, 'Proc. rep. Edward VI', 9.

[167] *H.M.C.*, Salisbury MSS., Pt 1, 51; Lodge, *Illustrations*, 1, 252–3; *Cal.S.P.Dom.*, 1547–80, Mary, xiv, p. 108.

[168] Bishop Wakeman (probably) and the second earl of Worcester (cer-

tainly) died during the 1549/50 session. *H.B.C.*, p. 227; *G.E.C.*, XII (II), 852. Bulkeley expired in mid-March 1553 (*H.B.C.*, p. 275) and Cotes in December 1555 (*ibid.*, p. 215). At the end of 1558 the Great Reaper of the Protestants swung his scythe to their evident satisfaction and, in the process, convinced them of the rightness of their cause. Archbishop Pole, stricken with a double quartan ague, died on the same day as Queen Mary. Griffith followed three days later, and Holyman before the year was out. *H.B.C.*, pp. 207, 211, 249.

169 He was about 62–65 years of age. L.J., iii, 1; *D.N.B.*, *sub* Thomas Goodrich.

170 Stone, *Crisis*, pp. 451, 715–16; G. C. Williamson, *George Third Earl of Cumberland, 1558–1605* (Cambridge, 1920), p. 5; *G.E.C.*, III, 567; *D.N.B.*, *sub* Henry Clifford, 2nd earl of Cumberland.

171 Even then, in 1548/9, he attended only three of the 73 sittings. L.J., ii, 111, 176, 209. His single recorded presence in 1549/50 has been treated as a clerical error (which indeed the entries of 1548/9 may also be). *Ibid.*, 272.

172 He may have come south to Westminster in October 1553 and November 1554 in order to attend the queen's coronation and his daughter's wedding, rather than with the specific purpose of attending parliament. Vertot, *Ambassades*, II, 246; *Machyn*, p. 82.

173 Miller, 'Attendance', 340; *L.P.*, Henry VIII, IX, No. 580; *ibid.*, XII (1), No. 803. Audley was an unlicensed absentee in 1547, 1548/9 and 1555, but he received an official exemption in 1554/5.

174 J. Smyth, *The Lives of the Berkeleys*, ed. Sir John Maclean, 3 vols (Gloucester, 1883–5), pp. 279–82.

175 Graves, 'The Mid-Tudor House of Lords', 1 (1), pp. 119–24; *Cal. S.P.For.*, Mary, No. 854 (p. 406).

176 Graves, 'The Mid-Tudor House of Lords', 1 (1), pp. 119–24.

177 *G.E.C.*, XII (II), 596; P.R.O., S.P., 15/1, fos 31, 33, 38.

178 It should also be noted that eleven of these royal servants remained on duty in Nov. 1558. So the exigencies of war, as well as a disinclination to attend in the closing days of the reign, contributed to the endemic absenteeism of Nov. 1558.

179 For a discussion of the technical problems relating to 'short-term' licences, see Graves, 'The Mid-Tudor House of Lords', II, 159. In a few cases there is an obvious correlation between a peer's appointment to office, the registration of his proxy, and his departure from the Lords. On 4 or 8 March 1552, Westmorland and Wharton were commissioned to treat with the Scots over the 'Debateable land'. Westmorland attended until 5 March, Wharton until the 8th. They registered their proxies on the 10th and 9th respectively. Their absence thereafter was the consequence of their new responsibility. Similarly Lord Howard of Effingham was present at the opening days of the session of April 1554. However, after 6 April he attended no more. By the 11th he was riding to the south coast to take up his duties as lord admiral. *Ed. VI's Chron.*, p. 114; *G.E.C.*, XII (II), 556, 597; *Queen Jane*, p. 74; L.J., ii, 235, 236; *ibid.*, iii, 1. Unfortunately the

journal does not record the date on which his proxy was registered.
[180] His proxy was registered on 2 January 1549, five days before the measure had its first reading. L.J., ii, 71.
[181] Gasquet and Bishop, p. 135; L.J., ii, 211, 272.
[182] Sampson's age – he was in his late sixties – may be sufficient explanation for his absence. He was also pardoned from Mary's second parliament. L.J., iii, 1.
[183] Between Christmas 1549 and 26 January 1550. *C.P.R., Ed. VI*, ii, 385; *ibid.*, iv, 14; Jordan, *Edward VI. The Young King*, p. 325.
[184] G. Anstruther, *Vaux of Harrowden* (Newport, 1953), pp. 43–4; *G.E.C.*, xii (ii), 220.
[185] He was 'so vehement in his religious conservatism that he dismissed one of his servants who [was] "of the new opinions" '. *D.N.B., sub* Thomas West, 9th Baron De la Warr; Miller, 'Attendance', 349; Ellis, *Original Letters*, ii, 123–5.
[186] 1539: 40 (41); 1540: 54 (59); 1542: 52 (60); 1543: 48 (68). During the thirties he had bombarded Thomas Cromwell with pleas for leave of absence: in 1531/2 because of poverty, in 1534 and 1536 because of his congenital speech defect. *G.E.C.*, iv, 156; P.R.O., S.P., 1/82, fo. 10; *ibid.*, 1/101, fo. 76. His late Henrician record reads as follows: 1544: 1 (55); 1545: 21 (26); Jan. 1547: 0 (11).
[187] 1547: 0 (35); 1548/9: 4 (73); 1549/50: 23 (66); 1552: 0 (60); March 1553: 0 (25).
[188] By 1547 he was 75 years old.
[189] L.J., iii, 1.
[190] Lords Seymour of Sudeley (1547 and 1548/9), Morley (1547–52), and (2nd) Windsor (1549/50). Windsor voted against the first and second bills of uniformity, clerical marriage, and the suppression of images. L.J., ii, 49, 80, 103, 126, 164, 188, 220, 255; Foxe, vii, 45. On Edward VI's death, he too appeared in arms for Mary. Dugdale, *Baronage*. ii, 308.
[191] L.J., ii, 103, 188.
[192] *Ibid.*, 235–6.
[193] *Ibid.*, 215.
[194] *Original Letters of the Reformation*, i, 87; *Ed. VI's Chron.*, pp. 44, 84–5, 101 and n. 197; *C.P.R., Ed. VI*, iii, 346–7; *D.N.B., sub* Richard 1st Baron Rich. For the curious and oft-repeated account of his resignation, see Burnet, *Reformation*, ii, 310, and P. Heylyn, *Ecclesia restaurata*, ed. J. C. Robertson, Ecclesiastical History Society (Cambridge, 1849), i, 251. Jordan rejected the story but in the process he muddled it. W. K. Jordan, *Edward VI: The Threshold of Power* (London, 1970), p. 56 n. 1.
[195] The earls of Bath (April 1554), (1st) Bedford (1554/5), (2nd) Bedford (1555), Huntingdon, Oxford, and (2nd) Sussex (all 1554/5), (5th) Westmorland (April 1554, 1554/5, 1555), 1st Viscount Hereford (April 1554, 1554/5), Talbot (1554/5), (8th) Audley (1554/5, 1555), Bergavenny (April 1554, 1554/5, 1555, Jan. 1558, Nov. 1558), (10th) Zouche (1554/5, Jan. and Nov. 1558).

196 Renard to Charles V, 3 April 1554, *Cal.S.P.Span.*, XII, 202; Noailles to Henry II, 12 March 1556. Vertot, *Ambassades*, v, 385.

197 Loades, p. 195.

198 *Cal.S.P.Span.*, XII, 202; *ibid.*, XIII, 134; Michiel to doge and senate, 21 Oct. 1555, *Cal.S.P.Ven.*, VI, Pt I, No. 251 (pp. 217–18).

199 *D.N.B.*, *sub* Thomas Stafford; Strype, *Eccl. Mems*, III, Pt II, 515–18.

200 L.J., iii, 1, 33, 87. He also departed with a licence from Mary's last parliament, but this time it was to take up his duties as lieutenant general of the north. *A.P.C.*, VI, 250; *G.E.C.*, XII (II), 557.

201 Graves, 'Politics of Opposition', 5 n. 32; Garrett, p. 75.

202 He also departed with a pardon in 1554/5 and January 1558. L.J., iii, 33, 129.

203 Garrett, pp. 275–6.

204 Antonio de Guaras, *The Accession of Queen Mary*, ed. R. Garnett (London, 1892), p. 132 n.

205 Loades, pp. 56, 58–9, 61, 64, 84–5.

206 L.J., iii, 1, 33, 87, 129.

207 Renard to Charles V, 3 April 1554, *Cal.S.P.Span.*, XII, 202.

208 Same to same, 17 Jan. 155, *ibid.*, XIII, 134. See chapter 8, pp. 196–8, of the present volume.

209 Huntingdon, Oxford, (8th) Audley, and Shrewsbury's heir, Lord Talbot. Huntingdon, a prominent Edwardian, had already been punished for his part in Northumberland's attempted coup. Oxford held 'reformed opinions', took a consistently anti-Spanish position, and was 'vehemetly suspecte' of treason in 1556. Audley and Talbot were suspected heretics and the former was the father-in-law of Sir Henry Dudley, who organised the abortive plot to spirit away the exchequer's cash holdings in 1556. *Machyn*, p. 37; *Wriothesley's Chron.*, II, 91; *Grey Friars' Chron.*, p. 81; *Two London Chrons*, p. 28; Holinshed, IV, 1; *A.P.C.*, IV, 330, 356; *ibid.*, v, 264; Foxe, VI, 541; *Queen Jane*, p. 27; *Cal.S.P.Span.*, XI, 307; *ibid.*, XII, 202; P.R.O., S.P. 11/7, fo. 24.

210 (1st) Bedford, (2nd) Sussex, (5th) Westmorland, (1st) Hereford, Bergavenny, Rich and (10th) Zouche.

211 Arundel, Cumberland, Pembroke, FitzWalter, St John, (9th) Cobham, Grey de Wilton, (2nd) Vaux and Bray.

212 *A.P.C.*, v, 42; Strype, *Cranmer's Mems*, 1, 493; *Cal.S.P.Span.*, XII, 96; Graves, 'Politics of Opposition', 5 n. 32; J. A. Froude, *The Reign of Mary Tudor* (London, 1913), p. 71.

213 *C.P.R.*, *Ph. & Mary*, 1, 65, 77, 176; Arthur Lord Grey of Wilton, *A Commentary of the Services and Charges of William Lord Grey of Wilton*, ed. P. de M. G. Egerton, Camden Society, old series, xl (London, 1847), p. 18; *Two London Chrons*, p. 28; *Queen Jane*, p. 13; imperial ambassadors to Charles V, 24 July 1553, *Cal.S.P.Span.*, XI, 116.

214 Vertot, *Ambassades*, II, 246; *Cal.S.P.Span.*, XI, 333, 363. For his loyal conduct over the exiles bill, see Michiel to doge and senate, 16 Dec. 1555, *Cal.S.P.Ven.*, VI, Pt I, No. 316. See chapter 8, p. 173, n. 3, of the present volume.

215 *C.P.R.*, *Edward VI*, III, 162; G. S. Thomson, *Two Centuries of Family History* (London, 1930), pp. 171, 174, 175 and n. 2, 183; *D.N.B.*, *sub* John Russell, 1st earl of Bedford; *Cal.S.P.Span.*, XII, 149, 315.

216 See chapter 8, pp. 191–4, of the present volume.

217 His last appearance was on 4 December. An erstwhile adherent of Northumberland, he had acquired monastic lands, embraced reformed doctrines, and suffered imprisonment for complicity in Wyatt's rebellion. Renard described him as a noble 'of French leanings'. *Ed. VI's Chron.*, pp. 97–8; E. Wingfield Stratford, *The Lords of Cobham Hall* (London, 1959), p. 59; *Queen Jane*, pp. 41, 91, 99; Foxe, VI, 386, 540; Renard to Charles V, 6 May 1554, *Cal.S.P.Span.*, XII, 239; Loades, pp. 59–62, 68, 82; *Machyn*, p. 58.

218 Hereford left after the sitting of 19 December, on the eve of the introduction of the bill for reunion with Rome. Bray departed during its passage.

219 The exception, Rich, was doubtless concerned about the preservation of his rich monastic pickings. He stayed for the reunion ceremonies but he was absent after 1 December. However he took care to protect his own interests: the bill for reunion with Rome at first specifically guaranteed to him (and to two other peers, Darcy of Chiche and Wentworth) lands which were formerly parcel of the bishop of London's property. This clause was later deleted when the Lords agreed to a Commons' request for the inclusion of a general confirmtion of secularised property. L.J., iii, 73; H.L.R.O., Orig. Acts, 1 and 2 Ph. & Mary, no. 8.

220 See chapter 8, pp. 196–8 of the present volume, for a full account.

221 L.J., iii, 37–84.

222 Renard to Charles V, 12 and 17 Jan. 1555, *Cal.S.P.Span.*, XIII, 133–4.

223 *Ibid.*, 134.

224 L.J., iii, 33.

225 14–16 January 1555. L.J., iii, 81–3.

226 Renard to Charles V, 3 April 1554, *Cal.S.P.Span.*, XII, 202; *Cal.S.P. Ven.*, VI, Pt I, No. 251 (pp. 217–18).

227 Thomas Edwardes to earl of Rutland, 16 April 1557, *H.M.C.*, Rutland MSS., I, 68.

228 *A.P.C.*, VI, 159–99.

229 *Ibid.*, IV, 256.

230 The surrender of his daughters to his wife, who was living apart from him, may have been a consequence of his sexual indiscretions. 15 June and 16 July 1557, *Cal.S.P.Dom.*, 1547–80, Mary, XI, Nos 10 and 28.

231 *H.M.C.*, Rutland MSS., I, 68.

232 E.g. Southampton, who had been dismissed from the chancellorship, attended 33 of the 35 sittings in 1547. *Cal.S.P.Span.*, IX, 197.

233 S. Haynes and W. Murdin (eds), *State Papers relating to Affairs in the Reigns of King Henry VIII, King Edward VI, Queen Mary, and Queen Elizabeth, 1542–70*, 2 vols (London, 1740–59), I, 84, 91; *D.N.B.*, *sub* Thomas Seymour.

234 Bodleian Library, Rawlinson MSS., D.1070, fo. 78–78v.

[235] L.J., ii, 32; Haynes, 82; J. G. Nichols, 'Duke of Somerset's 2nd patent as protector', *Archaeologia*, xxx (1844), 475–6, 480–1.

[236] *A.P.C.*, ii, 248; W. Cobbett, T. B. Howell *et al.* (eds), *A Complete Collection of State Trials*, 42 vols (London 1816–98), i, 485, 487, 497.

[237] *A.P.C.*, ii, 259.

[238] Haynes, 75–6, 106; *H.M.C.*, Salisbury MSS., Pt i, No. 300; *A.P.C.*, ii, 249.

[239] Haynes, 76.

[240] *Ibid.*, 76, 80–1; *H.M.C.*, Salisbury MSS., Pt i, Nos 263, 278; Jordan, *Edward VI. The Young King*, p. 373; Slavin, 'Fall of Lord Chancellor Wriothesley', 271–2.

[241] Dorset attended 67 of the 73 sittings, Rutland 69 and Northampton 51.

[242] Foxe, vii, 45; L.J., ii, 80, 220, 250, 255. Advices from Jehan Scheyfve, Jan. (?), 9 April, 12 May and 10 Dec. 1551, *Cal.S.P.Span.*, x, 215, 263, 291, 408.

[243] Their attendance record reads as follows: Derby: 1547: 23 (out of 35 sittings); 1548/9: 65 (73); 1549/50: 59 (66); 1552: 54 (60); 1553: 23 (35). Windsor: 1549: 33 (35); 1548/9: 67 (73); 1549/50: 64 (66); 1552: 50 (60); 1553: 22 (25).

[244] The tabular analysis is compiled from L.J., ii, 29, 33, 42, 80, 103, 188, 255; Foxe, vi, 126; Gasquet and Bishop, pp. 127–37. Although votes were not cast at the conclusion of the debate on the sacrament in December 1548, some of the bishops stated their doctrinal position.

[245] Proportion of daily sittings.

[246] See chapter 8, p. 197, of the present volume.

[247] These calculations are confined to sole proxies and first-named proctors, because they were the men who were most likely to exercise absentees' votes. Graves, 'Proc. rep. Edward VI', 25; Graves, 'The Mid-Tudor House of Lords', ii, App. Attendance, xi, xii.

[248] Strype, *Eccl. Mems*, ii, Pt ii, 252.

[249] Lodge, *Illustrations*, i, 252–3.

[250] L.J., ii, 209, 214, 236; *ibid.*, iii, 1, 33, 87.

[251] See p. 74 of the present volume.

[252] Gardiner was imprisoned after the writs had been issued, but six weeks before parliament assembled. P.R.O., Parl. Pawns, Petty Bag, C.218, Pt i, No. 4; *A.P.C.*, ii, 157.

[253] Muller, *Gardiner's Letters*, Nos 131 (p. 405), 132, 137 (p. 424), p. 443; *A.P.C.*, ii, 208–10; *Wriothesley's Chron.*, ii, 3; *Grey Friars' Chron.*, p. 56.

[254] See chapter 2, p. 23, of the present volume.

[255] Snow's contention – that some peers, especially royal servants, solicited proctorial powers from absentees – is supported by a solitary example, Lord Seymour's attempt to secure Rutland's voice in 1548/9. But any action by that harebrained noble can hardly be regarded as evidence of normal practice. It should be added that Seymour was soliciting Rutland's support, not his proxy. Snow, 'Proc. rep Edward VI', 21; Haynes, 81.

[256] Miller, 'Attendance', 332 n. 42, 335, 347–8.

[257] For example, the government did not follow medieval precedent and

fine unauthorised absentees. Roskell, 'Lords' Attendance in Medieval Parliaments', 170, 172, 199; Elsynge, *Ancient Method of Holding Parliaments*, pp. 96–7. In 1555, however, it did not initiate proceedings against members of the Commons for their unauthorised absence. Coke, *Institutes*, IV, 17–21.

258 In 1536 he advised the king 'to grant few licences for any to be absent from the Parliament'. Until his fall, four years later, even the poor and sick, aged and deaf were not excused. *L.P.*, Henry VIII, x, No. 254; Miller, 'Attendance', 341–3.

259 See pp. 71–2, 75 of the present volume.

260 In March 1553 Archbishop Holgate 'labored to have bene at home for dyvers sicknesseis and disseases which I had at that tyme and also fearinge that [the duke of Northumberland] wolde be in hande with me for Watton. But I coulde have no lycence for anye labour that I coulde by my selfe or my friendes maike, and so toike my journey to the parlyament.' Even this was an exceptional case. Northumberland was trying to extort the property of Watton from the archbishop and obviously wanted to exert personal pressure on him in a direct confrontation. A. G. Dickens, 'Archbishop Holgate's apology', *E.H.R.*, 56 (1941), 456.

261 Miller, 'Attendance', 332 n. 42; *L.P.*, Henry VIII, XXI (2), No. 523; *A.P.C.*, IV, 200; *ibid.*, v, 7.

262 *Ibid.*, II, 519; *ibid.*, III, 456; lord protector to Sir Thomas Cawarden, 28 Oct. 1547, *H.M.C.*, The Manuscripts of William More Molyneux, 7th Rep., App. (London, 1879), 605; P.R.O., S.P. 10/14, fo. 1.

263 *C.P.R., Ph. & Mary*, IV, 2, 60; Strype, *Eccl. Mems*, III, Pt II, 110; *H.M.C.*, Manuscripts of Charles Haliday, Esq., 15th Rep., App. Pt III (London, 1897), 66–8.

264 16 Oct. 1558, P.R.O., S.P. 11/14, fo. 2.

265 *Cal.S.P.Span.*, IX, 470.

266 Harbison, *Rival Ambassadors*, pp. 340–2; Graves, 'Politics of Opposition', 7–8, 9.

267 *Cal.S.P.Span.*, XII, 44.

Chapter 5: Cohesion and division

1 *G.E.C.*, IX, 113, 115.

2 *G.E.C.*, v, 9; *ibid.*, VI, 583–4.

3 These and the following examples of noble intermarriage are derived from *G.E.C.*; *D.N.B.*; Dugdale, *Baronage*; *Machyn*; D. Rowland, *An Historical Account of the Noble Family of Nevill* (London, 1830); *Wriothesley's Chron.*, I and II.

4 Compiled from *D.N.B.*, *G.E.C.*, and Dugdale, *Baronage*.

5 *Wriothesley's Chron.*, I, 50.

6 Scheyfve to Charles V, 12 and 30 May, 1553, *Cal.S.P.Span.*, XI, 40, 45–6; *H.M.C.*, Loseley MSS., 608, Col. 2.

7 *G.E.C.*, VI, 656.

8 Schenk, pp. 1, 172.

9 Rowse, 'Southampton', *H.L.Q.*, 111.

10 See pp. 100–2 of the present volume.

11 Gardiner to Somerset, 14 October 1547, Muller, *Gardiner's Letters*, No. 130 (p. 392).

12 Gasquet and Bishop, pp. 128–37; *Cal.S.P.Span.*, XI, 33.

13 The conflicts touched upon here are described and examined at length in chapter 8.

14 In 1529 the Upper House consisted of 49 lords spiritual and 51 lords temporal; in 1534 the respective totals were 50 and 55. Lehmberg, *Reformation Parliament*, p. 37 n. 1.

15 See App. A: Composition.

16 6 February 1547, *A.P.C.*, II, 13–14.

17 H.L.R.O., Orig. Acts, 1 Ed. VI, no. 2.

18 *A.P.C.*, II, 13–14; Pollard, *Protector Somerset*, p. 95; Gardiner to Paget, 1 March 1547, Muller, *Gardiner's Letters*, No. 118; P. F. Tytler (ed.), *England under the Reigns of Edward VI and Mary*, 2 vols (London, 1839), I, 23–5.

19 Hembry, pp. 80–1.

20 L. B. Smith, *Tudor Prelates*, pp. 298–300, 305.

21 *D.N.B.*, *sub* Gilbert Bourne; Hembry, p. 89.

22 *Athenae Oxonienses*, I, 582; L. B. Smith, *Tudor Prelates*, pp. 300–1.

23 *Narratives of Reformation*, pp. 238, 273, 274–5.

24 *D.N.B.*, *sub* Robert Ferrar and John Hopton; A. G. Dickens, 'Robert Holgate, Archbishop of York and President of the King's Council in the North', *St Anthony's Hall Publication*, No. 8, Borthwick Institute of Historical Research (York, 1955), p. 3; *Athenae Oxonienses*, I, 589; Gillow, III, 388.

25 Thomas Goldwell, Thomas Goodrich, William Repps, Richard Sampson, John Skip, James Turberville. *Athenae Oxonienses*, I, 594, 605; L. B. Smith, *Tudor Prelates*, pp. 11, 12.

26 J. G. Ridley, *Nicholas Ridley* (London, 1957), p. 8.

27 Sturge, pp. 3 and n. 1, 4, 5 n. 4 and App. I and II.

28 *D.N.B.*, *sub* John Taylor, William Glyn and Robert King; Foster, *Alumni Oxonienses*, II, 853.

29 Shirley, pp. 1–2.

30 G. S. Thomson, 'Background for a Bishop', in J. C. Davies (ed.), *Studies Presented to Sir Hilary Jenkinson* (London, 1957), pp. 414–17; L. B. Smith, *Tudor Prelates*, pp. 13–14, 303.

31 *C.P.R.*, Ph. & Mary, I, 22, 25.

32 J. G. Ridley, *Thomas Cranmer* (Oxford, 1962), pp. 46–7; Foxe VIII, 4; Garrett, p. 132; *D.N.B.*, *sub* John Hooper. As Cranmer married twice he may have suffered from an unnatural uxoriousness, or a driving urge to domesticity. When, during Mary's reign, he was interrogated about his first marriage, he was remarkably vague about worldly matters, even for a university don; he could not even recall his first wife's maiden name. Foxe, VIII, 58.

33 H.L.R.O., Orig. Acts, 2/3 Ed. VI, no. 19 and 5/6 Ed. VI, no. 12.

34 Hembry, p. 84.

35 John Bird, Paul Bush, Robert Ferrar, Henry Holbeach, Robert Holgate, John Ponet (twice) and John Scory. There is some doubt about the genuineness of Bush's reformed opinions. In reply to certain questions on 'the abuses of the mass', proposed in 1548, he opposed Cranmer and favoured solitary masses, services in Latin, and masses for the dead. Strangely enough, shortly before he married, he even voted against the bill 'for the maryage of preistes'. L.J., ii, 103; *D.N.B.*, *sub* Paul Bush.

36 *D.N.B.*, *sub* John Bird; Dickens, 'Archbishop Holgate's Apology', 451, 452, 454.

37 E.g. John Chambers, Robert King, Anthony Kitchin, John Salcot, Richard Sampson, Thomas Thirlby and Robert Warton.

38 H.L.R.O., Orig. Acts, 1 Mary, st. 2, no. 2.

39 *D.N.B.*, *sub* John Bird and John Scory.

40 *C.P.R.*, *Ph. & Mary*, I, 175; *D.N.B.*, *sub* John Scory; Garrett, pp. 285–6.

41 In March 1554. *C.P.R.*, *Ph. & Mary*, I, 175.

42 By 4 October, eleven weeks after Mary's accession, a commission was already 'acting during the vacancy of the see caused by the resignation of the bishop, William', *H.M.C.*, MSS. of Dean and Chapter of Wells, II, 276.

43 As Veysey had resigned in August 1551, he had to be reappointed by letters patent which were issued on 28 September 1553. *C.P.R.*, *Ph. & Mary*, I, 66.

44 *A.P.C.*, IV, 337.

45 *A.P.C.*, IV, 347; *Grey Friars' Chron.*, p. 84; *Queen Jane*, p. 27; *Wriothesley's Chron.*, II, 103.

46 Bird may have been ordered to stay away. See chapter 2, p. 28, of the present volume.

47 The social status of only five wives has been identified: one came from a merchant family, two were of gentle birth, and two were members of clerical families. There is no reason to think that the remainder would yield any spouses of noble birth.

48 *A.P.C.*, III, 427; A. G. Dickens, 'The Marriage and Character of Archbishop Holgate', *E.H.R.*, 52 (July 1937), 428ff.; Dickens, 'Archbishop Holgate's Apology', 452 and n. 3; *Machyn*, p. 8; *Grey Friars' Chron.*, p. 30; Ridley, *Cranmer*, p. 317. The same is true of Cranmer's two marriages. Foxe, VIII, 4–5, 58.

49 Gardiner's criticism of men of such diverse religious positions as Ridley, Cranmer, Barlow and Tunstall is indicative of the prevailing disunity. Muller, *Gardiner's Letters*, Nos 116, 117, 121 (p. 292), 125.

50 The parliamentary opposition to the Edwardian Reformation is examined at length in chapter 8.

51 See chapter 8. It is important to retain a sense of perspective about the parliamentary role of the bishops. On some of the great issues of the day, particularly religion and ecclesiastical authority, they were weak, divided, and the target of anti-clerical attacks. But in the daily grind of legislative business, which involved regular attendance and

participation on committees, many of them were, as we have seen, amongst the most active and effective members of the House.

52 *Ed. VI's Chron.*, p. 113.

53 *Cal.S.P.Dom.*, 1547–80, Ed. VI, xiv, Nos 1, 50; *Ed. VI's Chron.*, pp. 106, 144, 147. According to *H.P.T. Biogs*, Dudley was recalled at his own request.

54 *Cal.S.P.Span.*, x, 9. Northampton was one of Northumberland's supporters.

55 Foxe, vii, 45; L.J., ii, 80, 103, 188, 220, 255; Burnet, *Reformation*, ii, 561. The government's demand that Derby renounce his title to the Isle of Man in favour of the king may be a cause or consequence of his hostility to Northumberland's regime. *Cal.S.P.For.*, *Ed. VI*, 119; Hoak, *The King's Council*, pp. 67–8.

56 Both of them were sadly deluded, however, if they aspired to become the dominant influence over the queen. She preferred to place her trust first in the Burgundian, Simon Renard, then in her Spanish husband, Philip, and finally in the italianate Pole.

57 *A.P.C.*, ii, 248; Cobbett, *State Trials*, i, 485, 487. See also chapter 8, pp. 88–9, of the present volume.

58 Paget was a councillor and chancellor of the duchy of Lancaster.

59 *Cal.S.P.Span.*, x, 168–9, 214–15.

60 *Ibid.*, 166, 263, 279–81.

61 *A.P.C.*, iii, 328–9.

62 *Cal.S.P.Span.*, x, 425.

63 *Ibid.*, 546.

64 *Ibid.*, 579.

65 *Ed. VI's Chron.*, p. 150.

66 *Cal.S.P.Span.*, xi, 13.

67 See chapter 8, pp. 186–95, of the present volume.

68 Mary was now in the early stages of her first false pregnancy.

69 For a detailed account of the early Marian parliaments and the role of these peers between 1553 and 1555 see chapter 8, pp. 186–98, of the present volume.

70 The earls of Arundel, Cumberland, Northumberland, Oxford, Rutland and Shrewsbury, the 4th and 5th earls of Westmorland, the Lords Audley (2), Berkeley, Clinton, Dacre of the North, Grey de Wilton, Lumley, Stafford, the 8th and 9th Lords Scrope, Talbot, and the 8th, 9th and 10th Lords Zouche.

71 Northumberland, Somerset, Northampton, Winchester, Bedford (2), Pembroke, Southampton, Montagu, Bray, Chandos (2), Cromwell, Darcy of Chiche (2), Eure (2), Mordaunt, North, Paget, Rich, St John, Seymour, Sheffield, Warwick, Wentworth (2), Wharton, Williams, Willoughby, Windsor (2).

72 G. R. Elton, 'Thomas Cromwell's Decline and Fall', *C.H.J.*, 10, 2 (1951), 178 and n. 134.

73 *Ed. VI's Chron.*, p. 119.

74 *G.E.C.*, x, 276 n. (b); Jordan, *Edward VI. The Young King*, pp. 81, 101; *H.P.T. Biogs*.

75 *G.E.C.*, IX, 649; X, 774 and n (d).
76 James, 'Change and Continuity', p. 12; *G.E.C.*, XII (II), 594 n. (g).
77 *L.P.*, Henry VIII, XI, No. 705.
78 Powell and Wallis, p. 576, n. 71.
79 *D.N.B.*, *sub* William Herbert, first earl of Pembroke of the second creation. S. T. Bindoff, 'Parliamentary History, 1529–1688', *V.C.H.*, *Wiltshire*, vol. v (1957), 114.
80 M. E. James, 'A Tudor Magnate and the Tudor State: Henry, fifth earl of Northumberland', *Borthwick Papers*, XXX (York, 1966), *passim*; James, 'Change and Continuity', pp. 26–39.
81 M. E. James, 'The First Earl of Cumberland (1493–1542) and the Decline of Northern Feudalism', *Northern History*, I (1966), 44.
82 *Ibid.*, 64–7.
83 James, 'Change and Continuity', *passim*. Wharton's father had been a Clifford servant. *Ibid.*, p. 38.
84 *L.P.*, Henry VIII, XIII (2), No. 115.
85 *Ibid.*, XIV (1), No. 50.
86 *A.P.C.*, II, 553.
87 *H.P.T. Biogs.* When report of the bill reached Cumberland's ears, he was told that it had come as a complete surprise to his friends in parliament. A. G. Dickens (ed.), *Clifford Letters of the 16th Century*, Surtees Society, clxxii (Durham, 1962), 33–4, 101–2.
88 Unfortunately only the bill survives and so it is not possible to consider the other (and equally implausible?) side of the story. Henry earl of Cumberland *v.* Thomas Lord Wharton, Sir Henry Wharton *et al.*, Unlawful assembly &c at Wharton, co. Westmorland. P.R.O., STAC, 3, 6/46.
89 *A.P.C.*, V, 43.
90 Lord Dacre of the North must have become involved in the feud, doubtless on Cumberland's side, because he too participated in the ceremony. 15 December 1554, *ibid.*, 86–7.
91 Cumberland was absent throughout the session, but Wharton was present on the day and may have introduced the bill. L.J., iii, 142; *D.N.B.*, *sub* Thomas Wharton.
92 *A.P.C.*, VI, 291.
93 L.J., iii, 171–82.
94 E. Halle, *Chronicle: or The Union of the Two Noble ... Famelies of Lancastre and York* (London, 1550), p. 815; *L.P.*, Henry VIII, VII, 368–70.
95 James, 'First Earl of Cumberland', 47–8.
96 *G.E.C.*, V, 179–81.
97 *G.E.C.*, XII (II), 594–8; *D.N.B.*, *sub* Thomas Wharton; Reid, *King's Council in North*, App. II, Pt IV, p. 491.
98 28 September 1551. *A.P.C.*, III, 367.
99 *Machyn*, p. 12; *Cal.S.P.Span.*, X, 407. Machyn states that Dacre was 'carried to the Tower' but the *Acts of the Privy Council* refer to his enlargement from the Fleet. *A.P.C.*, III, 367–8, 447.
100 *A.P.C.*, III, 499–500.

[101] *Ibid.*
[102] L.J., ii, 209–68.
[103] *A.P.C.*, iii, 499–500.
[104] *G.E.C.*, xii (ii), 596–7.
[105] *C.P.R., Ph. & Mary*, i, 140, 177.
[106] *A.P.C.*, v, 13.
[107] *Ibid.*, 23.
[108] *A.P.C.*, v, 86–7.
[109] *G.E.C.*, xii (ii), 596–7.
[110] Strype, *Eccl. Mems*, iii, Pt i, 351–2.
[111] *G.E.C.*, ix, 619–20.
[112] Casady, pp. 67–8, 179–81.
[113] *Ibid.*, pp. 198–200.
[114] Loades, p. 212.
[115] P.R.O., S.P. Supplementary, 46/2, fo. 124; *G.E.C.*, vi, 142.
[116] *G.E.C.*, ix, 672.
[117] *Narratives of Reformation*, p. 312; Burnet, *Reformation*, ii, 518.
[118] Lord Grey testified to the privy council, at some time prior to 19 April 1551, that his ex-wife had conspired with one Randall Haward, with whom she was living, 'to murder him at his coming to London for the Parliament, but he did not come, so they conspired with Robert Battye to enter Powys's service to secure his murder'. When questioned Battye confessed to the charge. Petition to Privy Council by Edward Lord Grey of Powys, P.R.O., S.P. Supplementary, 46/2, fo. 124. Lady Anne later married Randall Haward. *G.E.C.*, vi, 143.
[119] L.J., iii, 105; C.J., i, 150, 150v, 156, 158.
[120] Lord Latimer's intent to commit rape may have had a similar effect. By June 1557 his wife Lucy, sister of the third earl of Worcester, was living apart from him. *G.E.C.*, vii, 484; see chapter 4, p. 87, of the present volume.
[121] The equivalent of a modern separation rather than a divorce.
[122] *A.P.C.*, ii, 164–5; Burnet, *Reformation*, v, 183–4; Ridley, *Cranmer*, pp. 276–7; Ridley, *Ridley*, pp. 144–5, 146–7; Jordan, *Edward VI. The Young King*, pp. 365–7; *C.P.R., Ed. VI*, i, 137, 261; also H.L.R.O., Orig. Acts, 34/35 Henry VIII, no. 39, 5/6 Ed. VI, no. 30. According to Ridley, Burnet's summary of Cranmer's notes on the Church's attitude to divorce is inaccurate. Ridley, *Cranmer*, p. 227 n. 1. Van der Delft to Charles V, 23 Feb. 1548. *Cal.S.P.Span.*, ix, 253.
[123] On 7 February 1556. G. Hinde (ed.), *The Registers of Cuthbert Tunstall, Bishop of Durham, 1530–59, and James Pilkington, Bishop of Durham, 1561–76*, Surtees Society, clxi (Durham, 1952), pp. 111–13, 149–64; *G.E.C.*, v, 181.
[124] *G.E.C.*, iv, 421.
[125] *Ibid.*, x, 411; *Cal.S.P.Span., Elizabeth*, i, 45.
[126] *Cal.S.P.Dom.* 1547–80, Ed. VI, i, No. 45; B. M. Ward, *The Seventeenth Earl of Oxford, 1550–1604* (London, 1928), p. 8; *G.E.C.*, x, 249.
[127] Pollard, *Protector Somerset*, pp. 181–2; Nichols, *Literary Remains*, ii, 215.
[128] Van der Delft to Charles V, 13 August 1549, *Cal.S.P.Span.*, ix, 429.

Chapter 6: The Lords' inheritance: clerks and
assistants to the House

[1] They were not, however, always masters of chancery prior to their parliamentary appointment. Pollard, 'Clerical Organization of Parliament', 40.

[2] M. F. Bond, 'Acts of Parliament: Some Notes on the Original Acts preserved at the House of Lords, their Use and Interpretation', *Archives*, vol. III, no. 20 (Michaelmas, 1958), 203; M. F. Bond, 'The Formation of the Archives of Parliament, 1497–1691', *Journal of the Society of Archivists*, 1, 6 (Oct. 1957), 151.

[3] D'Ewes, pp. 3–4, 14, 18; *L.P.*, Henry VIII, XIV, Pt I, No. 1181; John Vowell (alias Hooker), 'The Order and Usage howe to keepe a Parliament in England, in these Dayes', B.L., Harleian MSS., 1178, fo. 21; Pollard, 'Authenticity of the "Lords' Journals" ', 33–4. See also G. R. Elton, 'The Early Journals of the House of Lords', *E.H.R.*, 89 (July 1974), 481–512. In most respects this article supersedes Pollard's earlier work.

[4] L.J., ii. 130.

[5] Vowell, 'The Order and Usage', fo. 21; Smith, *De Republica*, pp. 52–3; Pollard, 'Clerical Organisation of Parliament', 43–5; D'Ewes, p. 35; A. F. Pollard, 'The Clerk of the Crown', *E.H.R.*, 57 (July 1942), 319. For much of the sixteenth century the nominal clerk appointed a *de facto* clerk to transact his duties. M. F. Bond, 'Clerks of the Parliament, 1509–1953', *E.H.R.*, 73 (Jan. 1958), 79. For the parliamentary functions of the clerk of the Crown, see Pollard, 'Clerk of the Crown', 312–33. The mid-Tudor clerks (1544–66) were Edmund Martyn and Thomas Powle. *Ibid.*, 328, 330. It appears that the clerk of the parliaments did not always enter the formula of assent at the closing ceremony but deferred the task to a later date and then forgot to do so. Probably this explains why some of the original acts of both Henry VIII (e.g. 26, 28, 31 Henry VIII) and Elizabeth (e.g. 1 Elizabeth, nos 15, 16, 35, 42; 13 Elizabeth, nos 18, 38, 40) bear no record of assent.

[6] G. R. Elton, 'The Sessional Printing of Statutes, 1484–1547', in E. W. Ives, R. J. Knecht, J. J. Scarisbrick (eds), *Wealth and Power in Tudor England. Essays presented to S. T. Bindoff* (London, 1978), pp. 80–4; Pollard, 'Clerical Organisation of Parliament', 45–8; Vowell, 'The Order and Usage', fo. 21v; D'Ewes, pp. 35–6.

[7] Graves, 'The Two Lords' Journals of 1542', 182–9.

[8] M. F. Bond (ed.), *The Manuscripts of the House of Lords*, vol. XI, new ser., Addenda, 1514–1714 (London, 1962), 3852(b).

[9] Bond, 'Clerks of Parliament', 82–3. Paget had held the clerkship jointly with Thomas Knight since 1543. Sir John Mason was appointed on 11 July 1550; it was regranted to him in survivorship with Francis Spilman in 1551 and when he died in 1566 Spilman continued as sole clerk for another eight or nine years. For further

evidence of clerical confusion in the mid-Tudor parliaments, see Bond, *ibid.*, 79.

[10] Pike, pp. 352–4; Pollard, *Evolution*, pp. 23–4.

[11] Vowell, 'The Order and Usage', fo. 21.

[12] *A.P.C.*, II, 258; Smith, *De Republica*, p. 51.

[13] Two of the mid-Tudor lords chancellor, Thomas Wriothesley, 1st earl of Southampton (1547), and Richard 1st Lord Rich (1547–51), were common lawyers, and Bishop Gardiner (1553–5) was a canonist and civilian, but Bishop Goodrich of Ely (1551–3) and Archbishop Heath of York (1556–8) had no formal legal training.

[14] The enrolments of these writs for the Edwardian and Marian parliaments have survived in the parliament pawns in the Public Record Office. P.R.O., Parl. Pawns, Petty Bag, C.218, Pt I, Nos 4–11.

[15] *Wriothesley's Chron.*, I, 187; Count G. T. Langosco da Stroppiana to the Bishop of Arras, 13 Nov. 1554, *Cal.S.P.Span.*, XIII, 82; Antoine de Noailles to M. d'Oysel, 21 Nov. 1554, Vertot, *Ambassades*, IV, 20.

[16] For example, before Mary's second parliament. *A.P.C.*, IV, 398; Simon Renard to Charles V, *Cal.S.P.Span.*, XI, 216, 220, 221, 222, 225, 238, 259. See pp. 190–1 of the present volume.

[17] *L.J.*, iii, 73; *C.J.*, i, 120–7v.; *Cal.S.P.Span.*, XIII, 82, 116, 120–1, 128–130; John Elder's letter in *Queen Jane*, p. 154; *Cal.S.P.Ven.*, VI, Pt I, No. 14 (pp. 9–12), and No. 32 (p. 27); W. Cobbett, *Parliamentary History of England from the Norman Conquest in 1066 to the Year 1803* (London, 1806–20), I, 622–3.

[18] *L.J.*, iii, 73.

[19] Vowell, 'The Order and Usage', fo. 21.

[20] *Cal.S.P.Ven.*, VI, Pt I, No. 282 (p. 251).

[21] D'Ewes, p. 16.

[22] P.R.O., Parl. Pawns, Petty Bag, C.218, Pt I, Nos 4–11.

[23] The lord chancellor, lord treasurer, lord president 'of the king's most honourable council' and the keeper of the privy seal 'being of the degree of barons of the parliament or above shall sit and be placed . . . above all dukes'. The great chamberlain, the constable, the marshal, the lord admiral, the great master or lord steward, and the king's chamberlain 'shall sit and be placed above all other personages being of the same estates and degrees that they shall happen to be'. H.L.R.O., Orig. Acts, 31 Henry VIII, no. 10.

[24] *Ibid.*

[25] Powell and Wallis, p. 580.

[26] Smith, *De Republica*, p. 51.

[27] See chapter 3, p. 55, of the present volume.

[28] H.L.R.O., Orig. Acts, 31 Henry VIII, no. 10.

[29] The parliamentary record of the secretaries, discussed in the following paragraphs, derives from the Lords' and Commons' Journals; P.R.O., Parl. Pawns, Petty Bag, C.218, Pt I, Nos. 4–11; *Return of the Name of Every Member of the Lower House of the Parliaments of England, Scotland, and Ireland, 1213–1874*, Pt I.

[30] Elton, *Tudor Constitution*, p. 241.

[31] There is no record of Sir William Cecil's election to the Commons in March 1553 in the *Official Returns* and according to Conyers Read he declined to sit. But he is not mentioned in the Lords' Journal for that session, the History of Parliament Trust Biographies record him as a possible knight for Lincolnshire (for which the *Official Returns* are missing) and, moreover, on 8 March a bill in the Commons was committed to 'Mr Cicill' and others. No other Cecil is recorded in the incomplete *Official Returns*, Pt 1, 378–80; C. Read, *Mr Secretary Cecil and Queen Elizabeth* (London, 1955), p. 81; *H.P.T. Biogs*; C.J., i, 58.

[32] L.J., ii, 20.

[33] *State Papers of King Henry VIII* (London, 1830–52), ii, 623–4; *L.P.*, Henry VIII, xvi, No. 437.

[34] *Ibid.*

[35] Elton, *Tudor Constitution*, p. 118.

[36] *Ibid.*

[37] *A.P.C.*, iii, App., 513; Strype, *Eccl. Mems*, ii, Pt ii, 159–61; iii, Pt ii, 160.

[38] See chapter 3, pp. 36–9, of the present volume.

[39] See chapter 8, p. 185, of the present volume.

[40] The judges and the attorney-general were in any case ineligible, whilst it was exceptional for a chief baron of the exchequer to sit there – only Clement Higham did so in 1558. No solicitor-general was elected during this period.

[41] *Official Returns*, Pt 1, 378–9, 397–8; *H.P.T. Biogs*.

[42] C.J., i, 17, 57, 61, 62v, 63v, 165, 167; L.J., ii, 3.

[43] Pollard, *Evolution*, p. 296.

[44] Smith, *De Republica*, p. 51.

[45] *A.P.C.*, ii, 37, 154; iii, 265; iv, 21; v, 22.

[46] *H.M.C.*, Salisbury MSS., Pt 1, 108–9, No. 424; D'Ewes, p. 3.

[47] C.J., i, 161v; D'Ewes, p. 203; B.L., Stowe MSS., 1029, fos 82–82v; L.J., v, 104; M. A. R. Graves, 'Freedom of Peers from Arrest: The Case of Henry Second Lord Cromwell, 1571–1572', *A.J.L.H.*, 21 (1977), 12–13.

[48] Pollard, *Evolution*, p. 252; Elton, *Tudor Constitution*, p. 242.

[49] *A.P.C.*, iv, 399; vii, 27.

[50] *Ed. VI's Chron.*, p. 100.

[51] 24 December 1554, *Cal.S.P.Ven.*, v, No. 975 (p. 598).

[52] 11 April 1537, *L.P.*, Henry VIII, xii, Pt 1, 901 (410).

[53] L.J., iii, 80.

[54] D'Ewes draws a distinction between the judges as 'joynt Committees with the Lords in ordinary Bills', and as 'Attendants upon them in matters of great Consequence'. D'Ewes, p. 22. But such a distinction is not made in the contemporary Lords' Journal.

[55] These totals have been calculated from L.J., ii, iii, *passim*.

[56] For example, L.J., ii, 20, 140, 232.

[57] *Ibid.*, 8, 9, 10, 15, 22, 23.

[58] *Ibid.*, 227, 235.

[59] That many cases went unrecorded seems probable from the startling

regnal difference. There is no reason to believe that the accession o
Mary coincided with a sudden change in procedural practice. Instead
one can only lament the relatively brief uninformative condition of
the Marian journals.

60 D'Ewes, p. 18.

61 L.J., iii, 55.

62 *Ibid.*, 156.

63 H.L.R.O., Orig. Acts, 1 Edward VI, no. 21; 2/3 Edward VI, nos 7
12, 28, 38, 39, 41, 47, 50, 52, 54, 60; 3/4 Edward VI, nos 8, 22-5
29-31; 5/6 Edward VI, nos 27-35; 7 Edward VI, nos 14-16.

64 *Ibid.*, 3/4 Edward VI, nos 22, 23, 25, 31. The act endorsed by
councillors in 1547 was the general pardon. *Ibid.*, 1 Edward VI, no. 21

65 Hoak, *The King's Council*, pp. 191-2, 336.

66 H.L.R.O., Orig. Acts, 3/4 Edward VI, nos 22, 23, 29-31; *ibid.*
5/6 Edward VI, nos 31, 32, 35.

67 One of these, the act 'to avoid certain Writings for Marriage to be
had betwixt the Earl of Oxford's Daughter, and One of the late Duke
of Somerset's Sons', is in a sense an exception. It commenced in the
Lords, but was replaced by a new bill in the Commons; yet the
engrossed original act bears Gryffyn's endorsement of examination.
Presumably the House sought Gryffyn's legal opinion on the Commons' new bill before registering their assent to it. C.J., i, 43-44v
48v, 49; L.J., ii, 237-9, 262-4; H.L.R.O., Orig. Acts, 5/6 Edward
VI, no. 35. Gryffyn's endorsement of the act 'for the assurance of the
Countess of Sussex Joynter' in the next reign indicates that his function was more than mere scrutiny. He composed a note to William
Basset on the dorse that 'I have penned the bille. I pray ye preserve yt
to be sygned [by the queen].' H.L.R.O., Orig. Acts, 4/5 Ph. & Mary,
no. 13.

68 L.J., ii, 172-5.

69 *Ibid.*, 34.

70 For a detailed treatment of the receivers of petitions, see Pollard,
'Receivers of petitions', 202-26.

71 The proportions of judges and masters were as follows: 1547, 4:5;
March 1553, 5:4; April–May 1554, 5:6; 1554/5, 5:6; 1555, 4:7;
1558, 5:7. Although the fifteenth-century clerk of the parliaments had
normally been included on the panels of receivers, only one was appointed in the mid-Tudor parliaments, and he, Sir John Mason in
1547, was then only acting clerk; he was not appointed a master of
requests until 1551. L.J., ii, 3, 273; iii, 3, 35, 89, 131; J. C. Wedgwood
and A. D. Holt, *History of Parliament, 1439-1509: Register of the
Ministers and of the Members of Both Houses, 1439-1509* (London,
1938), p. lx.

72 Pollard, 'Receivers of petitions', 219.

73 Adair and Evans, 'Writs of Assistance', 370.

74 'A Treatise of the Maisters of the Chauncerie', written 1596-1603,
in F. Halgrave, *Collectanea Juridicia, consisting of Tracts relative to the
Law and Constitution of England* (London, 1791), i, p. xl.

[75] M. Bateson (ed.), 'The Pilgrimage of Grace and Aske's Examination', *E.H.R.*, 5 (July 1890), 568.

[76] C.J., i, 107v, 115.

[77] The following analysis rests upon an examination of the Lords' and Commons' Journals.

[78] L.J., iii, 26, 166.

[79] C.J., i, 17, 127v, 183.

[80] In February 1552 a bill was taken down to the Commons by Mr Recorder and Mr Godsalve. The former may be a reference to Roger Cholmeley, chief baron of the exchequer, who had been recorder of London until 1545. In the following century it was certainly not unknown for judges to perform this routine duty. Hakewil, *The Manner how Statutes are Enacted*, p. 72; Smith, *De Republica*, p. 53.

[81] Neale, *Elizabethan Commons*, p. 372.

Chapter 7: The rules of business: procedure

[1] E.g. Notestein, 'Winning of the Initiative'.

[2] C. Russell, *The Crisis of Parliaments* (Oxford, 1974), pp. 38–40, 218–27.

[3] Elton, 'Points of Contact: Parliament', *passim*; 'Studying the History of Parliament', 4–14; 'Parliament: Functions and Fortunes', 255–78.

[4] See chapter 8 of the present volume, and cf. Read, *Burghley*, p. 34, and Neale, *Elizabethan Parliaments*, i, 40–1.

[5] *L.P.*, V, No. 124: B.L., Harleian MSS., 253, fos 32–6.

[6] Muller, *Gardiner's Letters*, pp. 420–1; R. Robinson, 'A Briefe Collection of the Queenes Majesties most High and Most Honourable Courtes of Records', ed. R. Rickard, *Camden Misc.*, 20 (1953), p. 10.

[7] Notestein, pp. 14, 17, 22–3; Neale, *Elizabethan Parliaments*, i, 11, 16, 27, 28, 40–1, 89ff., 421; *ibid.*, ii, 435–6; Neale, *Elizabethan Commons*, pp. 15–16, 372–3; Pollard, *Evolution*, pp. 160, 215, 277; Read, *Burghley*, p. 34.

[8] Notestein, pp. 8–10, 13–22.

[9] *Ibid.*, p. 23; Neale, *Elizabethan Commons*, pp. 376–9.

[10] Elton, *Tudor Constitution*, pp. 286–8.

[11] The classic example of this genre is J. E. Neale's 'puritan choir', based on a manuscript transcription which has no connection with either puritanism or parliamentary opposition. Cambridge University Library MSS., Ff. v. 14; Neale, *Elizabethan Parliaments*, i, 91–176.

[12] E.g. Neale, *Elizabethan Parliaments*, i, 40–1; Elton, *Tudor Constitution*, p. 244.

[13] E.g. Neale, *Elizabethan Parliaments*, i, 40.

[14] *Ibid.*, 16–29; Neale, *Elizabethan Commons*, pp. 372–3.

[15] The causes of disagreement and the names of the antagonists are never recorded.

[16] See pp. 170 and 172, of the present volume.

[17] M. A. R. Graves, 'Thomas Norton the Parliament Man: An Elizabethan M.P., 1559–1581', *H.J.*, 23, 1 (1980), 8–9; C.J., ii, fos 18–18v,

20, 23, 89v, 121; Hakewil, *Manner how Statutes are Enacted in Parlia**ment*, pp. A4v–A6v.

18 Neale, *Elizabethan Commons*, p. 309.

19 R. B. Merriman, *Life and Letters of Thomas Cromwell*, 2 vols (Oxford, 1902), I, 313.

20 Cambridge University Library, MSS., Ff. v. 14; Neale, *Elizabethan Parliaments*, I, 237; Neale, *Elizabethan Commons*, p. 410.

21 Smith, *De Republica*, p. 34.

22 See pp. 164–5 of the present volume.

23 On 31 January 1558 the House appointed a committee to examine 'as well by the ancient Records and Parliament Rolls of this Realm, as also by the Herald Books, and other Monuments', the claims of Lords Clinton and Stafford to be restored to the precedence of their ancestors. Until then they were duly recorded by the clerk as thirteenth and thirty-third respectively in the list of barons and presumably they occupied those positions on the benches. On 12 February, however, the committee declared its findings, as a result of which Clinton was 'restored and admitted' to fourth place and Stafford to thirteenth. L.J., iii, 148. As the clerk had made these adjustments to his attendance list two days before, it also tells us something about how and when he compiled his fair copy of the journal.

24 See p. 164 of the present volume. Henry Scobell's description of the Lords' procedure belongs to the next century. Yet his description of formal conduct, as distinct from actual rules of business, seems unlikely to have changed. For example that 'None but Members of the House might be covered in the Room . . . before the House sate . . . nor were any other persons to stay there, nor Attendant of any Nobleman, longer than whiles he brought in his Lord, and then retired . . . When the House was set, every Member that entred was to give and receive Salutations from the rest, and not to sit down in his place till he had made obeysance to the Cloth of Estate.' Or again, 'The Members were to keep their dignity and order in sitting as much as might be, and not to remove out of their places without just cause, to the hinderance of others that sate near them, and disorder of the House.' Scobell, *Remembrances*, pp. 14–15.

25 For their biographical details and dates at which they flourished, see *D.N.B.*

26 This is particularly true of Elsynge's *The Method of Passing Bills in Parliament* (London, 1685), *Harleian Miscellany*, v (London, 1745), e.g. pp. 211–12, and Scobell, *Remembrances*, e.g. p. 36. Both of these works have been used, where relevant, in the following examination of procedure. See also C. S. Sims, 'The Modern Forme of the Parliaments of England', *A.H.R.*, 53 (1948), 290.

27 E. Plowden, *The Commentaries, or Reports . . . containing Diverse Cases . . .*, 2 vols (London, 1792). I have also consulted C. Ericson, 'Parliament as a Legislative Institution in the Reigns of Edward VI and Mary', 2 vols, University of London, unpublished Ph.D. thesis, November

1973. Because the journal entries are so terse and uninformative that they can be interpreted in a variety of ways, we frequently disagree on details whilst sharing a common position on some of the more general aspects of procedural development and the legislative role of the two Houses.

28 Hoak, pp. 169–70, 171, 184.

29 The lord chancellor's adjournment of the House, entered in the journal, usually named the hour and day on which it would re-assemble. L.J., ii, 1–301. The adjournment notice is frequently omitted from the Marian journals. See chapter 8, n. 27, of the present volume.

30 These figures are calculated from L.J., ii–v.

31 W. B. Devereaux, *Lives and Letters of the Devereux, Earls of Essex*, 2 vols (London, 1853), i, 283.

32 Neale, *Elizabethan Commons*, p. 373.

33 Vowell, 'The Order and Usage', f. 20v. D'Ewes's and Elsynge's seventeenth-century accounts have nothing of importance to add. D'Ewes, pp. 10–11; Sims, 'Modern Forme of Parliaments', 296–7.

34 H.L.R.O., Orig. Acts, 31 Henry VIII, no. 10.

35 *C.P.R., Ed. VI*, i, 217; L.J., ii, 1.

36 Graves, 'The Mid-Tudor House of Lords', 1 (2), 458–66; see chapter 6, p. 127, of the present volume.

37 When Hakewil wrote that 'in this Chapter of passing of Bills, I was the more sedulous, because it is indeed the daily and most proper worke of that house' he was referring to the Commons, but it was just as applicable to the Lords. Hakewil, *Manner how Statutes are Enacted in Parliament*, p. A3v.

38 Neale, *Elizabethan Commons*, pp. 369–70.

39 Unless otherwise specified, the references to the Lords' proceedings on the following pages are derived from the manuscript Lords' Journals, ii, 1–301, and iii, 1–82, and Commons' Journals, i, 1–184.

40 As these readings were well spread, occurring on 30 Nov., 17 and 30 Dec., this could not have been a lengthy and continuous debate carried over from day to day.

41 The bill concerning pensions in April 1554.

42 E.g. bills still had four or five readings in 1554/5 and 1555.

43 E.g. in December 1554 the last of the six readings of a measure relating to herrings was identified as the third.

44 Acts constitute the only reliable test. Most abortive bills failed in one House or the other and were not victims of the royal veto. As they did not complete their passage through both Houses, they are of no use in a comparative analysis.

45 In three cases the same reading is recorded on consecutive days, but other bills interpose. E.g. the subsidy on 5, 7, 8 and 14 Feb., a cloth bill on 18/19 Feb., and another concerned with musters on 2/3 March.

46 Neale, *Elizabethan Commons*, pp. 372–3.

47 H. Elsynge, 'Expedicio billarum antiquitus: an unpublished chapter of the second book of the manner of holding parliaments in England',

in C. S. Sims (ed.), *Studies in History of Representative and Parliamentary Institutions*, XVI (Louvain, 1954), pp. xxxii, 15 and n. 1; Elsynge, *Method of Passing Bills*, p. 212.

48 *Ibid.*, p. 212.

49 Calculated from L.J., iii, 129–69; C.J., i, 165–79.

50 In March 1553 33.4% of bills passing the Lords and 36% of those proceeding through the Commons did not conform to the three-reading procedure.

51 E.g. the marquess of Northampton's restitution in blood which had two readings in April 1554. L.J., iii, 19–20.

52 By the time William Lambarde wrote, the clerical subsidy 'passed to the question upon the first reading thereof'. W. Lambarde, 'The Orders, Proceedings, Punishments, and Privileges, of the Commons – House of Parliament in England', *Harleian Miscellany*, ed. Thomas Park, 10 vols (London, 1808–13), v, 267.

53 Elsynge, *Method of Passing Bills*, p. 211.

54 Hakewil, *Manner how Statutes are enacted in Parliament*, p. 12. According to Hakewil, the reason for the single reading was 'because the subject must take it as the King will give it, without any alteration'. But it was certainly not unknown for the general pardon to be amended in the sixteenth century. H.L.R.O., Orig. Acts 3/4 Ed. VI, no. 24. Lambarde, writing in Elizabeth's reign and citing 25 Elizabeth, agreed that 'being once read, it is demanded, if they be contented to accept it, and so passeth to the question'. Lambarde, 'Proceedings', 267.

55 L.J., ii, 49–124.

56 Mid-Tudor parliaments were not always called in order to secure financial aid, e.g. 1547, Oct. 1553, and the two parliaments of 1554.

57 Shrewsbury's list included not only the subsidy, the very reason why parliament had been called, but also bills to preserve timber, prevent the export of bullion and the 'regrating of merchandise' and regulate spiritual leases. P.R.O., S.P. 10/15, fo. 73; Hoak, pp. 32, 143, 166, 190–2.

58 *A.P.C.*, IV, 398. In April Mary instructed five councillors to 'decide what was to be laid before Parliament'. *Cal.S.P.Span.*, XII, 197. See chapter 6, p. 132, of the present volume; Hoak, p. 192.

59 E.g. on 8 November 1547 committees were appointed to draft bills about the borders and the decay of arable farming. L.J., ii, 7.

60 Henry VIII's doubts about the loyalty of the spiritual bloc in the Lords in the early 1530s encouraged his council to submit anti-papal legislation to the Commons first.

61 *A.P.C.*, III, 471; Neale, *Elizabethan Commons*, pp. 383–93.

62 *H.M.C.*, City of Exeter MSS., 73 (1916), 41.

63 Aske's examination. 11 April 1537. *L.P.*, Henry VIII, XII (1), 10. See chapter 6, p. 131, of the present volume; W. Petyt, *Jus Parliamentorum*, 2 Pts (London, 1739), p. 136; *A.P.C.*, II, 37, 154, 265, 375, 379; *ibid.*, IV, 21, 39; *ibid.*, v. 22.

64 Vowell, 'The Order and Usage', fo. 21.

65 *Ibid.*
66 E.g. five bills on 13 Dec. 1547. They were a mixed bag: a Lords' bill which had been redrafted, another with a Commons' proviso, two which had only passed the Lower House, and one which had completed its parliamentary passage and was being returned into the lord chancellor's custody.
67 Vowell, 'The Order and Usage', fo. 20v.
68 Neale, *Elizabethan Commons*, pp. 393–4. Presumably, as in the seventeenth century, the House could override his decision to prefer one bill before another. Scobell, *Remembrances*, p. 7.
69 Elsynge, *Method of Passing Bills*, p. 211. Cf. Neale, *Elizabethan Commons*, pp. 393–4.
70 Scobell, *Remembrances*, p. 20.
71 Elsynge, *Method of Passing Bills*, pp. 211, 212.
72 None in 1547, 1548/9, 1554/5, Nov. 1558; one in 1549/50, March 1553 and Jan. 1558, three in 1552 and four in April 1554 and 1555. L.J., ii, 1–301; *ibid.*, iii, 1–182.
73 This excludes the occasions on which committal meant no more than the placing of bills in the hands of the lord chancellor for safe-keeping.
74 One of these did not refer to a revising committee. When a Commons' bill, freeing imported war materials from customs duties, was committed to Mr Attorney, the House was simply using the presence of the queen's legal counsel to ascertain her mind on the bill.
75 One bill, committed to the queen's solicitor after the second reading, has no recorded first reading. The clerk had either omitted it in error or entered it mistakenly as the second.
76 L.J., ii, and iii, *passim.* Ericson, pp. 103–4.
77 Elsynge, *Method of Passing Bills*, p. 212.
78 This was not the case in the seventeenth century, when the rules of debate had been tightened up and no man could speak twice at the same reading 'unless for explaining himself in some material part of his former Speech'. Scobell, *Remembrances*, p. 20.
79 Smith, *De Republica*, pp. 52–3.
80 Vowell, 'The Order and Usage', fo. 25.
81 *Cal.S.P.Span*, xi, 33. Cf. Neale, *Elizabethan Commons*, pp. 404–7 on the Commons' conventions in debate, and the frequent distance between theory and practice. *Miscellanea Antiqua Anglicana*, pub. Robert Triphook (London, 1815), p. 107.
82 Muller, *Gardiner's Letters*, p. 392.
83 Robinson, p. 10.
84 Muller, *Gardiner's Letters*, p. 377.
85 *Ibid.*, p. 392.
86 Jordan, *Edward VI. The Young King*, p. 168.
87 Gasquet and Bishop, pp. 127–9, 131–6.
88 Only one prelate, Cranmer, had the stomach to speak 'freely' against Tunstall's removal. Strype, *Cranmer's Mems*, i, 415; Ridley, *Cranmer*, pp. 335–6. See also Northumberland's threats against the bishops. *Cal.S.P.Span.*, xi, 33.

[89] Graves, '*Politics of Opposition*', pp. 17–19.

[90] See pp. 88–90, 104–5, 107, 181, 193–4 of the present volume.

[91] There is not a single recorded instance in the mid-Tudor Lords.

[92] Elsynge found 'many Bills to pass without Commitment, and some at the second Reading in the Times of Henry the Eighth, Edward the Sixth, and Queen Elizabeth. But now the constant Order is to read every Bill, save the Pardon, three Times.' Elsynge, *Method of Passing Bills*, p. 212.

[93] Elizabethan commentators, writing not many years or sessions after Mary's death, confirm that engrossment had by then assumed a settled and fairly consistent practice after the second reading and (if necessary) revision by a committee. Vowell, 'The Order and Usage', fo. 20v; Smith, *De Republica*, p. 53.

[94] L.J., ii, iii; H.L.R.O., Orig. Acts, Ed. VI and Mary.

[95] See chapter 1, p. 7, n. 25, of the present volume.

[96] Hakewil, *Manner how Statutes are Enacted in Parliament*, p. 23.

[97] Elsynge, *Method of Passing Bills*, p. 213.

[98] Hakewil, *Manner how Statutes are Enacted in Parliament*, p. 24. For the Lords, see Elsynge, *Method of Passing Bills*, p. 213.

[99] Vowell, 'The Order and Usage', fo. 21.

[100] Elsynge, *Method of Passing Bills*, p. 212.

[101] *Ibid.*

[102] *Ibid.*

[103] Not just those cited by Elsynge, but also e.g. *L.J.*, 1, 299, 301, 453, 482.

[104] See chapter 6, pp. 133–4, of the present volume.

[105] J. B. Davidson (ed.), 'Hooker's Journal of the House of Commons in 1571', *Transactions of the Devonshire Association*, 11 (1879), 478.

[106] Scobell, *Remembrances*, p. 23.

[107] *Ibid.*

[108] Elsynge, *Method of Passing Bills*, p. 213.

[109] Scobell, *Remembrances*, p. 24.

[110] Elsynge, *Method of Passing Bills*, p. 213.

[111] As these papers bear no identifying formulae, it is uncertain whether they derive from the Lords or Commons or, for that matter, whether they were drafted in committee, on the instruction of the House during the third reading, or as recommended alterations from one House to the other. However, their contents and format accord with Elsynge's description of the practice. Thus the 'Declaration of the repeale of the atteyndour of the late Cardynell Poole' (H.L.R.O., Orig. Acts, 1 Eliz., no. 29) is accompanied by a small paper which precisely identifies the points of emendation and the nature of the changes to be effected, e.g. 'In the xith and xiith Lines all thes wordes to be putt owt allthough that at the tyme of the making thereof the trewe meaninge was that it shoulde extende and take effecte But onelye from the tyme of the makinge of the saide date of repeale And not before.' Or 'In the xiiiith Lyne after thes wordes (or take effecte) to putt in thes wordes (as touching or concerning only anny estate right

tytle or Interest).' See also H.L.R.O., Orig. Acts, 1 Eliz., no. 30;
5 Eliz., nos 2, 11, 16; 13 Eliz., no. 36.

[112] The spokesman is only occasionally named, e.g. the bishop of
Coventry and Lichfield and Lord Morley on 3 and 4 January 1550.

[113] Most of the recorded entries concern *three* consecutive readings of a
proviso devised either during the third reading of a bill or by the other
house, but the principle remains the same, e.g. a proviso to the bill
'against Hunters', read thrice on 20 Jan. 1550. In the same session
the general pardon was passed after one reading, but a proviso to it
had three. However, on 27 Feb. 1552 the Lords did read a proviso
twice and annex it to a bill which had just completed its second
reading.

[114] Smith, *De Republica*, p. 53. After the engrossment the clerk 'ought to
indorse the Title thereof upon the back of the Bill and not within'.
Scobell cited Elizabethan cases in which the Commons returned bills
'for want thereof'. Scobell, *Remembrances*, pp. 26–7.

[115] D'Ewes, pp. 18–19.

[116] Even in early Stuart parliaments it was only put to the question 'If no
Lord speak against it.' Elsynge, *Method of Passing Bills*, p. 215.

[117] '[I]f any be disposed to object [it is] disputed againe among them.'
Smith, *De Republica*, p. 53. This was equally true of the Commons: the
bill to cancel letters patent of denization previously granted to
Frenchmen was read a third time on 15 February 1558, but debate
was resumed two days later before the bill was rejected in a division
on the 18th.

[118] E.g. The exiles bill on 13 Nov. 1555. L.J., iii, 105.

[119] For example, in 1548/9 there are minor alterations, interlineations
and deletions in H.L.R.O., Orig. Acts, 2/3 Ed. VI, nos 1, 4, 5, 7, 10,
14, 21, 23, 27, 31, 33, 41, 49. In 1549/50 the total is only four. *Ibid.*,
3/4 Ed. VI, nos 1, 2, 10, 23. But in 1552 there were more than twice
as many. *Ibid.*, 5/6 Ed. VI, nos 1, 2, 3, 9, 11, 12, 14, 18, 28, 31.

[120] Neale, *Elizabethan Commons*, p. 397; Coke, *Institutes*, IV, 35.

[121] Smith, *De Republica*, pp. 51, 53, 56.

[122] D'Ewes, p. 19.

[123] Smith, *De Republica*, p. 56.

[124] Vowell, 'The Order and Usage', fo. 21; Hakewil, *Manner how
Statutes are Enacted in Parliament*, p. 73. On this point he was in agreement with Scobell, *Remembrances*, p. 21.

[125] One is left wondering why a vote conducted in this precise way could
ever be inconclusive. Did not the clerk keep a tally of 'contents' and
'not contents'? Robinson averred that he did, and the journals confirm
that he recorded the latter if they constituted a minority.

[126] Elsynge, *Method of Passing Bills*, p. 215; Robinson, p. 4.

[127] Plowden, *Commentaries*, I, p. 126.

[128] Robinson, p. 4.

[129] The clerk then employed the formula 'Majore Procerum numero
assentiente conclusa est.'

[130] See also Scobell, *Remembrances*, p. 26.

131 'Majore Procerum numero dissentiente, rejecta est.'

132 In 1548/9 83% of all bills which passed did so unanimously; in 1552 the figure was 71%. Even in the more disturbed Marian conditions of 1555 and Jan. 1558 the totals ran at 61% and 59%. L.J., ii, 49–124, 209–69; *ibid.*, iii, 87–169.

133 'If any bill be demed impugned, and clear overthrowne, the same is no more to be thenceforth receyved.' Vowell, 'The Order and Usage', fo. 21.

134 E.g. H.L.R.O., Orig. Acts, 2/3 Ed. VI, nos 8, 54. Scobell, *Remembrances*, pp. 26–7. On 17 December 1547 the Commons would not receive a proviso to a bill 'because the Lords had not given their consent to the same'.

135 See chapter 6, pp. 138–40, of the present volume. Bills might be sent down singly, but frequently they were allowed to accumulate until several were ready for transmission to the Commons. The procedure of presentation to the other House is described in Smith, *De Republica*, p. 53 and Lambarde, 'Proceedings', 262; for a later account, see Scobell, *Remembrances*, p. 38.

136 *Ibid.*, pp. 38–9. With the exception of the subsidy which was returned to the Commons so that the speaker might present it to the monarch, all bills ended up in the Lords after the completion of their parliamentary passage. Vowell, 'The Order and Usage', fo. 20v; Lambarde, 'Proceedings', 266.

137 Scobell, *Remembrances*, pp. 27, 33.

138 H.L.R.O., Orig. Acts, 1 Ed. VI, no. 15.

139 Hakewil, *Manner how Statutes are Enacted in Parliament*, pp. 56–7; Scobell, *Remembrances*, p. 34; Elsynge, *Method of Passing Bills*, p. 218. See chapter 6, p. 124, of the present volume.

140 Lambarde, 'Proceedings', 262. In 1552 the Lords engrossed a proviso to the Commons' bill 'for the limitation of the duke of Somerset's lands' and sent them down with a a request that the amendment 'might be annexed'. See also H.L.R.O., Orig. Acts, 2/3 Ed. VI, nos 8, 27. In both cases the second chamber engrossed its proviso. The proprietary role of the House of origin is clearly set forth in the subscription on the latter act, a penal measure against buggery. It had commenced in the Lords, where the clerk duly endorsed it for despatch. The Lower House approved and returned it, with a proviso to which the originating chamber gave its assent. The endorsement of the Commons' clerk – *A ceste bill avecque le proviso annex les comuns sont assentus* – reads as if it had received both bill and amendment from the Upper House. In a sense it had, because the Lower House could only recommend the proviso. It was up to the Lords to determine whether it should become part of the bill and so annex it. It should be added, however, that inconsistencies and irregularities inevitably abounded. The examples cited here point only to the general procedural drift.

141 At times the proportion could rise to more than one-fifth of all bills (e.g. to 21% and 24% in the disturbed Marian parliaments of 1554/5 and 1555), but in 1547 it stood at only 4%.

142 See pp. 175 n. 15, 178–9, 183, of the present volume.

143 Scobell, *Remembrances*, p. 35.

144 Vowell, 'The Order and Usage', fos 21, 25; Scobell, *Remembrances*, pp. 29–30.

145 C.J., i, 183.

146 C.J., i, 165.

147 C.J., ii, 23, 121; Thomas Cromwell's parliamentary diary, Trinity College Dublin MSS., 1045, fo. 104v. In 1576 the Commons insisted that only the House 'wherein the Bill remaineth' could initiate a joint-conference. Scobell, *Remembrances*, p. 28.

148 E.g. in 1547 to 'treat and commune' of the repeal of treason laws. On 5 April 1552 the Lords, having doubts about a measure to regulate the manufacture of broadcloth, called for a joint-conference in order to obtain a 'better understanding of the said bill, and for their full instruction therein'. Most important of all, the bill for reunion with Rome in Mary's third parliament was drawn up by a committee of members from both Houses.

149 Smith, *De Republica*, p. 55.

150 Scobell, *Remembrances*, p. 31.

151 B.L., Harleian MSS., 253, fo. 35v.

152 Vowell, 'The Order and Usage', fo. 25.

153 C.J., i, 184.

154 Neale, *Elizabethan Commons*, pp. 335–6.

155 *Ibid.*, p. 335.

156 For the Commons see Hooker on the Bristol merchants bill (1571) and the restitutions of Norfolk and Tunstall in 1553/4. Hooker's Journal, 478; C.J., i, 96–9, 108. For the Lords see the proceedings against Somerset in 1549/50. L.J., ii, 170–5. When the House gave a second reading to a bill assuring certain lands to the sons of Lord Thomas Howard, the earl of Arundel moved that, as the matter touched his wife, she should be called before the House 'to declare there frankely, whither she was content with such mater as was conteyned in the saide bill'. The Lords concurred and two days later she duly made her appearance. The practice was not a mid-Tudor innovation. When a bill concerning Lord Mountjoy's estate came before the Upper House in Henry VIII's reign, it was resolved that 'the Cause should be heard openly in the House . . . by Council learned on both sides'. Scobell, *Remembrances*, pp. 21–2; Elsynge, *Method of Passing Bills*, p. 213.

Chapter 8: The legislative record of the mid-Tudor Lords

1 Neale, *Elizabethan Commons*, chapters 7, 9–11.

2 E.g. *ibid.*; Bindoff; *V.C.H., Wilts.*, v, 111–69. In 1547 the Commons included a dozen Seymour clients from Wiltshire alone. At least one Marian bishop, Stephen Gardiner, enjoyed a considerable following of friends, political allies, co-religionists and clients in the Commons. See p. 189, n. 86, of the present volume.

[3] There is not a great deal of evidence of this. On the other hand, it is difficult to believe that the duke of Norfolk's clients did not assist the invalidation of his attainder on its way through Mary's first parliament. C.J., i, 96, 97–97v, 98v, 99. H.L.R.O., Orig. Acts, 1 Mary, st.2, no. 27. See also the Musgraves' promotion of Wharton's bill against Cumberland, Chapter 5, p. 110, of the present volume; and Sir Christopher Hatton's ability to discourage legislation contrary to his interests as lieutenant of Corfe Castle. Neale, *Elizabethan Commons*, pp. 388–9. However there were limits to parliamentary loyalties. When the earl of Pembroke defended Sir Edward Hastings, the government's spokesman on the Marian bill to penalise exiles in 1555, he was deserted by many of the gentlemen in his service. Michiel to doge and senate, 16 December 1555, *Cal.S.P.Ven.*, VI, Pt I, No. 316. See also D. M. Loades, *The Reign of Mary Tudor* (London, 1979), p. 271. He denies any connection between clientage and political commitment.

[4] E.g. in 1554/5. See pp. 195–8 of the present volume.

[5] E.g. Willoughby's bill in 1554/5; the bill 'for Curriers and Cordwainers', which was redrafted in the Commons and went to four second readings there before proceeding to the Lords; and another for the assurance of the earl of Bath's lands which was rejected and redrawn in the Lower House, and altogether had twelve readings in the two Houses before passing into law: both in 1548/9; a bill for Chester in the following session was first redrawn by the Commons and then amended by a Lords' proviso; and in April 1554 a measure for the Calais cordwainers went to four readings in the Commons before being rejected by the Upper House. C.J., i, 7–32, 102–17, 137v–141; L.J., ii, 49–198; *ibid.*, iii, 1–29.

[6] See chapter 5, *passim*, and pp. 193–4 of the present volume.

[7] See pp. 184–94.

[8] See chapter 7, p. 172; Elton, 'Points of Contact: Parliament', 194 and n. 27, and 195.

[9] E.g. a bill 'for Cloth-making in the City of Worcester' is elsewhere described in more general terms as a measure 'Touching Clothmaking in Corporate Towns and Market Towns'.

[10] All but three of the 277 measures passed by the Edwardian and Marian parliaments, survive amongst the original acts in the House of Lords Record Office. The only lacunae are the act 'For Gavell kynde' (2/3 Edward VI), and the restitutions in blood of Lord Montagu's heirs and Sir William Parr (1 Mary 1553 and 1 Mary 1554). The texts of the two restitutions are on the parliament rolls. P.R.O. Parl. Rolls, C. 65, 162, nos 25 and 47.

[11] There were 17 Edwardian and 15 Marian restitutions (ten of which were enacted in October–December 1553). Twenty-two (possibly twenty-three) bore the sign manual and so fell into the category of grace acts. H.L.R.O., Orig. Acts, 2/3 Ed. VI – 4 & 5 Ph. & Mary. The additional possibility is the restitution of Montagu's heirs in 1 Mary (1553), the text of which does not survive in the original acts.

Unlike the restoration of Sir William Parr, the ex-marquess of Northampton, whose bill is recorded in the Commons' Journal as bearing the sign manual, the journal entries for Montagu's bill simply record that it had first passed the Lords. C.J., i, 112v, 113v, 115.

12 There were only six exceptions: the restitution of Isley in 1549/50, the confirmation of Sharington's attainder in 1548/9, and a clerical subsidy in Jan. 1558 went to more than three readings in at least one House; so did the bill to release the earl of Oxford from assurances made to the duke of Somerset. H.L.R.O., Orig. Acts, 5/6 Ed. VI, no. 35. Thomas Seymour's attainder involved a good deal of toing and froing between the Houses and protracted proceedings in the Commons in 1548/9, and the confirmation of Suffolk's attainder in 1 Mary (April 1554) actually stuck on a disagreement between the two Houses. It might be expected that estate bills (usually promoted by peers) were a formality justifying inclusion in this category but in practice this was not the case. Two were rejected (for Dacre in 1547, and the duchess of Suffolk in 1554/5), two were redrafted (for the earl of Bath and Edmund Lawson) in 1548/9, the Howard bill in the same session involved quasi-judicial proceedings in the Lords and a measure for the Cliffords went to more than three readings there. C.J., i; L.J., ii and iii; H.L.R.O., Orig. Acts.

13 This total includes the 14 abortive bills of November 1558, but none for October 1553 (owing to the lack of a Lord's Journal). Ericson's total of bills, again excluding Mary's first parliament, is 742, because he omits bills in 1547, 1548/9 and Nov. 1558.

14 E.g. committees were appointed by the Lords in 1547 to draw bills for the borders and against the decay of tillage. L.J., ii, 7.

15 There were also a number of measures which passed one House but were redrafted in the other. In such cases the workload was more equitably distributed between the initiating House and that which redrew it. Moreover the chamber which redrafted the measure often became the more formative influence on its final shape. The Lower House was more active in this role. For every one of its bills redrawn by the Lords, the Commons replaced four of those sent down to it. Nevertheless the numbers were insignificant, running at no more than two or three per session. They have not been credited to the redrafting House because, in many cases, it must have used the original bill as the model on which to base its own measure. See e.g. the Lords' original draft and the Commons' new version of the chantries bill in 1547. H.L.R.O., Orig. Acts, 1 Ed. VI, no. 15.

16 No bills of this kind commenced in the Commons.

17 These calculations, together with those in the preceding paragraphs, are compiled from the Lords' and Commons' Journals and the original acts. They are not entirely accurate because the record of abortive bills has not survived for the first Marian parliament.

18 A figure which includes the first Marian parliament.

[19] Excluding October–December 1553.

[20] They averaged nine weeks in Edward VI's reign and five weeks under Mary.

[21] Not that all local, sectional and economic measures began in the Commons. In 1552 the wardens of the woodmongers made 'earnest and dylygent sute to the Duke's grace of Northumberland and the resydewe of the lordes for the furtheraunce of the byll in the parlyment house concernynge the provysyon of woodes and ffewell for the cytie'. Corporation of City of London, Repertories of court of aldermen, Rep. 12, iii, fo. 470a; H.L.R.O., Orig. Acts, 5/6 Ed. VI, no. 28; *ibid.*, 7 Ed. VI, no. 7.

[22] In 1547 and 1553 (1 Mary) tunnage and poundage was granted. In November 1558 the passage of a subsidy bill was cut short by Mary's death. H.L.R.O., Orig. Acts, 1 Ed. VI, no. 20 and 1 Mary, no. 17; C.J., i, 183–4.

[23] H.L.R.O., Orig. Acts, 1 Ed. VI, no. 20; 2/3 Ed. VI, no. 37; 7 Ed. VI, no. 12.

[24] C.J., i, 183. For a full account of the proceedings, see chapter 7, p. 170, of the present volume.

[25] 'A Briefe discourse of the order ... used in the graunting of the Subsidy ... and the fiftenes to the King and quenes ma[jesti]es.' 4 & 5 Ph. & Mary, P.R.O., S.P. 11/12/31, fos. 67–70. See above, n. 23. These were not novel interventions. During the Reformation Parliament a Lords' delegation, once again headed by the lord chancellor, called for 'some reasonable ayde' which would enable the king to strengthen the borders in order 'to let the Scottysh men from their invasions'. 23 Henry VIII. Halle, fo. cciii. After lengthy debate the Commons revised the terms of the grant but this cannot erase the fact of the Lords' involvement. See Loades, *Mary Tudor*, pp. 408–9.

[26] This remained so in Elizabeth's reign, despite Neale's confident claim that 'if anything had become clearly established by [then] it was the prescriptive right of the Commons to initiate taxation'. In 1593 the Lower House was busily congratulating itself on its generosity in offering a double subsidy to the queen, when the Lords demanded three. The adoption of a face-saving formula by the Commons cannot obscure the fact that the Upper House won its point. Neale, *Elizabethan Parliaments*, II, 298–312; Roskell, 'Perspectives in English Parliamentary History', 469–70.

[27] See chapter 1, p. 7, n. 25, of the present volume, and Loades, *Mary Tudor*, pp. 274–6.

[28] See chapter 4, pp. 60–1 of the present volume. This can only be tested systematically for the Upper House. However, the Crown's prosecution of some of the knights and burgesses who departed without licence in January 1555 and the bills to penalise absent members, introduced in this and the following parliament, may point to a similar problem in the Commons. See pp. 197–8 and Loades, *Mary Tudor*, p. 272, for alternative explanations.

[29] One hundred and seventy (or 38%) if we take into account those bills whose passage was a formality.

[30] Or 53 (21%). See Table 3, p. 176, of the present volume.

[31] Or from 59% to less than 30%, if those bills which were a formality are discounted.

[32] The figures have been calculated from H.L.R.O., Orig. Acts. The Lords' initiation of 60% of all acts between 1539 and 1547 suggests that its Edwardian record was not an aberration, but rather that in Mary's reign there was a dramatic departure from an established pattern in which it had occupied the senior and superior role as House of origin. This view is further reinforced by Elton's description of the Commons' ascendancy in the 1530s as 'a few short and rather spurious years'. G. R. Elton, *England under the Tudors* (London, 1977), pp. 174–5.

[33] The Edwardian Lords threw out five bills in five sessions, whereas the Marian House dashed twice that number in fewer (four) and shorter sessions. The comparative Commons' figures are 12 and 17. The fact that two-thirds of those rejected by the Lower House originated there, whereas all but one of those turned down by the Lords had come up from the Commons, may reflect on the relative efficiency of the two chambers.

[34] From 9–10 under Edward down to 7–8 under Mary. Once again, however, it must be recalled that the Marian sessions were shorter.

[35] See pp. 193–4 of the present volume for a more detailed examination.

[36] Calculated from C.J., L.J., and H.L.R.O., Orig. Acts (1547–58).

[37] However, the last of these was rejected by the Commons in 1553 and only passed there in April 1554, after protracted quasi-judicial proceedings. C.J., i, 99, 108–9.

[38] See pp. 195–8 of the present volume.

[39] See pp. 198–200.

[40] E.g. The Commons gave a first reading to 130 bills in the 1548/9 session (compared with 93 in the Lords) and to 71 in 1555 (cf. 43 in the Upper House).

[41] With the possible exception of the Reformation parliament.

[42] See pp. 90, 104, of the present volume.

[43] See pp. 31–2, 91.

[44] See chapters 4, pp. 88–9 and 5, pp. 104–5.

[45] See p. 182. Acts were passed making it treason to plot the death of a privy councillor (a response to Wriothesley's attempted counter-coup), concerning Paget's property at West Drayton and the legitimisation of the children of Northampton and Elizabeth Brooke, three against Somerset, and an unsuccessful bill to punish Tunstall. H.L.R.O., Orig. Acts, 3/4 Ed. VI, nos 5, 25, 31; 5/6 Ed. VI, nos. 30, 35, 37; L.J., ii, 250; C.J., i, 46v. The only direct parliamentary effect of conciliar power-struggles was the absence of the losers: Wriothesley and Arundel were ordered into house arrest on 14 January 1550 and Somerset was executed just before the next session commenced. See Hoak, *The King's Council*, pp. 74, 257–8.

[46] Strype, *Cranmer's Mems.*, I, 415; Ridley, *Cranmer*, pp. 335–6. Hoak endorses Cranmer's opinion, that misprision was not the real reason for Tunstall's punishment. 'The bishop's real offence probably lay in his express opposition [in and out of parliament] to the radical direction of the government's religious programme.' Hoak, pp. 71–2.

[47] See Jordan, *Edward VI. The Threshold of Power*, p. 383; C.J., i, 46v; *D.N.B.*, *sub* Cuthbert Tunstall. Jordan misread the journals and identified two bills against Tunstall.

[48] E.g. in 1549 when the conservatives attempted to repeal sections of the act of uniformity and another measure, establishing a canon-law reform commission, met the resistance of virtually the entire episcopate. G. R. Elton, *Reform and Reformation, England 1509–1558* (London, 1977), p. 359.

[49] See chapter 5 of the present volume, *passim*.

[50] *A.P.C.*, II, 193–5.

[51] Five peers voted against the bill to suppress Catholic books and images. L.J., ii, 188. For the bishops' record of dissent, see chapter 4, p. 90, of the present volume.

[52] The Lords redrafted the Commons' bill on enclosures. H.L.R.O., Orig. Acts, 3/4 Ed. VI, nos 3, 15.

[53] The bill was endorsed not only by the king, his councillors, and legal counsel, but also by Somerset and his wife. H.L.R.O., Orig. Acts, 3/4 Ed. VI, no. 31; L.J., ii, 169–75.

[54] However, a few members of the Lords voted against three of them and the Commons redrafted a cloth bill.

[55] This analysis is based on an examination of C.J., i; L.J., ii and H.L.R.O., Orig. Acts, Ed. VI.

[56] See Loades, *Mary Tudor*, pp. 70–82.

[57] Muller, *Gardiner's Letters*, pp. 166, 170, 181, 218; *A.P.C.*, II, 131–2, 208–10; *Wriothesley's Chron.*, II, 3, 97; *Grey Friars' Chron.*, pp. 56, 82; Foxe, VI, 537; *D.N.B.*, *sub* Stephen Gardiner and William Paget; Graves, 'The Mid-Tudor House of Lords', II: Parl. Biogs *sub* Gardiner and Paget; Gardiner to Paget, 1 March 1547, Muller, *Gardiner's Letters*, no. 118.

[58] Graves, 'Politics of Opposition', pp. 3–5; Graves, 'Forgotten House of Lords', p. 26.

[59] Graves, 'Politics of Opposition', pp. 2–5, 10, 13, 14; Graves, 'Forgotten House of Lords', pp. 25–6; Loades, *Mary Tudor*, pp. 84–5.

[60] The Commons in Mary's first parliament included a sizeable group of crypto-Protestants. 'The names of the Knights and Burgesses of Parliament held at Westm[inster]. 5th October 1 Marie' with the addition that 'Those for the true religion are signed thus +', Bodleian MSS., e. Mus. 17.

[61] Particularly in view of Mary's known attitude to the expropriation of Church property. Baron Somers, *A Collection of Scarce and Interesting Tracts* . . . 16 vols (London, 1748–52), I, 55–6.

[62] P. L. Hughes and J. F. Larkin, *Tudor Royal Proclamations, 1485–1587* (New Haven and London, 1964–9), II, no. 390 (pp. 5–8).

[63] *Ibid.*, II, no. 392 (pp. 9–10).

[64] *Ibid.*, II, no. 393 (p. 12).

[65] *C.P.R., Ph. & Mary*, I, 70.

[66] C.J., i, 78v; Renard to Charles V, 23 Oct. 1553, *Cal.S.P.Span.*, XI, 314.

[67] If Renard's report of 19 October is accurate, parliamentary concern about religion, papal authority and the restitution of Church property was already being aired before the adjournment. Renard to Charles V, 19 Oct. 1553, *Cal.S.P.Span.*, XI, 305, 308.

[68] 3, 4, 6, 7 and 8 November. Loades claims that the repeal was smoothly carried out, but elsewhere he acknowledges determined and protracted resistance. Loades, *Mary Tudor*, pp. 156, 178, n. 44.

[69] Renard to Charles V, 8 Nov. 1553. *Cal.S.P.Span.*, XI, 349.

[70] *Ibid.*, 305, 308. When parliament enacted that Henry VIII's marriage to Catherine of Aragon was valid, it did so in a measure which made no mention of the papal authority on which Julius II's dispensation – and therefore the legitimacy of the marriage – rested. H.L.R.O., Orig. Acts, I Mary, st. 2 (1553), no. 1; Renard to Charles V, 15, 19, 21 Oct. 1553, *Cal.S.P.Span.*, XI, 298, 308, 309–10.

[71] The Lords did add a proviso to the bill. H.L.R.O., Orig. Acts, I Mary, st. 2, no. 2.

[72] The French ambassador named Suffolk, Pembroke, Cumberland, Clinton and 'plusieurs aultres des grands seigneurs' amongst Courtenay's supporters. Vertot, *Ambassades*, II, 246. For Gardiner's supporters, friends and clients in the Commons, see p. 189, n. 86, of the present volume.

[73] Renard to Charles V, 4 and 6, Nov. 1553, *Cal.S.P.Span.*, XI, 333, 343. Gardiner and members of both Houses accompanied the Commons' speaker, Sir John Pollard, when he presented the petition. In 1555 Pollard figured prominently in parliamentary opposition to the queen. Loades, *Mary Tudor*, p. 273.

[74] Renard to Charles V, 31 Oct. 1553, *Cal.S.P.Span.*, XI, 328; *ibid.*, 343, 348–9; Noailles to Henry II, 4, 9, and 14 Nov., 1553, Vertot, *Ambassades*, II, 234, 236–8, 241, 256; Loades, *Mary Tudor*, p. 120.

[75] Renard to Charles V, 28, 29 Nov., 3 Dec., 1553, *Cal.S.P.Span.*, XI, 395, 399, 412.

[76] Same to same, 8 Dec. 1553, *Cal.S.P.Span.*, XI, 416.

[77] Graves, 'The Mid-Tudor House of Lords', I, 88–9, 244–5; II, 270.

[78] H.L.R.O., Orig. Acts, I Mary, st. 1, nos 2, 3; I Mary, st. 2, nos 19, 21, 25–9, 31.

[79] Again, this was not unusual. Denizations, attainders and continuance bills rarely aroused criticism in either House.

[80] The repeal of treasons, and the declaration of the queen's legitimacy H.L.R.O., Orig. Acts, I Mary, st. 1, no. 1 and I Mary, st. 2, no. 1.

[81] The repeal of the Edwardian Reformation, the bill against disturbances during divine service, the release of the last subsidy, and the grant of tunnage and poundage for life. I Mary, st, 2, nos 2, 3, 16, 17.

[82] See below, n. 86.

[83] Dickens, *English Reformation*, p. 195.

[84] *A.P.C.*, II, 131–2, 157–8, 208–10; *ibid.*, III, 213–14; Muller, *Gardiner*, pp. 166, 170, 181, 218; *Wriothesley's Chron.*, II, 3, 46, 97; *Grey Friars' Chron.*, 56, 68, 82; Foxe, VI, 264–5, 537.

[85] The writs went out on 14 August. P.R.O., Parl. Pawns, C. 218, Pt I, No. 7.

[86] A few, such as Francis Allen and Thomas Martyn, sat for constituencies outside Gardiner's sphere of electoral interest, but most of them (e.g. James Bassett, Jacques Wingfield, John Norris, Sir Thomas White, Richard Bethell, John Beckensall and Oliver Vachell) were returned for Winchester, Hampshire, and the episcopal boroughs of Taunton (Somerset) and Downton and Hindon (Wiltshire), in which the bishops' bailiffs were the returning officers. Graves, 'The Mid-Tudor House of Lords', II, 200; Bindoff, *V.C.H.*, *Wilts*, V, 117–19; P.R.O., *Official Returns*, I, 381–99; Foxe, VI; *H.P.T. Biogs*; Price. Gardiner enjoyed an intimate association with the borough officers of Winchester. William Laurence, mayor and parliamentary burgess in 1553 and 1554, had given evidence in the bishop's favour during his trial. Richard Bethell, mayor in 1552, also represented the borough in Mary's first parliament. Nicholas Ticheborne, returned for Hampshire in October 1553, was the cousin of Sir Thomas White, who was Gardiner's servant. Will of Nicholas Ticheborne, esq., proved 25 July 1555. Hants R.O., Consistory Court, B 1555; B.L. Harleian MSS., 846, fos 4–4d. I am indebted to Ronald Fritze for these references. On most occasions Gardiner could also count on the support of Mary's household servants and fellow councillors such as Sir Francis Englefield, Sir Robert Rochester, Sir Edward Hastings, Sir Richard Southwell and Sir Henry Jerningham. Friends and allies in the Lords included the duke of Norfolk, Viscount Montagu (who had sat in the Commons in Mary's first two parliaments), Lords Stourton and Morley, Bishop White and other conservatives.

[87] At least 10 in April 1554, 8 in 1554–5, and 7 in 1555. These totals may be enlarged when the *History of Parliament Trust Biographies* are published.

[88] Muller, *Gardiner's Letters*, pp. 405, 424.

[89] His efforts had not always been crowned with success. In 1539 his efforts in the shire elections had been frustrated by Thomas Cromwell's agents. *L.P.*, Henry VIII, XIV (1), Nos 634, 662.

[90] See above, n. 86.

[91] Graves, 'Politics of Opposition', pp. 9–10.

[92] Henry Penning, *Cal.S.P.Ven.*, V, No. 813 (p. 431); *ibid.*, VI, Pt I, Nos 256, 258, 259; C.J., i, 74, 102, 120, 143; *Cal.S.P.Span.*, XII, 201; *ibid.*, XIII, 82; Vertot, *Ambassades*, III, 151–3; *ibid.*, IV, 20; *ibid.*, V, 173; L.J., iii, 6, 28, 84; Muller, *Gardiner*, p. 267; Cobbett, *Parliamentary History*, I, 613; A. M. Quirini (ed.), *Epistolae Reginaldi Poli* . . . 5 vols (Brescia, 1744–57), V, 46.

[93] *Cal.S.P.Ven.*, V, No. 813 (p. 431); Renard to Charles V, 28 Oct. 1553, *Cal. S.P.Span.*, XI, 324.

94 *Cal.S.P.Ven.*, vi, Pt i, No. 251 (p. 217).
95 *A.P.C.*, iv, 398.
96 Graves, 'Politics of Opposition', pp. 6–7.
97 *Ibid.*, pp. 7–9.
98 For a more detailed study of the preliminaries to the parliament of April 1554 and its progress, see *ibid.*, pp. 6–13; Graves, 'Forgotten House of Lords', pp. 26–8; Loades, *Mary Tudor*, pp. 83–4, 85, 86, 103 n. 71, 104, n. 73, 83, 135, 168–9.
99 Graves, 'Politics of Opposition', p. 11.
100 H.L.R.O., Orig. Acts, 1 Mary (1554), no. 1; Bodleian Library, Tanner MSS., 84, fos 211v–215v.
101 Graves, 'Politics of Opposition', pp. 14–15.
102 Graves, 'Forgotten House of Lords', pp. 27–8.
103 *Ibid.*, p. 28.
104 *Ibid.*, p. 28.
105 Graves, 'Politics of Opposition', p. 16.
106 *Cal.S.P.Span.*, xii, 220.
107 Graves, 'Politics of Opposition', pp. 16–17.
108 *Ibid.*, p. 17; Loades, p. 136.
109 *Cal.S.P.Span.*, xii, 230.
110 E.g. Rich.
111 E.g. Huntingdon, Pembroke, Rutland, Audley, Bray, Clinton, Cobham and Darcy of Chiche.
112 L.J., iii, 10; Graves, 'Politics of Opposition', p. 15.
113 *Cal.S.P.Span.*, xii, 238, 240, 251.
114 For the anomalous bill 'that the Bishop of Rome, or any other Bishop shall not convent any Person, for any Abbey-Lands', see Graves, 'Politics of Opposition', pp. 18–19. Loades argues that Gardiner proposed a *quid pro quo* – the restoration of papal supremacy in return for a guarantee to owners of secularised lands – and that, if it was introduced, it was incorporated in this measure. Loades, *Mary Tudor*, p. 169.
115 Bills relating to daggs, 'unlawful assemblies of masterless Men' and the sale of goods in towns, as well as the revival of one of the antiheresy laws and a measure concerning secularised property.
116 The repeal of a bill against the importation of foreign haberdashery.
117 Counterfeit steel, Calais cordwainers, distresses, and the bill against heretical opinions and books.
118 The Lords' legislative record in this parliament is derived chiefly from L.J., iii, 1–29, and C.J., i, 102–17.
119 *Cal.S.P.Span.*, xii, 221.
120 Dissenting votes were also cast against the restitution of the bishopric of Durham, bills against high wine prices, for causeways at Sherborne and between Bristol and Gloucester, and for sea-sands in Glamorgan.
121 Graves, 'The Mid-Tudor House of Lords', ii, 127.
122 Ericson, p. 48; Loades, *Mary Tudor*, p. 104, n. 75, 135–6, 169 and 272–3 (where Loades points up the importance of conciliar management).

[123] H.L.R.O., Orig. Acts, Ph. & Mary, nos 8 and 18.

[124] See Chapter 6, p. 132, of the present volume.

[125] Bills to prohibit priests from leasing benefices or becoming school-teachers, to confirm letters patent signed by Mary since her marriage and to punish treason by words, seditious rumours, heresy, and the absence of knights and burgesses from the Commons.

[126] Graves, 'The Mid-Tudor House of Lords', II, App. Attendance IV and V.

[127] Parliament was divided on the question. A number of lawyers in the Commons argued that a dispensation for lands was unnecessary, because kings of England had always exercised absolute authority over property donated to the Church. Many of the peers, however, were unsympathetic to this point of view – understandable because they were amongst the most important beneficiaries of the expropriations of the thirties and forties. Ericson, p. 213. See also L.J., iii, 60–2, 64–73, 81–3; Foxe, VI, 567–72, 573; C.J., i, 124, 125v, 126; *Cal.S.P.Span.*, XIII, 107–8, 116, 120, 121; John Elder's letter in *Queen Jane*, pp. 154–9, 160–1; *Cal.S.P.Ven.*, V, Nos 966, 975; *ibid.*, VI, Pt I, No. 14 (pp. 9–10); *Cal.S.P.Span.*, XIII, 124–5; *D.N.B.*, *sub* R. Pole.

[128] P.R.O., S.P. Mary, 11/5, fo. 1; H.L.R.O., Orig. Acts, 1 & 2 Ph. & Mary, no. 10; *Cal.S.P.Span.*, XIII, 125–34; L.J., iii, 54.

[129] *Cal.S.P.Span.*, XIII, 125–6, 130; Loades, *Mary Tudor*, p. 224.

[130] Loades, pp. 135–6; C.J., i, 132–3. Renard was informed that five peers departed because they were offended by the regency bill. *Cal. S.P.Span.*, XIII, 134; Graves, 'Forgotten House of Lords', pp. 28–9; Loades, *Mary Tudor*, pp. 223–4, 268–9.

[131] Graves, 'Forgotten House of Lords', p. 29; see chapter 4, pp. 86–7, of the present volume.

[132] Coke, *Institutes*, IV, 17–21.

[133] The Crown may have been distressed by absenteeism on such a scale as this, because it was bound to have a deleterious effect on the transaction of business – hence the proceedings instituted against some of them in king's bench during 1555. Despite the fact that absenteeism was a perennial problem, such drastic action was as rare as the mass walk-out itself. *Ibid.* See also Loades, *Mary Tudor*, p. 272. Loades cites J. Loach's conclusion that offending knights and burgesses simply resented an enforced stay in London over Christmas.

[134] Thirteen were returned from Devon and Dorset, including members from Tavistock (where the returning officer was Bedford's official), Bridport, Dorchester, Poole and Weymouth. Eight more were elected to Cornish constituencies. Six came from the earl of Arundel's county of Sussex and a round dozen from Wiltshire where the Herbert interest was strong – they included at least one of Pembroke's clients, William Clerke. Neale, *Elizabethan Commons*, pp. 196–200. Graves, 'Politics of Opposition', p. 19; Graves, 'Forgotten House of Lords', p. 29.

[135] Loades, *Mary Tudor*, pp. 135–6, 222, 268–9, 272.

[136] Neale, *Elizabethan Parliaments*, I, 23–6. Loades is right to criticise the

undue emphasis on both the 'too famous' defeat of this official measure and the general turbulence of the Lower House; he draws our attention to the Lords' rejection of a conciliar measure about liveries; and he refutes the notion of an organised opposition in the Commons. Loades, *Mary Tudor*, pp. 270–1, 273–4.

[137] See chapter 6, p. 125, of the present volume. The source of the posthumous charge that he had browbeaten and bribed members of the earlier Marian parliaments is suspect, and cannot be substantiated, but it is characteristic of contemporary opinion about his parliamentary 'busyness'. Loades, *Mary Tudor*, p. 273.

[138] See also Ericson, pp. 46–7.

[139] H.L.R.O., Orig. Acts, 2 & 3 Ph. & Mary, nos 4, 6; C.J., i, 143–62.

[140] See p. 177 of the present volume.

[141] Elton, 'Parliament: Functions and Fortunes', 260. He cites the distribution as 32:19 in favour of the Lords in 1563 and 17:20 in 1576.

[142] E.g. to 53% in 1559–71. In the parliament of 1572–81, the Commons initiated 78% of all bills and 60% of all acts. I am indebted to David Dean for this information.

[143] Many members of the Commons stood in awe of it. One of them, writing in 1581, disapproved of joint-conferences, because they intimidated the delegates sent up from the Lower House. B.L. Harleian MSS., 253, fo. 36; see chapter 7, p. 171, of the present volume.

[144] Coke, *Institutes*, IV, 35.

SELECT BIBLIOGRAPHY

Any study of the mid-Tudor parliaments must rest four-square on two sets of records in the House of Lords Record Office. The first of these consists of the journals, the working-manuals of the clerks who compiled them for the simple, down-to-earth, practical purpose of assisting and guiding them in their parliamentary duties. Inseparable from these must be the end-products of parliament and the alpha and omega of its existence: legislation or, expressed in more precise archival terms, the original acts engrossed on parchment. Although these sources frequently fail to tell us what we want to know, we cannot be without them and all other materials are subordinate to them.

House of Lords Record Office: Journals of the House of Lords, i (Henry VIII), ii (Edward VI), iii (Mary), iv, v (Elizabeth).

House of Lords Record Office: Journals of the House of Commons, i, 1 Edward VI – 9 Elizabeth.

House of Lords Record Office: Original Acts.

Equipped with these it is possible to construct a skeletal framework of the Lords' activity in each session. Despite the errors, inconsistencies, and other falls from bureaucratic grace which characterise them, they enable us to plot attendance patterns and the progress of bills and to identify the measures before parliament, the membership of many committees, and the activities of legal assistants. There are occasional bonuses too, such as the notes hastily scribbled in a journal or on the verso of an act, opening windows onto clerical practice and Lords' procedure. Together, these sources chart the way in which time, dedication and experience were endowing an assembly of amateur legislators with a touch of professionalism.

The official records are supplemented by the writings of a few practised and interested contemporaries. They ranged across the sub-noble spectrum from John Hooker (alias Vowell), the borough official, through Edmund Plowden, the lawyer, to Sir Thomas Smith, the long-time royal servant.

J. B. Davidson (ed.): 'Hooker's Journal of the House of Commons in 1571', *Transactions of the Devonshire Association*, 11 (1879), 442–92.

John Vowell: 'The Order and Usage howe to keepe a Parliament in England, in these Dayes', British Library, Harleian MSS., 1178, no. 16, fos 19–27.

E. Plowden: *The Commentaries, or Reports . . . containing Diverse Cases . . . in the Several Reigns of King Edward VI, Queen Mary, King and Queen Philip and Mary, and Queen Elizabeth*, 2 vols (London, 1792).

Sir Thomas Smith: *De Republica Anglorum. A Discourse on the Commonwealth of England*, ed. L. Alston (Cambridge, 1906).

These were practical men-of-affairs with personal experience of parliament: Hooker represented Exeter in the Commons in 1571; Plowden was one of the members charged with unlicensed departure in January 1555; and Smith's membership extended over several reigns.

Late in Elizabeth's reign they were joined by two other commentators:

R. Robinson: 'A Briefe Collection of the Queenes Majesties most High and Most Honourable Courtes of Recordes', ed. R. L. Rickard, *Camden Miscellany*, xx, 3rd series, lxxxiii (London, 1953).

W. Lambarde: *Archeion: or, a Discourse upon the High Courts of Justice in England*, ed. C. H. McIlwain and P. L. Ward (Cambridge, Mass., 1957).

W. Lambarde: 'The Orders, Proceedings, Punishments, and Privileges, of the Commons – House of Parliament in England' (1641), in *Harleian Miscellany*, ed. T. Park, 10 vols (London, 1808–13), v, 258–67.

Early Stuart commentators were half-a-century or more removed from mid-Tudor practice and so were correspondingly less relevant and reliable than contemporaries and Elizabethans. Nevertheless their value does vary. Henry Scobell, writing on the Lords and drawing on Tudor precedents, is clearly more rewarding than Henry Elsynge, William Hakewil and William Petyt, even though they can be mined for occasional nuggets.

H. Scobell: *Remembrances of some Methods, Orders and Proceedings heretofore used and observed in the House of Lords . . .* (London, 1657).

H. Elsynge: *The Ancient Method and Manner of Holding of Parliaments in England* (London, 1660).

H. Elsynge: 'Expedicio billarum antiquitus: an Unpublished Chapter of the Second Book of the Manner of Holding Parliaments in England', ed. C. S. Sims, *Studies Presented to the International Commission for the History of Representative and Parliamentary Institutions*, xvi (Louvain, 1954).

W. Hakewil: *The Manner how Statutes are Enacted in Parliament* (London, 1641).

W. Petyt: *Miscellanea Parliamentaria* (London, 1680).

W. Petyt: *Jus Parliamentorum*, 2 pts (London, 1739).

H. Scobell: *Memorials of the Method and Manner of Proceedings in Parliament in Passing Bills* (London, 1656).

A wide range of manuscript sources adds flesh to the bones. Prominent among them are the Harleian and Lansdowne MSS. in the British Library. The Public Record Office is even more rewarding: the parliament pawns provide a complete record of summonses to bishops, peers and legal assistants for the mid-Tudor period; Parliament Rolls throw some light on contemporary clerical practice, as well as filling one or two gaps in the Original Acts; the Close Rolls occasionally contribute information on the Henrician parliamentary record of Edwardian and Marian members; and the State Papers add important details about individual bishops and peers, parliamentary politics and legislative practice.

P.R.O., Parliament Pawns, Petty Bag Office, C.218.

P.R.O., Parliament Rolls, C.65.

P.R.O., Close Rolls, C.54.

P.R.O., State Papers, Edward VI, Mary, Elizabeth, and S.P. Supplementary, 46/2.

Once one has exhausted these major sources, it is a case of searching other collections for the occasional and precious gleanings. In the absence of the personal diaries and journals which illuminate the proceedings of the Elizabethan House of Commons there is no alternative. In 1964 I spent some time panning for gold in chilling rivers in Central Otago, New Zealand. There is a parallel pleasure in turning up unsuspected gold in archives, even if there are but a few grains – in time they accumulate. The most fruitful of these additional sources are:

Corporation of London	Repertories of the Court of Aldermen
Inner Temple Library	Petyt Manuscripts
Bodleian Library, Oxford	Dugdale, Rawlinson, and Tanner MSS.

The Repertories are particularly important for the sources of bills, the Petyt Manuscripts on procedure, and the Bodleian collections not only on the Marian parliaments in general but also on the activities of Stephen Gardiner in particular. The Loseley Manuscripts in the Guildford Muniment Room add a little more to our knowledge of Marian parliamentary politics and suggest significant links with the Upper House. I am grateful for permission to cite this material: in particular Loseley MSS., 1331/2.

The printed sources and secondary works, which have been used in the preparation of this book, have been cited in the appropriate places and do not justify repetition here. However there are certain exceptions which, by their very importance, warrant a mention: in particular the *Camden Society* publications which, together with *The Historical Manuscripts Commission Reports*, provide useful information on individual members:

Arthur Lord Grey of Wilton: *A Commentary of the Services and Charges of William Lord Grey of Wilton, K.G.*, ed. P. de M. G. Egerton, Camden Society, old series, xl (London, 1847).

W. D. Hamilton (ed.): *A Chronicle of England during the Reigns of the Tudors ... 1485 to 1559, by Charles Wriothesley, Windsor Herald,* Camden Society, new series, xi and xx (London, 1875–7).

C. L. Kingsford (ed.): 'Two London Chronicles from the Collection of John Stow', *Camden Miscellany*, xii, 3rd series, xviii (London, 1910).

J. G. Nichols (ed.): *The Chronicle of Calais in the Reigns of Henry VII and Henry VIII to the year 1540*, Camden Society, old series, xxxv (London, 1846).

J. G. Nichols (ed.): *The Diary of Henry Machyn, Citizen and Merchant Taylor of London, 1550–1563*, Camden Society, old series, xlii (London, 1848).

J. G. Nichols (ed.): *The Chronicle of Queen Jane, and of two years of Queen Mary* . . . Camden Society, old series, xlviii (London, 1850).

J. G. Nichols (ed.): *Chronicle of the Grey Friars of London*, Camden Society, old series, liii (London, 1852).

J. G. Nichols (ed.): *Narratives of the Days of the Reformation, chiefly from the Manuscripts of John Foxe the Martyrologist* . . . Camden Society, old series, lxxvii (London, 1859).

N. Pocock (ed.): *Troubles connected with the Prayer Book of 1549*, Camden Society, new series, xxxvii (London, 1884).

Other chronicles which serve a similar purpose include:

E. Halle: *Chronicle: or The Union of the Two Noble and Illustre Famelies of Lancastre and York* (London, 1550).

W. K. Jordan (ed.): *The Chronicle and Political Papers of King Edward VI* (London, 1966).

One item is impossible to catalogue. It is neither a chronicle nor a collection of official papers, a set of government directives nor a collection of parliamentary records. Indeed Stephen Gardiner's letters present something of a paradox: they are important in Edward VI's reign, when he did not attend a single parliament, but they have nothing of significance to offer in 1553–5, when he, more than anyone else, dominated the parliamentary scene.

J. A. Muller (ed.): *The Letters of Stephen Gardiner* (Cambridge, 1933).

Official papers provide important links between the government and the House of Lords: new creations and appointments to sees; the antecedents of official bills (e.g. proclamations); the government's preparations and the steps which it took to implement its legislative proposals:

Calendar of the Patent Rolls preserved in the Public Record Office, Edward VI, 6 vols (London, 1924–9).

Calendar of the Patent Rolls preserved in the Public Record Office, Philip and Mary, 4 vols (London, 1937–9).

P. L. Hughes and J. F. Larkin (eds): *Tudor Royal Proclamations*, 3 vols (New Haven and London, 1964–9).

The correspondence of parliamentary 'outsiders' must be treated with caution, but, as we lack the private members' diaries of a later age, we must make the best of what is available, especially the comment of foreign ambassadors and frustrated reformers. The former were often on the fringe of power or excluded altogether. The sole exception was Simon Renard, Mary's chief prop in 1553/4. Yet his access to the innermost secrets of government was counterbalanced by the twilight world of threatened descents, conspiracy and espionage within which he lived and tormented himself. The latter were a jaundiced crowd, impatient in Edward VI's reign and dismayed under Mary. Frequently, however, they provide the only evidence of what was being said and done on the great issues of the day, and for that reason alone they cannot be ignored.

W. B. Turnbull (ed.): *Calendar of State Papers, Foreign Series, Edward VI and Mary*, 2 vols (London, 1861).

M. A. S. Hume (ed.): *Calendar of Letters and State Papers Relating to English Affairs, preserved principally in the Archives of Simancas*, 4 vols (London, 1892–9).

R. Brown *et al.* (eds): *Calendar of State Papers and Manuscripts, Relating to English Affairs, existing in the Archives and Collections of Venice . . .* 9 vols (London, 1864–98).

R. A. Vertot d'Aubeuf and C. Villaret (eds): *Ambassades de Messieurs de Noailles en Angleterre,* 5 vols (Leyden, 1763).

H. Robinson (transl. and ed.): *Original letters relative to the English Reformation . . .* 2 vols, Parker Society (Cambridge, 1846–7).

Two works which really belong to the flanking reigns of Henry VIII and Elizabeth have much relevance for the mid-Tudor Upper House too:

J. S. Brewer *et al.* (eds): *Letters and Papers, Foreign and Domestic, of the Reign of Henry VIII, 1509–47,* 22 vols in 37 parts (London, 1862–1932).

Simonds D'Ewes: *The Journals of all the Parliaments during the Reign of Queen Elizabeth, both of the House of Lords and House of Commons* (London, 1682).

The first of these is important on the Henrician antecedents of the mid-Tudor Lords; the latter is invaluable as a record of the parliaments immediately subsequent to Mary's reign.

Secondary works

The dearth of books and articles on the institutional history of the Tudor Lords simply reflects the 'Commons orientation' of the past fifty years. Only a handful of brief monographs appeared before the late 1960s:

A. F. Pollard: 'The Authenticity of the Lords' Journals in the Sixteenth Century', *T.R.H.S.,* 3rd series, 8 (1914), 17–39.

A. F. Pollard: 'The Clerical Organisation of Parliament', *E.H.R.,* 57 (Jan. 1942), 31–58.

A. F. Pollard: 'Receivers of Petitions and Clerks of Parliament', *E.H.R.,* 57 (April 1942), 202–26.

A. F. Pollard: 'The Clerk of the Crown', *E.H.R.,* 57 (July 1942), 312–33.

M. F. Bond: 'The Archives of Parliament', *Genealogists Magazine,* 11 (1953), 338–48.

M. F. Bond: 'Clerks of the Parliaments, 1509–1953', *E.H.R.,* 73 (Jan. 1958), 78–85.

M. F. Bond: *The Records of Parliament: A Guide for Genealogists and Local Historians* (Canterbury, 1964).

In the mid-sixties the banner of revisionism was unfurled:

J. S. Roskell: 'Perspectives in English Parliamentary History', *B.J.R.L.,* 46 (March 1964), 448–75.

Renewed interest in the House of Lords was demonstrated in a spirited debate on the technically complex problem of proxies:

V. F. Snow: 'Proctorial Representation and Conciliar Management during the Reign of Henry VIII', *H.J.,* 9, 1 (1966), 1–26.

H. Miller: 'Attendance in the House of Lords during the Reign of Henry VIII', *H.J.,* 10, 4 (1967), 325–51.

V. F. Snow: 'Proctorial Representation in the House of Lords during the Reign of Edward VI', *J.B.S.,* 8, 2 (May 1969), 1–27.

M. A. R. Graves: 'Proctorial Representation in the House of Lords during Edward VI's Reign: a Reassessment', *J.B.S.*, 10, 2 (May 1971), 17–35.

V. F. Snow: 'A Rejoinder to Mr. Graves' Reassessment of Proctorial Representation', *J.B.S.*, 10, 2 (May 1971), 36–46.

The political vigour of the Upper House and its ability to adopt an independent stand were also rediscovered:

M. A. R. Graves: 'The House of Lords and the Politics of Opposition, April–May 1554', in G. A. Wood and P. S. O'Connor (eds), *W. P. Morrell: A Tribute. Essays in Modern and Early Modern History presented to William Parker Morrell, Professor Emeritus*, University of Otago (Dunedin, 1973), pp. 1–20.

M. A. R. Graves: 'The Mid-Tudor House of Lords: Forgotten Member of the Parliamentary Trinity', in F. McGregor and N. Wright (eds), *European History and its Historians* (Adelaide, 1977), 23–31.

The Journals of the Upper House enjoyed a reappraisal:

M. A. R. Graves: 'The two Lords' Journals of 1542', *B.I.H.R.*, XLIII (Nov. 1970), 182–9.

G. R. Elton: 'The Early Journals of the House of Lords', *E.H.R.*, LXXXIX (1974), 481–512.

So too did the rolls of parliament and the printed statutes:

G. R. Elton: 'The Sessional Printing of Statutes, 1484–1547', in E. W. Ives, R. J. Knecht, J. J. Scarisbrick (eds), *Wealth and Power in Tudor England, Essays Presented to S. T. Bindoff* (London, 1978).

Since then two important new volumes have appeared. Whilst they are not specifically studies of parliament, they shed fresh light on its workings in the mid-Tudor reigns:

D. E. Hoak: *The King's Council in the Reign of Edward VI (Cambridge, 1976)*.

D. M. Loades: *The Reign of Mary Tudor* (London, 1979).

During the 1970s G. R. Elton redirected the treatment of parliament (and therefore of the Lords) along institutional rather than political lines. The most important articles are itemised in chapter 1, n. 21. In addition he drew together much of his research and that of others in a more general study of Tudor England before Elizabeth:

G. R. Elton: *Reform and Reformation, England 1509–1558* (London, 1977).

Postscript: An article on the Marian parliaments appeared in print after the completion of this volume. Although it adds nothing to this study of the mid-Tudor Lords, it is in harmony with the present revisionist trend in parliamentary studies.

J. Loach: 'Conservatism and Consent in Parliament, 1547–59', in J. Loach and R. Tittler (eds), *The Mid-Tudor Polity, c. 1540–1560* (London, 1980), pp. 9–28.

INDEX

The entries for individual peers and bishops are accompanied by dates of (1) succession to (or creation of) noble title, or appointment to episcopal office, and (2) death, forfeiture, or (in the case of bishops) loss of office.

320

Index

Warwick, earl of, *see* Dudley, John

Watson, Thomas, bishop of Lincoln (1557–9), 210, 221

Wentworth, Barbara, 102

Wentworth, Thomas, 1st Baron Wentworth of Nettlestead (1529–51), 34, 56, 217, 227, 241n.37

Wentworth, Thomas, 2nd Baron Wentworth of Nettlestead (1551–84), 217; attendance record, 66, 227; education, 44, 47, 243nn.67 and 69; government of Calais, 66, 236nn.64–5; reunion with Rome, 263n.219

West, Thomas, 8th Baron West and 9th Baron De la Warr (1526–54), 11, 20, 81, 215, 261n.190; affliction, 41, 47, 81, 243n.75; attendance record, 78, 81, 225, 261nn.186–8; education, 47, 243n.69; opposition to Reformation, 81, 261n.185

West, William (created Baron De la Warr, 1570; died 1595), 11

Westminster, abbot of, *see* Feckenham, John (de)

Westminster, bishop of, *see* Thirlby, Thomas

Westmorland, earl of, *see* Neville, Charles; Neville, Henry; Neville, Ralph

Wharton, Sir Henry, 110

Wharton, Thomas, 1st Baron Wharton (1544–68), 50, 94, 95–6, 104, 108, 109, 201, 217; attendance record, 79, 111, 113, 114, 227, 253n.103, 260n.179; creation, 34, 35, 112; experience of Commons, 56, 247n.131; feuds, with Cumberland, 109–11, 269n.91; with Dacre, 109, 111–14; marcher warden, 37, 79, 109, 112, 113, 114; Northumberland's supporter, 113; royal service, 36–7, 109, 112, 260n.179; writs of summons, 79

White, John, bishop of Lincoln (1554–6), bishop of Winchester (1556–9), 49, 52, 210, 245n.109; attendance, 62, 221, 222; consecration, 235n.41,

257n.146; Gardiner's ally, 290n.86

White, Sir Thomas (Gardiner's servant), 290n.86

Whitgift, John, bishop of Worcester (1577–83), archbishop of Canterbury (1583–1604), 44

Williams, John, 1st Baron Williams of Thame (1554–9), 100, 217; attendance, 227; creation, 12, 36, 217, 257n.144; experience of Commons, 56, 247n.132; loyal Marian, 36, 37; royal service, 36, 37–8

Willoughby, William, 1st Baron Willoughby of Parham (1547–70/4), 12, 35, 40, 103, 227, 240n.8

Wiltshire, earl of, *see* Paulet, William

Winchester, bishop of, *see* Gardiner, Stephen; Ponet, John; White, John

Winchester, marquess of, *see* Paulet, John; Paulet, William

Windsor, Andrew, 1st Baron Windsor of Stanwell (1529–43), 34

Windsor, Edward, 3rd Baron Windsor of Stanwell (1558–75), 46–7, 107, 108, 217, 227, 243n.69

Windsor, William, 2nd Baron Windsor of Stanwell (1543–58), 217, 246n.130; attendance, 227, 264n.243; education, 46–7, 243n.69, 245n.100; opposition to Reformation, 89, 104, 261n.190

Worcester, bishop of, *see* Heath, Nicholas; Hooper, John; Pate(s), Richard; Whitgift, John

Worcester, earl of, *see* Somerset, Henry; Somerset, William

Wriothesley, Henry, 2nd Baron Wriothesley of Titchfield, 2nd earl of Southampton (1550–81), 18, 218

Wriothesley, Thomas, 1st Baron Wriothesley of Titchfield (1544–7), 1st earl of Southampton (1547–50), 49, 96, 97, 213,